COLLIERS ACROSS THE SEA

The Working Class in American History

Editorial Advisors
David Brody
Alice Kessler-Harris
David Montgomery
Sean Wilentz

A list of books in the series appears at the end of this book.

COLLIERS ACROSS THE SEA

A Comparative Study of Class Formation in Scotland and the American Midwest, 1830–1924

John H. M. Laslett

University of Illinois Press

Urbana and Chicago

⊛ This book is printed on acid-free paper.

Library of Congress Cataloging-in-Publication Data
Laslett, John H. M.
Colliers across the sea : a comparative study of class formation in
Scotland and the American Midwest, 1830–1924 / John H. M. Laslett.
p.   cm. — (The working class in American history)
Includes bibliographical references and index.
ISBN 0-252-02511-3 (cloth : alk. paper)
ISBN 0-252-06827-0 (pbk. : alk. paper)
1. Coal miners — Scotland — History — 19th century.
2. Coal miners — Middle West — History — 19th century.
3. Social classes — Scotland — History — 19th century.
4. Social classes — Middle West — History — 19th century.
I. Title. II. Series.
HD8039.M62S44   2000
305.5'62'0977 — dc21   99-6466
CIP

1 2 3 4 5 C P 5 4 3 2 1

*For Michael and Sarah, who both
know what union struggles are*

Contents

List of Figures, Maps, and Tables ix

Preface xi

List of Abbreviations xv

Introduction: Exceptionalist Paradigm or Comparative
Social History? 3

Part 1: Class Formation among Colliers in Southwest Scotland, 1830–70

1. Social Structure and Class in Early Scottish Mining
   Villages: Wishaw and Larkhall, 1830–70 15
2. Conflict and Accommodation in Lanarkshire, 1830–64 37
3. Crossing the Ocean: British Colliers Migrate to Northern
   Illinois, 1855–70 59

*Part 2: Growth of Class Hostilities in Scotland and the American
Midwest, 1865–1905*

4. Heyday of Pick Mining in the American Midwest:
   Braidwood and Streator, 1865–75 77
5. Strikes, Internal Conflict, and the Decline of the Class-
   Harmony Ideal, 1872–82 101
6. New Technology, New Immigrants, and Growing Class
   Conflict: Blantyre and Spring Valley, 1885–1905 125

Part 3: The Emergence of Mass Unionism and the Parting of the Political Ways, 1890–1924

7. Mass Unionism and Early Ventures into Politics   151
8. Moving in Tandem to the Left? Socialism and the
    Colliers, 1900–1914   173
9. Denouement: World War I, Labour Party Triumph, and
    the Collapse of the Left in Illinois, 1914–24   196

    Conclusion: Comparative Class Formation and the Colliers
    Who Crossed the Sea   222

    Notes   235
    Bibliography of Primary Sources   279
    Index   297

Figures, Maps, and Tables

Figure 1. Three Types of Mines Found in the Northern Illinois
    Coalfield, circa 1870   96

Map 1. The Lanarkshire Coalfield, circa 1865   2
Map 2. The Northern Illinois Coalfield, circa 1885   2
Map 3. Wishaw in 1864   16
Map 4. Larkhall in 1864   17
Map 5. Selected British Mining Settlements   66
Map 6. Braidwood and Satellite Mining Towns, circa 1870   79
Map 7. Streator, circa 1885   80
Map 8. Blantyre, 1889   127
Map 9. Spring Valley   129
Map 10. Ladd   134
Map 11. Coalfields in Downstate Illinois   155

Table 1. Coal and Iron Companies Owning More Than One
    Colliery in Wishaw and Larkhall and Valuation of Their
    Property Owned or Rented, 1861   19
Table 2. British Immigrant Coal Miners in Illinois, Maryland,
    Ohio, and Pennsylvania, 1870   65
Table 3. Birthplaces of Miners in Braidwood and Streator, 1860–80   81
Table 4. Miners' Occupations by Ethnic Group, Braidwood and
    Streator, 1870–80   88
Table 5. Coal Companies Owning One or More Pits in
    Streator, 1870   95

Preface

This book arose from my long-standing interest in comparative class formation and its relation to the much-debated issue of America's "labor exceptionalism." This is the idea that socialism has historically been much weaker
in the United States than in other advanced industrial societies and that
American workers have been less willing than their European counterparts
to challenge the dominance of capitalism. The study has been a long time
gestating, partly because of the difficulties of trans-Atlantic research and
partly because of my efforts to find a solution to what I call the "apples and
oranges" problem — the danger, particularly acute in writing a comparative
study that covers a long period of history, that the social and economic basis
for the comparison shifts over time, thereby throwing into doubt the validity
of the conclusions.

Using the modernization of the coal industry in Britain and America as a
common denominator, my solution was to see whether a group of migrating
Scottish coal miners who settled in the northern Illinois coalfield after 1865
experienced the same process of class-conscious alienation from society on
America's industrial frontier as they had in the already stratified mining communities of southwest Scotland.

My decision to use the experience of the "same" group of workers in two
different countries as a vehicle for exploring comparative class formation was
sparked by three unrelated events. The first was a year-long seminar in the
social history of British coal-mining communities that I attended in 1974 at

the Center for the Study of Social History at the University of Warwick, in England. That seminar resulted in much excellent scholarship, including Royden Harrison's *Independent Collier: The Coal Miner as Archetypal Proletarian Revisited* (New York, 1978). This book began the fashion of challenging the oversimplified view of the coal miner as an inherently militant worker. The second event was my chance discovery of the labor newspaper the *Glasgow Sentinel,* portions of which I read during a walking holiday in the Scottish Highlands in 1982. This journal, which reprinted numerous letters that Scottish immigrants to the United States wrote to family and friends in Scotland during the 1850s and 1860s, was brought to my notice by W. Hamish Fraser, of the University of Strathclyde.

The third event was reading Herbert Gutman's essay "Labor in the Land of Lincoln: Coal Miners on the Prairie" in Ira Berlin's posthumous collection of Gutman's work entitled *Power and Culture* (New York, 1987). Gutman's rich account of the labor republican ideals upheld by the Scottish miners who migrated to the northern Illinois town of Braidwood—a town that also figures in this study—made me seek the source of their labor republicanism. Was it acquired in the United States alone, or did it also reflect the radical traditions of the Scottish working class? At the same time, Gutman's exclusive concentration on the cultural sources of working-class protest made me want to add a deeper economic and political dimension to his discussion and to set it in a comparative context. Soon after this I conceived a research design and followed it up with several summers of field research in Edinburgh, Glasgow, and London. These trips were interspersed with numerous visits to research libraries and archives in various parts of the Midwest, which helped me not just to learn more about the lives of this remarkable generation of British immigrants but also to reconstruct the history of the three coal-mining villages I chose to study in northern Illinois.

My first thanks go to various Scottish friends who helped me at different stages of the research. Besides Hamish and Helen Fraser, these included Alan Campbell, a veteran of the 1974 research seminar at Warwick, whose excellent *Lanarkshire Miners* (Edinburgh, 1979) provided material for several of my Scottish chapters. Other Scottish friends who also came to my aid, either with their hospitality or their scholarly expertise, included Gordon and Alison Wilson, Robert Duncan, and Fred Reid. Thanks go also to my Scottish research assistant Martin Sime, who traveled back and forth to Glasgow from his remote croft in the Shetland Islands to carry out archival work. I am grateful, too, for the facilities extended to me by the archivists and librarians at the Scottish Record Office, the National Library of Scotland, and the Mitchell

Library in Glasgow, as well as at Glasgow University, Edinburgh University, and the University of Strathclyde.

In England I received help from my old friend Charlotte Erickson at Cambridge University, who knows more about the registers of ships carrying immigrants from Britain to the United States in the nineteenth century than anyone else alive. Thanks go also to Neville Kirk, of Manchester Metropolitan University, who welcomed me into his seminar and read a late draft of the manuscript. I would like to acknowledge, too, the help I received from the staffs of the British Library, the London University Library, and the manuscripts division of the London School of Economics.

On this side of the Atlantic, I received hospitality on several midwestern research trips from Richard Joyce, of Wilmington, Illinois; Ralph Stone, of Springfield; and the late Bobbie Herndon, also of Springfield. In the summer of 1994 Bobbie Herndon, a descendant by marriage of Abraham Lincoln's law partner, graciously invited me to stay in her lakeside home. Carl D. Oblinger; Stephane Booth; Amy Z. Gottlieb; the late Bernice Sweeney, of Spring Valley; and her daughter, Sarah Allen, also guided me to relevant sources for studying the now defunct mining communities of northern Illinois. I am grateful, too, for the help I received from staff at Springfield's Sangamon State University, the Illinois State Library, and various other repositories in the state capital. In addition, I made extensive use of library and research facilities at the Southern Illinois University, Carbondale; the University of Illinois, Urbana-Champaign; and Illinois State University, Bloomington-Normal. In Chicago I was helped by staff members at the Chicago Historical Society, the Chicago Public Library, and my old stamping grounds in the Regenstein Library at the University of Chicago.

I would also like to thank the American Philosophical Society, the Social Science Research Council, and the National Science Foundation for grants received in connection with the project. I have benefited, too, from numerous Academic Senate grants and sabbaticals accorded to me by UCLA. In addition, I wish to express my strong appreciation to the numerous research assistants I have employed over the years, particularly to Christopher Kenway, who spent many hours poring over the manuscript versions of the U.S. population census. Martin Sime performed the same task for me with the Scottish census. These research assistants also include my friends and former students Stephen Brier, Lawrence Lipin, and David Brundage. David Brundage participated in the Los Angeles Social History Group, to which I presented the drafts of several chapters. Special thanks go to my long-standing friends in that body. I am also grateful to Chip Hornick, a computer specialist at the Department of History at UCLA; to my stepdaughter, Olivia Banner; and to Richard Wentworth, Theresa L. Sears, and the various editors I worked with at the University of Illinois Press.

Finally, I was sustained in the final stages of this project by my beloved wife, Lois Banner, herself a distinguished historian, whose superb editing skills did much to improve the final draft of the manuscript. Any faults that remain are entirely my own.

Abbreviations

AFL	American Federation of Labor
AMA	American Miners Association
C&W	Chicago and Wilmington Company
CPPA	Conference for Progressive Political Action (U.S.)
CW&V	Chicago, Wilmington and Vermilion Company
ICR	Illinois Central Railroad
ILGWU	International Ladies Garment Workers Union (U.S.)
ISCD	Illinois State Council of Defense
ILP	Independent Labour Party (U.K.)
IWW	Industrial Workers of the World (U.S.)
JLLB	Joint Labor Legislative Board (U.S.)
LCMU	Lanarkshire County Miners Union (U.K.)
MFGB	Miners Federation of Great Britain
MNA	Miners National Association (U.S. and U.K.)
SDF	Social Democratic Federation (U.K.)
SLP	Socialist Labor Party (U.S.)
SMF	Scottish Miners Federation
SPA	Socialist Party of America
SVCC	Spring Valley Coal Company
SWPC	Scottish Workers Parliamentary Committee
SWRC	Scottish Workers Representation Committee
TUC	Trades Union Congress (U.K.)
UIL	United Irish League (U.K.)
UMWA	United Mine Workers of America

COLLIERS ACROSS THE SEA

Map 1. Lanarkshire coalfield, circa 1865 (*source: Third Statistical Account of Scotland* [1894]).

Map 2. Northern Illinois coalfield, circa 1885 (*source: Atlas of the United States* [1891]).

INTRODUCTION: EXCEPTIONALIST PARADIGM OR COMPARATIVE SOCIAL HISTORY?

Between 1865 and 1868 several hundred coal miners from the Clyde Valley in southwest Scotland crossed the Atlantic to take up new mining jobs in the United States.[1] They were part of a much larger stream of British artisans who responded to America's quickening demand for skilled labor as the nation industrialized rapidly in the decades following the Civil War. Some of these Scottish miners went straight to previously established enclaves of British colliers in eastern states such as Maryland and Pennsylvania,[2] but others took the "emigrant train" another nine hundred miles west to Chicago, looking for new work opportunities in the recently opened coalfield of northern Illinois.[3]

This book tells a human story about the fortunes of these migrant colliers and their families. It looks back in time at the development of mining as a way of life in three of the Lanarkshire mining towns from which they came and forward in time to the history of three of the communities they helped to found on the northern Illinois prairie in the years immediately following the American Civil War. The study also follows the history of all these communities and of the labor movements their miners helped to create in Scotland and the American Midwest until 1924. By that time the miners' unions that the colliers joined—the Lanarkshire County Miners Union (1879) and Illinois district 12 of the United Mine Workers of America (1890)—had come to exert a powerful influence on the internal life of the Miners Federation of Great Britain and the UMWA. Because of their large size and militant traditions, these two national unions also played a major role in shaping the political

3

and industrial development of the British and American labor movements as a whole.[4]

Most important, my purpose in this book is to use the example of these miners and their communities to shed fresh comparative light on the formation of the working class in Great Britain and the United States. Until recently most efforts to analyze American class formation have taken place within the framework of the debate over U.S. exceptionalism. According to this idea the United States, lacking a feudal tradition, underwent industrialization without major class conflict or the emergence of a major socialist movement like those that appeared in Great Britain and on the European continent. Louis Hartz, dean of the 1950s consensus school of historians, argued that America's origins as a liberal state froze Lockean individualism in place and guaranteed the permanent hegemony of free-market capitalism. Seymour Martin Lipset, focusing on American values such as liberty, equality, and laissez-faire, restated the position in somewhat different terms. He emphasized the uniqueness of the organizing principles and founding institutions of the United States. Others have emphasized the peculiarities of the American two-party system, the treachery of the labor leadership, the weakness of the American state, and the overweening power of the capitalist class as reasons for the absence of a revolutionary labor movement.[5]

Hartz, Lipset, and their followers among a younger generation of historians are not of course wrong to emphasize the broad appeal in American politics of democratic ideas such as personal liberty, free market economics, and a limited role for the state.[6] They fail to recognize, however, that liberalism was a historically contingent ideology that assumed different forms in different societies: it was neither writ in stone in the American experience nor confined to the United States alone. They err further in arguing that the liberal center remained unchallenged throughout most of American history and that its dominance precluded the emergence of a class system with strongly divergent economic interests.[7]

Some labor historians and sociologists, such as Gary Marks in his work on trade unions in general and Leon Fink and Kim Voss in their work on the Knights of Labor, have continued to use the exceptionalist paradigm, despite a number of effective criticisms of the concept.[8] Methodologically the most telling critique has been the observation that exceptionalism is an ahistorical, essentialist idea that describes one nation's pattern of development as a norm in relation to which all other cases are deviant. In terms of working-class history, depending on what variable is selected as the criterion of a "mature" working class, any number of countries can become the normative case, while all others are seen as deviant. For example, if the size of a socialist or labor party is taken as the criterion of normalcy, Germany becomes the standard bearer and the United States the pariah, with other nations falling in between. If voluntarist or antistatist labor movements become the norm, the situation is reversed, and the opposite model acquires legitimacy.[9] Selig Perlman and various Marxist scholars have developed other models that proceed along similar lines.[10]

Another criticism of exceptionalism emerges from a tendency among its proponents to rest their case on America's supposed peculiarities, such as mass immigration, the frontier, or a weak and divided state, while failing to subject them to rigorous comparative study. Sometimes they overlook institutions, such as chattel slavery, that do not fit the model.[11] In addition, with some notable exceptions a tendency exists among scholars to invoke the exceptionalist paradigm without paying sufficient attention to the societies with which the United States is being compared.[12] The latter weakness mars the work on the Knights of Labor carried out by Leon Fink and Kim Voss. Despite some interesting reflections on the similarities between the Knights of Labor and contemporary social movements in France, these two authors fail to provide the detailed historical narrative that is necessary to validate their conclusions. Indeed, the deep flaws in the exceptionalist paradigm lead me to agree with Sean Wilentz's 1984 suggestion that exceptionalism be abandoned as a mode of analysis and that it be replaced by a "truly comprehensive comparative history of American labor, one that is as open to analogies between events and movements in this country and those abroad as it is to the differences."[13]

In 1986 Ira Katznelson and Aristide Zolberg took a major step forward in the debate when they published *Working-Class Formation: Nineteenth-Century Patterns in Western Europe and the United States.* This work implicitly revealed many of the weaknesses in the exceptionalist paradigm. Positing an original, four-stage theory of class formation, Katznelson, Zolberg, and their collaborators wrote a series of compelling historical essays about the evolution of class relations in Germany, France, and America from the 1780s to the end of the nineteenth century. Their premise was that, despite some common features, capitalist institutions have assumed different forms in different countries. These institutions have thereby stimulated the emergence of different working-class movements that have responded in different ways to their separate national, state, and cultural traditions. Such an approach is clearly superior to the exceptionalist paradigm. It permits the historian to demonstrate the particular political and institutional characteristics of each nation's working class without forcing them, as do Hartz and Lipset, into a predetermined historical pattern.

As effective as the approach of the Katznelson and Zolberg volume is, however, it leaves several important problems unresolved. In the first place, the contributors largely ignore Great Britain. This is a surprising omission, since Britain was the first and for many years the most important industrialized country, and for a time it possessed the most highly organized and class-conscious labor movement in the world. In addition, of all the world's trade unions, Britain's were most similar to those of the United States. A second weakness is that all the essayists in *Working-Class Formation* end their narratives before 1914, even though it is generally acknowledged that World War I provided one of the great formative moments of Western working-class history. As I will show in this study, World War I played a critical role in differentiating the political development of the American working class from that of Great Britain. Zolberg himself points out, too, that it is impossible to account for the twentieth-century phases of class formation by a simple projection of pre-1914 trends.[14]

By ushering in mass production as well as modern consumerism on a large scale, the Great War and the years that followed it significantly affected both the size and ideological outlook of the working-class movement in nearly all the industrialized countries. In addition, the Russian Revolution of October 1917 permanently split most of the West's major socialist parties into feuding communist and social democratic factions, with profound consequences for the subsequent development of European party politics.

Moreover, the essays in *Working-Class Formation* reveal enormous variation in both size and trajectory among working-class movements in all the major Western countries. One manifestation of this variety was the differing number of workers belonging to trade unions, ranging from a high of 30 to 40 percent in Great Britain to only 15 percent in France. Another is that by 1919 only one of the advanced industrial countries — Germany — had developed a socialist movement large enough to secure the votes of a nominal majority of the workers. In the United States, however, the Socialist Party had by this time virtually collapsed. How comparable are labor movements that differ this enormously? Are we not dealing here with an "apples and oranges" situation in which the differences between the labor movements studied are so great that any conclusions are bound to be flawed?

Finally, despite a number of brilliant comparative insights, the essayists in *Working-Class Formation* for the most part adopt a "side-by-side" approach to the study of transnational labor movements that does not accord with comparative history in its true sense. Such an approach achieves less insight in revealing the factors that bring about the divergence between developments in two nations than do comparative studies that follow the history of a single social movement or set of ideas in two or more countries. Good examples of the latter genre are David Brion Davis's two-volume study of slavery in Britain and the Americas in the seventeenth and eighteenth centuries,[15] Richard J. Evans's comparative study of feminism in Europe, America, and Australasia,[16] and the comparative work done by Ann Orloff on the origins of the Anglo-American welfare state.[17]

More generally, the comparative historian of the working class, like other comparative historians, has an obligation to try to avoid the "apples and oranges" problem, especially if he or she sets out to trace the history of more than one labor movement over a long period of time. The difficulty here arises — as in other longitudinal studies of social movements — from changes, whether sudden or long-term, that occur in the national contexts in which labor movements grow. For example, comparing pre-1870 artisanal movements in France and Germany may be legitimate because of the statist but petty producerist nature of the two national societies. Comparing the French with the German labor movement after 1870 becomes much more problematic, however, partly because Germany industrialized much more rapidly than France and partly because the federal German state and its party system was so different from their counterparts in France that it becomes doubtful whether one is really comparing the same phenomena.[18]

The danger of comparing fundamentally different types can be seen as well in several transnational studies of coal miners' movements, even though in this industry the determinants of workplace solidarity vary little from country to country and the international tradition of mutual support between miners' unions is particularly strong.[19] One example of a study flawed in this way is the 1985 article by Eric Weitz in which he compares the development of class relations between colliers and their employers in Germany's Ruhr Valley with those in southern Illinois at the turn of the century.[20] Weitz was interested, as I am, in the effects of religious differences on the development of class consciousness among the miners, but he fails to point out that in Germany, unlike the United States, there were three separate miners' unions: one socialist, one liberal, and one nominally Catholic (*Kristliche*). By ignoring the German Catholic miners' union and dealing solely with the socialist one, Weitz omitted a crucial variable from his study. In addition, differences between the tradition of central government paternalism via the nineteenth-century German *Knappschaft*, as well as of state oppression toward the miners in the Ruhr, and the antistatism of the southern Illinois miners further undercuts the common ground between the two examples.[21]

The second comparative miners' study that in my view takes insufficient account of differences in national background is a recent book by Roger Fagge that contrasts the mining communities of West Virginia with those in South Wales between 1900 and 1922.[22] In this work the author argues, quite rightly, that the cultural homogeneity of the Welsh mining villages enabled the colliers there not simply to resist the depredations of the coal owners but also to become major players in both the miners' syndicalist movement and the British Labour Party. The multiethnic miners of West Virginia, however, who lived in feudal fiefdoms controlled by the coal operators, lacked a common culture that predated the coming of the coal industry. As with Weitz's study, Fagge's work fails to take sufficient account of the profound structural differences that existed between the two societies he chose to compare. The social, political, and ecological gap between the highly industrialized South Wales valleys and the autarkic, racially divided culture of pre–World War I Appalachia is too great to yield meaningful results.[23]

The best answer to the "apples and oranges" problem is not simply to limit the analysis to labor movements in two countries that had a great deal in common, such as Britain and America, but to ensure that the social and political contexts in which industrialization occurred were sufficiently similar that the overall comparison remains valid across time. Transnational comparisons with rather small differences in outcome are what provide the most illuminating case studies, not those where the differences are great. The historian pays a price for this approach, for it limits the ability to generalize from the chosen case, but it is a price well worth paying in the interests of historical accuracy. This was the solution adopted by James Holt in his comparative study of British and American steelworkers' unions[24] and by Jeffrey Haydu in *Between Craft and Class: Skilled Workers and Factory Politics in the United States and Britain, 1890–1922*. Haydu focused on the issue of deskilling as his main transnational variable and on skilled metalworkers' efforts to retain control over the work process in two discrete areas: Bridgeport, Connecticut, and Coventry, England. By carefully limiting his issues and cases, Haydu managed to draw compelling conclusions about the differing ways in which conflicts between employers and employees played out in these two locations while saying something important about the differences between the British and American labor movements.[25]

I, too, have chosen this method of limitation. Admittedly my subject of class formation is a good deal more complicated than the issue of deskilling or the comparative history of steelworkers' unions. Thus I deal not only with miners at the workplace but also with their political, social, and economic relations with the coal owners, as well as with the state authorities and with other workers in their local communities. Since my study covers one hundred years, a period of time longer than that chosen by any previous comparative labor historian, I have also had to provide considerable detail about the background and development of the mining industry in Britain and the United States as a whole.

It could be argued that groups of miners in Britain and America entirely independent of each other might provide a better comparison, because only then could we be sure that the similarities or differences in their behaviors derived from underlying differences in their respective societies rather than from the influence of one group on the other. Nevertheless, it is precisely because these miners shared common traditions, both at the workplace and in the community, while operating in distinct industrial societies that this comparison is worthwhile, for it throws into relief differences and similarities between the process of class formation in Britain and America in ways that examining two entirely different national groups of workers would not.

I do not claim that the comparative framework I have chosen for this study is perfect or that I have entirely eliminated the problem of comparing dissimilar entities. The mining population of these two areas was never exactly the same. Only a minority of colliers from southwest Scotland immigrated to America in the years between 1850 and 1870, and they never became a majority in the Illinois coalfield. English and Irish immigrants, along with a large number of Slavic and Italian miners, played a larger role in Illinois district 12 of the UMWA than did comparable groups of immigrant miners in the Lanarkshire County Miners Union. The geography and politics of the two areas were also somewhat different. Glasgow was nearer, both culturally and physically, to the Lanarkshire coalfield than Chicago was to the northern Illinois one. The Labour Party in southwest Scotland was a loose coalition of trade unionists and socialist societies whose main purpose was to elect labor leaders to the House of Commons. The Socialist Party of America, by contrast, was the U.S. equivalent of a continental social democratic party rather than a trade union party of the English type. Yet just as, functionally speaking, these two political parties performed the same role in Britain and the United States, the differences between the geography of the two areas and the nature of their mining populations were also relatively small.

Moreover, the mining industries in both southwest Scotland and the

American Midwest went through the same stages of economic and technological development in the same sequence: from shallow pits where coal was
mined on an informal basis to more disciplined methods of extraction later
on, and from skilled pick mining in 1830–70 to partially mechanized mining
in the years between 1880 and 1914. Both industries expanded rapidly in the
period under review, and both experienced marked increases in the division
of labor in the years leading up to and following World War I. With regard
to labor militancy and community solidarity, the differences in behavior between the miners in the Lanarkshire County Miners Union and Illinois district 12 of the UMWA were also small. Both the MFGB and the UMWA were
the largest industrial unions in their national labor federations, the Trades
Union Congress (1868), and the American Federation of Labor (1886). Both
miners' unions followed a policy of encouraging industrial militancy in the
early years of the twentieth century, and both attempted to secure protective
legislation, either from Parliament or from the legislatures of the various U.S.
mining states, to enhance the security of their members underground.

Finally, I chose to compare the three Lanarkshire coal towns with the
three in Illinois to reflect the particular variables that affected the development of the mining industry in southwest Scotland and in northern Illinois
between 1830 and 1924. In a longitudinal study such as this, it is important to
ensure that structural variables remain similar across time, for otherwise the
two cases may cease to develop along parallel lines at some point. Larkhall
was a single-industry mining town situated in a rural area on the south bank
of the River Clyde. Coal had been mined there since the eighteenth century.
Wishaw was a mixed coal and iron community on the northern side of the
river that developed somewhat later. Blantyre, the third Scottish community
to be studied, was another single-industry coal town, but it did not reach
industrial maturity until after the turn of the twentieth century.

The Illinois coal towns have been chosen with similar considerations
in mind. Braidwood, where the Scottish colliers first put down their roots,
was fashioned out of the raw midwestern prairie in 1865. Streator, twenty-
five miles to the west, was a mixed-industry coal town of colliers and glass
workers that came into being a few years later. Spring Valley, the third coal-
mining community to be considered, was not founded until 1886. All three
of these coal towns lay in the Illinois River valley and sold most of their coal
on the Chicago market, just as the River Clyde coal towns sold their prod-
uct in the industrial metropolis of Glasgow. It is true that by the turn of the
century the northern Illinois coalfield was largely worked out. By that time
many of the original immigrant Scottish, Irish, and English miners had either
left the pits, migrated further west, or moved into the southern part of the

state, where the Illinois coal industry's center of gravity then lay. The mid-Lanarkshire coalfield was also widening its field of operations. Hence the third part of this study broadens the focus to include the whole of the Illinois coalfield as well as the whole of the county of Lanark.

Interweaving the history of these mining communities on opposite sides of the Atlantic, the book tries to separate out the factors that differentiated the process of class formation in Scotland and Illinois. How and why did the social customs and political outlook of the mining population in southwest Scotland differ from those of colliers in the American Midwest? Did either the miners or the coal owners react differently to the industrial changes that pushed their interests apart? Did ethnic and cultural tensions among the colliers weaken community solidarity to a greater extent in Illinois than they did in Lanarkshire? What philosophical differences emerged in the attitude of the miners toward the state and toward third-party political action? Were certain stages in the class-formation process present in Scotland but absent in America?

In general, my contention is that the overall process of class formation was similar at the workplace in these two regions, although there were some differences in development at the community level. It was in the area of electoral politics, however, that the two groups of miners diverged most sharply. Because of their large numbers and dense geographical concentration, miners were vigorously courted by the British Labour Party and the Socialist Party of America between 1900 and 1914. For a time it seemed as though both parties would be equally successful in appealing to the miners. In the end, however, the Illinois colliers refused to follow the same political path as their Scottish comrades, even though many of them admired the Labour Party. This divergence was due partly to differences between America and Britain regarding the evolution of the franchise and the two-party system, partly to a number of material advantages that the miners enjoyed after they came to America, and partly to a series of adventitious events that took place during and after World War I.

Whatever the reasons for this parting of the political ways, the consequences were momentous on both sides of the Atlantic. In Britain the MFGB's support for the Labour Party was the most important factor that transformed the party from a minor irritant on the left wing of the Liberal Party into the majority party of the British working class. In the United States, by contrast, the UMWA's failure to throw its weight behind the Socialist Party of America helped to doom the party to political insignificance.

Despite the differences in political outcome, this book on balance rejects the exceptionalist paradigm.[26] I will argue that the process of class formation among the colliers who helped to establish the labor movement in the American Midwest was in most respects similar to that which occurred among the miners of southwest Scotland. The political outcome was indeed different, but this does not necessarily mean that the U.S. miners were "more conservative" than their Scottish counterparts. As I will show, it means rather that they used different means to secure similar, although not identical, ends.

PART ONE

Class Formation among Colliers in Southwest Scotland, 1830–70

1

SOCIAL STRUCTURE AND CLASS IN EARLY
SCOTTISH MINING VILLAGES: WISHAW
AND LARKHALL, 1830–70

In the early years of the nineteenth century, Wishaw and Lark-hall typified dozens of small Lanarkshire communities that were undergoing the first phases of coal mine development. By 1840 Wishaw, which was situated on the north bank of the River Clyde, was further along in that process than Larkhall. The latter town, located on the south bank of the river, retained a more rural aspect. Stretches of fertile farmland held their own against the encroaching mine shafts, and the remnants of a preindustrial economy coexisted uneasily with the outposts of modern industry. Both towns, however, were beginning to feel the influence of Glasgow, the burgeoning metropolis twelve miles downriver that was rapidly becoming one of Britain's largest industrial cities. By the middle of the century, supplying Glasgow with iron and coal for domestic heating, export, and manufacturing had become the main source of their industrial wealth.[1]

Before industrialization took a serious hold, both Wishaw and Larkhall were clusters of small farming settlements grouped around a larger township. Both towns had a commercial center, but Wishaw resembled an elongated triangle, with Cambusnethan as its market center and Newmains, Overton, and Craigneuk serving as industrial outposts (see map 3). Larkhall was even more spread out (see map 4). Stonehouse and Quarter, two of the rural settlements where miners' row housing was later built, were more than a half-mile from the village proper.[2] The towns housed a few artisans, clergymen, and tradesmen, but the only significant industry in either place was hand-loom weaving. In the 1830s most of the weavers, typically men rather than women,

Map 3. Wishaw in 1864 (*source: Ordinance Survey of Great Britain* [1864]).

worked on looms in cottages or outhouses or performed one of the many other tasks associated with the trade. Local inhabitants not engaged in weaving, at first a majority in Larkhall, were tenant farmers or laborers employed on the estates of the local lairds.[3]

These mid-Lanarkshire lairds, whose hereditary position, large landed estates, and control over mineral rights enabled them to dominate the region's social and economic life, were of two kinds. The first was typified by the duke of Hamilton, the largest and most powerful landowner in the region, and by Lord Belhaven of Wishaw House. Both men were traditional aristocrats whose wealth and power had come from investments in land and other property and who turned to manufacturing as a supplementary source of income. In the 1830s Lord Belhaven established a distillery, a stone quarry, a tile manufacturing plant, and two primitive coal mines on his estate. In the

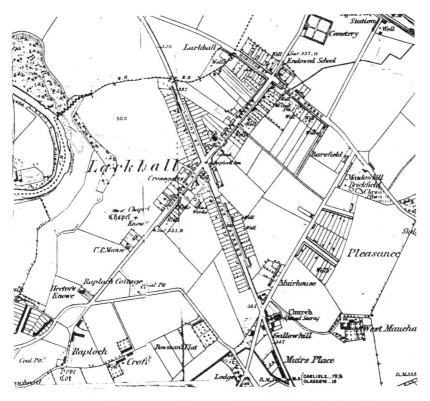

Map 4. Larkhall in 1864 (*source: Ordinance Survey of Great Britain* [1864]).

early days these shallow pits employed no more than a dozen men who used a horse and gin to raise their coal. Most of the duke of Hamilton's industrial wealth came from the royalties he secured from leasing coal lands to industrial entrepreneurs. Later he, too, established coal pits of his own on his estates.[4]

The second type of laird in the mid-Lanarkshire region was represented by Henry Houldsworth, a self-made Glasgow cotton manufacturer who hailed originally from Manchester. In 1836 Houldsworth purchased the Coltness estate from the aging landed aristocrat Sir Henry Steward. Soon afterward he established the Coltness Iron Works at Newmains, which together with Cambusnethan came to make up most of Wishaw. He also installed the blast furnaces at Coltness that were later to make the town one of the premier iron- and steel-producing centers in Scotland.[5] The Coltness Iron Works and other companies like it were made possible by two discoveries that, along with other innovations such as steam-driven machinery, undermined the preindustrial order in the Clyde Valley and helped to turn it into one of Britain's largest and most productive industrial regions. The first discovery occurred in 1801, when the manager of a small coal and iron company at Calder found that the local black stone, called "wild coal" by the local miners, was in fact iron ore. The second took place in 1828, when Glasgow engineer and chemist James Neilson revolutionized the iron-smelting process by inventing the hot blast. This new technique greatly improved the quality of the local iron, as well as its profitability.

The effect of these discoveries was immediate. In 1830 William Baird, who like Houldsworth was a self-made man, founded another great industrial empire when he established his iron works at Gartsherrie, near Coatbridge. (Coatbridge was located about twelve miles east of Glasgow and, like Wishaw, was located on the more heavily industrialized northern bank of the Clyde.) Baird's firm was followed by Merry and Cunningham, Wilson and Company, and ten or so other large iron producers. Two of these firms established blast furnaces in the Wishaw area as well. Unlike the traditional landed aristocracy, these new iron masters, although self-trained men, introduced up-to-date business methods, including modern accounting procedures, apprenticeship programs to produce skilled rollers and heaters, and the hiring of professional managers to whom they delegated considerable authority. The new iron masters also sank their own coal mines to supply their iron foundries with fuel. By 1854 the iron masters of the Glasgow region owned as many as eighty-two separate blast furnaces and produced 780,000 tons of pig iron per year.[6]

In 1844 Wishaw's industrial growth was further stimulated by the completion of the Wishaw and Coltness Railway. This line joined Newmains with Cambusnethan, encouraged other manufacturing companies to locate in the area, and linked Wishaw as a whole to major markets in Glasgow and the world beyond. In the 1840s and 1850s the Coltness Iron Works, as well as other local iron masters, began employing Irish unskilled laborers as pit-head workers and furnace fillers. From the 1850s on Wishaw's tangled web of railway lines, miners' row houses, belching blast furnaces, and desolate patches of open land marked it as typical of the mixed coal and iron towns that dotted the northern bank of the Clyde. By 1861 the town's population, only 3,373 in 1840, had jumped to 12,601.[7]

Larkhall, on the south bank of the Clyde, was more spread out and less advanced industrially than Wishaw. The coal industry there was dominated not by iron masters but by smaller-scale coal masters who produced nothing but coal. They sold it either to the iron companies for their smelters or

Table 1. Coal and Iron Companies Owning More Than One Colliery in Wishaw and
Larkhall and Valuation of Their Property Owned or Rented, 1861

	Name of Company	Number of Collieries	Property Valuation
Wishaw Iron	Coltness Iron Co.	8	£14,326
	Glasgow Iron Co.	4	4,904
	Shotts Iron Co.	2	120
	Merry & Cunningham	4	2,348
	Wishaw Iron Works	3	890
	John Wilson Co.	2	114
			£22,702
Coal	Boyd & Penman	2	£124
	Archibald Russell	2	88
	Robert Bell	2	72
			£284
Larkhall Iron	Colin Dunlop	5	£5,327
Coal	Hastie/Smith	4	£1,087
	Cochrine/Brand	4	1,000
	Hamilton/McCulloch	3	1,001
	Dunn Bros.	3	899
	Simpson, A.G.	3	762
	Robt. Cooper	2	664
	James Sym	2	119
	Alex Smith	2	90
	Merryton Coal	2	40
			£5,662

Sources: R. Hunt, *Mineral Statistics of U.K., 1860–1861,* 2 vols. (London, 1881), 1:114–15; Valuation Roll, Middle Ward of Lanarkshire, Scottish Record Office, VR 107/24; Alan Campbell, *The Lanarkshire Miners* (Edinburgh: John Donald, 1979), 214.

to other consumers of coal, such as local merchants, railroads, or larger coal companies that catered to Glasgow's domestic and export trade. The only iron works in the Larkhall district was built in the 1830s at Quarter, to the west of the town, on land that the duke of Hamilton leased to Colin Dunlop and Company. It was much smaller than the Coltness Iron Works at Newmains in Wishaw. Although the Dunlop Iron Works at Quarter was up to date, the coal pits that dotted the surrounding hay fields and orchards were smaller than the ones in Wishaw, and they used more primitive technology.[8]

These differences in scale between the coal industry in Wishaw and that in Larkhall are illustrated in table 1, which shows the value of coal properties belonging to coal and iron companies that owned more than one colliery. Some of the coal firms in Larkhall were quite large, but most of them had

fewer assets than the iron companies with pits either there or in Wishaw. The
turnover rate among coal companies was more rapid in Larkhall than it was
in Wishaw. The Larkhall coal masters also tended to live locally instead of in
Glasgow, Edinburgh, or even London, as many of the Wishaw iron masters
did. Both of these facts suggest that in the early days the coal masters in preindustrial Larkhall remained on more intimate terms with their employees
than the iron masters of Wishaw did.[9]

Understanding the process of class formation in Wishaw and Larkhall requires investigating the economic status, cultural background, and demographic characteristics of the growing number of colliers who flooded into
both towns in the middle decades of the nineteenth century. By 1871 Wishaw
and its satellite communities contained almost eight thousand male industrial workers, 77 percent of whom worked in the local coal or iron mines.
Larkhall, however, had just over half that number of industrial workers, the
majority of whom worked in the local coal pits.[10] Who were these Lanarkshire colliers, where did they come from, and how did they relate to the other
lower-class elements above and below them in the social hierarchy?

Because of their supposed rural isolation and their traditions of underground solidarity, no group of manual workers has been more subject to
occupational stereotyping than the miners. In the 1950s the favorite concept sociologists such as Clark Kerr and Abraham Siegel used to character-
ize the labor force in the mining industry was that of the "isolated mass."[11]
That concept, which focuses on the factor of physical isolation, was intended
to explain what supporters of the stereotype saw as the miners' automatic
predisposition to labor militancy manifested in high levels of unionization,
strike frequency, and political activism.

The isolated-mass hypothesis has rightly been criticized on a number of
grounds.[12] Not only does it leave little space for human agency, but it also is
an exclusively environmental argument that predicates the colliers' industrial militancy solely on the structural characteristics of the mining industry,
without reference to cultural or other exogenous factors such as the role of
the business cycle, individual labor leaders, or technological change. The
argument is also ahistorical. By taking the miners' presumed militancy as a
given in all places and times, the isolated-mass argument fails to distinguish
varying degrees of activism or social quiescence among different groups of
miners at different times. In reality miner behavior, like the behavior of other
workers, has varied greatly depending on time and place. Miners in some
countries have been politically conservative, whereas others have favored

third-party action. Some groups of miners have struck frequently, whereas others have eschewed strikes. In some regions miners have eagerly joined trade unions; in others—including southwest Scotland until the early part of the twentieth century—their unions have remained small and weak.[13]

These criticisms of the isolated-mass hypothesis apply just as forcefully to the colliers of Wishaw and Larkhall as to miners elsewhere. It is true that some of them lived in rural enclaves outside the main centers of the towns. For example, in both Stonecraigs Row, near Wishaw, and in the miners' rows at Quarter, outside Larkhall, colliers constituted an overwhelming majority of the residents.[14] Nevertheless, this type of residential segregation applied only to a relatively small number of colliers in the outlying districts of Wishaw and Larkhall. Most miners who lived in or near the centers of both towns did not reside in rural enclaves. They lived instead in urban housing that was occupationally quite mixed. For example, of forty-eight adult males living on East Main Street, Wishaw, in 1851, eleven were miners, twenty-one were tradesmen, four were professionals, three were tavern owners, and the rest were other workers. A similar pattern existed in the census years of 1861 and 1871, save that by this time the proportion of miners had declined somewhat.[15] The same kind of residential pattern prevailed in Hamilton Street, Larkhall, except that weavers outnumbered miners throughout the thirty-year period.[16]

Even in the geographically peripheral miners' rows, where colliers always constituted a majority of the male population, other workers were sometimes present. This was particularly true in the miners' rows situated near the local ironworks, where miners and ironworkers often lived side by side. For example, the occupations of thirty-four adult males living with their families in a row at Quarter in 1871 broke down as follows: seventeen miners, five furnace fillers, four laborers, three puddlers, two heaters, two rollers, and one engine keeper.[17] Among this group of workers, both the puddlers and the heaters, along with the rollers and furnace fillers, worked for the iron companies, not in the coal pits. This residential mixing suggests the possibility of a plebeian alliance between artisans, petty bourgeois tradesmen, and miners. It does not validate the notion of miners as an "isolated mass."

The isolated-mass argument also ignores the fact that as the Lanarkshire coalfield expanded rapidly in the middle years of the nineteenth century, its labor force was repeatedly restructured. One reason for this restructuring was the decline of hand-loom weaving in places such as Larkhall. As the power loom rendered weaving jobs obsolete, hundreds of hand-loom weavers left the area, some of them going abroad.[18] A second reason was the massive industrial development in nearby Glasgow. Every year its burgeoning textile, shipping, and engineering industries drew thousands of new recruits from the Scottish Highlands, Ireland, and the coal and iron towns that surrounded the city. At the same time these towns were attracting a flow of new recruits to their pits, reinforcing the fluidity of the industrial population.[19] Although the number of miners born in Wishaw and Larkhall rose during this twenty-year period, the proportion of locally born miners declined from 61 percent to 41 percent of Wishaw's population and from 79 percent to 62 percent of Larkhall's.[20] The proportion of locally born miners remained higher in Larkhall than it was in Wishaw, reflecting the greater social homogeneity of that town,[21] but the rate of turnover in Larkhall stayed high as well.

Further analysis of the data also points up the differences between short-distance and long-distance migration into the Lanarkshire coalfield. The newcomers who entered the mines from counties adjacent to Lanarkshire — some from agricultural areas such as Renfrewshire and Stirlingshire and others from semiurban mining counties such as Ayrshire, Midlothian, and West Lothian — came in roughly equal proportions to both towns. Most of the long-distance migrants, on the other hand, came from Ireland. These Irish immigrants rose more rapidly and constituted a much higher proportion of the total number of miners in the Wishaw pits than they did in those of Larkhall. In 1871 the Irish made up 26 percent of Wishaw's miners but only 10 percent of Larkhall's.[22]

In the 1830s and early 1840s most of these Irish migrants were young, single men and women from Ulster and Connaught who disembarked at ports such as Ardrossan and Stranraer on the Clyde coast. They either sought seasonal work as harvesters or took jobs as navvies in mobile construction camps helping to build industrial Scotland's network of canals and railways.[23] Initially most of these Irish "birds of passage" returned home after their seasonal work was done, but as time passed and the coal industry expanded, high wages led increasing numbers of them to take permanent jobs in the pits.[24]

In the later 1840s and early 1850s, these migrants were supplemented by a second wave of Irish immigrants. These were famine Irish who were brought in by large iron masters such as Baird and Company to break the strikes of the emerging miners' unions. Given the plight of Irish men and women fleeing the potato famines of 1845 and 1846, it was not hard to persuade them to replace the striking Scots, but their role as strikebreakers caused much bitterness among the native-born colliers. Combined with religious conflicts and differences over work and spending habits, this bitterness helped to create a political and cultural rift between the Protestant Scots and the Catholic Irish miners, both in the community and to some extent down the pit, that lasted well into the twentieth century.[25]

A final element in the restructuring of the mine labor force in Lanark-shire, one that repeated itself several times in Wishaw and Larkhall during the course of industrialization, concerns the persistence rate of individual miners. Contrary to Kerr and Siegel's isolated-mass hypothesis, a significant body of literature shows that miners generally moved quite frequently, doing so to find a better workplace or superior housing, to evade the employers' blacklists, or to earn a better tonnage rate.[26] In addition, especially if they were young and single, they would migrate from one coalfield to another or even from one country to another simply to see something of the world. It was this incentive that drove many young, single Lanarkshire miners to immigrate either temporarily or permanently to Australia, Canada, or the mining regions of the eastern United States in the period after the American Civil War.

Nevertheless, some historians still assume that because western Europe's working class was usually more "settled" than North America's, groups of workers in the United Kingdom moved less often than did their U.S. counter-parts.[27] This assumption has yet to be disproved for the labor force in both countries considered as a whole, but with regard to miners in Wishaw and Larkhall, the evidence on persistence rates calls it into question. The cen-sus data cited in the sample that follows must be treated with caution. Taken only once every ten years, the population census took no account of short- or long-distance movement in the interim. Short-term "flitting" from one neighborhood to another, as colliers looked for higher wages or more pro-ductive work rooms in different mines in the same neighborhood, was par-ticularly frequent in the mining industry.[28] The frequent use of similar names among the Scottish and the Irish miners also poses a matching problem. As a consequence, the sample chosen for analysis consists only of miners whose identity could be confirmed by other data, such as date of birth.

Nevertheless, data taken from the 1851 and 1861 Scottish population cen-suses suggest that the persistence rate among miners in Larkhall (defined as individuals found at the same address after a ten-year period) was only 14 percent. In Wishaw it was as low as 7 percent, possibly reflecting the larger number of young, single Irish miners who moved in and out of the Wishaw pits. In 1861–71 the persistence rate in both places fell even lower, standing at 9 percent for Larkhall and 4 percent for Wishaw.[29] As I will show in a subse-quent chapter, persistence rates were only slightly higher in southwest Scot-land than they were in the Braidwood-Streator area of northern Illinois. The development of face-to-face relationships over time is often thought to be a crucial element in the process of working-class formation. The fact that persistence rates were approximately the same in Lanarkshire and northern

Illinois suggests that — from this point of view, at least — the class-formation process did not differ as much between British and American coal miners as we have been led to believe.

A related and equally dubious stereotype frequently attached to coal miners portrays them as "archetypal proletarians." This stereotype, which has frequently been repeated by Marxist scholars, casts the miner as a quintessential proletarian who manifested the highest virtues of working-class solidarity.[30] It focuses less on the supposed physical isolation of the colliers and more on the argument that their sense of comradeship and mutual dependence fostered their presumed high level of labor militancy. According to this view, miners were a relatively uniform mass of unskilled or at best semiskilled workers. Their dangerous working conditions and intimacy down the pit fostered an inherently oppositional temperament that frequently placed them at odds with their employers. In the hands of contemporary critics, who were numerous among both patriarchal Scottish lairds and high-minded middle-class coal owners, the notion of miners as quintessential proletarians had a second and more sinister connotation. Instead of implying praise, it indicated a deplorable tendency toward illiteracy, violence, excessive drinking, and profligacy, both economic and sexual.[31]

Like the isolated-mass concept, the "archetypal proletarian" stereotype of the Scottish miner (and his English and American counterparts) has in recent years quite rightly been attacked as a partial and distorted image that bears only a limited relationship to reality. Alan Campbell and Fred Reid, in particular, have done much to debunk the negative aspects of the concept and to rescue the mid-nineteenth-century miner from the condescension of his critics. Far from being an unskilled wage laborer, they argue, the typical Scottish miner in these years was an "independent collier." He was a petty contractor who sold his labor at so much per ton for a designated period of time and who drew up a contract for this purpose with the coal owner or his agent. After the terms of the contract were fulfilled, the miner might renew it, move on to another mine, or take some time off to occupy himself with other matters.[32]

The idea that the early nineteenth-century Scottish miner was a petty contractor who took time off from working in the pits challenges the notion that he was from the beginning a class-conscious proletarian who was engaged from dawn to dusk in the dangerous and dehumanizing task of hewing coal. To the contrary, in places such as Larkhall, where miners lived next door to (and in some cases intermarried with) the daughters of farmers and farm laborers, many of them had a preindustrial association with the land. Some of the bigger miners' houses in Larkhall had gardens large enough to enable the residents to plant vegetables and keep chickens and sometimes even a cow. According to Naismith's *Hamilton Directory* for 1878–99, for example, many of the local colliers in the village of Quarter turned to "country wark [*sic*]" in the summer, when demand for coal for domestic heating slacked off. This work often involved using their traditional pick-mining skills in stone quarries and lime works, but it also included helping local farmers at haytime and harvest. "Being economical and thrifty," Naismith wrote, "they were mostly all 'bien' [prosperous] and well-to-do."[33]

Campbell and Reid also correctly assailed the idea that, because they lacked formal apprenticeships, miners were typically unskilled laborers. It is true that pick mining demanded great physical stamina of a sort not usually required of labor aristocrats such as engineers or carpenters. Nevertheless, the assumption that the premechanized pick miner was unskilled seriously underestimates his prowess. As he worked, often in semidarkness in his individual workplace or room, the Scottish collier had to accomplish a variety of tasks that required extensive knowledge, even if it was not learned from books. He had to know how to undercut a seam without causing it to fall on top of him, how to detect gas, how to interpret the creaks and groans in the rocks above him, and how and where to insert his blasting needle so as to explode his powder without killing his workmates and himself. "To hew coal is a peculiar and difficult task," wrote one observer of the Scottish miners in 1853. "The men have been brought up to it . . . through the successive grades of trapping, teaming and putting. Hewing is the top-most promotion — the colonelcy of the regiment."[34]

With regard to allegations of excessive drinking, Campbell and Reid acknowledge that consuming large quantities of liquor was then, as it still is, an integral part of the lifestyle of most coal miners not only in Lanarkshire but throughout Britain and in other countries. In Scotland the drinking of whiskey was prohibited underground for fear of accidents, but it was an integral part not only of social life in places such as Larkhall and Wishaw but also of the training process for a young collier. In the 1830s and even earlier, after a youth acquired the skills of a fully trained collier at around age sixteen, a brothering ceremony was held for the newly trained miner in which the participants exchanged loyalty oaths and drank a "social glass."[35]

It is also true that significant numbers of miners drank away part of their wages, especially on Saturday night after payday. To the consternation of the local coal and iron masters, as well as of middle-class reformers, the largest number of street brawls recorded in Wishaw and Larkhall took place on

Saturday nights after the public houses closed. Some of the altercations were mere fistfights, but others were more serious, involving stabbings or even murder by youthful hotheads who lost control of their tempers. When processions of Irish Catholic miners, commemorating prior struggles against the British Crown, marched through predominantly Protestant neighborhoods of native Scots, cries of "No Popery" sometimes escalated into full-fledged street battles. Mondays saw the largest number of colliers brought up before the magistrates in Wishaw or in Hamilton, where the Larkhall drunkards were arraigned. Campbell and Reid, however, also point to the large number of temperance societies that were established during this period not simply by the coal masters' wives and church leaders of all denominations but also by the colliers themselves. The miners' wives were frequently active in these temperance clubs, since they had even more to fear from the evils of drinking than their menfolk had. Wife beating was a common crime.[36]

The allegations of sexual impropriety Victorian critics leveled against the miners seem at first to find justification in the coal miners' illegitimacy rates, which were higher than those for most other kinds of workers. In fact, however, this high rate was due partly to the way men and women were thrown together in the pit before the 1842 Mines Act removed women from the mines and partly to the overcrowded housing conditions of the day. It was not due to inherent depravity. Reminiscing some years later about his time spent working down a Scottish pit, Kellog Durland noted that the three-room house in which he lodged was occupied by no fewer than fourteen people, including a miner's grown daughter who had to share a bed on a rotational basis with several male lodgers.[37]

The claim that miners were spendthrifts and uninterested in education also receives a balanced reply. There is much evidence, for example, of penny banks and miner-run insurance societies in the Lanarkshire coal towns at this time. Records deposited in the Scottish Record Office at Edinburgh show the Millheugh Friendly Society, Larkhall St. Thomas' Lodge, and four other Larkhall mutual benefit societies operating for long periods in the nineteenth century. At least three others, including a funeral society and the Wishaw Iron Works Society, were present in Wishaw.[38]

With respect to education, miners in both Wishaw and Larkhall did tend to take their sons out of school at an earlier age than did skilled workers in a number of other trades. But they did this partly because of the scarcity of schools, partly because of the hereditary nature of the pick miner's trade (which mandated that a boy follow his father into the pit at the age of ten or even younger), and partly because of the vitally needed extra earnings that a son could provide as soon as he was old enough to go down the mine. It was not necessarily because the miners were uninterested in education. In 1860 John Gordon, inspector of schools for the Lanarkshire district, commended local colliers who attended evening lectures, adding that "in some places, the works libraries are much used."[39]

All in all, Campbell and Reid's critique of the archetypal miner stereotype is largely accurate. Far from being instinctual rebels predisposed toward radicalism and violence, in the 1850s and 1860s the more thoughtful and literate Lanarkshire miners articulated a coherent labor philosophy that portrayed the colliers, along with the coal masters, as joint custodians of the wealth the coal industry created and that advocated restraint in their relations with the employers. This philosophy, which was group conscious rather than class conscious, was articulated most fully by Alexander McDonald, who was the most important Scottish miners' leader of the day. Since it was also carried across the Atlantic after the American Civil War by the colliers who immigrated to the United States, it is important to understand its meaning fully.

McDonaldism, as it can be called, was based originally on the idea of the coal miner as a petty contractor who, in terms of his skill and pride in craft — although not necessarily politically or socially — saw himself as the equal of the coal owner. In a speech reported in the *Glasgow Herald* in March 1867, Alexander McDonald rejected the laissez-faire market principles of the then fashionable Manchester school of political economists. "According to the popular teaching of those principles," he wrote, "capital rules labour." According to McDonald, however, this was not and should not be the case in relations between coal miner and coal owner or indeed between employers and other categories of workers. Instead, McDonald went on: "As the workmen view the matter money is the capital of the employer; labour is the capital of the workmen. The one capital is dependent on the other, while the union of both, their cooperation and partnership, is calculated to produce certain results popularly known as profits. . . . The great problem of the day is to devise the means which shall ensure an amicable adjustment — a fair division of profits among the respective capitalists [i.e., employers and workers]."[40]

McDonald advocated arbitration and conciliation for securing this "fair division of profits" and for settling disputes between owners and workers. In the 1850s and 1860s, before the Scottish miners' union had established permanent mechanisms for employer-employee negotiations, these arbitrations were carried out on a volunteer basis. Sometimes public officials in the coal towns, or even the mayor of Glasgow, would bring miners and coal masters together to settle disputes. At other times disagreements would be settled by direct negotiation between representatives of the miners and their employers.[41]

In adopting this approach, Alexander McDonald was to some extent advocating a doctrine of class collaboration, if not of outright class harmony,
between masters and men. This was a philosophy that was widely held on
both sides of the Atlantic in the middle decades of the nineteenth century.[42]
Both colliers and coal masters, McDonald believed, shared a common interest in extracting wealth from the minerals that lay beneath the ground. The
only real issue between them was how that wealth, whether in the form of
profits to the coal owners or wages to the coal miner, should be distributed.
Nonetheless, neither McDonald nor his followers were naive enough to believe that, in a world where the coal owners possessed all the mineral rights,
plants, and machinery, power relations between mine owner and miner were
truly equal and that the coal and ironmasters would voluntarily surrender a
major proportion of their profits to their men. Hence in practice the miners
employed two devices to protect their earnings and to secure their fair share
of the profits extracted from the pits. The first was the limited darg, or self-
imposed quota of coal, which the miner hewed and loaded into wagons each
day to be hauled away to the shaft bottom and hoisted to the surface.[43]

By restricting the amount of his darg, which amounted to between two
and three tons a day, the skilled Scottish miner could to some extent control
his output, the market price of coal, and the profits taken by the coal masters. At this time the market price for coal was largely determined by the state
of demand among coal exporters, Glasgow's coal merchants, and the large-
scale industrial purchasers of fuel, especially iron manufacturers. Since labor
costs accounted for approximately 40 percent of the coal owners' total expenses, by restricting the level of output the colliers could fairly easily induce
a shortage in supply. In turn — depending on the state of the business cycle —
this shortage drove up coal prices, thereby increasing both the profits that
could be made by the coal master and the wage (or price per ton) that the
individual coal miner earned.[44]

This policy of output restriction tended to discourage strikes, at least in
theory. If the miners could maintain or increase their wage levels by voluntarily limiting the output of coal and resolve disputes by discussing them
around a table with their employers, then strikes — which McDonald saw as
damaging and costly to both coal owners and miners — would be rendered
unnecessary. Contrary to Marxist historian Raymond Challinor, one ought
not to view this vision of class harmony simply as a class-collaborationist sell-
out by the Lanarkshire miners' union leadership abandoning the interests
of the rank and file.[45] Rather, it was a means of maintaining autonomy and
dignity for a wide range of miners while exerting sufficient pressure on the

coal owners to force them to acknowledge the legitimate interests of their employees.

The second mechanism the colliers used to protect their position involved controlling the labor supply. By limiting the number and the quality of the colliers who were allowed to work in the mines, the Lanarkshire miners sought to preserve their skills, influence output further, and protect themselves against the employment of inexperienced outsiders who might endanger lives by their ignorance of mining. Consistent with Alexander McDonald's philosophy, efforts to control coal output and the supply of labor in the pits became the main building blocks of the trade union policy pursued by the Scottish miners. It was already apparent in the mid-1840s, when William Baird and other iron masters began bringing in unskilled Irish peasants to work the pits in Wishaw, Coatbridge, and elsewhere. In response miners' leader William Cloughan defended the "restrictions of trade unions on apprentices and learners from other occupations as necessary to prevent the trade or calling from being overstocked with hands." The men's tasks and callings were their "private property," Cloughan argued, "and they had a right by union to protect it and keep it to themselves." [46]

Hence from the first not only the Scottish Coal and Iron Miners Association, which was established in 1855, but also the local colliers' unions in Wishaw and Larkhall included in their rules and regulations elaborate financial premiums and penalties designed to protect the skilled pick miners' jobs. Anyone joining the Wishaw Miners Association, which was founded in 1850, had to pay "entry money." If he had previously worked in the pits as a boy, the sum would be fifty pence. Anyone who had not previously worked as a miner was expected to pay the impossibly high entrance fee of £1.[47] These new rules also continued sanctions on "refractory men" that went from fines all the way up to expulsion from the union.[48] These initial tactics bespoke a form of group-conscious, rather than class-conscious, behavior in which the independence of each individual collier at the workplace was guaranteed in order to protect the common interests of the colliers as a whole.

Nevertheless, in their haste to rescue the colliers from the negative stereotypes associated with the archetypal proletarian concept, Reid and Campbell also presented a unidimensional portrait that unnecessarily romanticizes the Lanarkshire miners and limits our understanding of them as emerging members of the Scottish working class. A further review of the evidence suggests strongly that there were several different kinds of colliers working in the Scottish pits at this time, not all of whom conformed to the independent collier stereotype. Given the rapid turnover in the mines, the small size of the miners' unions, and the strict rules they imposed to prevent newcomers from getting jobs, it seems likely that Campbell and Reid described only an elite group of traditional pick miners at the top of the occupational hierarchy, not the entire labor force.

In the 1830s and early 1840s, before significant numbers of Irish and other newcomers entered the pits, the independent collier stereotype may well have fitted a majority of the native Scots who worked in the Lanarkshire mines. At that time the pits were still shallow, work habits were informal, and the all-around miners still constituted a significant proportion of all employees. By the 1860s and 1870s, however, when pits were being deepened and new technology was being introduced, a new division of labor had already begun to undermine the dominant position of the older generation of skilled pick miners and to create a more differentiated occupational hierarchy both down the pit and in the servicing jobs on the surface.[49]

By this time the skilled hewers constituted only about 60 percent of the labor force in the larger pits, with the number falling as time passed. Various other workers were now employed, both above ground and below it. Many of the newer workers were Irish in background, with a lower level of skills than their Scottish counterparts and with a different set of values. The heterogeneity of this new mine labor force, which also included other types of skilled artisans such as firemen, carpenters, engineers, and blacksmiths, throws doubt on the ubiquity of the stereotypic independent collier.

An article published by mining expert James Barrowman in May 1882 reviewed developments in the Lanarkshire coalfield over the previous twenty years. Barrowman distinguished between three broad categories of workers that, he said, had already emerged in the mine labor force during the 1860s. First there were the underground face workers and their helpers, who actually cut the coal. They constituted just over half the labor force. Second were the haulage workers, pit boys, and cage operators who moved the coal from the colliers' individual rooms to the surface. They made up about 20 percent of the work force. The remainder of the work force consisted of "oncost" men, who were usually not miners as such but engineers and wage laborers paid by the hour instead of by the ton. They were divided by skill level as well as by work site, either surface or underground. Among the new categories of underground workers were pit bottomers, who loaded the cages at the foot of the shaft; "brushers," or "redsmen," who cleared the underground roadways of falls and debris; and timbermen and firemen. The latter checked out the underground passages for gas before the shift began.[50]

Common sense suggests that the interests of all these workers were not always the same. The engineers who serviced the pithead machinery, for example, had skills very different from those of the coal miners; in fact, later in the century they belonged to a different trade union. Because they were paid by the hour at a fixed rate, neither underground nor surface oncost workers would automatically welcome an idle day called by the underground hewers, who might declare a work stoppage for their own reasons once they had completed their darg. In addition, petty jealousies often developed between the "oversman" (supervisor) and the hewer over the assignment of workplaces, between the hewer and the brusher over the correct way to keep the roadways clear, and between the fireman and the hewer over the proper way to inspect a workplace for gas.[51]

Also throwing doubt on the ubiquity of the independent collier are the changes to the traditional stoop-and-room method of mining prompted by the introduction of the longwall system. The independence that the skilled pick miner cherished under the stoop-and-room method, and that formed the basis for much of his work culture, was predicated in large part on the freedom of action he enjoyed as master of his own individual workplace or room and on his ability to come and go as he pleased, especially his power to summon the cage to travel to the surface when he saw fit. Under this early method of extraction, which predominated until midcentury, the pick miner worked alone or with a drawer or helper who was often his son. Under these circumstances the traditional pick miner could determine how much coal to cut, when to take breaks, and when and how to load his daily darg into the hutches. Under the longwall system, however, the coal was extracted in one operation by a line of men — perhaps as many as thirty — advancing simultaneously against the coal face. Whereas stoops (pillars of coal) had previously been left to sustain the roof and walls of separate workrooms, now the coal was collapsed in a controlled manner behind the line of men as they moved forward.[52]

Most coal owners preferred the longwall method because it facilitated supervision of their work force and enabled a greater division of labor at the coal face. By 1873 out of 169 pits operating in the eastern part of Lanarkshire (which included both Hamilton and Cambusnethan Parishes — i.e., all of Wishaw and parts of Larkhall), 87 were worked on the longwall system and 69 on the stoop-and-room technique.[53] This development, with the consequent increase in supervision, must have limited the skilled pick miners' workplace autonomy, which was a central part of the independent collier way of life. Also limiting the miners' autonomy were deeper mine shafts and the addition of cages that were now controlled not by the miners but by agents of the employers, sharply curtailing the traditional collier's ability to come and go from the pit as he pleased.

The increasingly varied character of the mining labor force in Wishaw and Larkhall similarly casts doubt on the ubiquity of the independent collier. The likelihood that the notion of the independent collier is a top-down concept, rather than one that can be applied to all mid-nineteenth-century colliers, is reinforced by the resistance that many of the lower-paid colliers displayed toward Alexander McDonald's policies regarding output restriction and strikes. In the 1840s and 1850s many of the native-born Scots miners accepted McDonald's call to limit their output (and hence exert an upward pressure on wages) by cutting a small daily darg. Recent recruits to the mines, on the other hand, whose inferior skills made them less productive, were less likely to do so. This was particularly true of young, inexperienced Irish immigrants. These men wanted to earn as much money as they could as quickly as they could, in order to accumulate savings they could send back to their families in Ireland or perhaps use to finance their own immigration to the United States.[54] To the irritation of their trade union leaders, therefore, they quite frequently acceded to the coal masters' calls for a "big darg," eschewing the "small darg" mandated by McDonald's philosophy.[55]

A similar point can be made with regard to the incidence of strikes. Despite McDonald's calls for restraint, strikes over unfair weighing practices, wage cuts, and other grievances remained endemic in the Lanarkshire coalfield, as well as in Wishaw and Larkhall. Gordon Wilson has tabulated the number of strikes in the coal-producing counties of western Scotland between 1842 and 1874. After 1854, he reports, "one feature of these new mining communities seems to have been their readiness to strike. There were three major strikes [each one lasting several weeks] in each district from 1855 to 1874, thirty lesser ones in Wishaw/Motherwell and twenty-two in Hamilton/Larkhall."[56] This was one of the highest levels of strike activity throughout western Scotland.

For all these reasons, any adequate description of class formation among miners in general — and those in Wishaw and Larkhall in particular — must abandon the notion of a single ideal type, whether it be isolated mass, archetypal proletarian, or independent collier. A more realistic appraisal of the Lanarkshire collier between 1830 and 1870 acknowledges the presence of at least three different elements, or groups, among them. The basis for making this three-way distinction is further validated in an article that a contemporary observer of the Scottish miners, Robert Haddow, wrote for the magazine

Nineteenth Century in September 1888.[57] Haddow described the differences between these three groups largely in cultural terms. To these differences I add the distinctions just made on the basis of generation, skill, and type of occupation at the workplace. Amalgamating these different levels of analysis, I argue that the mine labor force was divided into at least three basic groups: artisan-colliers, semi-proletarians, and newcomer-rebels.

The artisan-collier comes nearest to exemplifying Campbell and Reid's category of independent collier. Proud, responsible, and thrifty, these experienced pick miners saw themselves not as wage earners but as labor aristocrats who continued to reject underground supervision and negotiate individual contracts with mine owners after other elements in the trade had ceased doing so. In the days before the mass migration of Irish workers into the Scottish pits, most of these artisan-colliers were probably Lowland Protestant Scots. By midcentury, as Campbell and Reid point out, these men looked on their profession "as a sort of hereditary right, which had descended from generation to generation, for which they had to undergo a regular apprenticeship."[58]

This cadre of artisan-colliers produced most of the early leaders of the Scottish miners' unions, such as Alexander McDonald. "He has in most cases an education quite equal to that of a skilled artisan," Haddow writes of this type of miner. "He reads much; he thinks much, and has opinions of his own. . . . The colliers of this stamp are for the most part sober, steady and thrifty."[59] At the opposite end of the miner spectrum were the newcomer-rebels. Most of the men in this group were either young, single native Scots fresh from the countryside or first-generation Irish immigrants. These men sought to make money quickly either as helpers in the mines or as furnace workers or casual laborers in the iron works.[60] Contemptuous of authority, sometimes violent, and often a heavy drinker, the newcomer-rebel was disdained by the more respectable artisan-colliers and was often excluded from the miners' union until he had completed his apprenticeship. If he did become a fully trained miner, the newcomer-rebel tended to strike often and to favor a big darg. "In the pit he is an obstruction and a danger," writes Haddow of this group of men, "and in the social life of the village he is a nuisance; for he is always the noisiest and most quarrelsome of the noisy and inebriate who make a horror of the Saturday nights."[61]

Between the artisan-colliers and the newcomer-rebels was a third group I have labeled the semi-proletarians. This group was composed partly of older artisan-colliers whose skills were threatened by the growing division of labor and partly of newcomer-rebels whose ability to move up into the position of artisan-collier was being undermined by the same process. It also included the longwall mineworkers, as well as an increasing number of oncost workers who were paid a daily wage.[62]

The internal stratification of the mine labor force did not mean that the miners who composed it did not share a great deal in common. In the early days most of the artisan-colliers continued to defer to the existing social order. Both in the pit and the community, however, members of all three groups shared increasing feelings of alienation, if not of outright hostility, both toward the local lairds or landowners who made large sums of money by leasing their land to the coal owners and toward the coal and iron masters who employed them. When underground explosions killed or maimed their fellow miners, or when a lockout forced them to leave their company-owned houses, the three groups would forget their differences in a common effort to rescue the victims, bury the dead, and raise money for the families of miners who had been evicted from their homes.[63]

In addition, despite my criticisms of the isolated-mass and archetypal proletarian hypotheses, at least one generalization about the strong bonds of solidarity that developed among miners does hold up under scrutiny. This is the idea that they constituted an "occupational community." [64] Like loggers, longshoremen, or men aboard ship, the colliers of Wishaw and Larkhall at this time shared a mutual life not only at their workplace underground — where common danger forged many powerful links — but also above ground in their communities. There were, of course, important cultural and political differences between the Irish and Scottish miners in the two towns. For example, as far as can be ascertained, there was little intermarriage between the sons of Protestant miners and the daughters of Catholic ones, despite the important role that the women of both communities played in supporting their collier husbands both at home and on the picket line.[65]

Unlike big city workers, however, many of the male colliers in Wishaw and Larkhall saw each other every day after work as well as down the pit. They drank together at the same public houses, cheered on the same prize-fighters, married the same kind of women, and attended the same union meetings on the banks of the River Clyde. Many of the Scottish colliers also shared a hereditary way of life in which they would train their sons (or perhaps a neighbor's boy) to follow them down the pit. Another attribute helped the various elements of the Scottish mining communities to bond and hence to develop a strong sense of class identity early on: their low level of upward social mobility. Alexander McDonald, like James Keir Hardie, William Small, and others who succeeded them as Lanarkshire County union officers in the late nineteenth century, was (in the local vernacular) a "lad o' pairts" who managed to get himself educated and to climb up and out of the pits. Born in Damacoulter in 1821, after some years in the mines McDonald saved enough money to attend Glasgow University between 1846 and 1849. He then taught school, became the preeminent nineteenth-century Scottish miners' leader, and played an important role both in the British Trades Union Congress (1868) and in Parliament, which he entered in 1874.[66]

But McDonald's career was highly exceptional. Until the Scottish Education Act of 1872, only a small proportion of the coal miners' sons and daughters went to school for more than two or three years. A few of the boys might later become tavernkeepers or skilled artisans, and some of the girls, shop assistants or teachers. The vast majority of boys remained in the pits, however; only a handful of them were promoted to the position of oversman or mine manager, and still fewer graduated from the Glasgow School of Mines.[67] It was also rare for young colliers to marry the daughters of the local shopkeepers, tradesmen, or indeed anyone higher in the social hierarchy. I have traced the occupations of 106 fathers-in-law of miners who lived in Wishaw and Larkhall in the census years of 1851, 1861, and 1871. Most of these men were either weavers, laborers, farmhands, or furnace fillers from the local iron works. Only six were shopkeepers or professionals.[68] Nearly all the mine managers employed in the early days were either the sons of the coal masters or specialists brought in from the outside. Most of the colliers in Wishaw and Larkhall were part of a compact working class whose upper boundary was more rigid than it was in the case of other skilled British workers. As I will show in a subsequent chapter, this upper boundary was far more fluid in the case of American miners.

In the early years of the nineteenth century, therefore, the colliers of Larkhall and Wishaw constituted the lower segment of a clearly defined social hierarchy that contained few opportunities for social advancement. At the time, this social hierarchy was ruled by a small group of aristocratic lairds and middle-class iron and coal masters who, even if they did not always see eye to eye on politics or modern business methods, agreed in treating the miners as members of an inferior, semicriminal class who were in no sense their equals. The intervening stratum of shopkeepers, merchants, and professionals was quite small. It is also apparent from my references to strikes that the early nineteenth-century miners of Wishaw and Larkhall were already willing to register their protests against those coal owners who were unwilling to acknowledge the colliers' right to fair treatment down the mines. As my critique of the isolated-mass, archetypal proletarian, and independent collier concepts makes clear, however, no single stereotype satisfactorily encompasses all these colliers. Nor were they automatically radicals.

Instead, the growth of class solidarity among these colliers, like that among other groups of workers, must be seen as a historically contingent process that took place over time. As I will show in the next chapter, there is no doubt that by 1864 both the colliers of Wishaw and Larkhall and the coal and iron masters who employed them had developed a sense of themselves and their relations with each other quite different from the ones they had held in 1830. Over time the miners' shared predispositions, linked to a list of common grievances that they were soon to articulate, moved the colliers from the perception of themselves as a group apart to that of a body of men who were prepared to engage in collective action against their employers on a wide range of issues. But the transition from shared predispositions to collective action was not automatic. It had to be shaped by human agency.[69]

2

CONFLICT AND ACCOMMODATION IN LANARKSHIRE, 1830–64

During the middle decades of the nineteenth century, the miners of Wishaw and Larkhall accumulated shared grievances that by 1864 led them to take common action to defend their interests against their employers on a wide variety of fronts. These grievances were of two kinds. The first derived from the local coal and iron masters' efforts to introduce new technology and new forms of work discipline into the shallow, primitive coal pits that characterized the industry in the 1830s and 1840s. The second grew out of the coal owners' parallel effort to exert new forms of social and political control over the miners within their communities.

Given the single-industry nature of most coal towns, these two aims were closely intertwined. The problem of excessive drinking, for example, not only affected the private and public behavior of the colliers in places such as Wishaw and Larkhall; it also created safety problems for the coal owners. Nor was the miners' response to these efforts at social control uniformly hostile or class conscious in the modern sense. On such matters as temperance and education, for example, both of which the coal owners influenced considerably, most miners adopted what can best be called an accommodationist stance. Like their employers, they sought to take advantage of the reforming trends that affected mid-Victorian society. But the two factions often had very different views as to what direction those reforms should take.

On workplace issues the miners' opposition to the policies of their employers was also quite complex. For example, it is unlikely that many of the newcomer-rebels or semi-proletarians objected strongly to the owners' introduction of new technology in the early days, if only because they had no prior experience of the artisan-collier's long-standing traditions of work. In the 1850s and 1860s, moreover, the outlook of the artisan-colliers dominated both the ethos of the collier work force in general and the policies of their unions. The early miners' unions were united in their determination to preserve the collier's ability to set his own darg, to determine who should work in the pits, and to decide how the miner's output should be disposed of. In addition, when it came to such matters as underground discipline, safety, or the uses that the coal owners made of truck or company stores, the colliers displayed virtually unanimous opposition to their employers' policies. This chapter explores these matters in more detail, showing how they contributed to the process of class formation on both sides of the economic divide.

In the early days most Lanarkshire coal and iron masters failed to distinguish between the relative moderation — and strivings toward respectability — of the artisan-colliers, on the one hand, and the more truculent behavior of the semi-proletarians and newcomer-rebels, on the other. The condescending attitude of the coal-owning elite was captured in a comment made in 1844 by H. S. Tremenheere, the first government inspector of the mines, who frequently stayed with Lord and Lady Belhaven when he visited the Lanarkshire pits. He condemned the colliers for what he called their "moral degeneration." "Sensuality," he stated, "has produced indolence and a craving after more pay and less work. Dissoluteness of life, rudeness of manners, and contempt for the authority of parents [among miners' children] lead immediately to a contempt for, and opposition to, ... the legitimate authority of masters."[1]

Tremenheere's attitude was typical. As soon as mid-Victorian reformers such as Lord Shaftesbury began their paternalistic efforts concerning matters such as child labor in the mines, the entrepreneurs who controlled the Lanarkshire mining industry lost no time in asserting as much control as they could over the local working population in the name of modernization and moral uplift.[2] In the mid-1840s the coal owners became particularly alarmed about the influx of the famine Irish, who contributed a large proportion of the newcomer-rebel element in the mines.[3] After the Wishaw town council was founded in 1856, for example, one of the first targets of its new police force was the customary rights and practices that had come down to the colliers from their preindustrial past. Quite a few native Scots miners had for generations supplemented their diets by hunting rabbits or even deer on lands belonging to the duke of Hamilton or other local lairds. This practice was also taken up by the incoming Irish, who were if anything even more hostile than the Scots miners to the local aristocrats' manipulative behavior. The 1840s and 1850s saw an increasing number of arrests for these crimes. A desire to stamp out hunting may also have been present in one of the early rules posted by the Coltness Iron Company. The rule banned employees from keeping "dogs, swine, poultry or firearms on their premises on pain of instant dismissal."[4]

A second source of social control — and hence of growing class antagonism — derived from the influence that the coal and iron masters acquired over their employees' domestic lives by owning a large proportion of the housing stock, particularly in Wishaw and to a lesser extent in Larkhall. The most common type of coal company housing, which was later to become notorious, was the so-called miners' rows. Most of these rows were built near the pits or blast furnaces and rented out to the workers. The rent in these miners' rows was low, sometimes no more than a fifty pence a month, but it was deducted automatically from the miner's pay packet, and he and his family could be — and often were — evicted for breaking the company's rules or for going out on strike. In fact, the threat of eviction became one of the most powerful weapons in the mine owner's arsenal. In view of the importance that protests against bad housing assumed in twentieth-century Lanarkshire, and the insights they provide not only into the domestic lives of the Scottish miners but also into that of their wives, it is necessary to analyze their housing situation rather carefully.

Usually the miners' rows in the Lanarkshire coal towns consisted of one- or two-room houses set end to end and built around a central yard containing an ash pit, a water pump, and a communal toilet known as a "middens."[5] Sometimes larger two-story apartment buildings were erected, as in the Craigneuk area between Wishaw and Motherwell, where miners and low-grade ironworkers lived side by side.[6] In most cases the single-story rows had dirt floors, bare whitewashed walls, and almost no windows. The middens were supposed to be emptied daily by an agent of the coal company, but they rarely were. As the mining population increased, the miners' rows became fearfully overcrowded. Families of eight sometimes shared their two rooms with four or five male lodgers, keeping the beds in constant use on a rotating basis.[7]

The colliers' company-owned houses soon became worse than simply inadequate. They turned into breeding grounds for discomfort, disease, and social discontent. The burden of maintaining the miners' homes fell almost entirely on the colliers' wives and daughters. The lives of these women had always been hard, and they may well have grown still harder after 1850. This was when the demise of hand-loom weaving in places such as Larkhall consigned most girls, save for the relative few who worked as brickmakers, seam-stresses, or domestic servants in the towns, to work alongside their mothers in the never-ending task of caring not only for their husbands and fathers but also for the lodgers in the house. When he came home, the collier expected a hot meal, dry clothes, and a bath. According to one account, he "usually performs his ablutions in a tub placed in front of the fire." Often, "four or more are awaiting their turns for the tub, there being perhaps a father and two of his sons, and one or two lodgers, all working in the same pit." [8] For the miners' wives, the domestic dislocation became still greater when different miners living in the same house worked different shifts.

Besides suffering inadequate housing, the miner's wife had to deal with numerous other privations, some of which were worse than those faced by urban working women. [9] In addition to confronting never-ending house-work, she had to cope with exceptionally high childhood mortality rates, seasonal unemployment, and fluctuations in her husband's income due to strikes, pit shutdowns, and the termination of contracts. Perhaps worst of all, she lived under the constant fear of a severe injury or fatal accident to the family's main breadwinner, which could suddenly make her either a pau-per or dependent on charity. Kellog Durland remembered a Fife miner's wife who expressed such anxiety; when the whistle blew and her husband's shift came to an end, she said, "Aye tak's gud care to hae some wee bit thing to do aboot the window at the back o' twa o'clock," watching her "gude man" returning home safely. [10]

As holder of the collier family's purse strings, or at least of the allowance her husband made over to her every week, the miner's wife also bore the brunt of the third source of manipulation to which many Lanarkshire col-liers were subject. This was the fact that they had to purchase most of their goods at the employer-owned company store. By the late 1850s there were seven truck stores in the Wishaw area, most of them run by the iron masters. [11] The ostensible purpose of truck stores was to provide miners convenient ac-cess to nearby shops that would fulfill most of their families' needs. Their real purpose, however, was to intimidate miners into obedience by keeping them permanently in debt to their employers. To do this the coal masters often used a system known as "long pays" whereby the colliers were paid only once every two weeks, or even once a month, instead of once a week. Lacking sufficient cash to carry him to the next payday, the miner was often forced to secure credit slips from his company's pay office. These slips were redeemable only at the company store, which was often situated next to the pay booth. Miners who lived in downtown Larkhall or Wishaw could shop at stores owned by private merchants as well, but most coal owners frowned on this practice. The penalty exacted for persistent refusal to spend wages at the company store ranged from denial of further credit to assignment of bad working places underground or even outright dismissal.[12]

The employers enjoyed obvious advantages under the company store system. They could avoid making large cash outlays on their payroll, discipline those who showed signs of striking or joining a trade union, and— because the debts the colliers ran up at the company store usually required them to work for the same coal owner until their debts were paid—minimize the labor shortage problems caused by "flitting." Some Wishaw employers also made a profit by selling liquor to the miners at their truck stores, even though this practice was illegal. For example, coal master A. G. Simpson, who became mayor of Wishaw in 1850, continued to sell liquor at his store at Sunnyside for many years, even though doing so violated the 1831 Truck Act. (For a time Simpson tried to remain in technical compliance with the law by supplying his customers with whiskey through a convenient hole in the wall.)[13] Not only did truck store liquor sales pose a danger to the men who might be about to go down the pit; in addition, the hypocrisy of those coal and iron masters who preached the virtues of temperance and yet continued to sell liquor to their men constituted for the colliers one more source of anger toward their employers.

Closely linked to the question of drink were the issues of education and religious observance. Both the coal and iron masters, as well as most of the local clergy in Wishaw and Larkhall, used every available opportunity— public lectures, evangelist meetings, or sessions of the local temperance societies—to link acceptance of such values as sobriety, cleanliness, and punctuality to conformity to the word of God. The use of such moral strictures was, of course, a standard tactic all over mid-Victorian Britain.[14] In southwest Scotland, however, many ministers had a Calvinist background, which lent a peculiar ferocity to the rhetoric that they hurled from the pulpit every Sunday against the drunks, wife beaters, brawlers, and other renegades who had rioted in the streets the night before. It was softened only toward the end of the century when a few brave preachers in the more liberal denominations (Free Church, Congregationalist, and Baptist) began to attribute poverty not to individual moral weakness but to the industrial environment.[15]

Before the Scottish Education Act of 1872, which provided for publicly elected school boards, the miners had little if any choice regarding who taught their children in school.[16] Before that date the main responsibility for educating the colliers' children lay in the hands of the coal and iron masters, who established works schools that both boys and girls attended on a voluntary basis up to the age of twelve. By 1864 five such works schools had been established in Wishaw and at least one in Larkhall.[17] The privilege of appointing the teachers in these works schools also lay with the coal and iron masters. This was a task they usually discharged with relish, since it was their philanthropy that made the schools possible in the first place. In return for the education, between 1p and 2p per week was automatically deducted from the miners' weekly pay slips.[18]

The coal and iron masters' increased control over the miners' access to housing and schools, as well as to food and other supplies, was bound to cause resentment. Most of the masters probably meant well. They thought they were acting in the best interests of their men according to the social reform traditions of the day. Nonetheless, the miners, particularly the artisan-colliers, who occupied most of the leadership positions in the miners' unions and who cherished the independence their fathers had won in the years since the end of serfdom for Scottish miners in the 1790s, increasingly resented their employers' arrogance.[19]

The situation was worsened by the fact that most justices of the peace, as well as other state officials in both Wishaw and Larkhall, were either affluent tradesmen who entertained ambivalent feelings toward the colliers or coal and iron entrepreneurs. In the 1860s, for example, Lord Belhaven was appointed county commissioner of police in the Hamilton police court, where the major cases from Larkhall were tried. In Wishaw class rule was even more direct. In June 1866 more than a dozen workingmen who had been arrested for disturbing the peace after a Sunday night brawl were convicted by A. G. Simpson. Simpson was not only a justice of the peace; he was also mayor of Wishaw and a coal owner who employed several of the accused facing him in the dock.[20]

It must also be remembered that, unlike their counterparts in America, none of the colliers in mid-nineteenth-century Lanarkshire could express their opposition to their employers by voting against them in elections. Until the Second Reform Act of 1867, participation in British parliamentary and municipal elections was confined to those who owned significant amounts of property or who paid rent for housing at more than £6 per year.[21] This meant that not only economic power but also most of the political power remained in the hands of the same small oligarchy of local gentry and coal masters who controlled the mines. Even after the Second Reform Act of 1867, when the property qualification for British voters was reduced from £6 to £2 for renters, the great mass of Scotland's working population was still excluded from the franchise. It was not until the Third Reform Act of 1884 that most of them could vote. Hence, when the first municipal elections were held in

Larkhall in 1858, the voting rolls included only 68 men out of an estimated adult male population of 3,544.[22]

The 1855 electoral roll for Wishaw, which contained the names of only eighty voters out of an adult male population of 4,840, was even more narrowly drawn. Some of the self-employed tradesmen, merchants, and innkeepers were present on the roll, with approximately forty votes among them. The other half was divided between the coal masters—all eleven of whom were on the ballot—and a mixture of Protestant clergy, doctors, bankers, and farmers. The twelve town councillors who were chosen as the first popularly elected Wishaw city council reflected this same balance of class forces. James Miller, chief factor (manager) on Lord Belhaven's estate, was elected provost, or mayor. The remaining eleven councillors consisted of two coal masters, two merchants, one innkeeper, and six shopkeepers. Not a single coal miner was represented.[23]

Given their inability to vote, how did the coal miners of Wishaw and Larkhall, along with their allies in the iron and other skilled and semiskilled trades, react to the system of lopsided class rule that prevailed in the middle years of the nineteenth century? On some issues, such as housing and temperance, they reacted with moderation and a significant degree of accommodation combined with subtle forms of opposition. On others, however, such as truck stores, choice of schoolteachers, and political exclusion, they responded to the coal owners' hegemony with growing anger and hostility.

In the case of housing, there is little sign that in the early period the colliers staged overt public protests against the overcrowded and unsanitary miners' rows in which many of them were compelled to live. Such efforts would have to wait until the twentieth century.[24] For one thing, in the 1840s and 1850s the miners' rows, inadequate though they were, were still relatively new. For another, at least in Wishaw, few of the miners had prior experience of anything better. If anything, most of the famine Irish who entered the Wishaw pits in the mid-1840s had experienced even worse accommodations in their native country than they did in Lanarkshire, especially if they came from the poverty-stricken regions of western Ireland.

In Larkhall, however, which had fewer Irish immigrants, the quality of the miners' houses was somewhat better than it was in Wishaw, and the miners used home ownership to help them maintain a measure of independence from their masters. This was partly because Larkhall was less crowded than densely packed Wishaw, permitting the residents on some Larkhall streets to cultivate gardens of their own.[25] Primarily, however, it was because patterns of home ownership differed in the two places: whereas mine operators owned more than 80 percent of the miners' houses in Wishaw, in Larkhall the colliers themselves owned a significant proportion — perhaps one-third — of their accommodations. The practice of worker-owned housing had been started by the Scottish hand-loom weavers in their halcyon days between 1815 and 1835. Before the advent of machine weaving, they had established several cooperatively owned building societies in Larkhall, using their savings to purchase building shares. The miners continued this tradition, and by 1870 the colliers there owned as many as six hundred houses. This enabled their occupiers to avoid the eviction threats that the coal and iron masters were able to impose on colliers in Wishaw.[26] Privately owned housing, and the ability to act independently that it conferred, may also have been one of the reasons that Larkhall's miners' union was stronger than Wishaw's.

On temperance matters, too, the colliers shared a certain common interest with the coal owners, although they undoubtedly resented the constant lectures they received on the subject. For the miners' wives especially, restraint in the use of alcohol provided a way both of preserving hard-earned wages and of avoiding a drunken husband's sexual violence. Thus when temperance societies, sponsored at first by the Catholic clergy and then by various branches of the Presbyterian church, spread rapidly throughout the Lanarkshire coal towns in the 1850s, they often received the support of the colliers themselves. Interestingly, one of the leading temperance organizations that established itself in Glasgow and elsewhere in southwest Scotland in these years was the Independent Order of Good Templars. This temperance society originated in Syracuse, N.Y., in 1852 and set up branches on both sides of the Atlantic. By 1869 no fewer than 4,198 members, including large numbers of coal miners and ironworkers, were said to have joined the Order of Good Templars at Airdrie.[27] This town was only a few miles north of Wishaw and Larkhall, both of which had several temperance societies of their own.

Although the coal owners and miners had similar aims in promoting temperance, the long-term goals of the two sides differed significantly. The main interest of the iron and coal masters was to ensure public quiet in the streets and to render the miners obedient to the instructions of the oversman (foreman) underground. For the miner, however, taking the pledge not only preserved hard-earned wages but also lessened the risk of underground accidents caused by miners who might otherwise take whiskey with them to their workrooms for a drinking bout, or "fuddle." These were the two main motives that guided the Lanarkshire miners in their efforts to persuade coal masters to stop having mine managers pay employees in public houses. Safety considerations also prompted the colliers to pressure their employers to enforce the Truck Act of 1831 and to isolate employers such as A. G. Simpson who continued to sell liquor illegally in their company stores after the act was passed.[28]

In addition, the miners supported the temperance movement to boost the sense of manly independence that freedom from the slavery of drink gave them. At first sight this aim seems inconsistent with the alternative sense of manliness taught to younger colliers when they learned how to hold their liquor when drinking in the pub with their workmates after their shifts ended. For those who sought respectability and "true manhood," however, temperance enabled them to become loyal and intelligent members of their trade union. This rationale was quite different from the reasoning that prompted the coal masters to support temperance. Alexander McDonald touched on the trade union theme in a speech he made to a mass meeting of miners in Ayrshire in November 1862. Noting that the colliers in some local pits there made ten pence a day less than those in others, he attributed the difference to the fact that "the men had no spirit for union, but would rather accept a guzzle from their employer or spend in intoxicating drinks several times the amount of the [union] contributions required to make them independent." [29]

On matters of religious observance, however, the Lanarkshire colliers reacted to their masters' rhetorical pleadings to attend church not so much with hostility as with growing apathy and indifference. Figures published not long after 1864 show that overall church membership in Wishaw included only 21 percent of the adult working population. In Larkhall the percentage was even lower, standing at 15 percent.[30] These figures simply correlate church membership numbers with adult workers; they tell us nothing about church attendance rates. Nonetheless, the small numbers of members are consistent with other accounts of declining church attendance among Scottish workers in the second half of the nineteenth century.[31]

Thus on matters such as housing, temperance, and church attendance, accommodation coupled with a quiet determination to follow their own path ruled the day. When it came to appointing schoolmasters or legal officials such as justices of the peace, however, the Lanarkshire miners reacted with open anger to the arbitrary controls that the coal and iron masters tried to exert over their lives. Census figures for 1861 show that 54 percent of miners' children between the ages of six and twelve attended school in Larkhall, as did 32 percent of those in Wishaw.[32] This confirms the importance that many colliers attached to educating their children. Nevertheless, quite a few of these same colliers objected to the fact that their contributions to the cost of the works schools were automatically deducted from their pay slips, without giving them any say over the appointment of teachers or the content of the curriculum. This matter, which of course was not confined to Lanarkshire, became a major issue in the hearings in Parliament over the 1860 Mines Act, when some of the Scottish coal owners misled M.P.s by claiming that they alone paid for the works schools and that the miners influenced the appointment of teachers. In June 1860 Alexander McDonald exposed these fraudulent claims in the *Glasgow Sentinel*. He showed, for example, that at Legbrannock, not far from Larkhall, the miners had never been consulted about the appointment of their coal company school's teachers. "So far as the miners are concerned, they were never instructed otherwise than that they must pay for the teaching—and that was all."[33]

McDonald was equally scathing about the class biases of the elite group of mine owners and their allies who controlled the administration of justice in the Lanarkshire coal towns. Asked what he thought about the local justices of the peace when he was on a visit to London in 1866, he derided them as incompetent and lacking in any proper legal training. Most of the Lanarkshire JPs, McDonald complained, were "colliery managers, doctors attending the collieries, bakers, and some well-to-do grocers, who supply the truck shops with goods."[34]

The practice of deducting money automatically from the miners' wages to pay for their children's education particularly angered Irish Catholic miners at Wishaw, where they were more numerous than they were in Larkhall. In the 1840s and 1850s the Catholic diocese of Glasgow established a number of privately funded church schools in the coal towns that the sons and daughters of the Irish colliers were encouraged to attend. Much of this private funding came from the Catholic miners themselves. At the same time, however, these colliers continued to have part of their wages automatically deducted from their pay to help finance the separate works schools. These discriminatory deductions did much to exacerbate the bitterness that many Irish miners felt toward their largely Protestant employers. To resolve the dispute, Wishaw Catholics set up the Free School Agitation Committee, which sought to force the Coltness Iron Company to use the funds it collected from the Irish workers to help support their own schools.[35]

It was over the question of truck, however, and the various means the colliers employed to end it, that Lanarkshire miners engaged in what can be called their first collective political act in defiance of their employers. This was not so apparent in their initial tactic, which was to establish a network of cooperative retail stores as an alternative to the mine owners' company stores. But it certainly was true of their campaign during the 1850s and 1860s, however, when they attempted to have truck shops abolished by publicly exposing the system, as well as by lobbying Parliament for new legislation.

The system of retail cooperative stores in southwest Scotland, which fifty years later was to help draw the miners into support for the Labour Party, was not initially founded in response to the problem of truck. These stores derived instead from a long-standing tradition of cooperation that went back at least to the 1820s.[36] In 1821 a group of activist hand-loom weavers founded the Larkhall Victualling Society, which later came to resemble a modern cooperative store. This was the same body that sparked the building of worker-owned houses in the town. The Victualling Society employed a purchaser, who bought groceries and other goods wholesale; a salesman, who sold the goods retail; and a clerk. A one-pound, ten-pence deposit was required for membership in the society, along with evidence of good moral character. Propaganda on behalf of temperance was also undertaken by the early co-operators.[37]

It is not clear just when the miners of Larkhall began purchasing goods from the Victualling Society, but an 1854 minute from one of its meetings noted that a new store had just been rented in the Meadowhill area of town "to accommodate the miners at the old Buffy pit."[38] Their participation probably began earlier than that. At all events, from this small beginning grew several other cooperative retail stores, all organized on the Rochdale principle of dividends paid to the members, with the society eventually including several hundred Larkhall miners in its ranks.[39]

The Society of Equitable Pioneers of Wishaw, the retail cooperative society there, was not founded until 1860, almost forty years after the one in Larkhall, but it, too, espoused the principles of the Rochdale movement, which had moved north from Lancashire and was by this time flourishing in Glasgow and other nearby coal towns. By the summer of 1861 the Wishaw society had 220 contributing members. It also established branches not only in downtown Wishaw but in Cambusnethan and Shotts, a mining village to the east of the town.[40] These cooperative stores enabled the miners and their wives not only to earn a small dividend on the goods they purchased but also to avoid being pulled into the cycle of debt that dependence on the company stores brought about. Owenite missionaries such as Alexander Campbell, who was well known to the miners through the columns of the *Glasgow Sentinel*, also saw them as a first step in the rejection of competitive individualism and in the creation of a new form of society.[41]

The Scottish miners' lobbying campaign against truck stores was a long one. It began with efforts to force the mine owners to enforce the Truck Act of 1831, continued with public pressure over the issue on both Tory and Liberal candidates in the Lanarkshire parliamentary elections in the middle years of the century, and culminated with support for the 1887 act of Parliament that finally ended the practice of truck.[42] During this grass-roots campaign the miners created antitruck associations and publicly exposed the coal owners' unsavory practices. This experience also taught the colliers how to use extra-parliamentary direct action, which culminated in the syndicalist movement that emerged during the period of World War I. In 1870, for example, just before a new parliamentary investigation into the evils of truck was to begin, coal owner A. G. Simpson—who was still provost of Wishaw—suddenly had a change of heart about his company store. Faced with hostile demonstrations by miners and independent shopkeepers, Simpson closed his truck shop. No doubt chastened by the prospect of further parliamentary inquiries, he also announced that from then on he would pay his miners weekly instead of fortnightly.[43]

Nonetheless, the strongest evidence of the Lanarkshire miners' growing political awareness in the middle decades of the nineteenth century comes from the support they gave to the *Glasgow Sentinel*. The *Sentinel* was not just another Glasgow newspaper that found its way into the mining towns of the Clyde Valley. It was a radical, working-class newssheet that in 1860 came near to being purchased by the miners' union as their official organ. In June of that year the paper's editor and publisher, Robert Buchanan, went bankrupt, a calamity that, according to one report, "was talked about in all the mining districts of Scotland."[44] At a mid-August miners' delegate conference held in Glasgow, a proposal was made that rank-and-file miners each subscribe twelve and one-half pence to purchase the paper for the miners' cause. This proposal was rejected by the local miners' unions.

Soon afterward, however, Alexander McDonald, who by then had become the leading spokesman of the Lanarkshire colliers, acquired a controlling share in the *Sentinel*.[45] There is therefore good reason for thinking that the *Glasgow Sentinel's* politics were closer to those of the miners than were those of any other local paper. This belief is reinforced by the strong support the paper gave to several miners' strikes in the 1850s and 1860s. The *Sentinel* also championed free trade, cooperation, and parliamentary reform, all emerging liberal causes that were dear to the miners' hearts.[46]

Besides this, the *Sentinel* provided the colliers with information about the democratic reform movements then sweeping the European continent. While not espousing republicanism in quite the same sense as workingmen were doing at this time in the United States, the *Sentinel's* weekly pages were filled with reports on the political activities of Mazzini, Kossuth, and other 1848 revolutionary heroes. It called for a national system of secular education and for cooperative production along the lines advocated by socialists in France. In addition, it condemned the competitive individualism advocated by John Bright and other Manchester Liberals as "a worn-out carcass, having existed soulless for years."[47] Still more relevant to my story, during the 1850s the *Glasgow Sentinel* excoriated American slavery and expressed strong admiration for the democratic institutions of the United States.[48]

The importance of these community issues to the Lanarkshire colliers' growing sense of alienation from society was equaled, if not surpassed, by that of the mine owners' introduction of new methods of production and new forms of underground discipline that diminished the colliers' traditional workplace prerogatives. These efforts were driven by the coal owners' need to sink deeper shafts and to employ more up-to-date technology so that they could produce more coal and improve their competitive positions within the industry.

In the early days in the northeast corner of the Lanarkshire coalfield around Airdrie and Coatbridge, it was necessary to sink mines only to a depth of fifty or sixty feet. In these primitive pits, which sometimes had only one shaft and employed no more than twenty or thirty men, it was still possible for the artisan-colliers to make their own decisions as to when and how to complete their daily darg. Often they could operate by themselves the single cage that drew both men and coal up to the surface and thus come and go from the pit when they pleased. As mining operations moved further west into the Clyde Valley, however, it became necessary to go deeper underground to find commercially viable amounts of fuel. By 1840, in both Wishaw and Larkhall the three most extensively mined coals were Ell coal at 85 feet, Splint coal at 136 feet, and Kiltongue coal at 178 feet. All three required deeper pits and more complex winding gear to bring the coal to the surface than were needed in the older, shallower pits of the post-Napoleonic period.[49]

To operate these more complicated pits, dynamite replaced gunpowder as the primary explosive, steel hawsers and endless chains replaced hemp ropes for raising the cages, power-driven fans replaced furnaces burning at the bottom of the shaft as the preferred means of forcing air through the underground tunnels, and double cages replaced single ones in the shaft — one for moving men and equipment up and down the shaft and the other for bringing coal hutches to the surface. As far as the pick miner's control over his workday was concerned, it was probably the last of these innovations that caused him the most trouble. With the double cage system, a new specialist called a bottomer was called in to regulate the number of men who could travel in the cage. He alone operated the signaling system to the surface. Thus, instead of being able to summon the cage to leave the pit when he had completed his darg, the skilled pick miner now found himself obliged to wait at the bottom of the shaft, covered with dirt and sweat, until the bottomer authorized him to leave work.[50]

In addition, in the 1850s and 1860s the longwall system of mining described earlier, as well as other changes in the division of labor required by the new technology, began to deprive the artisan-collier of some of his former dominance and indispensability. Newly appointed enginemen controlled the steam-powered winches that drew the cages up and down the shaft. Company firemen inspected all underground workplaces for gas before the pick miner and his helper were allowed to begin their work. Roadsmen were introduced to inspect the state of the underground passages and roofs at the end of each shift. If an accident occurred, they could stop the movement of men and coal through the tunnels until needed repairs had been made.[51]

Above ground, too, the relatively informal work relations between earlier generations of coal masters and their employees, particularly in semirural places such as Larkhall, were replaced by more impersonal procedures and by a more hierarchical system of management and control. This was particularly true in the large-scale ironworks that owned and operated their own coal and ironstone pits, such as Dixons, Bairds, or the Coltness Iron Company in Wishaw. In these firms, the one or two managers (often the sons of the owners) who had formerly supervised the company's mines were now supplemented—and in some cases supplanted—by a large and specially trained cadre of engineers, accountants, and foremen, each of whom oversaw a particular department of the works. As the number of semi-proletarians in the labor force grew, Alexander McDonald's ideal of personal interaction and mutual respect between masters and workers began to fade.[52]

The coal and iron masters who introduced this new regime into the Lanarkshire pits in the 1840s and 1850s hoped not only to increase their total output of coal but also to bring about a rise in the individual collier's productivity, or output per person-shift. To some extent, this did indeed occur. The introduction of dynamite, for example, raised the amount of coal that could be brought down in a single blast, thereby increasing overall output.[53] But when the colliers balked at the threats that these new arrangements posed to their traditional system of workplace control, the masters began a concerted campaign to undermine their employees' restrictive practices. Their main target was the idea of the restricted darg.

In 1846 mine inspector Tremenheere delivered the first serious attack against restricted output when he expressed his frustration at the miners' unions for striking for a wage increase. The colliers might have secured some sympathy for their cause, he stated, if they worked hard for their money. "But the 'darg' to which they restrict themselves voluntarily is so light that . . . any industrious or able collier or miner could hew the quantity of coal, or get out the quantity of ironstone." The pernicious policy of output restriction, he argued, could be attributed either to willful ignorance of the laws of political economy or to a "species of communism, which induces them to fix their day's work at that which can be done with ease by the weakest and least able hands." [54]

The coal and iron masters were also angered by the colliers' insistence on preserving their right to determine the qualifications of a "full man" (i.e., a fully trained collier) and to limit—insofar as they could—what kind of workers entered the trade. By controlling not only the supply of coal but also the quantity and quality of men permitted to work in the pits, the colliers sought to maintain a level playing field on which to negotiate with the employers. Given the severe depression, the declining wages, and the social turmoil that characterized much of the 1840s, however, this task proved too much for them. Numerous strikes, most of them against wage cuts, took place in the Lanarkshire pits during that decade. They reached a climax during the Chartist agitation of 1847, when eight thousand Lanarkshire miners laid down their tools. During this strike, which affected both Wishaw and Larkhall, the coal owners made use of the two most dreaded weapons in their arsenal: evicting strikers from company-owned housing and importing cheap Irish laborers from abroad. [55]

In the 1847 strike eight hundred miners and their families were evicted from company-owned miners' rows in Holytown. (Holytown was Alexander McDonald's home for many years and was situated only a few miles from Wishaw.) [56] Shortly afterward iron master William Baird denounced the miners' behavior in language that summarized succinctly both the strategy the colliers employed to keep their wages up and the tactics the owners used to pull them down. "When our colliers reduced their 'darg' in the winter of 1846 by one-third," Baird wrote,

the price of coal rose in the Glasgow market to eight shillings [forty pence] per cart of twelve hundred weight. The consequence was that the sale left that port [instead of being sold locally] and the shipping went to Ayrshire and Fifeshire. At that strike, two hundred of our men turned out. We brought in Irish labourers who had been working in the pits as redesmen. In three weeks we had the output of coal increased. We were obliged to protect them day and night. The other men were very savage, and in one instance, not at our works, threw a policeman down a pit, and then cut the pit ropes.[57]

A third sign of growing class tensions between miners and mine owners in this period is seen in the disputes that arose over the increasing number of pit accidents involving new mining machinery and over who should be held responsible for them. In general, the reports of the inspectors of mines for East Scotland (which covered much of Lanarkshire) noted that deaths from mining accidents decreased during this period as mine safety legislation improved and the number of underground specialists charged with examining the pits increased.[58] They expressed concern, however, at the increasing number of accidents that resulted from the sinking of deeper shafts and the employment of new types of machinery. In 1854, for example, inspector Robert Williams noted several instances of accidents resulting from new steam-driven machines that disengaged while winding, causing the cage to plunge to the bottom of the pit.[59] In 1864 inspector Ralph Moore recorded the case of a fireman employed by the Shotts Iron Company, which was located just east of Wishaw, who was killed by a burst of steam from a newly installed pit pump, the first such incident Moore encountered.[60]

The main dispute between masters and men, however, arose over the assignment of responsibility for accidents. In turn this raised complicated questions concerning civil liability, monetary compensation, and control over litigation that became so serious they had to be resolved by Parliament. The coal owners tended to blame virtually all accidents on the miners' own carelessness rather than to accept any responsibility themselves. For example, one of the most hotly contested issues concerned who was responsible for the large number of accidents that resulted from falls of stone or coal from the mine roofs. These accidents were the leading cause of death in both Wishaw and Larkhall during most years from 1843 to 1864.[61] The coal owners, not unreasonably, denied responsibility for injuries that resulted from falls of coal occurring while the miner was working at the coal face, claiming that company-appointed roadsmen could not inspect these sites during an ongoing shift. The colliers, on the other hand, maintained that the companies were simply shirking responsibility by taking this position. A compromise of sorts was reached in the late 1850s, when responsibility for roof falls occurring in the miners' workplace came to be accepted as the fault of the miners, while responsibility for falls in the outside passages was accepted by management.[62]

Finally, as parliamentary oversight of the coal-mining industry grew, conflicts emerged over who was to draw up the miners' underground work rules and how they should be interpreted. The 1855 Mines Inspection Act, which laid down a number of general rules governing collieries in Great Britain, also mandated the adoption of special rules by the mining authorities in different parts of the United Kingdom. In Lanarkshire the Coal and Iron Masters Association of the West of Scotland was given authority to draw up these rules. The miners' representatives were given no say in the matter.[63] When the association published its list of special rules soon after the 1855 act was passed, the Lanarkshire colliers found to their dismay that the rules constituted a direct attack on their traditional system of workplace control. Rule 5, for example, sought to replace the miner's own intuitive set of work practices, in which he took much pride, with a new list of employer-driven requirements. "Colliers are required to place [pit] props within their working limits," the rule stated, "and in such manner as the employer or manager shall deem necessary."[64] Rule 6 required the roadsman to "report daily to the underground manager, any instances of neglect on the part of the colliers, in not carrying forward their coalface or walls, in accordance with the plan pursued in the working of the colliery."[65]

But it was special rule 3, which once more targeted the collier's limited darg, that drew the most anger. "On beginning work at every shift," rule 3 stipulated, "[miners] shall ... work at their appointed coal faces continuously and industriously, and without unnecessary interruption, while the shift continues."[66] Rule 3 generated such dismay among the miners that in February 1856 Alexander McDonald led a special delegation to London to protest the new rule to the home secretary, Sir George Grey. Lengthy discussion produced a new rule that left out the requirement that the miners work continuously and uninterruptedly at the coal face during the course of their shift, but they were still required to obey the orders of the underground manager "in all matters relating to their work, and the safety and ventilation of the pit."[67]

As they did in community matters, the Lanarkshire colliers responded to the coal masters' new program of increased control and discipline down the pit with a mixture of accommodation and resistance. There was little they could do to prevent the increasing division of labor, the introduction of new technology, or the sinking of deeper and larger coal pits. Regarding these developments, as with social issues such as temperance and education, they tried either to adjust themselves to their new situation or else to turn it to their advantage, thereby keeping class conflict less intense than it would become later in the century.

However, on matters such as preserving their traditional workplace prerogatives and maintaining their influence over wage levels and the supply of
labor, the colliers were determined to stand their ground. At first they placed
a good deal of faith in the ability of their newly established trade unions to
protect them against such employer tactics as the importation of Irish strikebreakers. Thus, as was mentioned in chapter 1, when the new Scottish Coal
and Iron Miners Association was established in 1855, it included an elaborate
set of rules and regulations designed to maintain and protect the skilled pick
miners' jobs.[68]

Indeed, during the 1850s and early 1860s the miners placed greater hopes
than ever before on local unions' abilities to protect and defend their wage
levels and traditional way of life. The wages of most Lanarkshire colliers fluctuated widely in this period, moving from a low of ten pence a day in the
depression of the early 1840s to twenty-four pence a day in 1854. The average
was about eighteen pence.[69] For the most part, the colliers adhered to Alexander McDonald's policy of restricting their output as the best way to keep
up wages. On this issue the efforts of the miners' unions were rewarded with
a certain amount of success. On other matters, however, neither the local
Wishaw and Larkhall unions nor the Scottish Coal and Iron Miners Association proved able to provide the colliers with an adequate and enduring
means of defense. In December 1858 the association boasted 9,000 members,
a number alleged to have grown to 20,000 the following year. In 1860, however, membership dropped back to 8,000, and by the mid-1860s the organization had largely disappeared.[70] The result was increasingly direct and open
tension between masters and men.

Particularly discouraging were two further strike defeats suffered by the
Lanarkshire miners in 1856 and 1863, with the main losers on both occasions
being the coal and ironstone miners of Wishaw. In 1856 the iron masters again
used eviction from company-owned housing to force the strikers into sub-
mission. In May of that year the Wishaw bailiffs forcibly emptied all or part
of the miners' rows at Simpson's Square, Sunnyside Rows, Bell's Rows, and
Cowie Square.[71] Colliers in several nearby towns voted relief funds, but since
they, too, were on strike, little extra money was available for the Wishaw
men. After twelve weeks the strike collapsed, throwing many miners' families into deep distress. The *Glasgow Sentinel* was indignant, accusing the iron
companies of "such indifference to the plight of the miners as would freeze
the heart of Ebenezer Scrooge."[72] The 1863 defeat was just as severe, leaving
many Wishaw colliers and their dependents, in the words of one historian,
"in a desperate plight of impoverishment, raggedness, and misery."[73]

It was no coincidence that Wishaw, not Larkhall, was the scene of these defeats. The miners' union in Wishaw was weaker than Larkhall's in part because large firms such as the Coltness Iron Company could exert their influence over their employees more easily than could the smaller-scale coal companies of Larkhall. This influence derived partly from the Wishaw iron masters' greater ability to enforce the special rules mandated by the 1855 Mines Inspection Act, but it also stemmed from the larger number of truck stores in Wishaw and from the greater degree of social control the iron masters were able to exert over their men in such socially isolated places as Sunnyside, Craigneuk, and Newmains.

In addition, Wishaw had a weaker union because its mixed-industry work force encompassed extensive cultural and occupational divisions that were largely absent from Larkhall's more homogeneous Scots-born work force. In Wishaw these divisions resulted partly from the presence of the iron industry. At the Excelsior Iron Works at Shieldmuir, for example, an upper echelon of respectable, well-paid English forehand puddlers, heaters, rollers, and shinglers manufactured rails, sheets of iron, and metal tubes. These men tended to look down on the native Scottish coal miners, both skilled and unskilled.[74] But the main social division in Wishaw was between the native Scots workers, whether they worked in the iron or the coal trade, and the incoming Irish. These cultural differences were exacerbated by the fact that some of the skilled workers in the Wishaw iron trades were Protestant Irishmen who had been recruited from the Belfast shipyards, whereas the unskilled mine laborers and furnace fillers in Wishaw neighborhoods such as Newmains tended to be rural Catholics from the southern and western parts of Ireland.[75]

The tensions that these cultural divisions sparked in Wishaw are significant not just for what they tell us about the greater weakness of the miners' union there compared to the one in Larkhall.[76] They are important as well for the comparative discussion of class formation in the British and American coal industries. One of the clichés about the weakness of the U.S. labor movement compared to its European counterparts is the oft-repeated view that ethnic and religious differences riddling the U.S. unions prevented their members from developing a high degree of class consciousness.[77] The evidence from this study, however, suggests that this view has been exaggerated.[78] Ethnic and religious tensions supposedly unique to the American labor movement were also widespread in western Europe, including southwest Scotland. A good example of these tensions and of the damage they could do to the idea of a united front among the Scottish miners is provided by the Order of Free Colliers in Lanarkshire, which was founded in 1863 largely by Protestant miners in a renewed attempt to protect the workers in the industry.

One of the purposes of the Free Colliers movement, which lasted from 1863 to 1866, was to defend the workplace autonomy of the native-born Scottish pick miner against the inroads of the employer. Paradoxically, it also tried to maintain the tradition of mutual respect between miners and coal masters that Alexander McDonald promoted and that had supposedly been widespread during the golden age of the artisan-collier in the immediate post-Napoleonic years.[79] Irish miners were not expressly excluded from the Order of Free Colliers, but most of its largest lodges were founded in the eastern counties of the Scottish coalfield, such as Clackmannan, Fife, and Midlothian, where few Irish miners were present.[80]

One sign of anti-Irish sentiment in the new Order of Free Colliers was the emphasis it placed on native-Scots ritual and symbols of brotherhood that commemorated the Scottish struggle against English oppression. For example, several of its lodges were named after Scottish heroes such as Robert the Bruce, and the anthem "Scots Wa Hae" was frequently sung at its meetings.[81] A second sign was the fact that the order was a secret society, something of which the Catholic church — and hence many Irish colliers — disapproved. Many Irish colliers expressed concern that the hostility they met on the streets of towns such as Coatbridge, Airdie, and Wishaw was but a precursor to ousting them from the pits altogether, and they feared that the order's activities would exacerbate this prejudice. One subscriber to a local newspaper in this period, who was probably a native Scot, spoke to these fears when he replied as follows to a letter from an Irish correspondent: "He speaks of Irishmen in days of yore being a rarity among the miners. I would consider it a blessing were Irishmen like him a rarity in the present day."[82]

The workplace philosophy of the Free Colliers movement became apparent when the order negotiated an agreement with a local coal owner, James Russell, at his Redding colliery at the end of 1863. In return for an invitation to join the Sir William Wallace lodge, Russell allowed his employees to determine their own working hours, thereby sanctioning a continuation of one of the colliers' most cherished methods of maintaining control over the conditions of their labor. Many members of the Order of Free Colliers welcomed this Redding agreement as indicating a return to earlier ideals of class harmony. In February 1864 a member of the Bo'ness, West Lothian, lodge expressed this sentiment in a letter he wrote to the *Glasgow Sentinel:* "I contend that the very foundation of free collierism is the welfare of all mankind;

it admits the employer in the same circle as the employed, for the purpose of engendering a friendly feeling between both parties."[83]

Nevertheless, the Free Colliers' agreement with coal master James Russell broke down almost as soon as it had been signed, exemplifying the growing tensions between coal owner and coal miners that by then had become widespread in the Lanarkshire coalfield. The agreement specified that if any of the miners at the Redding colliery dug more than the amount of coal to which they had agreed (i.e., if they exceeded their daily darg), their surplus earnings would be deposited in a special death and accident fund. Early in 1864, however, two colliers who refused to go along with this policy successfully sued the Redding Coal Company for their lost wages. This led to further trouble between miners and management, as a result of which Russell evicted his employees from their company houses, an act that precipitated just the kind of class conflict the Order of Free Colliers had struggled vainly to avoid.[84]

The Free Colliers episode was brought to an end in the mid-1860s when it became clear that the movement had served to divide the Scottish miners rather than to unite them and that it had failed in its mission to resurrect the old order of common interest between masters and men. A kind of obituary on this old order was pronounced in a series of letters that Baillieston miners' leader James King wrote to the *Glasgow Sentinel* in 1865. In a January 28 letter King criticized the secret character of the Order of Free Colliers in much the same way that the regular trade unionists were to attack the secrecy of the Knights of Labor in America in the 1870s. How were the Catholic colliers to be recruited, King asked sorrowfully, if the order kept its meetings private?[85]

King's most telling point, though, came when he attacked the order's leaders for letting their pursuit of harmony between the miners and their employers prevent confrontations with the coal masters over bread-and-butter union issues such as wages and hours. Although he did not cite the Redding agreement as an example, King might well have had it in mind. "The Grand Lodge," he wrote, "should be a worthy example to the humbler ones in everything that is just and expected to be beneficial. If so, what has it done for an advance of wages? What has it done for restriction of labour?"[86]

A new start and new policies were clearly needed if the Lanarkshire miners were to defend their position successfully. Early in 1865 a mass meeting of colliers held in Glasgow's city hall called for a general restriction of labor to begin throughout the Scottish coalfields on February 5, 1865, in hopes of forcing the coal owners to make some concessions.[87] Given the large number of colliers who remained outside the miners' unions, however, this campaign met no greater success than had its predecessors. Having tried conciliation and arbitration, parliamentary lobbying, the Free Colliers movement, and the limited darg, Alexander McDonald and the Lanarkshire miners were forced to look around for a new solution to the dilemmas they faced. The new solution they hit on was immigration.

Immigration abroad, as an alternative to unemployment and failed strikes at home, was just then being widely trumpeted by labor leaders throughout Great Britain.[88] Through it the Lanarkshire leaders hoped that they could remove enough colliers from the Scottish labor pool to keep up wages and at the same time improve the bargaining position of those who were left behind. Hopeful emigrants were encouraged to take ship from the Broomielaw, in downtown Glasgow, to a variety of destinations abroad. They could start mining again, or perhaps take up a new occupation, in one of the colonies of the British Empire such as Canada or Australia. Or they could immigrate to the new world in the United States. Wherever possible, the miners' unions would provide financial assistance to the colliers who decided to leave.[89]

The next chapter examines in detail why significant numbers of Lanarkshire miners immigrated to the United States. It describes the uneven fortunes of those who decided to take this momentous step. In particular, it explains how and why a small group of colliers from southwest Scotland, including some from Wishaw and Larkhall, ended up on the windswept prairie coalfield of northern Illinois.

3

CROSSING THE OCEAN: BRITISH COLLIERS MIGRATE TO NORTHERN ILLINOIS, 1855–70

Numerous motives besides a desire to regulate the flow of labor into the mines of southwest Scotland prompted the Lanarkshire miners' leaders to advocate immigration overseas during the 1860s. Another precipitating event was the prior movement of Glasgow's poverty-stricken hand-loom weavers to Canada, Australia, and other parts of the British Empire. Providing additional stimulus, British labor leaders in this period generally supported trade-union-assisted emigration. This policy was invoked in a variety of circumstances. It might be utilized to relieve a union of heavy unemployment expenditures or to provide a foreign outlet for individual workers whose jobs had been rendered obsolete by technological change. Or it might be used to help a particular union member who was unable to find employment because of an employer blacklist.[1]

Nonetheless, as already suggested, the most important motive behind such plans, which the Lanarkshire miners' union copied, was the desire to remove workers from the labor market in the country of origin so as to improve the bargaining position of those workers who remained at home. The wage-fund theory of Adam Smith, which posits that a reduction in the size of the labor force will automatically lead to higher wages, offered an intellectual rationale to justify the policy of emigration, as did the ideas of Thomas Malthus and John Stuart Mill regarding the need to check population growth. The latter argument seemed particularly relevant in the overcrowded mid-Lanarkshire coalfield. The most popular economic argument in favor of emigration, however, was the perceived need to limit the labor supply at home during periods when stocks of coal were high and to protect the bargaining position of the miners when their union was weak.[2] In 1877 a Miners National Union conference in Manchester adopted a resolution declaring that over-production was the cause of "the very low rate of wages that [had then] become general." One way of remedying the situation, the conference resolved, was to encourage miners to emigrate.[3]

A third, more immediate, reason for adopting the emigration policy was that the Lanarkshire coal masters threatened to impose a wage cut in the early months of 1865. This sort of threat was not new, of course. Many others like it had been made before. But the 1865 threat was made soon after the *Glasgow Sentinel* published a rash of letters from emigrant miners in America who extolled the virtues of the New World. On February 11, 1865, for example, "W. P.," of Schuylkill County, Pa., described the favorable response given to Scottish immigrant miners who had already settled near the bituminous mines of Maryland and Pennsylvania. W. P. was a friend of Alexander McDonald and came from Maryhill, just north of Glasgow. He reported that the immigrant miners in Schuylkill County made fifty pence a day, almost three times the wages in Scotland. (This exceptionally high wage was probably occasioned by the severe demand for coal during the final phases of the Civil War.) "I wish to God all my friends were here," W. P. wrote. "The men here go to work at 7, take dinner at 12, and are home by three or four o'clock, and during work you will not see the sweat pouring out of them, as at home." He summed up the prospects for immigrant miners in Pennsylvania as follows: "Plenty of work, good meat, good air, and the wee drop."[4]

Letters such as these, coupled with the other trade union precedents and the knowledge of American mining conditions that Alexander McDonald had gained by his extensive correspondence with Scottish miners who had already gone abroad, sparked an emigration fever in the Scottish coalfields. At a large meeting of miners' representatives held in downtown Glasgow on April 9, 1865, that included delegates from both Wishaw and Larkhall, McDonald proposed that emigration committees be set up in every Lanarkshire mining district to raise money to pay for the miners' passages. Because these committees were unlikely to raise enough money for all those who wished to leave, he also suggested that a random selection method be used to decide who should go. McDonald urged that "6d per week [two and one-half pence] be the amount of [the] subscription, [and that] those who contributed 1/- [five pence] receive two chances in the ballot for emigration."[5] Miners who had been blacklisted by their employers would be given priority. The proposal was greeted enthusiastically and adopted unanimously. At another delegate meeting three days later, McDonald announced that he had secured the names of one hundred miners who wished to emigrate through the subscription method. He had initially intended, he said, that the men chosen to leave should be selected from all parts of the Scottish coalfields. "But if a strike were forced upon the men he would . . . consider it his duty to ask the miners to join with him in an endeavor to clear out an entire firm. Let these men be sent to America, and let their masters find workmen anywhere they pleased. (loud cheers)."[6]

It is unlikely that the miners' emigration policy actually did much to limit the labor supply available to the Scottish coal operators or to maintain a higher level of wages in the Lanarkshire coalfield than would otherwise have been the case. Wages there continued to fluctuate just as much as they had before the policy of officially supported emigration was adopted. Moreover, too many miners were entering the coalfield's pits from Ireland, as well as from elsewhere in Scotland and even from England, to create a serious shortage of labor. Equally misleading were the erroneous conclusions about emigration's effects on the labor market that Alexander McDonald reached as a believer in Adam Smith's wage-fund theory. This theory ignores the point just made, namely, that any diminution in the ranks of the miners resulting from emigration abroad could easily be made up by newcomers entering the pits. In 1873 McDonald claimed that after 1864 the surplus in the Scottish mines "began to be drawn off,"[7] but there is no real evidence that the policy of assisted emigration had the effect of clearing out an entire coal company, as McDonald claimed in his speech of April 12, 1865, let alone that it prevented a coal owner from recruiting new workers to replace the old.

Given the emigration fever then sweeping southwest Scotland, however, such criticisms of the plan were dismissed. Having made the decision to leave, miners in Hamilton, Larkhall, Wishaw, Motherwell, and numerous other Clyde Valley coal towns bought steerage tickets from the local agent of a transatlantic steamship company. Having said their farewells, they then traveled by horse-drawn cart or rail into Glasgow, walked down to the embarkation point at the Broomielaw, and took a local steamer down river to open water at Greenock or to the assembly point at the mouth of the Clyde called the Tail O' the Bank, where the ocean-going vessels awaited them. Sometimes the miners took their wives and children with them. More often, however, they went alone or, if they were married, with one of their sons who was already in training to become a collier. Having arrived at the Tail O' the Bank, the colliers transferred themselves and their baggage to the ocean-going vessel and descended to the lowest level of the ship, along with other steerage passengers from Glasgow's burgeoning working class. Apprehensive but excited, they departed on their ocean voyage. Some of them would go back and forth across the ocean several times before settling down. Once they had saved up enough money to pay the fare, however, most of the colliers — like other immigrants in this period — would send for the rest of their family members.[8]

In the days of sail that preceded the American Civil War, the voyage across the Atlantic from Glasgow to New York or Philadelphia — or sometimes to Nova Scotia, where quite a few Scottish miners put down roots — was a hazardous undertaking. It usually took four or five weeks, but adverse winds or bad weather could extend it considerably. Even when Alexander McDonald took his first trip to America on board the U.S. steamship *Iowa* in September 1867 to visit the miners he had helped to emigrate, the voyage took sixteen days.[9] When hundreds of people were crowded together for weeks on end in the cramped, dimly lit, poorly ventilated compartments of a wooden sailing vessel, the voyage was not only uncomfortable; it could also be dangerous. The passengers had to bring their own food and cook it on communal stoves. Sea sickness, tainted water, and an almost complete lack of privacy contributed to the general discomfort. Worst of all was the danger of epidemics, fires, and shipwreck. Typhus and cholera were common on pre–Civil War sailing vessels, fires frequently broke out in the crowded wooden hulls, and even steamships were quite often lost during severe weather. In the stormy winter of 1854, for example, the iron-hulled steamship *City of Glasgow,* sailing from Liverpool, went down with 480 passengers on board.[10]

Conditions such as these, as well as the high cost and length of the voyage, often deterred British miners from emigrating, but the more widespread use of steam-powered ships in the post–Civil War period and the introduction of stricter safety laws brought a marked improvement. In 1873 a report on American steamship lines declared that the supplanting of sail by steam had brought "shorter voyages, increased space, improved accommodation, more light, better ventilation, [and] more abundant supplies of more wholesome food and water."[11] The incidence of shipwrecks and shipboard epidemics declined. Better facilities were installed at the sites of embarking in Scotland and debarking in Boston, Philadelphia, and New York, although tricksters and thieves continued to prey on travelers coming ashore. Above all, the transatlantic voyage became cheaper as well as shorter. In the early days of steam, fares for steamships were higher than those for sailing ships, but a few years after the Civil War, the large profits to be made from the booming emigrant trade, coupled with keen competition between British and American shipping companies, brought the cost of the transatlantic fares down markedly.[12]

Why did emigrating Scottish colliers choose America instead of coal-producing regions in the British Empire or elsewhere in the world? Higher wages, the appeal of cheap land, and the overseas recruitment campaigns undertaken by agents of the coal, iron, and railroad companies all were important. Then there were the letters written back home and the drawing power of the networks of miners and their families who had already migrated to the eastern United States in the antebellum years. Reformers in Edinburgh and Glasgow also looked to the higher wages and free public education in the United States to deliver the immigrant Irish colliers and their families from the bonds of poverty and ignorance.[13]

Political considerations, too, were involved. From the time of the American Revolution Scottish radicals had admired U.S. democracy, while dissenters and freethinkers among them extolled the absence of an established church. Some of the radicals on the left wing of the British Chartist movement in the 1840s who influenced the miners were also republicans of one stripe or another. Hence they praised the absence of a monarchy in the United States as well as equal manhood suffrage and the lack of property qualifications for the vote.[14] From this it was but a short step to supporting the American version of labor republicanism, as is apparent in an article in the *Glasgow Sentinel* of October 1865 written by "Americanus" — the pseudonym for a Lanarkshire miner who had emigrated from Larkhall. "America," he wrote, "is a republican country with fair compensation, and where the workingman is well regarded by his master."[15]

This sentiment not only reflected the democratic aspirations of many Scottish colliers but also echoed Alexander McDonald's doctrine of mutual respect between miner and mine owner. Such ideas also fitted well with the U.S. labor republican ideal that the true interests of labor and capital, when not distorted by grasping capitalists, were similar and could easily be reconciled. This class harmony idea was not, of course, confined to McDonald and other Victorian trade unionists in England and Scotland. At midcentury it was advocated by numerous labor reformers in the United States, including the celebrated American economist Henry Carey, whose opinions were reprinted in the columns of several Scottish working-class newspapers, the *Glasgow Sentinel* among them.[16]

The link that Chartist reformers forged between the Scottish and American labor movements is particularly intriguing. Lanarkshire miners gave relatively little support to the Chartist movement for political and economic reform in the 1840s, but significant contacts were developed between British immigrant miners and well-known ex-Chartists who fled to America after the collapse of the movement at the end of the decade. The list of seventy-six Chartists in America drawn up by Ray Boston in his 1971 book on the subject includes only four coal miners, but three of them played influential roles in developing collier trade unionism in the American Midwest. Yorkshire-born John Bates, who left England for Pittsburgh in the latter part of 1848, founded the first Pennsylvania anthracite union with more than a local following. According to Boston, Bates's union was run on Chartist principles. More important was Thomas Lloyd. "Formerly a very active Chartist," Lloyd emigrated from Staffordshire to the United States in 1858.[17] In 1860 he traveled west to the burgeoning Belleville coalfield in southwestern Illinois to help fellow Chartist Daniel Weaver found the American Miners Association, an organization that exercised an important influence over the policies adopted by the infant miners' unions of northern Illinois later on in the same decade.[18]

Table 2 provides a snapshot, frozen in time, of the distribution of British immigrant miners in the four states where they settled in the largest numbers. Pennsylvania, not Illinois, attracted the largest number of immigrant colliers, but with 624 Scots-born colliers in 1870, Illinois contained the same percentage of Scottish miners as did Maryland. These figures date from 1870, however, when most of the British-born colliers living in Illinois resided in the south-central Illinois coalfield, in St. Clair County, near St. Louis. Hence

Table 2. British Immigrant Coal Miners in Illinois, Maryland, Ohio, and Pennsylvania, 1870

	Illinois	Maryland	Ohio	Pennsylvania	Totals
Miners in the state	6,954	2,838	15,501	47,997	73,290
British-born miners	3,261 (47%)	1,393 (49%)	3,709 (24%)	13,964 (29%)	22,327
English	1,541 (22%)	628 (22%)	1,816 (12%)	4,013 (8%)	7,998
Irish	926 (13%)	400 (14%)	975 (6%)	4,714 (10%)	7,015
Scottish	624 (9%)	261 (9%)	729 (5%)	2,416 (5%)	4,030
Welsh	170 (2%)	104 (4%)	189 (1%)	2,821 (6%)	3,284

Sources: Ninth U.S. Population Census (1870), vol. 1, 731, 738, 752, 754–55. See also Amy Z. Gottlieb, "The Regulation of the Coal Mining Industry in Illinois, with Special Reference to the Influence of British Miners and British Precedents, 1870–1911" (Ph.D. diss., University of London, 1975), 59.

the table does not explain why, five years earlier, significant numbers of Scots had been attracted to the northern Illinois coalfield, fifty miles southwest of Chicago and more than two hundred miles north of St. Louis. At that time much of the area surrounding the northern coalfield was still bleak, open prairie. It had few amenities and was in many ways still part of the frontier. Why did the emigrating miners settle there?

One reason for the appeal of the northern Illinois coalfield, as can be seen from map 5, was its location, at the western edge of the expanding coal-mining frontier. Skilled colliers were still scarce there. Initially, therefore, despite greater physical discomfort, wages were higher in northern Illinois than they were in the eastern coal-mining states or even in the established coalfield in St. Clair County. Incoming miners had the pick of the best jobs without having to compete with established colliers. In addition, mining had already been started in 1856 at the town of La Salle, approximately fifteen miles northwest of what was to become Streator, so the area was not entirely unknown.[19]

In addition, there was the opportunity to purchase cheap plots of the open prairie land that still covered much of La Salle, Will, and Grundy Counties, where the northern Illinois coalfield lay. In 1856, too, the attractions of the area were noted in a series of booster articles about the American Midwest that appeared in the Scottish press. One of them claimed that, because of

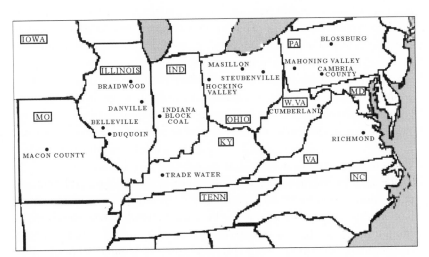

Map 5. Selected British mining settlements (*source:* Edward Wieck, *The American Miners Association* [New York: Russell Sage Foundation, 1940], 1).

its superior communications, northern Illinois was a better place to settle than either Wisconsin or Minnesota. This article stated that tracts of virgin Illinois prairie could still be bought at fifty cents to two dollars an acre. Its coalfields were just opening up, and mining wages were more than double those in southwest Scotland. Waxing lyrical about the beauty of the Illinois countryside, the article concluded by comparing it favorably — but with little sense of geography — to Perthshire in Scotland, "with the Mississippi taking the place of the Tay, and the mountains of the Upper Mississippi that of the Grampians." [20]

Despite its scenic exaggerations, the booster article about northern Illinois was correct in at least one respect. Railroad communications there were indeed better than those in Wisconsin or Minnesota. This was especially true of the links between the St. Clair County coalfield and the northern Illinois one, which had been facilitated by the completion of the Illinois Central Railroad in 1856, as well as by the opening of the St. Louis, Alton, and Chicago line. The Illinois and Michigan Canal, constructed earlier, connected Lake Michigan to the Illinois River, enabling merchants to ship coal east to the industrial cities of the Great Lakes basin. These improvements were due in part to a group of Irish immigrant laborers who had been brought over from the United Kingdom to help build the local railroads and canals. Some of these men bought land on the northern Illinois prairie after their laboring work was done, while others went into the mines.[21] A still more direct conduit between Scotland, Ireland, and northern Illinois was opened up in May 1863, when the Illinois Central Railroad contracted with an agent of the Foreign Emigrant Aid Society of Boston to distribute five thousand posters in various parts of Britain advertising ICR land for sale.[22]

There was a third reason for northern Illinois' appeal: miners were in short supply there because many colliers from the central part of the state had enlisted in the Union army during the Civil War. Some of these Union army volunteers were important figures in the mining world. For example, even though he was over forty years old, American Miners Association president Thomas Lloyd, who was known to be a foe of slavery, volunteered to mine coal for the Union army near Chattanooga, Tennessee, in order to help supply General Sherman's forces with fuel. John Hinchcliffe, a Yorkshire-born tailor who had become an American lawyer as well as editor of the *Weekly Miner,* was appointed captain in the commissary department of the Union army. Several hundred other Illinois miners from St. Clair County served in the northern armies as well.[23]

Finally, two of Alexander McDonald's brothers had migrated from southwest Scotland to the Midwest before the Civil War, and they wrote flattering accounts of the region in letters they sent back to the *Glasgow Sentinel.* One of these brothers, James McDonald, reporting from Ohio in October 1863, stated that he was earning sixteen dollars a week (the equivalent of three pounds, fifty pence) working as a roadsman. Soon after this brother Charlie reported from Gardner, Illinois, that he was earning four dollars a day as a hewer of coal.[24] Gardner was no more than two miles from where Braidwood was shortly to be built.

The next step in the emigration process involved the propaganda efforts of the Foreign Emigrant Aid Society of Boston. The stated purpose of this body, which was founded in 1863, was to seek out and recruit skilled artisans from the United Kingdom to help develop America's burgeoning industries and to accelerate production in those industries, such as coal, that were particularly important in the prosecution of the Civil War. Evidence suggests, however, that the society also sought to recruit soldiers for the Union army. By May 1864 the Boston society had raised enough money to appoint an agent to seek out would-be emigrants from Europe. The agent's name was Peter Sinclair, a former Scots emigrant who before the Civil War had already paid several visits to Glasgow attempting to lure Scottish skilled workers abroad.[25]

On August 15, 1864, Sinclair spoke to a meeting of the Glasgow Trades Council about the aims of the Foreign Emigrant Aid Society. He explained the methods by which the society helped would-be emigrants to get jobs in the United States, pointed to the higher wages that could be earned there, and appealed to the delegates to inform workers in their various trades of the numerous vacancies. Several representatives of the Lanarkshire miners' union were present at the trades council meeting. At first, however, they reacted cautiously to Sinclair's suggestions, partly because they had learned, from other sources, that coal operators had used British miners they had imported into the St. Clair County region to break a strike there. They were also wary because of rumors that despite its denials, the Foreign Emigrant Aid Society of Boston was indeed engaged in recruiting soldiers for the Union army.[26]

These fears appeared to be confirmed when, a few weeks after the Glasgow meeting, reports circulated that the American embassy in London was drawing on a secret service fund to pay Peter Sinclair to propagandize on behalf of the Union cause.[27] However, Sinclair made a more favorable impression when he spoke to a mass meeting of miners held a few days later in the open air at Bogle's Hole, on the banks of the River Clyde. Sinclair said he had been told by the American manufacturers who acted as his sponsors that U.S. coal owners had immediate vacancies for between five hundred and one thousand experienced colliers. He claimed (rather improbably) that miners in Pennsylvania were being paid seven dollars a day. In response to questions, moreover, Sinclair denied emphatically that he had instructions to recruit soldiers for the Union army.[28]

These statements appeared to assuage the doubts of many in the audience. The clinching argument at the Bogle's Hole meeting came when *Glasgow Sentinel* reporter Alexander Campbell read out portions of a letter he had just received from Robert Rankin, a Lanarkshire miner who had immigrated to the south-central Illinois coalfield several years before. In his letter Rankin acknowledged that the inflation caused by the American Civil War was quite severe and that the Lincoln administration had imposed some new war taxes. "But this I can say," Rankin concluded, "that this country is a long way better off for a workingman [than Scotland]. He is a long way better paid for his labour. We can make from four to five dollars per day, and the work is no harder than in Scotland for that sum." [29] At the end of the meeting several miners asked Sinclair about enrolling under the emigrant society's plan.

Few Lanarkshire miners actually followed through on the Boston society's scheme. It is hard to say whether this was because they distrusted Sinclair or because they learned that his plan involved a contributory system of payment whereby most of the money for the transatlantic fare would come from the miners themselves. Probably it was a combination of both. Instead, most of them chose either to emigrate privately, if they did so at all, or to follow Alexander McDonald's plan for union-supported emigration. By this time McDonald had established personal contact with a number of individual U.S. mining companies, including the Hampshire and Baltimore Company of Maryland. In the summer of 1864 he engaged in extensive negotiations with that company's representatives about the possibility of sending a group of Lanarkshire miners across the ocean to work for the firm. This plan was in addition to the previously noted general union scheme to support miner emigration.[30]

Given the miners' fears about being misled, in negotiations with U.S. coal companies McDonald tried to ensure that the offers he recommended to Scottish miners would protect their interests. In June 1864, for example, he warned colliers against signing a sample contract that had been sent to a Bothwell concern by the Fallbrook Coal Company of Pennsylvania. The contract stated that Fallbrook would pay the miners' passage across the Atlantic, as well as from New York to Pennsylvania, and that the miners would be able to repay their cost of passage on an installment plan. It said nothing about the wages the miners would be paid, however; it required them not to join a union; and it specified that anyone who had not paid off the passage money by a certain date would be fined $125.[31]

Thus, before recommending that miners accept the Hampshire and Baltimore Company's offer, McDonald first sought to check out the bona fides of the firm via his brother Charlie.[32] He also tried to ascertain on his own behalf just what the company would do for its immigrant employees. In reply, the Hampshire and Baltimore Company informed him that the seams at the company's Maryland mines were twelve feet thick and hence would yield a profitable tonnage; that the company would provide miners with three-room detached cottages, along with land for grazing animals; and that it would have no objection to the miners' erecting their own schools and churches.[33]

Apparently satisfied, in October 1864 Alexander McDonald urged up to forty Lanarkshire miners to sign a contract with Thomas Gemmell Sr., the vice president and general manager of the Hampshire and Baltimore Company. In the following six months several boatloads of Lanarkshire miners migrated to America either under contract to Gemmell or as a result of alternative arrangements. They formed part of a much larger emigrant stream of colliers that reached its peak between 1865 and 1868. Despite McDonald's care, however, his negotiations with the Hampshire and Baltimore Company backfired, as did several of the contracts that craftsmen in a number of other Glasgow trades signed with American employers through Sinclair and Boston's Foreign Emigrant Aid Society.[34] The reasons for this are best seen in the experience of McDonald's admirer and one of his chief lieutenants, John James, who will later play a prominent part in my story.

John James was a typical artisan-collier. He was born at Nitshill, a few miles southwest of Glasgow, in 1829. James attended school between the age of six and ten, when he entered the pits. Hard times drove the family to nearby Jonstone when he was still an adolescent. There he met McDonald, became an agitator for a mine inspection bill in Parliament, and joined the local miners' union. Subsequently blacklisted, James tramped to nearby Elderslie, where he married. His reputation as a union activist continued to dog him with employers throughout the 1850s. Having found work at the Inkerman mines, near Glasgow, he was again discharged for criticizing the management. Following the "flitting" habits that characterized others in his trade, James then returned to Elderslie and secured a job at the Balaclava pit under an assumed name, but his identity was soon discovered. Now desperate, he went on the tramp again, ending up at the Denny works in Ayrshire. It was there that he decided to go to America, and he saved up the money for his passage.[35]

At McDonald's urging, John James became one of twenty-eight Lanarkshire miners who signed a contract with the Hampshire and Baltimore Company in the early months of 1865. Sailing from Clydeside on May 10, 1865, he and his party landed in New York and went by train to Baltimore, only to be told by Thomas Gemmell that the Hampshire and Baltimore Company could not employ any of them. To justify himself, Gemmell claimed that since concluding his negotiations with McDonald, but before James's arrival, he had written to McDonald advising him not to send any miners. Offering an alternative, Gemmell directed James and his party to a coal operator he knew at Newburgh, West Virginia, who had supposedly said that he would find jobs for the new immigrants. James and his fellow miners went on to Newburgh, only to find that the local miners were on strike and that he and his party had been brought in as strikebreakers.[36]

Predictably, as a loyal trade unionist James refused to break the strike at the Newburgh mine. Instead he and his fellow immigrants lent their support to the strikers, who offered to board them until they could find "honourable work."[37] The Newburgh strikers also issued a statement bitterly denouncing Gemmell and the Hampshire and Baltimore Company for importing strikebreakers and for trying to break up their trade union. Several of their number, the strikers stated, had fought for "Union and Liberty" in the Union army during the Civil War and had lost family members as a result. Now they were being asked to forfeit the very liberties for which they had made sacrifices. They refused to do so. They were, the strikers said, "willing to lose all they had before they would submit to give up the principles of their organization."[38] With a versatility typical of his breed, John James recouped his losses by working for a local Newburgh farmer. Then he signed on at a Pennsylvania mine; went to Rock Island, Illinois, on the false promise of high wages; returned to work in the Pennsylvania pits; and finally ended up in Braidwood, in the northern Illinois coalfield, in the fall of 1867.[39]

Meanwhile, the ill fortune that had struck John James and his party of twenty-eight caused a furor back home in southwest Scotland. The immediate issue was whether Alexander McDonald had actually been warned by Thomas Gemmell not to send any miners, or more precisely, whether he had been warned in time to prevent James and his party from taking up the Hampshire and Baltimore Company's offer. The misfortune was seized on by all those in the Lanarkshire mining community who had disapproved of McDonald's emigration policies in the first place. Chief among these was James King of Bargeddie, the Irish-born miners' leader who had been one of McDonald's main critics over the anti-Irish tendencies of the Order of Free Colliers. On July 1, 1865, King published a blistering attack on McDonald in the columns of the *Glasgow Sentinel*. He began by reviewing the various steps that the emigration policy's champions had taken. "There followed in quick succession," James King wrote, "departing feasts, testimonials of good feeling, Scotch convoys, pathetic speeches on the Clyde, and off goes the emigrant riding like a cork on the broad Atlantic sea, with a full soul and an empty stomach, landing in the 'beautiful west' just in time to become — what? A landowner? No. A colliery shareholder? No; but a duped, deceived, dependant pauper!" [40]

McDonald did not reply directly to James King's allegations, but he defended himself in other ways. First, he claimed that in giving advice to departing emigrant miners, he had carefully avoided describing their prospects in the glowing terms that James King said he had used. Accompanying one party of miners on the first stage of their journey down the Clyde in April 1865, McDonald warned them about the dangers they would face in America. "You are not to think for one moment," he said to those gathered about him on the deck, "that you are going to paradise." [41] Second, he took advantage of his influence in the office of the *Glasgow Sentinel* to print favorable comments alongside some of the positive accounts of life in America that were reported in the paper. On October 28, 1865, for example, the *Sentinel* reproduced a letter from John McTavish, who had emigrated from Wishaw to Mckees Port, Pennsylvania, in which he reported that in one day he could fill four big hutches of coal at a dollar and a quarter apiece. "Four waggons, at a dollar and a quarter," McDonald noted sarcastically at the bottom of the page, "is four dollars a day. Truly, that must be a land of suffering!" [42]

Third, and most important, McDonald prevailed on John James himself to help him to redeem his reputation. James obliged. In a letter written to the *Glasgow Sentinel* from Mercer County, Pennsylvania, on September 16, 1865, James acknowledged that Thomas Gemmell had not in fact written to McDonald warning him not to send any miners to the Hampshire and Baltimore pits. He further stated that Gemmell had deliberately misled McDonald as to the availability of work in the hope of importing strikebreakers to defeat the union at the Newburgh mine. James added that Gemmell was a "charlatan, who would stop at nothing to get his way." Displaying the admiration for, and confidence in, Alexander McDonald — and McDonaldism — that he was to manifest throughout his future career as a miners' leader in the American Midwest, James concluded: "I will never forget Mr. McDonald, as I believe through his advice in coming to this country I will have made a happy change, and never doubted the purity of his motives." [43]

Given James's reputation as a miners' leader in southwest Scotland, it is not surprising that other Lanarkshire colliers chose to follow him to the northern Illinois coalfield in the late 1860s and early 1870s. Braidwood had been growing rapidly since 1865, and the fact that its founder, James Braidwood, also hailed from the Glasgow area added to its appeal. In addition, by this time quite a few Scottish, Welsh, and English as well as native-born American miners had begun to drift west to Illinois from the bituminous coalfields of Pennsylvania, Maryland, and Ohio.[44] Some of these migrants ended up in Braidwood and Streator as well. Most important of all, before the decade was out, Braidwood witnessed the arrival of Daniel McLaughlin, the second of the two influential Scottish miners' leaders to settle in the region. In view of the important role McLaughlin was to play in subsequent American labor history, it is worth describing the process by which he, too, ended up in northern Illinois.

Daniel McLaughlin was born in Scotland in 1831, two years after John James. He was the son of an Irish stonecutter, however, not a native Scot. Like James, McLaughlin entered the pits at the age of nine. He worked for most of his early life in Maryhill, just north of Glasgow, where he took part — at the tender age of eleven — in a successful miners' strike in 1842. In 1847 McLaughlin was again on strike, and it was then that he met Alexander McDonald and, according to one account, "made his first public appearance as an agitator and an enemy to injustice and oppression."[45] In 1851 McLaughlin helped to elect McDonald to a local union position, possibly in Holytown. McLaughlin also served as both president and secretary of the Maryhill miners' union. As a result he, too, made enemies among the local coal owners. From 1847 to 1868 McLaughlin took "an active and prominent part in all matters of reform in the interests of the wage-workers of Britain," gaining a "national reputation, so much so that . . . he found it almost impossible to get employment in his native land."[46] Finally, like John James before him, McLaughlin tired of the discrimination and blacklisting his union activities provoked. In August 1869, four years after James had left Scotland, McLaughlin too crossed the Atlantic ocean to the United States.[47]

After a brief period in Boston, Daniel McLaughlin moved straight on to northern Illinois, where he was convinced to stay by none other than John James himself. In early October 1869 McLaughlin was working in a Braidwood pit during what he thought would be a short visit to the town. "On my way to the station," he later recalled, "I called on John James to bid him good-bye, on account of the kindness he had shown me. He pressed me to stay; but it would not do — I must get employment. . . . He went and got two or three of the men from the old country together, and the result was that two of the men took one of his brother's workplaces, and I got in [i.e., shared his workplace] with John himself."[48] More political than James, McLaughlin rose to become mayor of Braidwood in the latter part of the 1870s.

Such were the reasons that prompted a growing number of Scottish colliers to move to the American Midwest. By 1869 the Civil War, and with it the fear of being conscripted into the Union army, was long gone. The fact that both John James and Daniel McLaughlin, two of Alexander McDonald's best-known lieutenants, had settled in Braidwood helped other emigrating British miners to feel more confidant about the northern Illinois coalfield. So, too, did the consistently high wages and the possibility of moving further west under still more advantageous circumstances.

PART TWO

Growth of Class Hostilities in Scotland and the American Midwest, 1865–1905

4

HEYDAY OF PICK MINING IN THE AMERICAN MIDWEST: BRAIDWOOD AND STREATOR, 1865–75

At the end of the American Civil War, most of the flat prairie land in northern Illinois, where Braidwood and Streator were built, was still in its virgin state. Some of the land surrounding both town sites, which were situated twenty-five miles apart in the Illinois River valley fifty miles southwest of Chicago, had been inhabited by homesteaders for more than a generation. In 1865 the coalfield itself was described by a local resident as "nothing but a sea of tall grass, or in winter a boundless field of snow, reaching out to meet the horizon, with scarcely a cabin intervening."[1] Besides the recently arrived Scottish, Irish, and English colliers, a small group of miners had already arrived from Pennsylvania and points east looking for better jobs.[2] What did the future hold for these immigrant colliers on the edge of the industrial frontier?

Braidwood was the first northern Illinois mining camp to be transformed from a frontier settlement into an industrial town. The town itself was incorporated in 1865. James Braidwood, after whom the town was named, was a skilled pick miner with engineering skills who immigrated to the United States from southwest Scotland in 1863.[3] Streator was founded three years later, when a group of Ohio capitalists learned about untapped coal lands twenty-five miles west of Braidwood. Early in 1866 they dispatched Col. Ralph Plumb to buy up coal lands on behalf of the newly founded Vermilion Coal Company. Since Ralph Streator of Cleveland provided most of the capital, it was from him that Streator got its name.[4]

Braidwood and Streator grew quickly because of the rapidly increasing demand for coal in the nearby industrial city of Chicago, the speedy arrival of skilled engineers and mine sinkers, and the willingness of eastern capitalists to invest their money in the local coalfield. By 1870 twenty freight and passenger trains a day hauled coal and other commercial products from Braidwood and Streator north to Chicago. Food, machinery, and other materials needed for development, as well as miners seeking jobs, filled the trains on their return journey from the metropolis.[5]

Among the Braidwood coal firms, the Chicago and Wilmington Company, which was founded in 1866, was by far the most important. Building its own branch line to the Chicago and Alton railroad, the company invested $475,000 in its Braidwood operations between 1866 and 1868. These advantages helped to turn Braidwood, for a period of about ten years, into one of the most important coal-producing centers in the Midwest. The growth in its output was extraordinary. During 1866 Braidwood's mines shipped ten thousand tons of coal on the Chicago and Alton line to St. Louis, Chicago, and elsewhere. By 1873 two thousand tons a day were leaving pits dotted all over Reed Township. As can be seen from map 6, additional coal came from a number of Braidwood's satellite towns, such as Braceville, Diamond, and Gardner, which rapidly cropped up in neighboring Grundy County.[6]

Streator's growth spurt began somewhat later than Braidwood's. Indeed, in building a railroad link to the new city, Col. Ralph Plumb, secretary of the newly formed Vermilion Coal Company, encountered difficulties similar to those experienced by Lord Belhaven and Henry Houldsworth in constructing the Wishaw and Coltness branch of the Scottish Caledonian railway twenty years before. Acting on behalf of Ralph Streator and the other members of the board of directors back in Cleveland, Col. Plumb began sinking what became known as the "Old Slope Mine," north of the city park, in the spring of 1866. At the same time, however, he had to raise enough capital to build the fifteen-mile "Stub End Road" that led westward from Streator to Wenona and a junction with the Illinois Central Railroad.[7] Plumb and his fellow entrepreneurs also had to plat the land, lay out the streets, build stores and homes, and attract miners from the east. They did this by booster tactics similar to those employed earlier by the Foreign Emigrant Aid Society of Boston. The Vermilion Coal Company lacked the money to send its own agents to Europe to secure miners under contract. Instead, it notified steamship offices of new jobs that were opening up and persuaded local railroad companies to carry notices of Streator's promise (see map 7).[8]

Another tactic used to attract miners to the two northern Illinois towns was to offer them housing lots they could keep as their own. In the late 1860s both the Chicago and Wilmington Company in Braidwood and the Vermil-

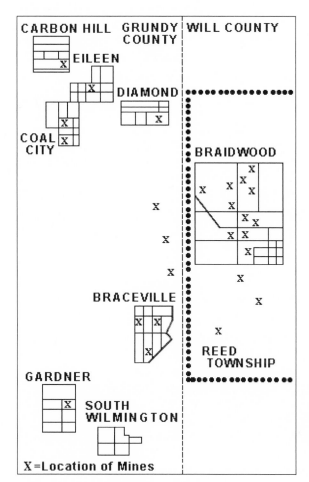

Map 6. Braidwood and satellite mining towns, circa 1870 (*source: Combination Map of Will County* [1873]; *Platt Book of Grundy County* [1874]).

ion Company in Streator sold land to incoming colliers at ten dollars or less per acre. The coal companies, however, kept the mineral rights to the land. The low prices enabled quite a few first-generation colliers to build houses on their own land, raise fruit and vegetables, and even keep chickens, a pig, or a cow.[9] This ability to purchase housing, as well as other material advantages I will discuss later, made the initial prospects of the incoming miners much better than those of the Lanarkshire colliers who had entered the Wishaw and Larkhall pits thirty or forty years before.

By 1870 dozens of new settlers were coming to Braidwood and Streator every week. In that year Streator's overall population, at 1,486, was still much smaller than Braidwood's, which stood at 2,421. By 1880, however, Streator

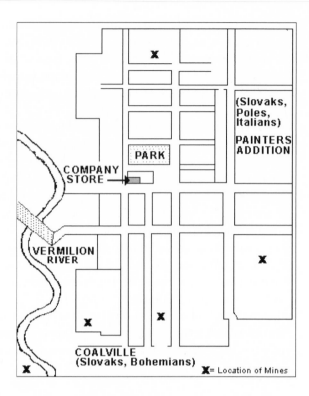

Map 7. Streator, circa 1885 (source: Platt Book of La Salle County [1886]).

had come near to catching up. At 5,157 (Braidwood had 5,524) Streator's citizenry had more than tripled in ten years.[10] It is difficult to say just what proportion of the Scottish element in the two towns came from Wishaw and Larkhall. Nevertheless, some evidence on this point is given in the list of Scots whose places of origin Alexander McDonald noted on his two visits to northern Illinois in 1867 and 1869. These were Airdrie (4), Rutherglen (4), Wishaw (4), Hamilton (2), Larkhall (2), Glasgow (2), Maryhill (1), and Newmains (1). Even if only a small proportion of the miners in Braidwood and Streator came from Wishaw and Larkhall as such, all the other towns mentioned in this list were within a ten- to twelve-mile radius of the two originating Lanarkshire towns.[11]

The important role Scottish and Irish miners played in both Braidwood and Streator is confirmed by table 3, which breaks down by place of origin the two cities' mining population between 1860 and 1880. In Braidwood the Scots made up 22 percent of the miners in 1870 and 14 percent in 1880. In Streator English miners played a more dominant role and both Scottish and Irish miners a lesser one. The difference was made up by a higher propor-

Table 3. Birthplaces of Miners in Braidwood and Streator, 1860–80

	1860	1870	1880
Braidwood			
Native-born	2 (100%)	224 (32%)	551 (25%)
English	0	128 (19%)	382 (18%)
Irish	0	114 (17%)	248 (12%)
Scottish	0	155 (22%)	294 (14%)
Welsh	0	29 (4%)	49 (2%)
Other European	0	41 (6%)	614 (29%)
	2 (100%)	691 (100%)	2,138 (100%)
Streator			
Native-born	1 (25%)	176 (25%)	674 (29%)
English	0	243 (34%)	489 (21%)
Irish	3 (75%)	104 (15%)	293 (12%)
Scottish	0	118 (17%)	198 (8%)
Welsh	0	31 (4%)	91 (4%)
Other European	0	32 (5%)	612 (26%)
	4 (100%)	704 (100%)	2,366 (100%)

Sources: U.S. Population Census, Will and La Salle Counties, Illinois (1860, 1870, 1880).

tion of native-born American miners, many of whom were sons of British immigrants, as well as by a growing number of so-called new European immigrants from southern and eastern Europe.[12] In Braidwood these new Europeans were primarily northern Italians, Bohemians, and Poles. In Streator they were largely Slovakian peasants from the Austro-Hungarian Empire.[13]

Census data also permit further comparisons between the demography of the two northern Illinois towns and the two Lanarkshire ones. A slight majority of the British miners in Braidwood and Streator were married, and they had an average age of twenty-six. The average number of children in the immigrant miners' families was 3.2, a figure somewhat smaller than the one for the families back in Wishaw and Larkhall. The fact that a significant number of the Irish miners' children in both Braidwood and Streator had been born in Scotland confirms the fact that quite a few of the Irish migrants had spent time working in southern Scotland before coming to the United States. One local newspaper reporter, commenting on the accents of immigrant workmen disembarking from a train that arrived in Braidwood from Chicago in the fall of 1868, "found it hard to distinguish the voices of men who came from Old Scotia from those who came from the Emerald Isle."[14]

❖

To gain insight into the process of class formation in the Lanarkshire and northern Illinois coalfields, it is necessary first to compare the different social and economic conditions under which both groups of miners lived. Because Braidwood and Streator, like Wishaw and Larkhall, were mainly mining towns, all four of them displayed much the same social geography. As in Lanarkshire, the streets near the core of both Braidwood and Streator were the main commercial centers. In addition, in the early years the miners' houses in the U.S. coal towns were interspersed with those of tradesmen and professionals, like their counterparts in Wishaw and Larkhall. As in Scotland, too, the coalpits in Braidwood and Streator were sunk either inside or near to the main residential neighborhoods, within easy walking distance of the colliers' homes. This permitted the same frequent "flitting" (i.e., exchange of jobs) of colliers and the same sense of miner solidarity. In the early 1870s this sense of community was enhanced in both towns by the construction of streetcar lines, which brought each town's neighborhoods closer together. In Braidwood special cars were set aside for miners traveling to their morning shift.[15]

The incoming British colliers found some features of early life in Braidwood and Streator alien and unattractive. The so-called new European immigrants who began to arrive from northern Italy and various provinces of the Austro-Hungarian Empire in the late 1870s were more alien to the newly arrived Scots than were the fellow Celts who had crossed the Irish sea to work in Lanarkshire in the 1840s and 1850s.[16] As in southwest Scotland, the semi-proletarian or newcomer-rebel element among the colliers exhibited a tough, combative attitude toward mining that could easily lead to blows. What distressed the more sober among the artisan-colliers, however, was the greater readiness of malcontents in the United States to settle their disputes with firearms. An ordinance against carrying concealed weapons was passed in Braidwood in 1871, but according to one source, it was largely ignored as "a farce and a laughing stock." In 1879 another resident claimed that "at least 500 revolvers are carried here to-day."[17]

In addition, the danger of fires was greater in America than in Scotland. The majority of homes and businesses in Braidwood and Streator were built of wood, not the stone or brick used in the Clyde Valley. The more frequent use of wood in northern Illinois was due in part to the short life of the shallow mines that dotted the area and to the need for light, balloon-framed houses that could easily be moved from one part of the coalfield to another when worked-out mineral deposits necessitated a shift in the surface community.[18] Both private houses and most places of business were vulnerable to fire, especially in the long summers, which were drier than Scotland's.

As a consequence, both Braidwood and Streator suffered extensive property damage from conflagrations.[19]

The absence of effective safety legislation in the early years meant that, for a time, the Illinois pits were more dangerous to work in than the Scottish ones.[20] The wide-open prairie that lay just beyond the city limits of both Braidwood and Streator also posed problems. The western prairie was appealing because of the fertile land that could be bought for a relative pittance, but it was also forbidding because of its total lack of amenities and extreme climatic conditions. An anonymous letter appearing in the *Glasgow Sentinel* in February 1867, for example, described the fate of a group of immigrant miners who had set out from Braidwood by wagon, bound for a new mining camp that had been opened in Kansas a few months earlier, only to come back penniless: "Yes, my friends, [they] came back penniless, with broken health and spirits. Do you ever think about the extreme heat and cold that this climate is subject to? Have you any idea of the thermometer at the height of 100 or 101, or of the cold 32 degrees below the freezing point?"[21]

Do these early hazards mean that the quality of life — and hence the likelihood of the miners' early alienation — was worse in Braidwood and Streator than it had been in Scotland? The answer is a decided no. First of all, it must be remembered that despite a different terrain, Larkhall and Wishaw had also been preindustrial towns in the 1830s and that their rapid growth in the following two decades had been accompanied by many of the same social ills that characterized the emergence of Braidwood and Streator twenty years later. Early residents of Braidwood and Streator complained frequently about the lack of paved roads, the absence of municipal services, and the inability of law-enforcement officers to control the drunks who roamed the streets. These complaints differed little, however, from those that had appeared with monotonous regularity in the columns of the *Wishaw Press* and the *Hamilton Advertiser* twenty years before.

Second, complaints about the adequacy of drinking water and other sanitary facilities were rarer in northern Illinois than in Lanarkshire. This meant, in turn, that the fear of epidemics resulting from bad sanitation was less prevalent in Braidwood and Streator than it was in Scotland. This was an important matter. Outbreaks of typhus were not uncommon in the substandard Scottish miners' rows.[22] In addition, by 1876 both of the U.S. towns had installed extensive systems of street lighting. This was more than could be said for the remoter parts of Wishaw and Larkhall.[23]

By 1875, moreover, Braidwood and Streator boasted just as many churches and temperance societies to combat the evils of violence and drink as southwest Scotland had. These societies included several chapters of the ubiquitous Order of Good Templars. In fact, ministers and other community leaders in northern Illinois acted much like those in Lanarkshire regarding the subject of drink, but without quite the same expectations of social deference that accompanied the ministers' sermons in Scotland.[24] In addition, miners' wives in the northern Illinois coal towns deplored drunkenness for the same reasons that miners' wives did in Wishaw and Larkhall.[25] And H. K. Barnard, who wrote the life of Anton Cermak (a Bohemian immigrant who spent his boyhood in Braidwood and later became mayor of Chicago) explained the colliers' drinking in terms of the same masculine culture that predominated in the mining towns of Lanarkshire. For the prairie collier of the 1860s and 1870s, writes Barnard, the saloon was "a virtually indispensable institution. It was the miner's social club, political forum, meeting place, and theater all in one. . . . Here he might feel more a man among men than a human mole; here he might achieve social status among his peers by virtue of his capacity, strength, or wit."[26]

So far I have treated Braidwood and Streator as a single entity, without considering the differences between them, yet some of those differences were just as important for the issue of class formation as those between Wishaw and Larkhall. In general Streator was wealthier, occupationally more diverse, and culturally more sophisticated than Braidwood.[27] The main reason for this difference was Streator's more extensive manufacturing base. Besides containing coal, Streator's soils possessed a combination of clay and shale suitable for making bricks, tile, and drain pipes. Braidwood, on the other hand, remained a single-industry coal town throughout this period. Aside from boasting a couple of small bottling companies and ethnically specific businesses such as Peter Rossi's macaroni factory, it contained few other sources of employment besides the seventeen or eighteen coal pits dotted throughout the township.[28]

Streator's more diverse occupational structure can be demonstrated statistically. Whereas miners and mine laborers constituted 78 percent of Braidwood's male labor force in 1880, they made up only 65 percent of the workers in Streator.[29] In addition, well over half of the 12 percent of Streator's labor force designated as "casual workers" in the 1880 census were brick and shale workers. As in Lanarkshire, many of these brick workers were young girls and women.[30] Considered disreputable by the town's middle-class leaders, these female brick workers carried out a wide variety of tasks. Some stirred the brick paste, which was made of yellow clay and hemp rope bits; others shoveled it into molds; and a third group stacked the bricks into kilns for firing and later removed them when the kilns had cooled down. In general, however, jobs outside the home for the miners' wives and daughters were no more numerous in Braidwood and Streator than they had been back home in Scotland.[31]

The occupation that most differentiated Streator from Braidwood, however, was glass making. According to the 1880 census, 22 skilled bottle blowers lived in Streator at that time, along with 84 helpers, 114 sheet-glass workers, and some ancillary tradesmen. Their numbers grew still larger by the end of the century.[32] Streator's skilled glassworkers more or less paralleled the skilled element among Wishaw's ironworkers in dividing the towns' male labor forces into an upper and a lower echelon. Few even among the artisan-colliers could command either the same high wage levels or the same degree of respect among their fellow workers as the skilled glass makers and iron-workers. In fact, in the hierarchy of workers that prevailed on both sides of the Atlantic, none occupied a higher or more respected position than skilled glassblowers and trained iron rollers and heaters.[33]

Did the labor aristocratic lifestyles of the Streator glassworkers threaten the growth of working-class solidarity there more than the middle-class life-styles of the trained rollers and heaters endangered the development of inter-occupational bonds in Wishaw? The answer is no. It is true that the interests of Streator's glassworkers sometimes differed from those of its coal miners. For one thing, they earned more money. The top daily wage for glassblowers was $4.49, almost twice as much as that for the best-paid colliers. This enabled the glassblowers to buy quite large houses in a select area of Streator known as Twister Hill. In 1873 this residential segregation led one miner to call the glassblowers "the plutocrats of the working class."[34] Besides wage differentials, there were also cultural and religious differences between the Continental glassworkers and the British-born miners. Most of the glassworkers in Streator were German or Belgian artisans brought there from Pittsburgh or Charleroi, in Belgium. Most, too, were Catholics whose religious outlook and drinking habits offended the temperance views of the Protestant leaders of the artisan-colliers.[35]

Despite these differences in income and lifestyle, however, there is little to suggest that tensions between Streator's glassblowers and pick miners were more damaging to the growth of a common class consciousness than were the differences among the Scottish miners, their Irish helpers, and the cadre of skilled English iron rollers and heaters who lived in Wishaw. For example, when the miners carried out a brief strike in Streator in 1879, the coal supplies needed to heat the glass-melting pots were threatened much as the coal supplies used to fuel the iron smelters in Wishaw were threatened when the miners struck there. Nevertheless, when a much longer strike wave drew Streator miners into conflict with their employers in the latter part of the 1880s, these divisions did not prevent the glassblowers from giving the colliers their full moral and financial support.[36]

Although the social geography of the downtown areas of Braidwood and Streator was similar to that of Wishaw and Larkhall, residential patterns among the ethnic minorities who worked in the northern Illinois towns differed somewhat from those of the Irish minority who lived in Lanarkshire. For example, the married Scottish colliers in Wishaw and Larkhall tended to live side by side with Irish colliers and their families in the same miners' rows. The young, single southern and eastern European peasants who began working in Braidwood and Streator in the 1870s, however, lived for the most part in rental units or boardinghouses on the edges of town.[37] In Streator most of the boardinghouses were located in the Coalville or Painters Addition neighborhoods, which were situated on the extreme northeastern and southwest sides of the city.[38] These differences in residential patterns between Scotland and northern Illinois raise additional questions about the issue of miner solidarity and class formation.

The boardinghouses in Coalville and Painters Addition were crude in construction and often overcrowded. Twenty to thirty young, single miners would find a suitable house, agree on a common rent, and appoint a *burdos gazda* (Slovakian for "housekeeper"; sometimes a married couple and other times a miner's wife), whose job it was to buy provisions, cook and clean, and fill the miners' lunch buckets every day.[39] A common evening meal of home country food would be served in the kitchen, but there was little privacy in the bedrooms, where two or three miners would sometimes share the same bed, rotating between shifts. This same practice had been followed by the Irish in the miners' rows in Lanarkshire. The crucial question, however, is whether this segregated pattern of living, when coupled with the cultural differences between the British miners and their new European immigrant counterparts in the United States, inhibited the growth of solidarity among them to a greater extent than did the differences between the Scottish and Irish colliers in Lanarkshire.

Cultural tensions certainly existed between the British miners of Braidwood and Streator, on the one hand, and the Slovakian, Italian, and Bohemian colliers, on the other.[40] Evidence on this point can again be found in the early life of Anton Cermak. As a boy Cermak frequently found himself derogated not simply by the Irish and English boys in his neighborhood but also by the recently arrived immigrants in Upper Braidwood. "In those days," writes Cermak's biographer, "clashes between at least five groups were common, and Bohemians didn't dare put their heads out after dark."[41] Such divisions were exacerbated in both towns by the reproduction of long-standing European national and religious enmities that sometimes set ethnic minorities from the czarist and Austro-Hungarian Empires against each other. Bohemians, for example, had a lower social status than Germans; Poles disliked Russians; and Slovaks carried bitter memories of the authoritarian rule of the Hungarian elite in the dual monarchy of the Austro-Hungarian Empire.[42]

An additional cultural division stemmed from each ethnic group's tendency to reestablish its Old World churches and voluntary associations in order to bring order and familiarity to the workers' new lives. As one historian of Streator puts it: "The advent of each nationality to fit into the town's economy was followed always by the founding of a church of that particular ethnic group."[43] This patchwork quilt of ethnic neighborhoods was also reflected, in the early years at least, in an ethnically determined occupational hierarchy in the mines. The figures given in table 4, which correlates national origins with job level, provide insight into the occupational distinctions between the skilled British artisan-colliers and the unskilled semi-proletarians and newcomer-rebels from eastern and southern Europe. (The *newcomer-rebel* term fits well with the undisciplined work habits of the Slovaks and Bohemians when they first entered the northern Illinois pits. Until they learned the ropes, these men — like the Irish in Lanarkshire during the 1840s — were willing to work harder than the British artisan-colliers for a quick dollar in order to send money back home. Consequently, like the earlier Irish miners in southwest Scotland, they were unwilling for a time to take as much care with their work as the more experienced men.) The extent to which British-born miners in Braidwood and Streator dominated in the possession of skilled jobs is striking. In 1880, 31 percent of the foremen and 24 percent of the checkweighmen were either English or Scottish, while out of a total of 1,577 skilled pick miners, 1,058 were of British or American stock. Most of the mine laborers, drivers, and helpers, however, were Italians, Bohemians, or Slavs.

Contrary to received opinion, however, the northern Illinois colliers' greater tendency toward ethnic diversity no more weakened the miners' willingness to act collectively than did similar cultural differences in Lanarkshire. Several countervailing tendencies in Braidwood and Streator reinforced a sense of common purpose among the miners and neutralized the divisive impact of occupational segregation underground. First, despite the presence of a number of Catholic parochial schools, there was a widespread desire — shared by new and old immigrants alike — to establish a common, tax-based free public education system that would enable all the local miners' children to go to the same school. The aim, in the words of one historian, was to en-

Table 4. Miners' Occupations by Ethnic Group, Braidwood and
Streator, 1870–80

	Braidwood		Streator	
	1870	1880	1870	1880
Skilled miners[a]				
Native white	48	140	88	214
English	90	110	38	109
Scottish	81	116	42	64
Irish	46	81	31	118
Welsh	18	38	30	68
French	12	21	0	4
Italian	8	102	33	89
Bohemian	11	41	12	68
Slavic	0	88	14	106
	314	737	288	840
Unskilled miners[b]				
Native white	56	86	16	118
English	41	22	54	81
Scottish	34	27	18	68
Irish	42	23	18	72
Welsh	17	14	23	82
French	0	32	30	18
Italian	43	444	157	561
Bohemian	132	415	16	64
Slavic	12	338	84	462
	377	1,401	416	1,526

Sources: U.S. Population Census, Will and La Salle Counties, Illinois (1870, 1880).
a. Pick miners, foremen, engineers, checkweighmen, and firemen.
b. Drivers, laborers, helpers, and shovelers.

able children of all nationalities to "acquire the common language and to learn the value of American citizenship."[44] At first this was more easily said than done, because land and property values were too low to provide a significant tax base. At least in Braidwood, however, the miners overcame this problem in 1874 when they prevailed on Scottish immigrant city attorney William C. Mooney to get a bill passed in the Illinois state legislature permitting municipal governments to allocate part of their saloon tax to finance the public schools.[45] The fact that the immigrant miners in these towns were able to vote as soon as they got their citizenship papers also meant that they assumed the burdens of civic responsibility earlier than their Scottish equivalents. These developments tended to draw the community together rather than to divide it.

Second, although ethnic and religious differences could and did divide the coal town communities on political lines, they could also bring them together. Because they were the first on the ground, British immigrants at first dominated the political process, but once the southern and eastern European immigrants began registering to vote, it became necessary to forge cross-ethnic alliances to ensure that the miners' voices would be heard. This was particularly important in the election of local officials such as sheriffs and judges. By choosing whether to issue or enforce court injunctions, these officials played a crucial role in determining the outcome of strikes. In Scotland the judges and police officials were appointed by higher authorities, not elected by popular vote. This transatlantic difference in political practice gave the British colliers in the United States a powerful incentive to work together with other ethnic groups in electing candidates favorable to the miners' cause. As one Braidwood paper put it in 1873, local political tickets had to be ethnically balanced, because "to secure the support of every nationality, each must have a fair representation."[46]

Third, although its size fluctuated, the local labor movement in the northern Illinois coal towns was both larger and more all-encompassing than were the miners' unions in southwest Scotland at this time. In Braidwood and Streator the movement took the form first of branches of the Miners National Association (1873) and then of the Knights of Labor. By bringing to their meetings the same sense of cross-cultural solidarity that the miners of different nationalities had built up underground, union locals provided a powerful antidote to cultural separatism in the community. The Knights of Labor played an especially integrative role. By 1882 its district assembly 22, which included Braidwood but was based in Streator, contained no fewer than seventeen affiliated assemblies, twelve of which were mixed assemblies containing railroad workers, blacksmiths, teamsters, and building tradesmen as well as miners. By 1880 district assembly 22 contained approximately 800 members and included many ethnic groups.[47] Such occupationally mixed unions were unheard of in Scotland at this time.

Last, although each nationality had its own voluntary associations, there were other social institutions in the Illinois mining towns that cut across ethnic and religious divisions and drew together citizens from a wide range of ethnic groups. An 1884 report on Streator noted the following: "The lodges of the different friendly societies, which abound here, offer evening entertainment to miners and their families of different nationalities every night of the week. Social parties, balls and outings are not uncommon, and music is studied with delight."[48] Braidwood too had its separate Masons, its Knights of St. Pythias, and its Phil Kearney post of the Grand Army of the Republic for those colliers who had served in the Civil War. Nonetheless, in July 1877 an out-of-town newspaper commented favorably on the positive manner in which the many different ethnic groups in Braidwood interacted. Despite its "incongruity of race," reported the *Chicago Times,* "there is remarkable unanimity among the miners" of Braidwood. This was because they viewed themselves as "members of a proud Republic . . . and well disposed to tolerate each other."[49]

It would be going too far to suggest that ethnic and religious differences among the miners in southwest Scotland, where the Irish and Scots were the only two large cultural groups, were just as great as they were in northern Illinois. Problems there stemmed not only from the larger number of ethnic groups involved but also from language barriers in the polyglot coal towns of the U.S. Midwest, at least until the eastern and southern European miners learned to speak English. Nevertheless, as I will show in more detail in a later chapter, once Illinois district 12 of the United Mine Workers of America (1890) organized most of the southern and eastern European miners into the UMWA, a significant degree of interethnic (although not always of interracial)[50] harmony was achieved. Ethnocultural differences may have retarded the growth of class-conscious sentiments in the northern Illinois coal towns to some degree, but compared to the conflicts that separated the colliers of southwest Scotland into rival groups, they were not large enough to constitute the main reason that class formation did not develop as quickly in the American Midwest as it did in Lanarkshire.

If ethnocultural differences did not constitute a more serious barrier to the initial growth of class-conscious sentiments among the miners of northern Illinois than they did among the colliers of southwest Scotland, then what did? The answer lies in a number of social and economic advantages that, for a number of years, at least, the British immigrant miners of Braidwood and Streator enjoyed over their counterparts in Larkhall and Wishaw. In fact, in material terms the fifteen-year period between 1865 and 1880 can be described as the heyday of pick mining in the American Midwest.

The most obvious material advantage that the northern Illinois miners enjoyed compared to their Scottish counterparts was superior housing. "The type of miner's home most frequently met with," stated a report of the Illinois Bureau of Labor Statistics in the early 1880s, "is a one-story frame, painted and plastered cottage, standing on a lot 50 × 150 feet deep. The house is commonly about 16 × 24 feet, with an addition of 12 × 14 feet." This was larger even than most of the cooperatively owned miners' homes in Larkhall. Some of the Streator miners' houses were worth more than $500. "Their furniture usually consists of tables, chairs, bedsteads, sewing machines, bureau or stand, a rag carpet, and pictures and other household goods. There are cabinet organs in a number of miners' homes, and two or three [have] pianos."[51]

In addition to this, in the 1870s and early 1880s the proportion of home-owning miners was greater in Braidwood and Streator than it was in Wishaw and Larkhall. A survey of miners' housing carried out by the Illinois Bureau of Labor Statistics in 1884 showed that 200 miners in Streator (20 percent of the total), 170 in Braidwood (33 percent), and 200 in the nearby village of Braceville (38 percent) owned their houses.[52] Other evidence of material well-being was also recorded. In Streator, the 1884 report noted, sixty-eight miners held stock worth $7,304 in local building and loan associations. Quite a few of the miners possessed surpluses in the accounts they held with commercial banks.[53] Their diet also appears to have been superior to the one in Scotland. Miners demanded "the very best" in the way of meat and groceries, the 1884 report noted, adding that "in this respect they are more particular and use a better quality than artisans or farmers."[54] These food purchases were supplemented by liberal quantities of fruits and vegetables, as well as by the chickens and pigs that the colliers raised in their backyards. Not even the Larkhall miners, some of whom owned their own houses with gardens out back, could match this.

Besides cultivating the plots of land attached to their houses, a number of the early miners in northern Illinois also bought or rented farmland in nearby rural areas while still working in the mines, something that had been impossible in southwest Scotland. Anecdotal evidence suggests that the number of colliers who took up farming successfully in the United States was quite large. For example, of twenty-two former miners who moved away from Braidwood between 1874 and 1876, six became farmers.[55] One of them, a Scotsman named Thomas Stewart Cumming, divided his time between homesteading in Kansas and mining in northern Illinois. When Frank Newsam, another British miner, retired, he was able to settle on a farm of 320 acres.[56]

The most obvious basis for these immigrant miners' superior standard of living, however, was their higher level of wages. Comparing the wage levels between miners working in Britain and America at that time is difficult. Besides variations in tonnage rates in different pits, numerous other factors influenced the individual miner's pay packet. These included the miner's age and skill level,[57] the number of days he worked in a year,[58] the money deducted from his earnings by the employer,[59] and the earnings of sons living at home who worked down the pit.[60] Nevertheless, it is possible to take these variations into account and roughly compare the average money wage that a miner earned in Streator between 1880 and 1890 with the earnings of his counterpart in Wishaw during the same period. (Reliable comparative data are unavailable for the period before 1880.)

The average daily amount earned by a skilled pick miner in Wishaw in 1880–90, based on a daily output of approximately three tons of coal, was $1.08 (22p). The typical Streator miner, on the other hand, earned $2.40 per day for the same output. Given the exchange rate from dollar to pound ($4.83 = £1), the Streator miner brought home the equivalent of 49p. This was more than twice the Wishaw miner's daily wage. Adding in the average amounts contributed by the sons' earnings, the estimated average yearly family wage of the Wishaw miner during this decade was £65 91p, or $318. Using the same methods of calculation, the typical Streator miner's family earned $510. The difference between the two sums is $192. This means that during the 1880s the typical Streator miner earned approximately 60 percent more than did his Wishaw counterpart.[61]

Care must be taken with these figures, since they reflect money wages, not real wages. They do not take into account the higher American cost of living. (Data presently available are insufficiently detailed to permit calculations of real-wage differences between the two coalfields.) It must also be remembered that, although the 1880s were a deflationary period in both Britain and the United States, prices at this time were falling more rapidly in America than they were in Great Britain.[62] Nevertheless, this evidence reasonably suggests that even if the miners in Streator were not—because of more rapid U.S. deflation—as much as 60 percent better off than their Wishaw fellows, their wage levels were significantly higher than those of the miners they had left behind.

Another index of relative well-being among the immigrant colliers concerns the cordial relations they initially enjoyed with tradespeople and other middle-class elements in Braidwood and Streator—relations that appear to have been superior to those in Scotland. "It is asserted by friends and foes [of the miners]," reported the *Chicago Tribune* in June 1874, "that very little unpleasantness has ever occurred between the miners and the trades people." [63] These superior relations were probably due in part to their common social origins. Out of thirty-five shopkeepers or merchants in Braidwood in 1878, for example, no fewer than twenty-five had started life as wage earners. Twenty of these had been coal miners, and eighteen of them were either English or Scots by birth.[64] In turn, these figures show that the first generation of miners who settled in the northern Illinois coalfield were much more upwardly mobile than were the colliers of southwest Scotland. Only a few "lads o' pairts," such as Alexander McDonald or the handful of miners who graduated from the Glasgow School of Mines, became pit bosses or managers in the Lanarkshire mines at this time. Although the exact total cannot be determined, a number of miners in Larkhall and Wishaw did become shopkeepers or tradesmen,[65] but these numbers were small compared to the much larger number of first-generation colliers in Braidwood and Streator who managed to leave the pits and enter the ranks of the property-owning middle class.

The evidence for Braidwood on this matter is largely anecdotal. It comes from two volumes of biography that were published in 1878 by the town's boosters as a means of attracting investment capital and new settlers.[66] Although not statistically representative of Braidwood society as a whole, vignettes of the town's forty-five leading citizens included six former Scottish miners who turned to other careers: three mine managers, one politician, one insurance agent, and one attorney.[67] The 1878 series also contained interesting details concerning the lives of a number of the other leading residents of Braidwood. Several of these leading residents had worked in the pits for some time before rising in the social hierarchy. Take, for example, William Maltby, superintendent of the Eureka Coal Company. Born the son of a mining official in Staffordshire, England, in 1840, Maltby emigrated to Canada at the age of twelve. He then moved from job to job in Michigan, Pennsylvania, and New York before settling in Braidwood in 1866. "Mr. Maltby came to America as a poor boy," states the collection's author. "To-day he has risen from the lad that was engaged in driving the mule to the plough, to a Superintendent of one of the largest coal companies in the West."[68]

Anecdotal sources reveal less about upward mobility rates among the miners of Streator, but the careers of Welshman John Williams and his associates, who met as a study group to discuss economic and philosophical questions in the early 1870s, provide some insight. Born near Merthyr Tydfil in South Wales in 1853, Williams immigrated to America with his parents at the age of nine. He worked as a miner in the Streator pits for about fifteen years and then became in turn a newspaper reporter, a fire insurance agent, a theater manager, and a labor arbitrator.[69] The *Rotary Spokesman* later called Williams "the leader of a class of English, Scotch, and Welsh miners who engaged in the study of many subjects, with such success that practically all of its members were called to positions of responsibility as mine managers and mine inspectors."[70] The latter point is confirmed by the fact that at one time or another a large number of Streator miners—perhaps as many as ten— were appointed by the governor as mine inspectors for the State of Illinois.[71]

Anecdotal material on upward mobility for Streator is weak, but the statistical evidence taken from city directories is strong. Out of 208 Streator miners who changed their jobs between 1872 and 1888, for example, 53 (25 percent of the total) left the pits but maintained their position within the skilled segment of the working class. This category included several pit bosses, blacksmiths, and building tradesmen. No fewer than 117 (56 percent), however, moved up and out of the working class altogether. Occupationally this group of former colliers broke down as follows: 8 mine owners, 14 mine managers, 37 merchants, 13 saloonkeepers, 11 engineers, 7 railroad officials, 6 schoolteachers, 6 city officials, 5 farmers, 4 salesmen, 3 clerks, 2 attorneys, and 1 clergyman.[72] During this period some of the most enterprising British immigrant miners went to local land grant colleges or even to the University of Illinois. Among the miners in Scotland, only Alexander McDonald achieved something comparable. At least three miners from northern Illinois — Samuel Drew, William Mooney, and David Ross — used their college education to study law and secure admission to the Illinois bar.[73]

Moreover, these immigrant miners who moved up into the middle reaches of U.S. society did so within a social hierarchy that was already much less stratified than the one in southwest Scotland. It is true that in Streator, which was the more socially stratified of the two U.S. towns, leading families such as the Plumbs, the Heenans, and the Fawcetts owned a significant proportion of the businesses and available land by 1875,[74] but these families were headed by self-made entrepreneurs, most of whom came from humble origins. Their wealth and influence, though considerable, did not make them comparable in status or political power to men such as the Bairds, the earl of Belhaven, or the duke of Hamilton. It is true, as I will show in a subsequent chapter, that the social advantages that the first generation of northern Illinois miners enjoyed would soon suffer a significant decline. But for the first ten years of their residency, at least, there is no doubt that their material conditions were far superior to those of the Lanarkshire miners they had left behind.

Besides reaping the material advantages conferred on them by higher wages, superior housing, and rapid rates of upward mobility, the immigrant colliers of Braidwood and Streator were able — for a time, at least — to assert the same control over their underground work habits that miners a generation earlier had enjoyed in the coalfields of Great Britain. Large-scale Lanarkshire coal and iron companies such as Dunlops, Bairds, and Merry and Cunningham had used their economic power in the 1840s and 1850s to modernize the mining process, thereby disrupting the preindustrial collier's work rhythms. In the early years of the northern Illinois coalfield, however, the ability of the mining companies to do this was limited by the smaller scale of their opera-

Table 5. Coal Companies Owning One or More Pits in Streator, 1870

Company Name	Number of Pits	Number of Employees	Valuation of Company
Vermilion Coal Co.	4	380	$92,480
Acme Coal Co.	4	228	80.316
Atkinson Coal Co.	2	61	43,900
E. J. Fairburns	2	74	28,630
Kangley and Sons	2	84	16,900
Perkins and Harp Fuel	1	23	7,220
Riverside Co.	1	16	4,200
Williams Bros.	1	12	3,000
Frank Taylor	1	12	2,898
Lee Coal and Brick	1	8	1,028
McCormick Coal Co.	1	7	898
Davies Coal Co.	1	7	714
Shaughnessy Coal Co.	1	4	328

Sources: City Directory of Streator, 1872; Illinois Bureau of Commerce and Manufacturing, 1870.

tions and by the more primitive level of their technology. In effect, in the immediate post–Civil War period the coal industry of northern Illinois was at the same stage of development as the mining industry of Lanarkshire had been thirty years before. For example, the coal companies of Streator in 1870 were smaller and more diffused in ownership than even the Larkhall ones had been a generation before. Table 1 (p. 19) showed sixteen mines in the hands of the three leading mining firms of Larkhall. Table 5, however, shows that in Streator in 1870, the three top coal companies owned only ten mines.

Table 5 also demonstrates that many of the early coal firms in Streator owned only one mine and employed very few colliers. These small companies had a much smaller dollar valuation figure than their equivalents in southwest Scotland. In addition, the smaller size of the mining companies in Braidwood and Streator points up the informal character of the early mining operations in the American Midwest. Writing about the latter part of the 1860s, one historian of early Braidwood states that some of the pits were "so small as to be operated by man-power, as were the gin mines operated by [mine owner] . . . George Woods, who acted as digger, car pusher, hoisting engineer and salesman."[75] Many of the early pits in Streator were small drift mines that were burrowed out of the banks of the Vermilion River at the eastern edge of the town. As is evident from figure 1, in drift mines (and sometimes in slope mines, too) colliers could walk to and from their work without need of mechanically operated cages. This meant that coal company officials could not yet subject them to the same degree of discipline as they could in the shaft-operated mines of southwest Scotland, where cage operators con-

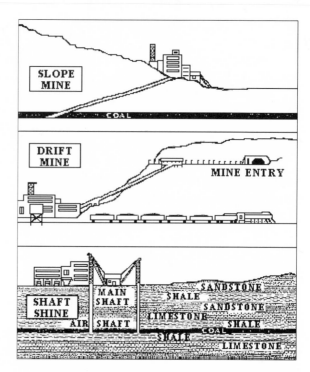

Figure 1. Three types of mines found in the northern Illinois coalfield, circa 1870 (*source:* Bituminous Coal Institute, *Bituminous Coal Annual* [Washington, D.C.: National Coal Association, 1949], 34).

trolled entrance and exit from the pit. The absence of longwall methods in the early Illinois pits, and the reliance on hand-skill techniques, also meant that the immigrant colliers could easily assert individual control over the amount of coal they raised each day.[76]

In fact, the high incidence of slope and drift mines in northern Illinois during the immediate post–Civil War period probably meant that the immigrant pick miners enjoyed more workplace autonomy than they had possessed in Scotland. In turn, this helps to explain the euphoria with which British miners described their freedom of action during their first years in the area. Author Tom Tippett caught the easy social relations of these early midwestern coal camps in his novel *Horse Shoe Bottoms*. Horse Shoe Bottoms is a fictitious mining camp located about seventy miles southwest of Braidwood and Streator near the Illinois River. It closely resembles the actual early coal towns that were situated further north. One of the main characters in the novel is "Old Bill," an English miner who drove a slope mine into the bank of Kickapoo Creek, much as the real-life colliers did along the banks of the Vermilion River in Streator. "Old Bill did not hold himself apart from his men," wrote Tippett. "He lived as they lived and he supplied them with work for which he paid them wages. He fashioned a community with the means at hand."[77] Describing the building of an air shaft by one of the miners, Tippett pointed to the same intuitive skills of which the Scottish artisan-colliers had been so proud in the 1830s and 1840s. "George Dodd did not have a plan [for building the air shaft]; he could not read and write; he never had gone to school; but back in his head he understood the laws which governed the air system."[78]

After a few years the slope mine at Horse Shoe Bottoms is worked out, and a small shaft mine replaces it. Because of the empathy he feels for his employees, however, Old Bill makes no attempt to control the number of hours a day his colliers work. At one point John Stafford, the novel's hero, expresses pleasure that even in the shaft mine he can hew his daily output at his own pace and in his own time. "He was a coaldigger," wrote Tippett, "and, in his own room, doing his own work, with no head man to give orders on how this or that must be done, the time to John, passed more interestingly, and more quickly too."[79]

Given their ability to reproduce — or even to improve — their status as artisan-colliers, it is not surprising that this first generation of immigrant miners in northern Illinois articulated a belief system similar to the one they had espoused at home. The class-harmony doctrine, in particular, seemed to fit social relations in the early mining industry in Braidwood and Streator even more closely than it had in Lanarkshire. In southwest Scotland this ideal had always been to some extent compromised by the fact that the colliers were born into a system of marked social inequality, as well as by the emergence in the 1850s and 1860s of large-scale coal and iron masters who threatened to reduce the status of the skilled pick miner from semi-independent contractor to semi-proletarian. Industrial capitalism was of course emerging in the American Midwest, too, but in these early years there was no clear evidence that it would develop into the same system of overweening economic power that prevailed in Lanarkshire.

Thus in the early days of Braidwood and Streator, when the coal industry required little capital to enter and the town pits were owned by local entrepreneurs whose backgrounds differed little from those of the miners, the colliers believed that they had achieved not only social equality with the coal operators but something like economic equality as well. Welsh immigrant collier John Williams of Streator put it this way: "Work is the great unifier; when master and man touch elbows in a common task there is born a spirit of fellowship which no disparity in wealth and station can neutralise. The absentee employer, like the absentee landlord, is the true creator of class divisions, the begetter of class pride, the fomenter of class hatred. In Streator he is practically unknown."[80]

Consistent with this position, the American Miners Association, which was established in Belleville, near St. Louis, in 1861 and included a number of northern Illinois miners in its ranks, adopted many of the same class-harmony policies that Alexander McDonald and his supporters had earlier espoused in Scotland, including voluntary restriction of output.[81] The union advocated this practice both to assert the principle of the owners' and workers' joint control over the work process and to ensure that the individual collier would be able to limit his hours of work. At its La Salle convention held in northern Illinois in 1863, near where Streator would soon be founded, the AMA took another familiar step. It mandated that before any applicant could be admitted to a branch of the union, "he must prove by [evidence given] by members of said Lodge, or by letters from any mining district from which he may have come, that he is a [qualified] miner."[82] An accompanying resolution establishing the regulations for admitting boys as apprentice miners shows clearly that its purpose was to control the influx of inexperienced men into the mines, just as the Scottish miners had done with respect to the Irish in Lanarkshire.

Further evidence of the influence of mid-Victorian British trade union principles upon the Illinois miners can be found in the policies adopted by the Miners National Association, the AMA's successor. This body, which sought to become nationwide in scope, was founded at a convention held in Youngstown, Ohio, in October 1873. The MNA's constitution was modeled almost exactly on that of the Miners National Association of Great Britain, of which Alexander McDonald was the main architect. So too were its basic principles, which included arbitration, conciliation, and cooperation. Strike action, while not prohibited entirely, was discouraged. John James of Braidwood became a prominent leader of the new union. As national secretary of the MNA James was responsible for drawing up most of the rules that governed the union.[83]

The Scottish immigrant miners also sought to combine strands from their own radical political tradition with elements from the American republican ideal. This meant fusing rudimentary ideas from Scottish Jacobinism, Chartism, and antimonarchism with the complex of ideals — concerning political and economic equality, limited government, and civic virtue — that were embodied in U.S. working-class republicanism. As with other American skilled workers, the immigrant colliers were much exercised by the need to defend their equality and status against large-scale holders of wealth.[84]

Like many other groups of American workers at the time, these pioneer miners also linked the ideals of working-class republicanism to the humble — or supposedly humble — origins of several of America's leading statesmen. The Scottish colliers added a special twist, however, by associating U.S. labor republicanism with national heroes of their own. This can be seen in a letter John James wrote to the *Workingman's Advocate* in Chicago soon after arriving in Braidwood. Mingling Scottish and American national icons in his pantheon and betraying confusion about their social origins, James asserted, "Our great men were but workingmen." He included Francis Bacon, James Watt, George Stephenson, Jesus Christ, and Alexander McDonald in his eclectic list. On another occasion James just as romantically associated the power of workingmen with that of America's founders: "We forget that George Washington left the plough to fight the battles of his country. We forget that 'Old Abe' Lincoln split rail fences, yet did he steer the helm of the nation through one of the most gigantic civil wars in the annals of history. We forget that 'Ben' Franklin was but a workingman, yet does he stand as an ornament in literature and philosophy." [85]

The colliers did not espouse artisanal republicanism simply out of a general commitment to social and political equality. They did so for two specific reasons related to mining. The first was their hope that America's republican ideal, devoted to equality of economic opportunity, would help persuade the coal owners to share the profits of their enterprises with the miners. The second was their belief that America's republican tradition, which had initially frowned on excesses of wealth, would help prevent the country's homegrown capitalists from attempting to impose their political will on the colliers, as Scotland's coal owners and capitalists had done in earlier decades. An immigrant Scottish collier writing to the *Belleville Democrat* in May 1863 put it this way:

> It may be the case in a country under Monarchical Government, but in this Republican country where "equal rights" is our motto — why should the laboring man be governed by capitalists? Government by capitalists must not be tolerated by any freeman, because if it is tolerated it would belie the principles of the founders of this great Republican nation. I would ask of any man, can he doubt the principles advocated by such men as the signers of the Declaration of Independence? I think any man who would for a moment doubt that such men as they were, intended that this country was to be governed by capitalists, is not a friend either to himself, his fellow man, or his country. [86]

Illinois's artisan-colliers were not naive enough to believe that abstract principles alone would protect them against the inequalities threatened by large-scale entrepreneurs. Nevertheless, they did appear to think that republican institutions, if vigorously defended by an educated citizenry with the economic and political advantages of the early miners of Braidwood and Streator, would be able to do so. John Hinchcliffe, the influential tailor turned attorney who edited the *Weekly Miner* in Belleville, put the matter succinctly in an editorial he wrote in June 1864. "Upon [the] labor and intelligence of laboring men," Hinchcliffe wrote in the vein of Lincoln, "depends the stability of the republican form of government and the greatness of a democratic people." [87]

Such was the optimistic outlook concerning the position of the American workingman, and of the relations between labor and capital, that was espoused by the Illinois miners during the heyday of the pick-mining era, between 1865 and 1875. It saw the United States as an experiment in republican democracy that was superior in every way to the class-ridden societies of Western Europe. America seemed to have resolved the problem not simply of political equality for its citizens but also of industrial equality. In addition, the material prosperity that attended their first years in America, coupled with this optimistic labor philosophy, reinforced the skilled pick miners' belief that they had found a permanent new haven in the United States that would enable them to maintain their status as artisan-colliers or independent contractors indefinitely. These beliefs seemed warranted for as long as the post–Civil War coal industry boom lasted. But what would happen to the colliers' optimistic outlook when that boom came to an end and America's mining industry began to take on many of the same exploitive characteristics that had emerged in the British mining industry ten or twenty years before?

5

STRIKES, INTERNAL CONFLICT, AND THE DECLINE OF THE CLASS-HARMONY IDEAL, 1872–82

In 1872 the doctrines of class harmony, peaceful industrial re-lations, and joint stewardship of the coal industry shared by masters and men appeared to be riding high on both sides of the Atlantic. As a result of a boom in the coal trade, the Lanarkshire miners succeeded in raising their wages, which had fallen to less than twenty pence a shift in 1869, to the un-precedented level of fifty pence a day. In consequence Alexander McDonald's reputation rose to new heights. "If you hold fast to your policy of lessening the chance of strikes, and of bringing about friendly intercommunication between Capital and Labour," he told a meeting of colliers in Hamilton in January 1871, "there is no reason why your standing should not continue to rise." [1]

In fact, the coal boom generated so much optimism in Scotland that some miners came to believe that the days of low pay and indignity down the pit were gone forever. Thus a collier who attended a delegate meeting in Glas-gow in December 1872 disputed the coal owners' belief that the typical miner was arrogant because he aspired to "ride in his own carriage, and to bring home a bit of beef. Why should the collier not eat beef, the delegate asked? Who had a better right to a bit of beef than the hard-working miner?" [2]

In northern Illinois in the early 1870s the prospects seemed to be even more encouraging. The coal trade was booming, wage levels were going up, and the Ohio-based Miners National Association, with John James as its sec-retary, was at the height of its powers. Early in 1874 President John Siney and Secretary James of the MNA met in Cleveland with coal and iron magnate Mark Hanna, who as head of the National Civic Federation (1899) was later to become one of America's leading advocates of peaceful industrial relations. The two union leaders told him that they sought goodwill between masters and men and that they would discourage strikes wherever possible. In return Hanna and a number of other midwestern coal operators agreed to recognize the Miners National Association. Siney and James were delighted. "Mr. Hanna not only kept his promise," commented a sympathetic observer, "but to the end of his life he labored to harmonize the interests of capital and labor in every branch of industry. The workingmen of America never had a better or a truer friend than Mark Hanna." [3]

By the end of the decade, however, the situation had turned from triumph to something near disaster. The coal and iron boom had broken, a rash of strikes had broken out on both sides of the ocean, and the immigrant Scottish colliers' hopes of restoring in the New World the workplace independence they had lost in the Old seemed to have crumbled to dust. Even John James, who had reaffirmed his faith in the class-harmony ideal when he defended Alexander McDonald against his anti-emigration critics in the mid-1860s, recognized that America could not provide a haven against the degrading consequences of modern capitalism forever. "Capitalists are the same the world over," he reported sorrowfully in a letter to Alexander McDonald in January 1876. "The same desire to trample roughshod over the man who toils is evidenced here to a large extent. . . . I am thoroughly satisfied," James added, "that whether it be under a republic or an empire, labor, if it will have fair, honest dealings at the hand of its employer, must put itself in a position to command it." [4]

In Lanarkshire itself McDonald was also being challenged by a new generation of critics who no longer accepted his industrial policies at face value. The most articulate of these critics was the young James Keir Hardie, who later became a member of Parliament and an influential leader of the British Labour Party. In an article published in the *Miner* not long after James had written to McDonald expressing his misgivings about capitalism, Hardie indicted the coal and iron owners' exploitation of his fellow miners in southwest Scotland. "The remedy is simple," wrote Hardie, "if only the nation had sense enough to apply it. Get rid of the idea that the capitalist is an indispensable adjunct of the capitalist system and the problem is solved." [5]

What had gone wrong? Why were policies that had guided the miners for more than a generation being challenged in favor of ideas that, in Scotland at least, were putatively socialist? The purpose of this chapter is to find out.

❖

The economic reasons for the miners' new-found skepticism about the future of the coal industry were threefold: the arrival of a new stage in the modernization of the coal industry, the downward pressure on miners' wages generated by the international economic recession of the mid-1870s, and the failure of the miners' traditional methods of peaceful negotiation to defend their interests successfully in disputes with employers.

The economic transformation that accompanied the next stage in the modernization of the coal industry took place a couple of decades earlier in southwest Scotland than it did in the American Midwest. The same features drove it in both places, however: technological innovation, increasing competition, and a further rapid expansion in the market for both iron and coal. In the 1850s and 1860s the Scottish iron masters' own coal mines had supplied not only their own fuel needs but approximately half the coal required for both domestic heating and the railroads in the Clyde Valley. The 1868–72 boom, however, saw the establishment of many new sale companies (companies that produced only coal), some of which were large enough to compete with the iron masters on their own terms. Thus the Lanarkshire iron firms found their share of the coal market shrinking. At the same time, large iron companies such as Bairds, Glasgow Iron and Steel, and Merry and Cunningham, which had previously enjoyed secure export markets, found themselves challenged by newer, more up-to-date coal and iron companies on the European continent and in the United States.[6]

The economic problems of the Scottish iron industry were compounded by the fact that it switched from iron to steel more slowly than its competitors. This lag had serious consequences in Wishaw, whose metal products were the second largest source of income in the town. The giant Coltness Company and the Glasgow Iron Company faced particularly difficult problems. In the 1870s the local ironstone they had used to make their products began to run out, forcing the two firms to spend extra money bringing in iron ore from elsewhere. In addition, Scottish pig iron also proved to be ill suited to the newly invented Bessemer process of steel making.[7] Unlike Scottish coal, little U.S. coal was exported overseas at this time, but by the mid-1880s the midwestern bituminous market had expanded with such astonishing rapidity that it had created a central competitive field stretching all the way from western Illinois to eastern Pennsylvania. Given the huge size of this market, the competitive pressures it exerted on the coal companies in northern Illinois were very similar to those that had caused the expansion of the coal and iron companies of Wishaw and Larkhall at an earlier date.[8]

To deal with these new economic forces, the coal firms of Braidwood and Streator — just like those in southwest Scotland twenty years earlier — found it necessary to improve their access to capital, reform their managerial techniques, and expand the basis of their mining operations. At the end of 1873 the Wilmington Coal Mining and Manufacturing Company sank a deep shaft mine in the newly laid out village of Diamond, immediately southwest of Braidwood. In 1874 the Coalfield Coal Company purchased 1,000 acres of land along the railroad in Grundy County to the west of the town. It leased 640 of these acres to the Wilmington Star Coal Company and laid out the town of Coal City. In the early 1880s the sleepy village of Braceville was awakened when the Chicago, Milwaukee, and St. Paul Railroad purchased 14,000 acres of coal lands in the vicinity and started new large-scale mining operations there.[9]

No coal company in the American Midwest reflected this transition to modern corporate methods more clearly than the Chicago, Wilmington and Vermilion Company. This large corporation resulted from the 1872 merger of the Streator-based Vermilion Company and Braidwood's Chicago and Wilmington Company. Capitalized at two million dollars, by 1876 the CW&V's five shafts in Braidwood and Streator gave employment to more than half the miners who lived in the two towns. By 1878 the coal companies of Will and Grundy Counties, which covered much of the northern Illinois coalfield, were producing 478,000 tons of coal a year with a labor force of 5,422 men. For a brief period this made them the two largest coal-producing counties in the state.[10]

In addition, absentee ownership now became a marked feature of coal company management in the United States, just as it had at an earlier date in Scotland. This development undermined the sense of common endeavor between masters and men that had characterized the industry in the immediate post–Civil War years. For example, the CW&V's new stockholders were absentee owners who lived in Boston and other eastern cities, and both its president, James Monroe Walker, and its general manager, A. L. Sweet, lived in Chicago, more than fifty miles northeast of Braidwood. A Boston capitalist, Frances Bartlett, replaced Walker as president in 1881, and members of a Boston banking firm run by the Thayer family took over many of the positions of leadership that had earlier been in the hands of local men.[11] Masters and men no longer "touch[ed] elbows in a common task," as Welsh immigrant collier John Williams of Streator had said they did a few years before. The growing divorce between ownership and control caused industrial reformers such as Henry Demarest Lloyd to charge that, in Braidwood, "babies, and men and women, wither away to be transmigrated into dividends of a millionaire coalowner of Beacon street, Boston."[12]

Faced with the competitive pressures of a rapidly expanding market, the newly minted mining corporations of Braidwood and Streator, just like their counterparts in southwest Scotland, lost no time in pressing their employees for greater industrial discipline so as to compete successfully with other regional coal companies. In the spring of 1873 the Braidwood managers of the CW&V asserted their unilateral right to shut down their pits at any time. They required their men to "perform a full day's work of ten hours" unless they had special permission to do otherwise.[13] In addition, they insisted that terms of employment would be determined by the company's officials alone. "No person will be allowed to interfere with the employers' just right of employing, and discharging from employment any person or persons whom the Superintendent may consider proper," the new season's contract read. Nor would miners who rejected the CW&V's terms be permitted to interfere, "by threats of menace, or otherwise," with those who wished to accept them. The operators made it clear that they opposed the formation of union locals. The new contract contained a clause refusing to deal with "any committee purporting to represent any league, organization or combination of workingmen."[14]

Such were the new industrial policies threatening the relatively harmonious relations between miners and mine owners that had obtained in northern Illinois since the Civil War. They were compounded by a severe depression in both the British and the American coal industries that began with the financial panic in New York during the summer of 1873 and led to the most drastic round of wage cuts to be inflicted on colliers on either side of the ocean for more than twenty years.[15] The bottom fell out of the north Atlantic coal and iron boom toward the end of 1873. By the end of that year coal and iron prices had collapsed all over Britain and North America. Despite some intermittent relief, they continued to fall until 1887. The resulting wage cuts drove the Lanarkshire miners' earnings down from forty pence a day in 1873 to about twenty pence in 1874 and fifteen in 1878.[16] The resulting human suffering was extensive. In the autumn of 1879, for example, large numbers of striking miners from Wishaw, Larkhall, and several other Lanarkshire mining towns were evicted from company housing owned by Dunlop's and other big iron companies after they had protested a wage cut. Those who could not stay with relatives or find jobs in nearby mining communities were forced to live in tented encampments without proper sanitation and sometimes even without sufficient food.[17]

Slack times among the Braidwood miners in northern Illinois began as early as June 1873. By December of that year John James reported sadly that only two out of five colliers were working in the local pits. Commenting on the situation in Braidwood in April 1874, the *Wilmington Advocate* noted "many families at the mines . . . in want of the necessities of life."[18] In Streator miners were being discharged at the rate of twenty a week, leading many of its miners to migrate further west or even go back to their countries of origin. Several dozen Braidwood miners moved to the Colorado mines at this time, causing a local newspaper to ask, "Will Braidwood and Gardner be depopulated?"[19]

The third factor prompting miners on both sides of the Atlantic to rethink their political and economic strategy was the growing class divide that emerged between mine owners and their employees. This class divide was, of course, in part a function of the industrial developments just described. One of its manifestations was the mine operators' growing unwillingness to settle disputes according to the methods of conciliation and arbitration that had for years been practiced both by Alexander McDonald in southwest Scotland and by his disciples in northern Illinois. This combination of falling wages and operator hostility, coupled with the prolonged depression of 1873–79, caused an unprecedented number of (coincidental) large-scale strikes to break out in both the Lanarkshire and the northern Illinois coalfields. Since the loss of these strikes on both sides of the Atlantic played an important role in the collapse of the class-harmony doctrine, it is necessary to describe them in some detail.

The first in the series of coal strikes took place in Lanarkshire in December 1872–March 1873. It began when over a thousand miners from Wishaw, Larkhall, Motherwell, and the Hamilton area struck unsuccessfully against a wage cut of 10p in some areas and 5p in others. The strikers were forced back to work without the cuts being rescinded. The second Lanarkshire walkout occurred about a year later, in the spring of 1874, when a wage cut imposed by the coal and iron companies produced an almost identical result. Miners who worked for large-scale iron companies such as Bairds, Merry and Cunningham, and Dixon's endured another 10p cut, while those who worked for the sale coal companies lost another 5p a day.[20]

The third strike took place in northern Illinois between June and September 1874. It was the only one that could be called a standoff rather than an outright defeat for the miners. On June 1, 1874, the CW&V cut its mining pay rate from $1.25 to $1.10 per ton, and the price for "pushing" coal cars (drawing or hauling them from the miner's workplace to the bottom of the main shaft) was cut in half. On this occasion the local miners' union was able to drive a wedge between the smaller and the larger coal companies, enabling it to gain the upper hand. In late August 1874 the Wilmington Star and Diamond Coal Companies agreed to a compromise settlement, with the Eureka Coal Company signing on a few days later. This isolated the CW&V, forcing it to settle on September 4. The terms of the settlement involved a small cut in the digging rate, but the company withdrew its demand that the miners sign a restrictive contract, and it agreed to rehire all the strikers without discrimination.[21]

In the summer of 1877, however, the northern Illinois coalfield witnessed a further major, districtwide strike that resulted in a humiliating defeat for the miners. It began on May 1, 1877, when the CW&V managers in both Streator and Braidwood announced that the pick-mining rate for the following season would be 25 percent lower than it had been in 1876. The company also refused in advance to negotiate with the miners' union, insisting instead that the colliers sign yellow-dog contracts repudiating any attempt at union organizing. The proposed contract demanded that the miners "not stop work, [or] join any 'strike' or combination for the purpose of . . . causing the company to pay their miners an advance of wages." [22] Angered by this demand, as well as by those of other coal operators in Braidwood and Streator, more than 1,500 miners walked out. In response Alanson Sweet, the CW&V's general manager, imported first white strikebreakers from Chicago and then a larger number of blacks. The Illinois state militia was brought in to protect the African American strikebreakers, a move that doomed the stoppage to defeat and caused considerable bitterness among the white miners. Although it limped on until November 1877, the miners were forced back on the employers' terms amid much suffering.[23]

The final strike in this series took place in Lanarkshire in 1879–81. In November 1879 the Lanarkshire Coal Owners Association cut employees' wages by an additional 2½p a day, with further cuts threatened in the weeks that followed. Several hundred miners promptly walked out of the pits. Alexander McDonald urged the other leaders of the Lanarkshire County Miners Union to accept the 2½p-per-day cut, meanwhile sending agents into Fife, Clackmannan, and other mining counties to urge the miners there to press for wage increases. The idea was to undermine the employers' rationale for cutting wages in Lanarkshire by equalizing wage levels throughout southwest Scotland. Desiring a more militant response, rank-and-file miners refused to go along with McDonald's strategy. Instead, increasing numbers went out on unofficial strike. The coal masters were not to be intimidated, however. At the beginning of December, they imposed a third reduction, also of 2½p, which brought wages in many pits down to 15p a day. This level was as low, if not lower, than the one colliers had been forced to accept in the late 1860s.[24]

The response to these new cuts in Lanarkshire was an even more extensive strike. But it was to no avail. Early in 1881 several iron masters in the Wishaw, Coatbridge, and Motherwell area put their furnaces out of blast. This move, coupled with the introduction of extra police to keep pickets away from the mine gates, forced the miners back to work amid much suffering.

The 1879–81 stoppage was the first major struggle in which the young James Keir Hardie played an important role. In an effort to keep the strike going, he persuaded the shopkeepers in Hamilton to provide strikers with potatoes on credit, thereby giving the stoppage the name the "Tattie strike." When the strike collapsed, however, the LCMU repudiated the debt with the shopkeepers. As a consequence of this, McDonald branded Hardie an "irresponsible agitator," thereby bringing in the open the disagreement between himself and the putative leader of a new generation of radical miner activists. Keir Hardie had grown up in the village of Newarthill, only a couple of miles from Holytown, where McDonald lived. At first the older man was the younger one's mentor, having appointed him agent for the LCMU only a short time before the "Tattie strike." By the strike's end, however, the two men had drifted apart.[25] As the gap between them widened, the disagreements between Alexander McDonald and James Keir Hardie came to symbolize a major new stage in the growth of class-conscious militancy among the Scottish miners.

The new unwillingness of the coal operators on both sides of the Atlantic to rely on the earlier policy of arbitration and conciliation to settle labor disputes was demonstrated in at least two of the strikes just described. One was the 1872 stoppage in Lanarkshire. When the Lanarkshire iron masters announced their 10p pay cut, Alexander McDonald and his supporters looked for some way of resisting the employers' demands short of an official stoppage. On December 8, 1872, for example, the leaders of the LCMU wrote the operators urging that the dispute be "settled by a court of conciliation and arbitration, [made up] of equal numbers of workers and employers, and an independent umpire who could adjudicate in case of deadlock." The relationship between miners and mine owners, the letter concluded — in a bow to the class-harmony doctrine — "should be [one of] mutual trust." The employers rejected the proposal out of hand.[26]

A similar development took place during the events that led up to the northern Illinois strike of 1874. In 1873 the CW&V had insisted that it had the unilateral right to shut down its pits at any time and that it would not negotiate with any union organization set up by the men. Responding to the new rules the coal company had laid out, the miners suggested as an alternative that a joint committee of colliers and CW&V representatives draw up the 1873–74 contract. They also proposed that a board of arbitration made up of three miners, three operators, and an unbiased umpire adjudicate any ongoing grievances between the miners and the enlarged corporation. Like the large coal and iron companies in Wishaw and Larkhall, however, the CW&V peremptorily refused to go along with this procedure. Instead, it attempted to impose its will on the miners through unilateral action.[27]

The Scottish mine owners' reluctance to continue utilizing arbitration and conciliation during this period not only demonstrated their abandonment of the idea that their employees had a right to help determine the industry's future course. It also signaled their clearer awareness of their own separate interests as part of the employing class. This was shown by the establishment of the Iron Masters Association in Glasgow in November 1872 and of the Associated Society of Scottish Mine Owners soon afterward. Shortly after its founding, the latter organization announced that it would "resist unreasonable claims and demands made by miners and other workmen." [28] Additional evidence of growing class consciousness on the part of the coal owners was given at the founding meeting of the Associated Society of Scottish Mine Owners. It established a twenty-four member council to consult with all the firms in the Clyde Valley whenever their joint interests were threatened. The society also stipulated that when the pits of one of its members were struck, no other member would give jobs to the strikers; that the other members would aid the struck coal master financially; and that all members would adopt whatever wage policy the society's council approved. It did not follow from this that the Scottish mine owners were henceforth always to be united in a common cause. The iron masters still had interests that were in some respects different from those of the sale coal masters. Nevertheless, it was an important sign of the times.[29]

The growth of a sense of class identity that separated miners from their employers proceeded more slowly and ambiguously in northern Illinois than it did in southwest Scotland, a matter that is significant for my theme. No separate associations of coal owners were established there until the mid-1880s. In part, this time lag simply reflected the fact that the coal industry in Braidwood and Streator was younger than its counterpart in Wishaw and Larkhall. Hence, with the exception of the CW&V, most local coal firms were still small-scale affairs owned by individual coal owners who were just emerging into entrepreneurial status. Out of a total of eighteen coal companies present in Braidwood and Streator in the mid-1870s, for example, eleven employed fewer than twenty men. As was mentioned in the last chapter, many of these mines were little more than deep holes or passages driven into the banks of rivers or streams that produced only a few hundred tons of coal a year.[30] By this time few if any of the mines in Wishaw or Larkhall were operating on such a small scale.

In addition, the social hierarchy continued to be more fluid in the two American towns than in Scotland, blurring class distinctions between masters and men. In the 1874 strike, for example, the merchants of Braidwood, many of whom were former miners themselves, extended credit to the out-of-work miners for a considerably longer period of time than their counterparts did in Wishaw and Larkhall. Moreover, a number of local attorneys, schoolteachers, and church leaders in northern Illinois identified themselves publicly with the miners' cause. For example, at a July 4, 1874, picnic and rally held in Streator's town park on behalf of the striking colliers in nearby Braidwood, Streator public school principal W. H. Hewitt asserted that "unless the strike is won, no parents will be able to hold their heads up in front of their children." Hewitt was followed by Rev. E. R. Davis, minister of the First Presbyterian Church of Braidwood, who averred, "God, with all his avenging might, will one day bring low the grasping money-seekers who now threaten to deprive our fellow human toilers of their just deserts."[31]

Ironically, the ideals of labor republicanism also lent an ideological dimension to these cross-class ties between merchants and miners that was lacking in southwest Scotland. On June 4, 1874, after the Eureka Coal Company ordered its employees who were not already on strike to work ten hours a day rather than eight, one of its employees blamed the coal company for attempting to deny miners "the freedom the founders of this free Republic intended for all classes."[32] Statements such as this were commonplace among the better-educated miners in Braidwood and Streator at this time. More interesting were the almost identical sentiments expressed only two days later by the large retail store owner H. H. Heenan, who was one of Streator's leading citizens and a close associate of the wealthy Irishman Charles Devlin, the town's first mayor and principal founding father. "When our mining population first came here to work the coal that lies beneath the city," Heenan stated, "they did so in the righteous belief that they were building their dignity as free citizens of a free Republic. But now" — because of the unfair treatment the mine owners were meting out to the colliers in the strike — "our biggest coal owners are denying them that right."[33]

In Lanarkshire, by contrast, there were fewer vehicles to prevent the bitterness engendered by the strike defeats from spilling over into antagonism between the classes. Before the 1872 Education Act, most schoolteachers there were Church of Scotland ministers who tended to identify with the local lairds.[34] With few exceptions, the local shopkeepers in Wishaw and Larkhall looked down on the miners as their social inferiors.[35] After 1886, too, the Catholic priests — who, as leaders of the most proletarianized element among the Lanarkshire miners, had been concerned to maintain good relations with the coal owners — became increasingly preoccupied with the divisive issue of home rule for their native Ireland.[36] It was not until the 1884 Reform Act drew a significant number of miners into the franchise that Gladstonian liberalism created an active political coalition in which both activist miners and middle-class social reformers could share a common cause.[37]

As the 1870s proceeded, however, and the bitterness of the strike defeats sank in, the attitudes of the different social classes in Braidwood and Streator began to change in ways that presaged the crystallization of more permanent feelings of class separation on the U.S. side of the ocean as well. This was hastened by the savagely fought national railroad strike of July 1877, which was seen as a watershed in the development of corporate capitalism in America and to which both miners and railroad workers in Braidwood gave their moral and sometimes financial support. CW&V general manager A. L. Sweet, by contrast, who was anxious to continue transporting his coal to market, supported the railroad owners, a development that appeared to have a significant polarizing effect. On August 24, 1877, the *Chicago Tribune* reported that many merchants in Braidwood were no longer willing to extend credit to the miners and that two of their leaders, Daniel McLaughlin and Frank Lofty, had found it necessary to appeal for help outside the town. The Will County sheriff, whom the Braidwood miners had opposed during a recent election campaign, sided with the coal companies in the 1877 strike — a fact corroborated by a Chicago newspaper reporter when he remarked succinctly that "no love [was] lost between the Sheriff and the miners." [38]

Another sign of growing class tension in the Illinois coalfields was the bitterness many of the 1877 strikers felt toward the coal operators, who had persuaded Governor Shelby Cullom to send the state militia to Braidwood to break the strike. In theory the militia was sent in to protect the African American strikebreakers who had been forced out of the mines by the local colliers. It soon became clear, however, that the main effect of the military intervention would be to defeat the stoppage as a whole. One newspaper used the following language to describe the hostility that the strikers felt toward the militiamen: "They called them 'a regiment of clarks' [*sic*] . . . who would not hesitate — even were anxious to shed gore for the capitalist." [39]

At the same time, to protect their jobs and communities against the assaults of the larger coal companies, miners in both Braidwood and Streator began to think more seriously about establishing trade unions. By far the most important of these unions were the local assemblies of the Knights of

Labor. In one sense the mixed trade assemblies of the Knights, which sometimes included petty bourgeois elements, blurred the focus of their class appeal. In another sense, however, they made possible the establishment of
numerically larger plebian bodies to defend the interests of both the colliers and their community allies against the overweening power of the coal
companies.

In January 1877 the Pittsburgh office of the Knights of Labor sent Harry W.
Smith to organize miners and other workers in the northern Illinois coalfield.
Within eight months he had established thirty assemblies, most of them con-
sisting of miners, railroad workers, and skilled craftsmen.[40] Unfortunately,
few details are available concerning the activities of these assemblies in the
Braidwood and Streator areas. Much more is known about them in the following decade. Nevertheless, a report published in the *Wilmington Advocate*
(Wilmington was a small town just south of Braidwood) on October 9, 1879,
gives a strong clue. "No fewer than five local assemblies of the Most Noble
Order of the Knights of Labor have come into being in the Wilmington field
over the past six months," ran the report. "Coal miners, carpenters, railroad
men and teamsters are flocking to them in droves. Last night, after a meeting
of five hundred miners and others held at Free Gardners Hall [in Braidwood],
a motion was unanimously passed 'That we resist the endeavors of the coal
companies to force us into wage slavery.' "[41]

The growing concentration of economic power within the coal companies of
both Lanarkshire and northern Illinois, coupled with the disastrous series of
strike defeats just described, prompted a wide-ranging debate on both sides
of the ocean over the industrial tactics the miners should adopt to reverse
their declining fortunes. This debate was more vigorous in southwest Scotland than in northern Illinois, probably because the Illinois miners already
had at their disposal, in the form of the Knights of Labor, a defensive tool
more broadly based and powerful than the Scottish miners' labor groups.[42]
Another likely reason was that although Braidwood colliers' leaders such as
Daniel McLaughlin and John James possessed as much prestige among the
U.S. miners as Alexander McDonald did among those in southwest Scotland,
they never asserted their will over the rank and file as autocratically as the
venerable — and now increasingly conservative — Scottish leader did. Hence
the disagreements between the older and the younger generations of miners'
leaders in northern Illinois never acquired the same degree of open rancor
that the disagreement between men such as McDonald and James Keir Hardie
did in southwest Scotland.

As the disputes of 1872–82 unfolded, the most important question discussed in the Lanarkshire coalfield concerned the use of the strike weapon itself. This issue also became, of course, a major debating point between Grand Master Terence V. Powderly and his lieutenants in the Knights of Labor in the United States a few years later on.[43] Since strikes signaled a complete breakdown of trust between coal masters and their employees, the question of how and when they should be used went right to the heart of the argument over the viability of the class-harmony ideal. It also became the central issue in a debate between Alexander McDonald and his critics in the Lanarkshire coalfield. McDonald had never rejected the use of strikes as such, but he saw them as a last resort, a weapon to be used sparingly and only when all other means had failed.

McDonald also appeared to believe that the unevenness between the pay scales of the iron masters and the sale coal companies was as much a cause of the problem as were the wage cuts themselves. Thus in both the 1872 and 1874 disputes, he followed a policy of selective strike action. For example, McDonald requested all the miners who worked for the sale coal companies to accept the 5p wage cut that had been imposed on them. At the same time he urged a walkout for those colliers who worked for iron masters in selected pits where a 10p cut had been imposed.

Hence the first overt disagreement between Alexander McDonald and his opponents took the form of a quarrel between his followers and the supporters of a local leader from Holytown named Henry Malcom. The only means that had any chance of reversing the 1872 wage cuts, Malcom argued, was not McDonald's policy of selective strikes but a broadly based stoppage that would unite the local sale and iron miners in a common cause and bring out the rest of the colliers in southwest Scotland along with them. This proposal for a general, or regional, strike ran directly counter to the LCMU's established policy of sanctioning only district- or at most countywide strikes, and then only under exceptional circumstances. Nevertheless, at a mass meeting held in Hamilton on December 8, 1872, a resolution supporting Henry Malcom's call for a general miners' strike was adopted by a large majority.[44]

McDonald and his supporters, who were largely older Scots-born artisan-colliers, were horrified by the very idea of a general strike. They also believed that the small size and local character of the miners' unions made such a tactic unlikely to succeed. Hence McDonald responded to Henry Malcom and his followers by attacking them as irresponsible troublemakers whose precipitous acts were likely to alienate a large number of employers and bring the whole edifice of conciliatory collective bargaining down around their ears. Angered by what seemed to them a narrow and ineffective policy, Malcom and his followers decided to ignore their aging leaders' criticisms. Defying McDonald's plea for caution, they tried to rally as many rank-and-file miners as they could in support of a general strike. In the first two weeks of December 1872, the towns of Wishaw, Larkhall, Motherwell, and Holytown witnessed an unusual spectacle. Several thousand angry colliers, marching from pit to pit with banners flying and fifes and drums playing, urged all the local miners to come out on strike with them and to accept no wage cuts at all.[45]

For a brief time it seemed as though the Malcom faction might carry the day. At a mass meeting held in Watson's Hall, Wishaw, just before Christmas, it was reported that sale masters Robert Brand and A. G. Simpson had agreed to rescind the 5p cut. In January 1873, however, the basis of Malcom's support began to crumble. For one thing, despite his marching campaign, by no means all the local pits came out on strike. In fact, the majority of the local mines, those run by both sale and iron masters, remained at work. A second factor was the strike's unpopularity with the general public owing to the shortage of coal during the Christmas season. Third, there was the difficulty of getting the oncost men (furnacemen, carpenters, enginemen, and engineers who serviced the mines when they were shut down) to come out in support.[46] Further, it came to light at a meeting of colliers' representatives from other parts of Scotland that most Lanarkshire miners earned more than miners elsewhere. This gave the miners from other areas little incentive to support a strike on behalf of the Lanarkshire colliers.[47]

Thus in the 1872 dispute Alexander McDonald and the official leadership of the LCMU were able to turn the tables on the insurgents.[48] The problems created by the defeat of the 1874 Lanarkshire strike, however, were a different matter. On this occasion McDonald's selective strike policy turned out to be even more disastrous than it had been a year earlier. Unemployment had grown worse in the meantime; the ironworkers of Ayrshire, Fife, Midlothian, and East Lothian were preoccupied with their own problems; and since local wages continued to be higher there than they were in the Clyde Valley, miners in other parts of western Scotland had even less incentive than before to come out in solidarity with their Lanarkshire fellows. To make matters worse, McDonald himself pursued a vacillating policy. While publicly supporting the selective strike, he privately sought to negotiate a sliding-scale agreement with one of the largest coal companies in the area, the purpose of which was to permit coal miners' wages to rise and fall according to the price of iron on the Glasgow iron market.

This was the first time that the sliding scale, which was later to play an important role in the miners' affairs, was seriously considered as a method of determining wages. Up to this time, the "price" (or wage) per ton that each collier earned had been determined either by separate negotiations between the pit boss and himself or by the company's list of prices for mining different grades of coal. The idea behind the sliding scale, however, was to let wages move up and down according to fluctuations in coal prices and, in turn, iron prices on the Glasgow market.[49] In accordance with the class-harmony ideal, this method accepted the impersonal role of the market in determining wages, but it also sought to minimize conflict between miners and mine owners by providing an automatic adjustment in wage levels. Although the coal owners would be permitted to cut wages when coal prices fell, they would in theory also be required to raise them again when prices were high and profits were good.

Such a system might well have seemed attractive to miners when wage levels were high, as they had been in the 1868–72 period. By early 1874, however, the price of pig iron had fallen so low on the Glasgow market that had the sliding scale for coal been adopted, it would have pulled wages down to approximately 17½p a day. This was not much higher than the rock-bottom level that wages had reached in the mid-1860s, before the 1868–72 boom set in. On hearing of McDonald's proposal for a sliding scale, therefore, many colliers — particularly the younger rebel-newcomers who had favored a more militant policy all along — dismissed it out of hand.[50] In Larkhall the sliding scale was attacked as a "piece of trickery." The miners of Maryhill, just north of Glasgow, also rejected it.[51] This put McDonald in a quandary. Faced with a glutted coal market and spreading skepticism as to whether his selective strike policy would succeed, he abruptly reversed course. On March 28, 1874, McDonald persuaded those local miners' leaders who still trusted him to abandon the strike altogether and to return to work on the masters' terms. In most places this meant accepting both the 10p and the 5p wage cut.[52]

For many rank-and-file miners, this was the last straw. Hostile to the idea of a sliding scale and fearful that the depression would now push their wages below those of the previous decade, they jettisoned what remained of their deferential attitude toward their longtime leader and openly condemned him for his contradictory and ineffectual tactics. One of the forms this anger took was a protest against the bureaucratic way in which McDonald had arrogated to himself much of the decision-making power in the Lanarkshire miners' union. In turn this confirmed the increasing radicalism of the rank-and-file miners and showed their determination to secure a more democratic, as well as a more militant, type of trade union.

In the early days the Lanarkshire miners' method of governing themselves was somewhat informal. In the 1840s and 1850s the colliers of the Clyde Valley would meet en masse in a field or a quarry outside town to hear reports from their district leaders and to vote on policy. At peak seasons of coal production, when employment was at its height, more than 5,000 men would participate in such local meetings, tramping in from nearby villages or outlying rural pits. From the 1860s on, however, the mass meetings were more likely to elect representatives from each pit or local district to represent the colliers at a delegate meeting in Glasgow, where the final policy decisions would be made. How far these delegate meetings actually guided Alexander McDonald in his actions as president of the LCMU and how far he abused these powers by making important policy decisions himself is unclear.[53]

Whatever the exact source of McDonald's authority, by early 1874 it had become clear that a significant proportion of the union membership was no longer willing to accept what many perceived as his policy of handing down decisions from above. Angered at the strike defeats, his more vocal critics now went on to challenge not only McDonald's authority as leader but the whole delegate system of LCMU governance. They wanted some form of direct democracy instead. John Beveridge, a miner from Larkhall, was one of the spokesmen for this group. Beveridge said that he could no longer accept a process in which delegate conferences meeting in Glasgow took the entire responsibility for making decisions affecting the miners, especially when such decisions were often taken without consulting the colliers themselves. At one of many mass meetings held to discuss the issue, Beveridge said he "did not see why forty human beings should be allowed to rule the whole of Scotland by conferences." In the future, he suggested, "The miners should be allowed to settle their own affairs."[54]

Nor was this all. By the early 1870s a new element had been added to the union's system of governance: the paid miner's agent. The function of these agents was partly to carry out union policy and partly to make it. In the crisis of confidence that overtook the Lanarkshire miners in 1874, they found themselves forced to choose between McDonald and his critics. While most of the agents deferred to McDonald's long experience as a leader, a minority decided to distance themselves from his failed policy of selective strikes. During the course of a delegate meeting in April 1874, for example, agent Michael Brown of Wishaw stated caustically that he had "the misfortune to be a miners' agent and should, perhaps, have continued digging coal." He then added, in a radical departure from McDonald's own views, that the best policy would be either that all the miners—both those employed by sale coal masters and those employed by firms that manufactured iron—strike together or that none of them should strike.[55]

Agent Brown's reference to the need for some form of general strike if the 1874 cuts were to be rescinded was accompanied by a growing recognition that the miners' unions of southwest Scotland needed to add more members and to draw them from a broader geographical base. In principle this was not a controversial issue. Alexander McDonald himself had sometimes advocated enlarging the miners' unions in these ways. The disagreement arose over the role such an expanded union should play. McDonald wanted to use an enlarged union to keep wages high by the traditional method of the limited darg. Michael Brown and the other critics of the class-harmony doctrine, however, wanted to use an expanded union as the basis for far more militant policies. The most dramatic of these was the idea of inducing the government to support a minimum wage.

It was Keir Hardie, however, who articulated the idea of state intervention most forcefully. The thrust of his thinking was made clear in a speech he delivered to an open-air meeting of more than a thousand miners near Irvine, Ayrshire, on August 18, 1880. Keir Hardie first expressed his reservations about the sliding scale as McDonald had proposed it. He then went on, in an unprecedented departure from traditional thinking, to link his critique of the sliding-scale idea to the desirability of state support for a minimum wage. "There were two different kinds of sliding scale," Keir Hardie stated. "There was the sliding scale that was always sliding down, and there was a fair one, and they [the miners] did not object to the latter." The point of a fair sliding scale, he went on, was to enforce a minimum level of wages below which the miner's pay should not be allowed to fall. "In Australia," he noted, "the sliding scale had been brought into force by the Government, who had also appointed a Minister to look after the mining community."[56]

By making this suggestion Keir Hardie moved the terms of the debate over miner strategy beyond the issue of industrial tactics onto the broader plane of political economy. In doing so, he implied the need for a revolution in the Lanarkshire miners' thinking that was to lead in the direction of state intervention and, beyond that, to some as yet ill-defined concept of social democracy.

The class-harmony ideal did not break down as much or as quickly in northern Illinois during the late 1870s and early 1880s as it did in southwest Scotland. The Knights of Labor, which during the 1880s drew strong support from coal miners all over America, was in most respects a militant and progressive organization. Nonetheless, it sought to avoid some of the more extreme consequences of class separation by opposing large-scale strikes and maintaining a commitment to arbitration and conciliation as the best way to negotiate disputes. Moreover, although a sliding scale was adopted in many northern Illinois pits, no one in the 1870s drew from its introduction the radical conclusions to which Keir Hardie had come.

Nevertheless, the midwestern coal operators witnessed several manifestations of the transforming effect that the defeats of the 1870s had on the outlook of those colliers who still sought to defend the class-harmony ideal and to maintain amicable relations with their employers. One such manifestation was the anger and disillusionment that many northern Illinois miners expressed at the way in which the CW&V exploited its 1877 victory to increase industrial discipline over its colliers and to fire or blacklist their trade union leaders. Some of these expressions of discontent, while not going so far as to suggest state intervention in the coal industry, nevertheless implied a loss of confidence in the prevailing economic system's ability to provide the miners with an acceptable standard of living. In January 1879, for example, an anonymous Braidwood collier wrote to the *National Labor Tribune* in the following terms: "It is possible that low wages, poverty and enforced idleness may be ... carried too far. There is a limit to human endurance, and it would be well for those at the helm of the ship of state to think carefully [about the miners' plight]. ... Continued and worsened suffering might even cause an uprising that would startle the world." [57]

The CW&V also took advantage of the upper hand it had gained to open four truck stores near its pits, two in Braidwood and two in Streator. No precedent existed for such stores in these two midwestern coal towns, in part because friendly shopkeepers had earlier been willing to supply sufficient credit to tide the miners over during hard times. By now, however, many of these store owners had either lost their sympathy for the colliers or gone out of business as a consequence of the prolonged industrial depression. The introduction of company stores, which were all too reminiscent of the ones in Great Britain, angered the miners, but they had little in the way of an alternative. Those unwilling to take some of their wages in "store pay," one disillusioned miner reported, learned that they could "take up their beds and walk," [58] meaning that those miners who refused to use scrip at the company stores would be fired. These firings angered the miners still further: they viewed such enforced subservience as a threat to their republican liberties. In response the miners of Braidwood, like the colliers in Lanarkshire, established and equipped a cooperative store of their own. In January 1878, however, a fire burned it down, and the miners lacked funds to rebuild it. "Poverty," one of them commented sadly, "is too deep-rooted and widespread to reaccomplish this glorious undertaking. We must look to a different system." [59]

A third, if indirect, piece of evidence about the way the struggles of the

1870s led the northern Illinois miners to acknowledge the permanency of class separation can be found in the concluding chapters of Tom Tippett's novel *Horse Shoe Bottoms*. During the course of his fictitious tale, Tippett recounts John James's visit to the mining camp. James bears a message from John Siney advising the miners to join the American Miners Association. The plight of the miners James describes on his visit was almost identical to that of the colliers in the real-life towns of Braidwood and Streator. After Old Bill's coal company sinks several new shafts in the mid-1870s and acquires the attributes of a modern corporation, Bill decides to sell most of his interest in it to a group of urban investors represented by a professional mine manager named Don Simpson. After they hear this, the local miners go out on strike, only to be fired and blacklisted for their pains.[60]

This puts Old Bill in a quandary. On the one hand he still owns part of the mine and remains a director of the new coal company. On the other hand, having been a miner himself, he sympathizes with the unemployed colliers. Old Bill, Tippett tells us, "resented also the idea of Don [Simpson] so ruthlessly trampling over his coal-diggers. Had he the full control of his business in his own hands, his attitude might have been otherwise, but he realized the directors of the company had never completely accepted him as a man like themselves."[61] Old Bill ponders Siney's message urging the miners to organize and finally decides to break with manager Don Simpson and the other directors and throw in his lot with the colliers instead. In effect, Old Bill chooses sides in an emerging class war.

In the concluding chapter of Tippett's novel, mine manager Don Simpson expresses his incredulity at Old Bill's decision to support the miners' union, arguing that Siney's call to organize will raise the coal company's costs and that it runs counter to the interests of the company. "And I say," replies Old Bill, "that Siney is a fine fellow. I've heard of Siney. Why shouldn't the men protect themselves from the corporation? If I was a miner I'd lead them, and so would you if you had a grain of sense." "But I'm not a miner," replies Don. "I'm a coal operator, and you ought to decide which of the two you are. We have the interests of the company to look after, not the miners."[62] Fictitious though it is, Tippett's novel clearly illustrates the need for self-made, old artisan-miners like Old Bill to choose sides in the hardening class divide that was beginning to take shape in American industrial society.

Further evidence of the way that the breakdown of the class-harmony ideal polarized attitudes in both Lanarkshire and northern Illinois can be found in the increasing bitterness that characterized personal relations between those labor leaders who still clung to the mid-Victorian conciliatory brand of trade unionism and those who favored a new and more militant approach. In Lanarkshire it was once more Alexander McDonald who suffered the brunt of these attacks. The disagreement between MacDonald and Keir Hardie over the 1879 "Tattie strike" was but one in a series of quarrels that took place between the venerable leader and his foes. At a mass meeting held near Hamilton in April 1874, for example, John Beveridge returned to the topic of McDonald's autocratic ways not simply as a union leader but also in his personal relations with individual colliers. McDonald's high-handed manner, said Beveridge, made him and his fellows feel like "slaves in a Scotch Siberia under an Emperor Alexander." Beveridge urged his fellow miners to "free themselves from his rule." [63]

The episode that symbolized most clearly the ideological gulf separating McDonald from the younger generation of militants in the LCMU, however, was the reaction to his 1874 purchase of the luxurious fourteen-room mansion Wellhall, just outside Hamilton, which was the site of the LCMU headquarters. McDonald bought the house in conjunction with Samuel Thomson and Robert Alston, two local businessmen who planned to sink coal shafts on the estate. This implied that McDonald was going into business as a coal owner on his own account.[64] Such an action would not necessarily have been considered reprehensible fifteen years earlier. Self-improvement by whatever means possible had been one of the bedrock elements of the artisan-collier philosophy since the 1830s. Coming when it did, however, in the middle of an industrial depression when large numbers of colliers were unemployed, McDonald's purchase of the Wellhall estate was too much to bear. As luck would have it, moreover, the purchase was made at a time when the Dixon Coal Company was ejecting a number of rank-and-file miners from company housing as a result of the 1874 strike. Hence soon after Alexander McDonald bought Wellhall, a storm of criticism broke around his head. One critic accused him of having become "a capitalist," a sobriquet burdened with a pejorative meaning it had not carried before. Now that McDonald had become a landowner as well as a putative coal owner, the critic asked, "how could he be expected to work in the interests of labour?"[65] Language such as this was unprecedented in the internal discussions the Lanarkshire miners had so far held about their trade union philosophy. In effect, McDonald's critics were calling him a class traitor.

These 1874 attacks did not entirely put Alexander McDonald in the shade. He remained president of the LCMU for six more years, but his reputation with most ordinary miners had been irrevocably sullied. McDonald was a proud man, and these blows to his reputation, coupled with the strenuous life he had led as president of the British Miners National Association, leader of the Scottish miners, and M.P. for Stafford in the English Midlands, took a toll on his health. Early in 1881, after repeated bouts of illness, he was diagnosed with heart disease and during the following months was increasingly confined to his bed. McDonald died on October 31, 1881, just after receiving the news that his brother James had passed away in Clay County, Indiana, to which he had immigrated some years before.[66]

Despite his unpopularity with the militants in the LCMU, Alexander McDonald had by now become a national figure, and so November 6, 1881, the day of his funeral, was declared a special day of mourning by miners throughout the Clyde Valley. Blinds were drawn, local shops were closed in Hamilton's main streets as a mark of respect, and a large crowd stood somberly by as McDonald's funeral cortege passed in front of them. Starting in the market square, the procession wound its way eastward through the grim pit heaps and railway embankments of Motherwell, Holytown, and Airdrie, an area that had been largely open countryside when McDonald was born in 1821. The procession finally halted at the graveyard of the small village church in New Monkland, near to his place of birth. McDonald was buried there, beside his parents, less than twelve miles from Hamilton and only a short distance from the farm where he had come into the world some sixty years before. It was the end of an era.[67]

In northern Illinois it was not a generational split like the one between Alexander McDonald and James Keir Hardie that symbolized the new division between the militants and the conservatives in the miners' unions. It was, rather, an ideological parting of the ways between Alexander McDonald's two most famous American protégés, Daniel McLaughlin and John James. Sometime in 1876, despite increasing tensions between the mine operators and the colliers in Braidwood, John James took a job as agent for one of Braidwood's coal companies.[68] This decision was not seen as evidence of class treachery in quite the same way that McDonald's purchase of Wellhall was later seen in Scotland—a fact that throws further light on the somewhat weaker sense of class separation present in northern Illinois at this time.

Nevertheless, James expressed disapproval of the miners' decision to quit work at the outset of the great 1877 coal strike, and he quarreled openly with his longtime friend Daniel McLaughlin, who was now both mayor of Braidwood and the most important leader of the stoppage. After the state militia had come to Braidwood, James expressed regret at the bitter class antagonisms that the conflict had stirred up. He repudiated the Braidwood miners' decision to lend their support to the Greenback Labor Party, and he was incensed when Supervisor John Young decided to impose a property tax on the hitherto untaxed coal lands of the mining companies, seeing it as a deliberately provocative act. James also accused Young of various fiscal improprieties, including, as he put it, having "prostituted his office" by using Braidwood's tax revenues to feed the strikers.[69] This not only irritated Young; it also incensed Mayor Daniel McLaughlin, who responded by telling his former comrade-in-arms, "Your day of . . . fooling the people, especially the mining classes, is gone."[70] But this only widened the split. James even went on to repudiate the establishment of Knights of Labor assemblies in Braidwood, arguing that they were part of a secret organization whose clandestine nature was bound to offend the employers.

It so happened that John Siney — the real Siney this time, not the fictional one — was visiting Braidwood while this split between McLaughlin and James was developing. James and Siney had become friends in Cleveland between 1873 and 1876, when the Lancashire-born Siney and the Scots-born James were president and secretary, respectively, of the Miners National Association.[71] In an act redolent of support for the now discredited class-harmony ideal, Siney lined up alongside James in his quarrel with McLaughlin and the Braidwood rank and file. The once powerful Siney was now in a weakened situation himself, however, and was in no position to give James much help. Two years before, as leader of the anthracite miners in Pennsylvania, Siney had suffered a fate quite similar to the one that befell McDonald in Scotland. In 1875, after Siney had struggled unsuccessfully to persuade the bituminous coal operators in Pennsylvania and Ohio to settle a series of coal disputes through arbitration, his leadership had been repudiated by the "wilder spirits" of the MNA's rank and file.[72] A strike broke out but ended in total defeat, and Siney himself was arrested and tried on criminal conspiracy charges in Clearfield County, Pa. Although he was ultimately acquitted, the humiliation Siney suffered as a consequence of his trial and the repudiation of his leadership of the MNA brought his union career to an end.[73]

Ostracized by McLaughlin and his other former friends, James stood by anxiously as the northern Illinois miners went down to a humiliating defeat in the 1877 strike. He left Braidwood for good sometime in 1880. Like many other skilled British miners who had come to America in the 1860s, James spent the rest of his working life either as a mine manager or in some other supervisory capacity.[74]

Daniel McLaughlin, on the other hand, was radicalized by the 1877 strike defeat. He did not abandon the class-harmony ideal altogether, and he never became a socialist, as Keir Hardie did. McLaughlin also remained critical of strikes, and he upheld the idea of a sliding scale. Nevertheless, he fully supported the program of the Greenback Labor Party, which achieved considerable success in Braidwood between 1876 and 1878. In the winter of 1877, moreover, McLaughlin articulated a vision of the future that went beyond the piecemeal reforms he had advocated before. "It does not require much logic or reason," McLaughlin stated, "to prove that the wage workers and wealth producers are defrauded and robbed out of the just share of the wealth they create. The basis of our social system requires to be remodelled and founded upon industrial equality." [75]

The economic crisis of the mid-1870s and the unsuccessful strikes that polarized mining communities in both Lanarkshire and northern Illinois did not bring about a complete repudiation of the class-harmony ideal. Miners' unions on both sides of the Atlantic continued for some years to uphold the policy of arbitration and conciliation in their relations with coal owners and to treat the strike as a weapon to be used sparingly. Nor did the increased industrial discipline that had taken hold on both sides of the ocean mean that the artisan-colliers had all been transformed into semi-proletarians. The artisanal habits and workplace autonomy of the skilled collier, which were to continue until the introduction of the mechanical coal cutter at the turn of the century, continued for some years to maintain his self-image as an independent artisan. Other aspects of Alexander McDonald's legacy continued to exert a powerful influence over miners in both Britain and America for a considerable period of time.

But a number of things had now changed irrevocably. The calls for a general strike by Scottish miners in 1872 and 1874, coupled with the coal owners' efforts to organize separate associations of their own, showed that not only the colliers but also the coal owners had now recognized their separate interests as a class. Doubts were also being raised among the miners about the efficacy of output restriction as the primary means of regulating wages and prices. Instead, in Lanarkshire at least, rank-and-file miners were now groping toward the idea of a "fair" wage that would remain stable over time instead of being determined only by the vagaries of the capitalist market. Alexander McDonald himself had espoused the idea of a fair wage, as had his disciples on the American side of the ocean. Nevertheless, whereas the older miners' leaders believed that a fair wage could be achieved by means of a limited darg, arbitration of grievances, and consultation with the employers, the new generation of miners' leaders, such as James Keir Hardie, were unwilling to accept that point of view. Instead, they had begun to believe that part of the responsibility for the regulation of miners' wages lay with the state.

In the 1880s and 1890s, in southwest Scotland at least, these developments resulted in the growth of a more militant and broadly based form of trade unionism and, among a minority of miners, in a move toward political socialism. In Illinois, although there was a similar, if not equal, degree of class-conscious militancy at the workplace, the political outcome was more ambiguous. As I will show in a subsequent chapter, in the mid-1890s a small number of northern Illinois miners, building on the traditions of the Greenback Labor Party, sought briefly to establish a Labor-Populist alliance, but they remained a small minority. It was not until after the turn of the century that the socialists succeeded in attracting a significant number of U.S. miners to their cause.

But this is getting ahead of my story. Before these political developments could come to fruition, the coal industry had to pass through another stage of modernization. This stage took it beyond the level of economic development that had been reached either in Wishaw and Larkhall in the 1860s and 1870s or in Braidwood and Streator between 1872 and 1882. The new stage significantly increased the separation of class interests between the miners and their employers and led to the development of militant mass unionism among the colliers in both Lanarkshire and Illinois on a scale beyond anything that had occurred before.

6

NEW TECHNOLOGY, NEW IMMIGRANTS, AND GROWING CLASS CONFLICT: BLANTYRE AND SPRING VALLEY, 1885–1905

At the turn of the century both the Lanarkshire and the northern Illinois coalfields came near to reaching peak production. Between 1870 and 1913 both output and employment almost doubled in southwest Scotland, from 11.9 million tons produced by 34,732 miners in the former of these two years to 20.4 million tons raised by 58,420 colliers in the latter.[1] A similar development occurred in northern Illinois, although on a smaller scale. By 1903 the mines around Braidwood and Streator were producing 7.4 million tons of coal per year, dug by over 4,000 miners.[2]

The demand for coal in both the Clyde Valley and the American Midwest, however, continued to soar. In the Scottish case this was due partly to a rise in coal exports and partly to ongoing growth in the shipbuilding, engineering, and other heavy industries of the Glasgow region. In northern Illinois it was due to a similar development of heavy manufacturing in Chicago, as well as to a new burst of population growth and urban infrastructure in East St. Louis and Springfield, in the central part of Illinois. To consolidate or enhance their position in the industry, the larger coal companies on both sides of the Atlantic again found it necessary to develop new sources of capital, build deeper and larger coal pits, and purchase more up-to-date equipment. The new technology included the first coal-cutting machines to be used on either side of the ocean.[3]

As a consequence, in the last two decades of the nineteenth century, new and deeper shaft mines were sunk in many places on the south bank of the River Clyde in Lanarkshire, as well as in the coal lands further west along the

Illinois River valley in northern and central Illinois. Two new coal towns, in particular, fully exemplified these modernizing tendencies. They were Blantyre, an old agricultural settlement on the edge of the Clyde, not far from Larkhall and Wishaw, that was transformed in 1870 by the discovery of coal, and Spring Valley, a new mining community that sprang up in the mid-1880s about twenty miles northwest of Braidwood and Streator.[4]

The new mining era typified by Blantyre and Spring Valley was marked not only by larger and deeper coal pits and the more widespread use of new technology. It was also characterized by the employment of a larger and more proletarianized labor force than had been present in the industry earlier on. A few northern Italians and peasant Slavs from various provinces in the Austro-Hungarian Empire had already begun to work in the pits in Braidwood and Streator in the late 1870s. In the 1880s and 1890s this influx of new European immigrants turned into a flood. Slavic and Italian mine laborers, some of whom came west to Illinois from the bituminous coalfield of western Pennsylvania and others of whom immigrated directly from southern and eastern Europe, made up a much larger proportion of the mine labor force in Spring Valley than they had in either Streator or Braidwood.[5] A few Poles and Lithuanians from eastern Europe also found their way to Blantyre and other Lanarkshire coal towns.[6]

Before the mining era Blantyre was known chiefly for the large water-driven cotton-spinning and Turkish dye works that had been built in earlier days at the eastern edge of the community, on the south bank of the River Clyde. Some of the offspring of these mill workers, many of whom were Irish, intermarried with the town's miners after coal was discovered in 1870. The Blantyre textile works was a self-contained company town, however, in some respects like Robert Owen's eighteenth-century model mill village at New Lanark, a few miles further up the Clyde. Its employees had little to do with the lairds and clergy of High Blantyre, whose handsome houses stood on a hill in the center of town, or with the grimy, overcrowded miners' rows that the mining companies built in Stonefield in the 1870s on a stretch of formerly agricultural land between the eastern and western ends of the parish.[7]

By the end of the nineteenth century the construction of large-scale mining enterprises in the Blantyre district was just about complete (see map 8). The William Dixon Company had four pits at High Blantyre. Baird's was operating the Craighead and Whistleberry collieries, just west of Stonefield, as well as the Bothwell Castle colliery, a half-mile to the north. Merry and Cunningham had sunk its two pits, along with the accompanying surface buildings, near the hamlet of Auchinraith. These mines were much deeper and more complex than the same companies' pits in Wishaw and Larkhall.

Map 8. Blantyre, 1899 (*source: Ordinance Survey of Great Britain* [1899]).

In 1895 the Bothwell Castle colliery employed no fewer than 339 men in its two mines, Merry and Cunningham had 459 employees, and William Dixon Company employed 548 men in its four shafts. The grand total of 1,346 men working in these pits produced more than a half-million tons of coal per year. Taken together these Blantyre enterprises constituted one of the largest concentrations of miners' rows, coal pits, railway sidings, and brick works to be found in southwest Scotland.[8]

The output of each collier in the new deep shaft mines on both sides of the Atlantic was still limited by the use of hand shovels to load the mined coal into coal cars.[9] Other innovations helped to alter key parts of the coal-mining process, however. Electrical signaling devices replaced communication by hand; first pit ponies and then electric engines took over from human muscle as the main method of moving coal cars from the shaft bottom to the surface. Important innovations also resulted from the manufacture of up-to-date drilling and mine-sinking equipment. "Instead of sinking shafts of the usual size of 16 feet broad and 5 feet wide," wrote Scottish mine inspector Robert Moore in 1893, "some of them were 24 feet long and 8 feet wide."[10]

Only the largest and wealthiest Scottish coal and iron companies could raise the capital and buy the equipment needed to build these new mines. "In the fittings commenced after 1870," as inspector Moore put it, "the first workable seam—the ell coal—being at a depth of from 100 to 200 fathoms, a large amount of capital had to be expended, and it was necessary to raise large outputs in order to make the collieries profitable."[11]

Much the same thing happened at Spring Valley, which was located on the northern bank of the Illinois River near the western edge of the northern Illinois coalfield. Unlike Blantyre, Spring Valley sprang up virtually full-blown from the raw midwestern prairie, like Braidwood and Streator before it. Until the mid-1880s the area was largely agricultural. In 1884, however, Charles Devlin, a mine manager from nearby La Salle, made borings on the sloping ground running down to the river. He found that the ground contained an even four-foot seam of coal at a depth of 380 feet—almost two hundred feet deeper than the coal seams at Braidwood and Streator. Devlin then persuaded his father-in-law, Henry Miller, who was one of the richest men in surrounding Bureau County, to buy five thousand acres of the coal-rich land.[12]

Thereafter industry developed just as rapidly in Spring Valley as in Blantyre. Devlin and Miller persuaded a number of other absentee industrialists to help develop their newly purchased coal lands. The investors included E. N. Saunders of St. Paul, a director of the Chicago and Northwestern Railroad; coal operator John Taylor of What Cheer, a Welsh mining town in eastern Iowa; and Congressman W. L. Scott of Erie, Pa., who had property interests in that state's extensive coalfield. All these men were capitalists on a much larger scale than that of the self-made entrepreneurs who founded Braidwood and Streator in the immediate post–Civil War years. Late in 1884 two new corporations were set up. One was the Spring Valley Townsite Company, owned by Henry J. Miller, which laid out the town in the usual gridlike manner and sold housing lots to the incoming miners (see map 9). The other new corporation was the Spring Valley Coal Company, of which Charles Devlin became vice-president and general manager.[13]

The Spring Valley Coal Company was to play an even larger role in the lives of the local mining population than the CW&V had in Braidwood and

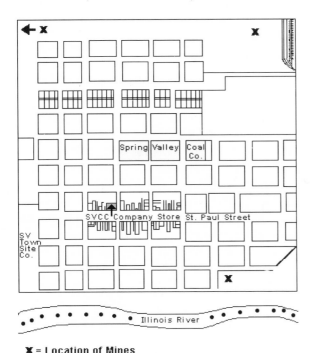

Map 9. Spring Valley (*source: Platt Book of Bureau County* [1890]).

Streator. This was because, once its four main pits had been completed, the SVCC employed about 80 percent of the town's labor force, which gave it enormous political and economic power. Symbolic of this power was the fact that one of Charles Devlin's first acts when he settled in the town was to establish a company store. Again, company stores were common in Lanarkshire, but they had only recently been introduced into the northern Illinois coalfield.

Perhaps because they feared the disruptive effects of modern deep-shaft mining, the citizens of Spring Valley at first expressed a mixture of pride and apprehension about the size and depth of the SVCC's new pits. "The engine house is 55 + 48 feet in diameter," wrote the *Spring Valley Gazette* proudly about the city's pit no. 1 in June 1888. "It has a 110 horse power hoisting double-second motion engine, with a double drum, made by Bullock & Co. of Chicago.... In No. 1 mine between six and seven hundred are employed."[14] This was a work force even larger than that employed by Dixon's at Blantyre. A second reporter, however, commenting a little later about another new deep shaft mine that had just been dug at Carbon Hill, outside of Braidwood, remarked: "The work day [there] was long and hard, with ventilation poor and the dangerous gasses present. There were many crippling accidents and deaths."[15]

The more complex technology of the deep shaft mines also allowed large-scale coal companies such as Baird's and Merry and Cunningham to impose their concept of industrial discipline on their employees more effectively than they had been able to do in Larkhall and Wishaw. This trend was enhanced in the Blantyre region because mining employees were concentrated in the densely packed miners' rows that lay in the interstices between the middle-class housing of High Blantyre and the working-class neighborhoods of Stonefield and Auchinraith. Nonetheless, the social and economic power of the coal operators was noticeable in Spring Valley as well, where two members of the same family, Charles Devlin and Henry J. Miller, controlled the two largest corporations in town.[16]

It should also be remembered that an even larger proportion of the new mining companies that were established in the northern Illinois coalfield in the 1880s and 1890s were owned and controlled by absentee directors and investors. Streator activist John Williams had earlier pointed to absentee ownership as the factor most likely to provoke class conflict. Both the densely packed miners' rows and the growing power of the absentee coal operators increased the social distance that separated employers from employees in the coal industry and stimulated the miners' desire to develop effective trade unions and to increase their sense of common identity down the pit.

Aside from the larger number of miners involved, what was the social and economic impact of deep-shaft mining on the long-term process of class formation among the miners of southwest Scotland and northern Illinois? In particular, how did the introduction of new technology, especially the deployment of coal-cutting machines, affect the skilled pick miner? Attention must also be paid to the social consequences of the expansion of the coal-mining industry. Was not the relatively high standard of living of the British pioneers in the northern Illinois coalfield undermined as a new generation of European peasant immigrants, accustomed to working harder for lower rates of pay, moved into the pits? And how did both the Scottish and American colliers respond when, in the mid-1890s, these social and economic changes were compounded by a new industrial depression and another round of bitter strike defeats?

The new coal-cutting machines were intended to increase productivity by removing the most time-consuming part of the miner's job. They enabled him to make a surgical incision at the base of the coal face and then proceed immediately to blasting the coal, instead of spending several hours under-cutting the coal face with handtools.[17] In 1882 the CW&V introduced three Harrison coal-cutting machines into one of its Braidwood pits. In 1887 the SVCC brought two Legg machines, an advance over the Harrison model, into its no. 2 mine at Spring Valley. Thereafter, as the machines improved in efficiency, they were used more widely in the northern Illinois pits. In 1891 the Bureau of Labor Statistics reported that in the first and second districts of Illinois — which included Braidwood, Streator, and Spring Valley — "there [were] thirty-eight different machines in use, cutting more than 80,000 tons of coal per annum." This was 23 percent of the overall output.[18] Coal-cutting machines were not introduced into southwest Scotland until after the turn of the century. This was partly because the seams in the older Lanarkshire pits were narrower and more angular than the ones in northern Illinois and partly because — save for a few of the larger firms — the Scottish coal and iron entrepreneurs were slower to experiment with new mining technology than were their U.S. counterparts. Nevertheless, the machines were quite widely introduced into the Lanarkshire pits in the years leading up to World War I.[19]

For as long as the hand-loading era lasted, the introduction of coal-cutting machines did not affect the fundamental control that the individual miner exerted over the pace and rhythm of his work. Save for those working under the longwall system, most colliers still worked alone or with the aid of a single helper in their own workplaces or rooms.[20] Nevertheless, the intro-duction of coal-cutting machines harmed the older generation of artisan-colliers on both sides of the Atlantic in at least four ways. First, it undermined their monopoly of skill. Undercutting the coal face by hand did not simply necessitate great strength and suppleness of body. It also required the collier to know how far he could go with his pick without bringing the entire coal face crashing down on top of him. Artisan-colliers had prided themselves on these skills for generations. The machine tender who operated a coal cut-ter needed almost none of them. The machine he used obviated them at a stroke.[21]

Second, the new machines made the miner's task more dangerous. For one thing, they were extremely noisy and so prevented the collier from hear-ing noises warning him that the roof was "working" (i.e., shifting and groan-ing), which when audible would let him get out of his workroom before the roof collapsed. Equally serious were the larger quantities of coal dust the cutting machines churned up, thereby increasing the danger both of pneu-moconiosis and of explosions from firedamp.[22]

Third, the new machines increased the division of labor both above-

and below ground. This helped to fragment the mine labor force and create potential conflicts of interest between those working underground and a growing cadre of specialists on the surface who serviced the new machinery and ensured the smooth running of the mine.[23]

Finally, the use of coal-cutting machines resurrected the danger of unskilled workers entering the industry without a full understanding of mining operations. Indeed, the short time required to train new Italian and Slavic recruits on the new mining machines was one of the main reasons U.S. coal operators used them increasingly in the last two decades of the century. The problem here was not the operation of the coal-cutting machines themselves but rather the work habits of the new European immigrant machine operators, who endangered the lives of others through their inability to read English and their failure to grasp the dangers presented by firedamp, inadequate roof supports, and other hazards.[24] Reminiscing on his earlier days as a collier, W. D. Stewart, a Scot, referred to this problem when he wrote that coal-cutting machines caused "the elimination of the most skilled part of [the Scottish miner's] work, . . . thus making it possible for unskilled men to enter the mine freely and in a short time to take their place alongside the skilled collier."[25] A northern Illinois miner turned mine inspector summed up the matter more succinctly in a report he wrote in 1888: "The mining machine is in fact the natural enemy of the coal miner. It destroys the value of his skill and experience, obliterates his trade, and reduces him to the rank of a common laborer or machine driver."[26]

While these new developments were threatening the former independence of the artisan-collier down the pit, life on the surface was undergoing other changes that made it considerably less attractive than it had been for northern Illinois's first generation of immigrant miners. As noted previously, when Spring Valley was founded in 1886, Henry J. Miller's Spring Valley Townsite Company sold housing lots to the incoming miners much as the founders of Braidwood and Streator had sold them to the British colliers who settled there in the late 1860s. It seemed, on this basis, as though Spring Valley might also become a bastion of home-owning miners who could depend on their ownership of property to protect them from coal company manipulation. But it did not turn out that way. An 1892 survey of miner-owned housing in Spring Valley put the figure at 35 percent, a significantly smaller proportion than that of colliers who owned their own houses in Braidwood.[27] In addition, by this time there were few, if any, new private plots of land available for purchase either in downtown Spring Valley or in the immediate vicinity.

As a consequence of this housing shortage, the Spring Valley Coal Company began building its own houses and renting them out to its employees just as the coal companies did in southwest Scotland. The new company houses were much inferior to the privately owned ones the first group of miners had acquired when they arrived in Braidwood a generation before. In fact, they strongly resembled the bare, comfortless structures that the eastern coal companies built in the company towns of mining states such as Pennsylvania or West Virginia. According to one report, the SVCC's company houses were constructed out of vertical planks, "without weatherboarding . . . plaster or wallpaper, . . . no central heating, no running water, and one privy served three or four houses." [28]

Housing conditions began to deteriorate similarly in Streator as the century drew to a close. In 1891 the Illinois Bureau of Labor Statistics conducted a survey to determine what proportion of the miners in that township still owned their own homes. The survey found that 20 percent did so, a significantly lower percentage than had owned homes in 1884. In fact, the percentage was only slightly higher than it was in Wishaw that year, where 15 percent were home owners.[29] As if this was not enough, by the turn of the century both Streator and Spring Valley were flanked by satellite villages that were unquestionably company towns, even if the parent cities themselves were not. In 1891 a Streator coal operator named Edward Kangley purchased several thousand acres of nearby coal land on which he built a company store, a school, and company housing sufficient to house all his employees. He named this satellite village after himself. Significantly Edward Kangley was also the inventor of a new brand of coal-cutting machine, which he used extensively in his pits.[30]

The growth of satellite company towns was even more marked in the case of Spring Valley. Between 1889 and 1895 Ladd, Seatonville, and Dalziel were all established in an arc of small mining communities around the city a few miles to the north and west. The CW&V owned the single mine at Seatonville, while the one at Dalziel was in the hands of the SVCC. In all these places the great bulk of the company-owned housing was constructed on the same sparse, crude model as was used for the new company housing in Spring Valley itself.[31]

Map 10 shows Ladd, located about two miles north of Spring Valley. This wind-swept village was the sole creation of the Whitebreast Coal Company, which sank two shafts, both more than five hundred feet deep, close by the tracks of the Chicago, Burlington and Quincy Railroad. In 1892 612 miners worked in them. The only prominent building on Main Street was the coal company store. The Whitebreast Coal Company also donated the land for the Ladd public school and for its only church. All this made Ladd a classic company town and enabled the coal company to exercise an even greater de-

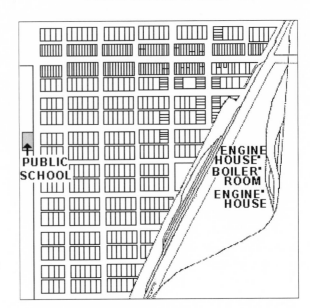

Map 10. Ladd (*source: Platt Book of Bureau County* [1890]).

gree of control over its labor force than the mine owners could in the socially more diverse coal towns of southwest Scotland.[32]

In December 1897 a disgruntled collier who hailed originally from Hamilton, in Lanarkshire, complained bitterly about the narrow, wooden company-built shack in which he was compelled to live at Ladd, as well as about the town's lack of public recreation facilities: "The cold wind whistles off the prairie right through the wooden planks of my kitchen, and when we venture out there is naught to do. In Hamilton, we had many fine parks, taverns and sporting fields to idle our time in, as well as outings up the river Clyde. Here we have but one park, and spend our leisure hours staring out at the frozen prairie."[33]

It would be going too far to say that housing conditions in Spring Valley, Seatonville, and Ladd were as bad as they were in the miners' rows around Wishaw and Blantyre. The damp, dark residences there, without any separate bedrooms or proper sanitation, were among the worst miners' accommodations to be found anywhere in Great Britain.[34] Nevertheless, the appearance of the company town in the northern Illinois coalfield, and the increase in coal company power that accompanied it, symbolized an ominous loss of the republican freedoms that the post–Civil War immigrant colliers had taken as their right.

In part, the deteriorating housing conditions at Spring Valley, like those in the miners' rows at Blantyre, resulted from neglect and the mine owners' desire for a quick profit. But they were also a consequence of the overcrowding that resulted from an ongoing influx of new immigrant miners. In the case of Blantyre, the new arrivals were relatively few in number, consisting mostly of new groups of Irishmen who came either from other Lanarkshire mining towns or from Ireland itself.[35] During the 1880s, however, a small number of Polish and Lithuanian colliers also found their way into the Scottish pits.

Given that U.S. industrial cities were the preferred destination of most southern and eastern European emigrants in the 1880s and 1890s, how did it happen that a minority of them ended up in southwest Scotland? The answer was usually a question of money. It was a habit among young, single emigrating Poles and Lithuanians to stop somewhere along their routes and get temporary employment so as to earn enough cash to finance their passage to the United States. Having traveled from Riga to Hamburg, however, a minority of these emigrants — probably numbering no more than a few hundred in all — found they could not raise enough money for the Atlantic crossing. They sailed instead to the United Kingdom and disembarked at Glasgow, which was Britain's northernmost industrial port. Most of these Poles and Lithuanians stayed there only long enough to earn the money to continue their journey to America, but some of them settled in southwest Scotland and took jobs in the Lanarkshire coal pits.[36]

The thousand or more new Slavic and Italian immigrants who entered the northern Illinois coal mines in the last two decades of the century represented a much larger influx. Not all of them, of course, went to Spring Valley. Many of the Slovaks settled in Streator, as did a number of Poles, Lithuanians, and Bohemians.[37] It was largely the northern Italians who went to Spring Valley. Some of these Italian immigrants, who hailed mostly from the provinces of Turin, Modena, and Bologna, possessed skills that were useful in mining, for they had learned how to use explosives while helping to build tunnels through the Alps. Most, however, were former peasants or small farmers whose illiteracy, religious beliefs, and cultural habits marked them as quite different from the skilled British pick miners who had hitherto dominated the midwestern coal towns.[38] Did this new wave of European immigrants weaken the prospects for the growth of solidarity among miners to a greater extent in the American Midwest than in southwest Scotland?

There is no doubt that when they first arrived in the northern Illinois coalfield, both the Italian and the Slavic immigrants were treated by the British and native-born colliers with a mixture of suspicion and contempt. At the mine itself, complaints brought against them included the assertion that they held down wages, deprived native-born workers of their jobs, and made working underground more dangerous. These complaints were registered not only at the local level but also at the national conventions of the United Mine Workers of America (1890). "The situation is alarming," stated a resolution adopted by the UMWA at its 1892 convention. "These immigrants are being forced upon us in great multitude, and we are being deprived of the opportunity to earn our daily bread." [39]

At the community level, the social condemnation that greeted the new arrivals in northern Illinois was even worse than the complaints that were registered down the pit. George Ward, an ex-miner from Streator, authored part of a report issued by the Illinois Bureau of Labor Statistics in 1894. The Italians and the Slavic miners, he wrote, constituted an ignorant and undisciplined element who used physical violence instead of reasoned argument to settle their marital disputes. They clustered together "in neighborhoods respectable citizens fear to enter. The homes of these miners," Ward continued, "are usually situated on the outskirts of the towns and in close proximity to the mines, sometimes hidden from view by piles of refuse or slack. These homes are in many instances much overcrowded, making it extremely difficult to maintain a proper standard of health or morality." [40]

A demographic analysis of residential patterns in Spring Valley confirms that the new European immigrants there did indeed congregate in separate ethnic enclaves. Italian miners predominated in the northeastern sections of Spring Valley and Lithuanians resided in the northwest, while the English-speaking miners continued to predominate in the downtown area. [41] Nevertheless, there is little evidence to suggest that the British — or Scottish — miners' prejudice against the newcomers was any worse or any more destructive to miner solidarity in Spring Valley than it was in southwest Scotland.

To begin with, complaints expressed against newly arrived Poles and Lithuanians during this period were no less vociferous in the Lanarkshire coal towns than they were in northern Illinois. The first evidence of their presence in southwest Scotland appeared in November 1884, when Merry and Cunningham hired seventeen "spare furnacemen" (shovelers and wheelbarrowmen) to work in their steel works at Glengarnock, in Ayrshire. Later on a larger group of Poles was employed in the Coatbridge area, as well as at the steel and iron works at Craigneuk, between Wishaw and Motherwell. Some were hired at the Blantyre pits, too. In 1884 miners' agent James Keir Hardie, who interviewed the Lithuanians at the Glengarnock iron works shortly after they had arrived there, alleged angrily that they had been brought in deliberately to keep wages low. The employers in the case, Merry and Cunningham, denied the charge, but the protests continued. At a mass meeting held at Irvine, in Ayrshire, for example, a resolution calling for the removal of the "Poles" was passed unanimously.[42]

Cultural slurs, coupled with reports of the eastern Europeans' drunken behavior and arrests for street fighting, also appeared in the local Scottish press. During a three-week period in 1903, for example, the *Lanarkshire Examiner* printed seven such stories. Two of them were headlined as follows: "Pole Assaults a Female" and "A Filthy Toungued Pole." [43] These criticisms of Poles and Lithuanians in Blantyre differed little from those directed against the Italian and Slavic miners in Streator and Spring Valley.

Nevertheless, officials in the Lanarkshire County Miners Union and in Illinois district 12 of the UMWA soon came to realize that these cultural divisions between the British-born colliers and the Poles and Lithuanians were unhealthy both for community relations in the mining towns and for future trade union growth. They feared, not without reason, that the coal operators would exploit these ethnic differences to their advantage. Thus soon after the new European immigrants arrived in the Lanarkshire coalfield, LCMU leaders began to play down ethnocultural differences in the interests of civic harmony and union solidarity. In the mid-1890s Lithuanian miners were admitted to full membership in the LCMU, and within a short time they came to be accepted by the established colliers as reliable and responsible partners underground. In 1905, for example, a strike broke out at Loganlea, a pit where quite a few Lithuanian miners were employed. In its half-yearly report, the union went out of its way to praise the support given to the strike by the eastern Europeans (whom it misidentified as Poles): "This is the first dispute in the County in which such a majority of the Polish miners engaged, and it is satisfactory to find that those workmen are quite as determined fighters for justice as the Scottish miners are." [44]

More remarkable, however — given prevailing assumptions about greater ethnic prejudice in the U.S. labor movement than in the British — was the fact that the leaders of the United Mine Workers of America also quite quickly adopted a policy of mutual tolerance and restraint in their dealings with the new European miners, even though such immigrants were far more numerous there than in Britain. This official policy of integrating the new arrivals did not mean that the UMWA supported the open immigration policies being pursued by the U.S. government in general. The UMWA gave strong support to the AFL's demands for immigration restriction.[45] By the turn of the century, however, Illinois district 12 of the UMWA had succeeded in creating both an organizational structure and a union philosophy that had largely defused the ethnic issue, putting together a united front that was just as solid as the one in Scotland.

How was this multiethnic unity secured? It did not stem from the superior humanitarian instincts of the Anglo-Saxon miners in the United States. It derived instead from the same pragmatic motives that prompted the leaders of the Miners Federation of Great Britain to come to terms with the much smaller number of Polish and Lithuanian miners who entered the Scottish coalfields. These motives included the miners' mutual dependence on one another for safety underground, the need for uniform wage rates if the coal operators were to be prevented from playing the native-born workers against the immigrants, and the desire to recruit all the colliers into a single union if UMWA district 12 was to become a statewide organization capable of resisting the power of the large new mining corporations that were now emerging all over the state. Flowing from this was a growing conviction, stimulated in part by the Illinois miners' earlier commitment to the Knights of Labor, that they should now establish a full-fledged industrial union rather than a semicraft trade union consisting only of the miners who worked underground.

Over time the first of these three needs was met by state legislation mandating appropriate training for all workers — including new European immigrant mine laborers — in the coal industry.[46] The second was met when, in its annual contract negotiations with the coal companies, district 12 obtained an agreement that required the same pay scale for the same job irrespective of who carried it out. This was particularly important for those skilled British pick miners whose pay rates had been undercut by the lower rates paid to new European immigrants imported under contract to work on the new mining machines.[47] The third objective was achieved when the UMWA's national leadership recognized that it had to organize all the workers who worked in and around the mines, irrespective of their skill level or ethnic background, into one big industrial union if the union was to negotiate successfully with the coal operators at the national level. To attract the new European immigrants to its banner, the union realized, it was essential to appoint Slavic and Italian organizers who could speak to the newcomers in their own languages and minister to their own particular needs. The result, by the time of World War I, was a militant, class-conscious trade union that by the turn of the century had become the most advanced industrial organization in the AFL.[48]

These advances did not come all at once, of course. They took more than a decade to complete. Nonetheless, they were given a significant boost by the constructive role that Italians, Slavs, and other new European immigrant miners played in the U.S. national coal strikes of 1894 and 1897. The common suffering that these immigrants endured side by side with their English-speaking comrades in the 1894 defeat, as well as the tenacity they displayed in bringing the 1897 strike to a successful conclusion, in Illinois as well as elsewhere in the country, allayed many American-born miners' doubts that the newcomers were capable of giving the union their full support in a prolonged industrial struggle. Colliers of all nationalities, stated a special report on the 1897 strike, "engaged in missionary work with all the zeal of a holy cause."[49] Equally supportive was a comment made by Illinois district 12 president W. D. Ryan, a native of Streator, in the 1898 district convention's postmortem on the strike. "We have been laying the blame of blacklegging at the doors of the colored man, and the Pole, the Hun and the Italian," Ryan stated. "Let me now say that those [groups] will bear favorable comparison with the English and the native-born American miner."[50]

Soon after this the Slavs and Italians received their reward within the official union hierarchy. By the turn of the century, growing numbers of them had been either elected or appointed to local, if not yet statewide, office throughout the UMWA. In Spring Valley itself the long monopoly on local offices held by English, Scottish, and Irish miners in local 8215 was broken in the 1898 elections. Two Italians, Enrico Bargini and Tomaso Farcetti, were elected to the union's executive board. Similar changes took place in the UMWA locals in Braidwood and Streator.[51] By 1904 this trend of electing new European immigrants to union office had gone far enough to permit John R. Commons, the famed labor historian, to note: "The policy of the mine workers union is to distribute the offices among the different nationalities, in order to have interpreters at their meetings, and agents to keep the several nationalities in line."[52]

The new ethnic order was canonized in a speech made by UMWA president John Mitchell at a welcome-home ceremony held in his honor in Spring Valley on December 4, 1902. Mitchell had by this time become a hero to coal miners throughout the United States because of the leadership he had displayed in the recently won Pennsylvania anthracite strike. Born in Braidwood in 1870, Mitchell had for most of his career made Spring Valley his home. Having held office in district 12 and acted as a UMWA organizer elsewhere, in 1898 Mitchell was elected president of the UMWA at the surprisingly young age of twenty-nine. He had then been catapulted to national fame as the leader of the 1902 Pennsylvania anthracite strike, which President Theodore Roosevelt helped to settle. Significantly, that victory was due as much to the tenacity of the Slovaks and the other new European immigrants in the anthracite region as it was to the efforts of the American and British-born miners in the UMWA.[53]

Despite a constant rain, fifteen thousand colliers from all over north-

ern Illinois crowded around the small platform erected near the Spring Valley railroad station to welcome President Mitchell back to his hometown.
Mitchell's speech was long and somewhat rambling, but toward the end of it
was a passage that the new European immigrant miners in his audience must
have been glad to hear: "I want to thank for their efforts in Pennsylvania not
only our long-standing and faithful brothers from England, Scotland, Ireland and native-born America. I want to appreciate the solidarity of the new
arrivals, the Hunkies, the Italians and all manner of Slavs. They, too, are the
backbone of our union." [54]

The relatively rapid integration of the new European immigrants into the
UMWA in the opening years of the twentieth century was not characteristic
of the U.S. labor movement as a whole.[55] Nor did it mean that ethnic and racial
prejudice in the UMWA had been entirely overcome. Black miners, for example, continued to suffer from a significant degree of racial prejudice, even
in northern Illinois.[56] In addition, the culturally sensitive native-born colliers who lived in the southern Illinois counties collectively known as Little
Egypt, some of whom came from the South, continued to distrust the Italian
and Slavic miners who moved into their area. Outbursts against foreigners
now tended to occur more in the community than they did down the pit,
however, and the election of new European immigrant miners to union office
in the UMWA confirmed that cultural differences were less an obstacle to the
growth of class consciousness in the American trade union movement than
is usually supposed.[57] The eruption of xenophobic sentiments against Poles
and Lithuanians on the part of the native-born Scottish miners in the 1880s
and 1890s also showed that ethnic prejudice—and the dangers it posed to
the development of class solidarity—was no more likely to occur in Britain
than it was in the United States.

The deterioration of social and economic conditions in both the workplace and the community continued to create serious disaffection among the
more militant colliers on both sides of the Atlantic. In the late 1880s and early
1890s, these problems were compounded by an even more serious period
of economic depression, as well as by a series of confrontations between
miners and mine owners that clearly indicated increasing class polarization
not simply in southwest Scotland but also in the American Midwest. There
were four major incidents, two in Lanarkshire and two in northern Illinois.
Although they were not, of course, causally linked, their simultaneous appearance fitted the more general pattern of worsening industrial relations in
both the British and the American coal industry at this time.[58]

The first of these labor confrontations took place in Blantyre. By the end of 1886, according to a survey carried out by the *Glasgow Weekly Mail*, average colliers' wages in the Blantyre district had fallen to 75p for a five-day week, or 15p a day. Deductions for rent, powder, pick sharpening, check-weighing, and other services reduced them still further. "The Lanarkshire coalowners are engaged in the propagation of misery and the manufacture of paupers," wrote the *Mail*. "They make their money by keeping the mining population next door to starvation, and ultimately throwing them on the hands of the ratepayers." [59] Early in 1887 Keir Hardie, who was now secretary of the Lanarkshire County Miners Union, proposed introducing the old McDonaldite tactic of restricting coal output to secure a wage increase of 2½p a day, but large numbers of miners in the Blantyre area, as well as elsewhere, went on strike instead. In Ayrshire and Fife the colliers soon went back to work, leaving the Lanarkshire men to struggle on alone. The result was overall defeat. [60] Before it came, however, the resentment of the striking miners in the Blantyre region boiled over into open violence.

At the beginning of February 1887, officials of both Bairds and the Dixon Coal and Iron Company in Blantyre began bringing in scabs to work in their pits. On the evening of February 8, a rumor spread that a child had been killed in a clash between the mine pickets and the mounted police escorting the blacklegs to work. Hearing this, a crowd of strikers marching back to Blantyre from a mass meeting in Rutherglen looted a bread van, broke into several grocers' shops in Stonefield, and seized large quantities of whisky, cheese, and ham. In response a force of over one hundred special constables was sent out from Hamilton and Glasgow, accompanied by more than twenty hussars. On February 9 these officers forced their way into the company houses on Dixon's rows in Auchinraith, beating resisters and forcing the residents to allow the local scabs to leave for work. More than fifty miners were arrested, and several were badly hurt. Captain McTeague, commander of the hussars, was well known as a Protestant Orangeman. He took particular delight in punishing the Catholic Irish miners who had taken part in the riot. [61]

This incident seemed on the face of it to be fairly minor. No one was killed, and the summoning of troops to maintain public order in the Scottish coalfields was by no means unprecedented. For many exasperated colliers, however, the Blantyre riots proved to be a turning point in their lives. Among other things, it led to a further escalation in the running battle between militant rank-and-file miners and their union's leaders. Fearing that it would damage their reputation with the public, the LCMU's leaders condemned the Blantyre riot and called on the membership to repudiate it. At a mass meeting called to consider the outbreak, the LCMU officers proposed the following resolution: "That the County Board and assembled mass of Lanarkshire miners . . . express their unqualified disapprobation of the conduct pursued in Blantyre by the lawless mob wrecking and looting." The motion was howled down, however, "there being cries to burn it." An alternative motion was then carried. It endorsed "a vote of congratulations on the Blantyre men." [62] The days of deference toward the coal owners and the more cautious of the leaders of the LCMU were now over. If either group stood in the way of the rank and file, they would now be defied.

The Blantyre riot and the defeat of the 1887 strike also helped to move putative socialist James Keir Hardie still further to the left. At the outset of the strike, recall, he advocated Alexander McDonald's old tactic of output restriction to raise wages, but he soon came to realize that this approach no longer commanded sufficient support to make it the main basis of union policy. What most miners now wanted was mass strike action. The intervention of the police and the use of soldiers to protect scabs also had a radicalizing effect. If state authority could be used to force the miners to submit to the will of the mine owners, Hardie reasoned, then why should the miners not retaliate by making the state work on their behalf as well? In several of his speeches following the Blantyre riots, Keir Hardie proposed national legislation to provide state insurance for miners. He even came out in favor of an eight-hour workday for miners to be mandated by Parliament.[63]

The second major episode in this series of events took place in the northern Illinois coalfield about eighteen months after the Blantyre riot when the Spring Valley Coal Company imposed a lockout in all its pits. Since the SVCC was by far the largest employer in Spring Valley, this action had disastrous consequences for all the local colliers and their families. The Spring Valley lockout was implemented in two stages. The first step was taken on December 12, 1888, when without notice or explanation the SVCC suddenly shut down pits 2 and 4, throwing about one thousand men out of work.[64] Their fellow miners in pits 1 and 3, aware that the families of the locked-out miners would suffer severely without any income, shared their own workplaces with the locked-out men. The second blow came on April 29, 1889, again without explanation. General manager Charles Devlin shut down pits 1 and 3 as well, throwing virtually the entire male labor force of the town out of work.[65]

In the following weeks the colliers of Spring Valley made several attempts to find out why they had been discharged and to persuade the SVCC to reopen its pits, but to no avail. With no money coming in and summer produce scarce, the miners' families quickly used up their savings, and destitution became widespread. Wagons were sent out to nearby farms in search of food, and more than 1,500 of the town's 2,200 miners traveled to other coalfields looking for work. Relief committees were also set up in the nearby towns. But even these measures were insufficient. Chicago mayor Dewitt Cregier and a local congressman, Frank Lawler, appealed to the general public for aid. The local and national press also took up the cause. On June 24, for example, the *Chicago Tribune* reported that five hundred miners' families had become entirely dependent on charity for survival. On August 3 the *New York World* stated that two babies in Spring Valley had died from starvation, and on August 19 Father Huntingdon, a Catholic priest nationally well known as a humanitarian, traveled through the area and reported that an epidemic of diphtheria had broken out among Spring Valley's children.[66]

It was at this point, on September 3, 1889, that the well-known muckraking reformer Henry Demarest Lloyd visited Spring Valley. By threatening public exposure, he forced the SVCC to reveal the real reason for the lockout. The ostensible reason was that the company's costs were higher than those of its competitors so that it could no longer afford to operate its Spring Valley pits. After researching the matter, Lloyd showed these claims to be false. Contrary to the company's public statements, Lloyd demonstrated that the SVCC made a $10,000 to $12,000 monthly profit when operating and that its company store brought in more than $40,000 per year. The real reason for the lockout, Lloyd showed, was to force the company's employees to accept a rate of pay lower than that paid by the other coal companies in the region so as to raise the firm's profits still higher.[67]

The SVCC showed its true colors on August 22, 1889, when it offered to reopen its mines at a wage rate of 75 cents per ton, which was 15 cents lower than the rate the men had been paid before the lockout began. Even this offer was deceptive, however, since it included a provision that three miners share a single room, thereby limiting their output, and that they cut thirty inches of brushing (removing the rock stratum above the coal before mining) without extra pay. Taken together, these requirements would have reduced the effective mining rate from 90 to 45 cents a ton. It was far less than a living wage.[68]

The Spring Valley miners indignantly rejected this "infamous proposition" and refused to go back to work.[69] The national press denounced the grasping tactics of absentee owner William M. Scott, SVCC's president. Henry Demarest Lloyd himself took the lead. Addressing himself directly to Scott in a pamphlet entitled *To Certain Rich Men,* Lloyd accused Scott of having deliberately induced miners from all over the country to settle in Spring Valley and then of having sacrificing them on the altar of profits. "You made commercial war on them, their wives and children, to add to your millions at the risk of misery, disease and death to them."[70] But the SVCC would not be moved. By November the miners had run out of all forms of relief, and they were forced back to work on the company's terms. It was a devastating defeat.

The significance of the great 1889 Spring Valley lockout was twofold. First, it demonstrated that in the age of large-scale firms operating in a competitive market, the small local miners' unions would have to form a much more broadly based and militant trade union if they were to protect themselves against the class-conscious tactics of the mine owners. John McBride, then president of the National Federation of Mine Owners and Mine Laborers (one of the UMWA's immediate predecessors), distributed a thousand copies of Lloyd's *Certain Rich Men* pamphlet at the union's next national convention, and he spoke at length from the podium about the need for a single, nationwide miners' union.[71] Second, the cynical tactics employed by the mine owners during the lockout were exposed for all the world to see by Henry Demarest Lloyd in his celebrated muckraking book *A Strike of Millionaires against Miners* (1889). His account showed the extent to which the U.S. miners and mine owners had moved away from the class-harmony ideal of the immediate post–Civil War period and the depth of the class divide now separating them. Lloyd's book also gave a boost to the imminent Populist reform movement, in which, as I will show shortly, the Illinois miners also played an important part.

However, the episodes that demonstrated most clearly the growth of class-conscious antagonism between miners and mine owners on both sides of the Atlantic in the waning years of the nineteenth century were the two national coal strikes that took place in 1894, first in the United States and then in Scotland. The American strike ran from April to June of that year; the Scottish one, from June to October. Both stoppages were the first national coal strikes for either country. The U.S. strike also took place during the United States' worst depression to date.

With a market glutted with coal even before the depression began, hundreds of coal mines were closed all across the United States during the opening weeks of 1894. So many miners were thrown out of work, in fact, that the governors of several midwestern states, including Illinois, issued public appeals for aid. In an attempt to avert further wage cuts, the UMWA national convention meeting in Indianapolis in January 1894 ordered a general strike to begin on April 21. With only 13,000 paid-up members in the union and $2,600 in the national treasury, it was a desperate gamble. Nevertheless, over 100,000 miners came out in support and stayed on strike for eight weeks. Illinois district 12 of the UMWA was the most solid region behind the stoppage. "The miners are on strike because they must," wrote Daniel DeLeon in *The People*, the official organ of the Socialist Labor Party. "Their condition is unbearable."[72] He went on to cite, as an example, the near-starvation conditions in which a family of miners was living in Ohio.

The U.S. national coal strike was an almost total failure. Wage reductions were temporarily checked in some of the coalfields, but UMWA president McBride was forced to abandon his hope of a nationwide conference with the coal operators, and the union emerged from the conflict severely weakened. Some of the unemployed miners went to the cities in search of jobs; others joined "General" Jacob S. Coxey's famous march on Washington.[73] Most of the embittered colliers stayed near the pits, however, scraping together food from their own backyards and from what little local charity was available. After the strike was lost, the UMWA temporarily lost most of its influence, and hundreds of local strikes broke out instead, driven by frustration and rage. "We would strike [for] three, four, six weeks," recalled one Ohio miner years later, "go back to work when starved to it; work until we had a barrel of flour and a side of bacon ahead, and then we would give them another tussle." Another collier, this one from Kansas, remembered this period as the worst time in his life: "Out of work more than half the time; ill paid and disheartened while working; insecure at all times; not knowing whether we would strike or be forced to strike; no certainty of a home anywhere" — this was an experience he wished never to repeat.[74]

The circumstances surrounding the Scottish national strike, which began on June 26, 1894, and lasted until October 20, were somewhat different. Conditions there were not quite as depressed as they were in America, since a lockout of English miners the previous year had created a nationwide shortage of coal, thereby driving up the price of fuel in Scotland. Nevertheless, once the English lockout was over, coal prices fell once more, and early in 1894 the Scottish coal owners demanded a wage cut of 5p a week. This amounted to 25 percent of the average collier's weekly pay. The newly established Scottish Miners Federation responded with a national stoppage to restore the full amount, on the understanding that the English miners would give them financial aid. Within a few days over 70,000 were striking, even though no more than 30,000 were members of the union. It was another unprecedented example of miner solidarity.[75]

The MFGB did agree to levy its members south of the border to provide monetary support, but only if the Scots asked for a restoration of almost half the pay cut, meaning 2½p rather than 5p. This angered much of the Lanarkshire rank and file, and during the remainder of the strike a dispute developed within the Scottish Miners Federation between President Robert Smillie and Secretary Chisholm Robertson and his supporters. Robertson insisted that the men hold out for the full 5p, while the rest of the SMF leadership favored going along with the MFGB's terms. In the end, however, neither side had its way. In September the MFGB's support from the English and Welsh miners dried up, and most of the strikers were forced to go back on the employers' terms. The Scottish strike, like the American one, ended in a humiliating defeat.[76]

The size of the turnout in these strikes and the tenacity with which many thousand of miners hung on until the end in both Britain and America showed that there were now national unions in both countries willing to take on the full weight of the employers. The two strikes were remarkable in several other respects also. Miners from all six of the towns considered in this narrative, in both Lanarkshire and northern Illinois, played a prominent role in the stoppage. Late in July 1894, for example (some weeks after the American strike was officially over), several hundred colliers from Spring Valley were reported to be "firm as bands of steel" in their determination to stay out and secure their former rate of pay.[77]

In addition, elements on both sides of the class divide engaged in considerable violence during the two strikes. At Oglesby, Illinois, strikers wrecked a coal train by piling rails across the tracks of the Illinois Central Railroad. At Minonk miners put ties, bolts, and other debris on the tracks, leading Governor John Peter Altgeld to bring out the Illinois state militia to protect the passing trains. Both these places were within walking distance of Spring Valley.[78] Similar violent incidents accompanied the Scottish miners' strike. As the financial aid provided by the English coal miners diminished and the turnout began to crumble, increasing numbers of pickets were deployed along the miners' rows in various Lanarkshire towns to prevent the colliers from going back to work. In response, the Lanarkshire Coal Owners Association persuaded the authorities to send a special detachment of police from Glasgow, supplemented this time by additional policemen from England. Almost inevitably, violent clashes occurred between the two sides. On September 16, for example, LCMU agent David Gilmour reported that when his men were picketing peacefully outside the miners' rows at Larkhall, they "were brutally attacked by the police, and a number fell beneath their blows." [79]

On the Scottish side it was once more Keir Hardie who drew the most far-reaching conclusions from the failure of the 1894 strike. On October 20, just after the stoppage ended, he published an analysis of it in the *Labour Leader*. The class lines between masters and men could not have been more sharply drawn, Hardie stated. "On one side were the miners, their wives and children; on the other, fighting against you, were hunger, the masters, the law, backed by policemen and soldiers, [and] the Government." The lesson was clear: labor must establish its own separate political party to challenge the forces of the state on their home ground. Support your union, Hardie exhorted the miners. "But after you have done all this, carry your principles to their logical conclusion by acting politically as you do industrially. It is foolish to form a union to fight the coalmasters and then send one of these masters or his friend [to Parliament] to make laws for you." [80]

It is fair to conclude from the strike actions just described that class antagonisms between coal miners and coal operators on both sides of the Atlantic became more marked than ever before as the nineteenth century drew to a close. The violence displayed by the miners in the Blantyre riots, the callous disregard of the colliers' interests shown by the operators in the Spring Valley lockout, and the miners' humiliating defeat in both 1894 national strikes show how polarized the coal industry had now become not only in Britain but in America as well. All four of these events were marked by much personal suffering among the miners and their families. Finally, the creation of two large national unions, the Scottish Miners Federation (1887) and the United Mine Workers of America (1890), shows an unmistakable trend toward rising militancy and solidarity on the part of an increasingly proletarianized labor force.

These incidents also created a legacy of bitterness that did much to undermine the optimistic outlook that the earlier generation of Lanarkshire colliers had brought with them when they first settled in northern Illinois. Although wages remained higher on the U.S. side of the ocean, many now doubted whether mining conditions in America were superior to those in Britain. These doubts were reflected in a review of Lloyd's *Millionaires against Miners* published by a London newspaper early in 1891. "Both continents are downtrodden by the rich men who own the raw material out of which wealth is created by human labor," the review stated. "Wages may be higher in America, but the increased cost of living there will nearly equalize the condition of the two continents. While for swindling, lying and merciless oppression, many American capitalists leave their European brethren far behind." [81]

To put it mildly, comments such as these do not fit well with the exceptionalist paradigm. At the same time, however, the political fallout from this series of confrontations seems to have been a good deal more radical in Scotland than it was in the American Midwest. Keir Hardie was not alone in expressing the view that Scotland's miners should join in establishing a national political party devoted solely to the interests of labor. Robert Smillie, William

Small, and a number of other Lanarkshire colliers' leaders were urging the same thing.[82]

How did northern Illinois miners view the political consequences of the escalating industrial conflict? By the mid-1890s a small group of radicals in the Illinois labor movement was also considering independent political action. One of its leaders was the radical progressive Henry Demarest Lloyd, who in 1894 sought to promote a third-party coalition of Populists, socialists, and labor — including district 12 of the UMWA — to contest local elections up and down the state.[83] Up to this point, however, little evidence had emerged to suggest that Illinois miners as a whole had an interest in third-party politics. Does this mean that the American miners lagged behind their Scottish counterparts on the question of independent political action and that the high level of class-conscious solidarity they had achieved at the workplace was not matched by a comparable interest in socialist political ideas? The following three chapters will provide an answer to this question.

PART THREE

The Emergence of Mass Unionism and the Parting of the Political Ways, 1890–1924

7

MASS UNIONISM AND EARLY VENTURES INTO POLITICS

The failure of America's national coal strike in the summer of 1894, coupled with the Scottish colliers' defeat the same year, dealt a serious blow to the cause of mining trade unionism on both sides of the Atlantic. Before the strike the Lanarkshire County Miners Union had 8,261 members, and UMWA district 12 had put down strong roots in northern Illinois. After the strike, both unions temporarily lost most of their members.[1]

By the early years of the twentieth century, however, the situation of both unions had been transformed. Capitalizing on the rapid growth of the labor movement in both Britain and the United States, they emerged as two of the leading district organizations in their respective national trade unions. By 1910 Illinois district 12, with 47,242 members in eighty-eight locals spread up and down the length of the state, had become the largest and most powerful district union in the national UMWA.[2] Two years later, after the bitterly fought British minimum wage strike of 1912, the LCMU also became a mass organization. Working from their county headquarters in Hamilton at the center of a network of over thirty miners' lodges, the LCMU's experienced cadre of county agents brought 39,412 miners—more than 70 percent of Lanarkshire's colliers—under their sway.[3]

The mass unions that emerged early in the twentieth century also made it possible for both the Scottish and the American colliers, motivated by a similar desire for safety legislation, to consider the possibility of independent political action. Concentrated as they were into densely packed mining towns, the miners in both countries possessed an almost unique ability—

second only, perhaps, to that of the textile workers — to influence the political process. What determined the basis for political action among this critical block of working-class voters? How did matters differ between Scotland and Illinois? By 1900 to what extent had differences emerged in the way Illinois and Lanarkshire miners responded to the demands of socialists and others that they participate in establishing an independent working-class political party? Most important of all, how did the differential response to the issue of independent political action affect the process of class formation among miners on both sides of the Atlantic?

Before answering these questions, it is necessary to describe briefly the further expansion of mining trade unionism that took place on both sides of the ocean at the turn of the century, especially in the American Midwest.

Between 1890 and World War I the most productive area of the Scottish coalfields moved slowly east from the Clyde Valley toward newer coalfields in eastern Scotland. This change reflected both the exhaustion of mid-Lanarkshire's thickest and most easily cut seams and a shift in the export markets for Scotland's coal, from the Atlantic to the Baltic. The Clyde Valley coalfield became an area of high-cost production, providing the coal and iron companies an incentive to cut costs by resisting wage raises and increasing the use of coal-cutting machines. In turn, this action further hardened class lines between miners and coal operators and prompted the Lanarkshire County Miners Union, under the umbrella of the Scottish Miners Federation, to expand its links with the county unions to the east.[4]

The restructuring of the Illinois coalfield was even more dramatic. By the turn of the century the old northern Illinois pits could no longer compete with the larger, more modern mines that had been established in the southern part of the state. Braidwood, where the Scottish immigrants had originally settled, reached its peak output in the early 1880s and began to decline soon after that. By 1900 Streator's coal mines had been outpaced by its glass and metals factories. Although Spring Valley remained an important mining center until after World War I, its bituminous output, too, leveled off after 1900. By that time many of the narrow seams in the northern Illinois coalfield were either worked out or no longer profitable.[5]

As a result of the decline in the northern Illinois coalfield, the colliers there either pursued alternative sources of employment or migrated along with the coal industry to more profitable areas downstate. In the Spring Valley area the exodus was hastened by the Cherry mine fire of 1910, in which

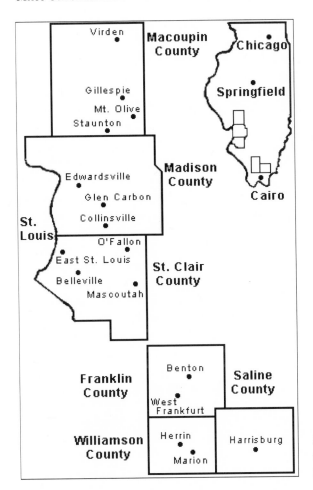

Map 11. Coalfields in downstate Illinois (*source: World Maps*).

more than two hundred miners lost their lives. This fire resulted in the departure of many old-guard British colliers, along with newly arrived Slavs and Italians, either to new industrial jobs in cities such as Chicago or Detroit or to alternative mining positions in the lower regions of Illinois.[6] Once there, they joined other Poles, Lithuanians, Slovaks, and Italians who had been brought in separately under contract from eastern and southern Europe to work the deep shaft mines that now dotted the cornfields all across the southern half of the state (see map 11).[7]

For the English, Scottish, and Irish miners of the northern Illinois coalfield, many of whom were now of a second generation, the opening of the

new downstate coalfields also brought a further readjustment. No longer re-
plenished by newcomers from the British Isles, some of the remaining first-
generation British colliers migrated further west to other coal-mining states,
such as Colorado and Wyoming, where pick miners were still needed. Others
took supervisory positions in the existing mines or skilled jobs in the new
pits opening up in central and southern Illinois. Most of the newly arrived
immigrants from southern and eastern Europe, on the other hand, started
as machine miners in entry-level posts.[8]

The years of experience the British colliers had gained in the post–Civil
War period guaranteed them a disproportionate number of the local and
statewide offices in Illinois district 12 of the UMWA after it was formed in
1890. According to a survey conducted by labor historian John R. Commons, of the 493 men who held office in district 12 between 1897 and 1912,
114 had been born in either England or America. They were closely followed
by the Scots, who occupied 91 of the local and district offices. A number
of mining towns in the central and southern parts of Illinois, such as Gillespie in Macoupin County, still possessed major Scottish enclaves.[9] Third in
terms of office holding came the Irish, with 63 positions. The remaining 225
local union offices were divided up between miners of Welsh, German, and
Austro-Hungarian descent.[10]

The two most influential districtwide officers with a continuing Scottish
background were Duncan MacDonald, who served as secretary-treasurer of
district 12 between 1910 and 1917, and John H. Walker, who was the union's
president between 1906 and 1912. Later on Walker occupied the still more
important position of president of the Illinois State Federation of Labor. In
that role he became influential in a wide range of areas, varying from state
politics to national AFL affairs and from consulting with leading Illinois industrialists to balancing the interests of UMWA district 12 with the powerful
Chicago Federation of Labor.[11] For many years, too, Walker was a leading
member of the Socialist Party of America.

The first new coalfield that Illinois district 12 succeeded in organizing during the closing years of the nineteenth century lay in Macoupin and Madison
Counties (see map 11). This field was located in central Illinois between the
declining northern coalfield at the top of the state and the long-established
St. Clair County coalfield to the southwest. In 1910, 63 percent of its mining population came either from Austria-Hungary or from czarist Russia.[12]
Staunton, the largest mining town in the area, where the headquarters of subdistrict 5 was set up, was largely German. Adolph Germer, for many years
president of subdistrict 5, hailed from nearby Mount Olive. Madison County,
to the immediate south of Macoupin County, contained a similar ethnic mix.

Subdistrict 6's headquarters were located in Edwardsville, even though most of the surrounding population were farmers.[13]

Unlike those in northern Illinois, most of the new coal towns in down-state Illinois began their lives as company towns. For example, until the 1897 strike gave the UMWA some degree of countervailing power, the town of Glen Carbon was wholly dominated by the Madison Coal Company, complete with company housing, payment in scrip, and a company store. The reason for this domination by the companies was that — to a greater extent than in southwest Scotland — much of the land and infrastructure in the new coal towns belonged either to the coal companies themselves or to large-scale railroad corporations such as the Illinois Central and the Chicago and North-western. In fact, when they were first established, coal towns such as Virden, Gillespie, and Mascoutah were little more than clusters of mine tipples and mine shafts built on railroad spurs leading out across the prairie from the state's main railway lines.[14] This meant that many of the miners in downstate Illinois answered either directly or indirectly to the same employers as did Illinois' railroad workers. Besides encouraging common bonds of solidarity between these two groups of workers, their joint antipathy toward monopolistic corporations was to play an important role when it came to political protest.

A second area of new or (in this case) expanded settlement was the St. Clair County coalfield centered on Belleville, located about twenty miles southeast of St. Louis. In 1897 Belleville became the headquarters of subdistrict 7 of district 12. Dominated since the Civil War by British and German miners of cosmopolitan background, it was the only large coalfield to be located near a big city. East St. Louis, along with Belleville and Granite City, contained numerous glassblowing and stove-making shops and was served by an interurban railway that linked all three cities to the outlying coalfields. By 1912 two-thirds of the coal mined in this area was dug by machine, and one-half of its pits were powered by electrically driven haulage systems. Of all the coal-mining areas in downstate Illinois, the St. Clair County district came nearest to resembling the dense industrial region of Scotland's Clyde Valley.[15]

Further south in Illinois, near the confluence of the Ohio and Mississippi Rivers, lay the third large new coalfield, and the last one to be developed. Taking its name from the nearby city of Cairo, this area was called "Little Egypt." Encompassing Franklin, Saline, and Williamson Counties, by 1917 Little Egypt contained some of the largest, deepest, and most up-to-date mines in the state. By 1915, 58 percent of the coal in these three counties was cut by machine, and the mining labor force there was the most proletarianized in the state.[16] Coal town culture in Little Egypt also differed from that in upstate Illinois. Unlike the northern and central parts of the state, many of its coal-mining communities had been settled by poor dirt farmers from the hill country of Kentucky and Tennessee. Most of them were Baptists or evangelical Protestants who found the Catholic faith and foreign habits of the more recently arrived Italian and Slavic miners difficult to accept.[17]

The key to district 12's rapid growth throughout Illinois in the opening years of the twentieth century was the victory it helped secure in the 1897 national coal strike. Between 1894 and 1897, much like its Lanarkshire counterpart, district 12 had been prostrated by industrial depression, but all this changed as a result of the 1897 stoppage, which UMWA president Michael Ratchford described as "nothing less than the spontaneous uprising of an enslaved society."[18] Starting on July 4, with an exhausted treasury and only a few hundred miners belonging to the union, by September 3 the mass outpouring of miners in support of this second national coal strike finally forced the Illinois Coal Operators Association to the bargaining table. The Central Competitive Field Agreement, which followed in January 1898, mandated wage increases, union recognition, the eight-hour day, and the six-day week.[19] The agreement was renewed each spring in joint negotiations between district 12 and a number of other district unions, on the one hand, and the soft coal operators in Illinois, Indiana, Ohio, and Pennsylvania, on the other. It gave the union legitimacy on a wide range of fronts. The agreement's most important feature was the checkoff of union dues at the pithead, which guaranteed district 12 a closed shop throughout almost the entire state of Illinois. A similar development took place at about the same time in southwest Scotland, where the Joint Conciliation Board, representing both miners and owners, was established in 1899 to adjust wages up or down on the basis of the 1888 wage scale.[20]

It was a dramatic weeklong march southward from Mount Olive to Belleville, carried out by "General" Alexander Bradley and four hundred of his supporters, that brought victory in the 1897 coal strike. Encouraged by the moderating of the industrial depression, Bradley and his men marched from town to town making speeches, recruiting volunteers, and galvanizing support. He was accompanied at the head of his march by a Slavic fellow miner carrying a large American flag. The pairing of these two men symbolized the new-found unity in district 12 between the older generation of Anglo-Saxon pick miners and the more proletarianized machine miners from southern and eastern Europe. This pairing was not unlike the alliance that had grown up in southwest Scotland two generations before between the native-born Scots colliers and the incoming Irish. In district 12 this ethnic alliance, even though for a time it excluded most of the African American miners who had moved to Illinois from the South,[21] became the UMWA's most formidable weapon in fashioning modern industrial unionism throughout the state.[22]

In other respects, too, Alexander Bradley was a transitional figure among the Illinois miners. Born in England, Bradley wore a top hat and a Prince Albert coat to symbolize his origins as an artisan-collier. In his speeches Bradley also used the same biblical language of righteousness and moral uplift that Alexander McDonald had invoked earlier in southwest Scotland. Like McDonald, he eschewed class conflict.[23] Nevertheless, to the new generation of miners' leaders who came to power in Illinois district 12 in the years after 1890, the labor republican sentiments of Alexander Bradley seemed somewhat old-fashioned.

After the bitter national coal strikes of 1894 and 1897, most miners' leaders on both sides of the Atlantic, particularly socialists such as Robert Smillie in Scotland and John H. Walker in Illinois, abandoned their earlier rhetoric about republican values and the miners' and owners' joint stewardship of the coal industry. Instead they spoke the language of militant industrial unionism and the highest possible wage. For example, in negotiations between the leaders of district 12 and the Illinois Coal Operators Association in 1904, the union's leaders used the closed shop to force the employers to grant their members the highest wage conceded to any statewide union in the Central Competitive Field. District 12's growing sense of class-conscious solidarity was also expressed in 1907 when it allied with other unions in the Illinois State Federation of Labor to oust from its ranks the Mine Managers' Association, which was composed mainly of former colliers who had become mine supervisors. It did this on the ground that "bosses and foremen had no place in a working class movement."[24]

The annual negotiations that took place after the turn of the century between the LCMU and the coal operators in Lanarkshire, and between district 12's leaders and the Illinois Coal Operators Association in the United States, were far more complex than they had been before. Formal negotiating procedures replaced informal bargaining, grievance committees were set up, and the terms of the contracts were strictly enforced. Although the negotiations usually resulted in a compromise, the two sides no longer had any doubts that they were divided from each other by a wide class barrier. For example, both the strike that resulted from the breakdown of negotiations between the miners and the coal owners in Illinois in 1910 and the nationwide stoppage that took place two years later in Scotland over the issue of a minimum wage created much bitterness on both sides.[25]

When it came to major strikes such as these, leaders and rank-and-file members usually gave each other strong support within both the LCMU and

Illinois district 12. Nonetheless, the new and more complex negotiating machinery that had been brought into being in the Central Competitive Field, along with the commitment that both unions and management made to settling disputes by means of arbitration, frustrated a growing minority of rank-and-file miners on both sides of the ocean. They wanted greater freedom of action to challenge the employers than the cumbersome negotiating machinery permitted.[26] This factor, too, contributed to rising class tensions in the years preceding World War I.

On the Illinois side the desire for more open class confrontation between labor and management was especially prevalent in subdistricts 5 and 7, where young militants such as Edward Wieck and Adolph Germer voiced rank-and-file grievances against what they saw as the excessively class collaborationist policies of the official union leadership. By calling them collaborationist they did not mean that their leaders were attempting to resurrect the Victorian ideal of joint partnership between coal masters and men. Such ideas by now were clearly obsolete. They were referring, instead, to the willingness even of nominally socialist leaders such as district 12 president John H. Walker to give up too many of the union's negotiating aims to the Illinois Coal Operators Association in return for maintaining industrial peace. Dissidents expressed similar resentment against President Robert Smillie and other leaders of the LCMU in southwest Scotland. For example, at large-scale collieries such as the ones in Blantyre, insurgents such as Manus Duddy complained about the refusal of local grievance committees to call strikes over such issues as lower pay scales for machine mining and inadequate compensation for injuries.[27]

Another source of discontent in the Lanarkshire union was the increasingly bureaucratic manner in which the LCMU was governed. Although individual LCMU unions, or lodges, enjoyed a considerable amount of autonomy, their full-time agents were appointed for life. Echoing protests that had first been voiced in the Alexander McDonald era, in 1912 a rank-and-file demonstration of miners at Hamilton demanded the election of all county agents, "in order that the miners of the county might have more say in their own affairs." [28]

Illinois miners, too, sometimes had differences with their leaders. In district 12 the favored means of voicing rank-and-file complaints was through the miners' pit committee. Elected by the colliers in each mine, the pit committees could intervene in the assignment of workplaces and challenge the wage rates paid by mine bosses for deadwork and machine mining. Sometimes they would even call wildcat strikes to protest particular clauses in the Illinois state agreement, even though such strikes were illegal while the agreement remained in operation. Increasingly these pit committees became a thorn in the side of district 12's official leadership. In 1904, for example, a new clause was inserted in the statewide agreement providing for the removal of any pit committee member who violated the contract. It read: "Any pit committeeman who shall attempt to execute any local rule or proceeding in conflict with any provision of this contract shall be forthwith deposed." [29] Similar efforts were made by the leaders of the LCMU to control the more headstrong elements in the Scottish rank and file.[30]

In one sense the militant rank-and-file movements that emerged in both the LCMU and Illinois district 12 in the first decade of the twentieth century helped to propel the miners of both unions to complete their transition from the craft union traditions of the nineteenth-century artisan-collier to the mass industrial unionism of the modern semi-proletarian miner. One outcome of this, as already indicated, was the election of socialists Robert Smillie and John H. Walker, respectively, to the presidencies of the LCMU and Illinois district 12. Smillie held office between 1898 and 1912 (and again after World War I); Walker, between 1905 and 1912.[31] In another sense, however, these conflicts led dissidents such as Manus Duddy in Lanarkshire and Edward Wieck in Illinois toward a syndicalist interpretation of the purpose of trade unionism. According to this view, direct action against the employers at the pithead would prevent both overly restrictive bargaining agreements and excessive state intervention in the mining industry. At the same time, however, these differences between union leaders and the rank and file also helped to shape the attitude that the Scottish and the Illinois miners adopted toward electoral politics.

However, many historical influences besides differences over trade union policy determined the miners' attitudes toward political action. What were these influences, and how did they affect the colliers' involvement in state and national politics? By the time of World War I, the rise of mass unionism had given the MFGB and the UMWA more political clout than almost any other group of workers in the transatlantic working class possessed. To answer these questions, and to understand the different political paths the LCMU and Illinois district 12 ultimately took, it is necessary to go back to the period before the American Civil War, when Lanarkshire miners first began coming to the United States.

The main structural factor differentiating the Lanarkshire miners' politics from those of the miners who migrated to Illinois in the early days was the fact that only the latter could vote in public elections. It was not until the Scottish

Reform Act of 1868 that the right to vote, which in Britain was based on property qualifications, was extended much beyond the land-owning gentry to include a limited number of tenant farmers and middle-class city dwellers. The 1868 act did allow a small number of colliers to vote for the first time, but it was not until 1884, when the Third Parliamentary Reform Act was passed, that large numbers of them were admitted to the ballot.[32]

Exclusion from the franchise did not mean that the Lanarkshire miners took no interest in politics. To the contrary, their earlier efforts to press for the enforcement of the 1831 Truck Act demonstrated a long-standing interest in political reform. The colliers' frustration at being excluded from the franchise was also strengthened by the defeat of the Chartist movement of the 1840s.[33] This broad-based social movement, which among other things called for manhood suffrage throughout the whole of Great Britain, did not directly involve the miners of Wishaw and Larkhall. But enough Chartist clubs were founded in the nearby mining towns to suggest that the colliers from these two places were influenced by the militancy of the Chartist movement, if only indirectly. For instance, Chartist clubs were set up not only in Hamilton but also in Shotts, which was less than two miles east of Wishaw, and in Stonehouse, which fell within the Larkhall miners' district. A reciprocal relationship also developed between a body known as the Coal Miners' Chartist Association and several major, sometimes violent, miners' strikes that swept through Lanarkshire during the depression year of 1842.[34]

Miners from the Lanarkshire coalfield also played a role in agitating for a further expansion of the franchise during the 1860s. The main vehicle for this agitation was the National Reform League, which held large meetings in Edinburgh, Glasgow, and elsewhere in southern Scotland.[35] There is no direct evidence that colliers from Wishaw and Larkhall participated in these meetings, but miners from places such as Rutherglen, which was only a few miles from the two towns, certainly did. Besides signing petitions, these colliers marched in street parades and traveled by train to participate in large demonstrations organized by the National Reform League on Glasgow's famous green.[36]

This long-standing struggle against political exclusion in southwest Scotland did much to consolidate the earlier — and more extensive — development of a separate sense of grievance against the state that was significantly stronger among the Scottish colliers than it was among their counterparts in northern Illinois. It also presented a striking contrast to the political opportunities available to the British colliers who migrated to the American Midwest just after the American Civil War. Having been excluded from the ballot in Great Britain, most of these men quickly became U.S. citizens and took an active part in the political life of their adopted country. They were particularly attracted to the opportunity, which had been denied them in Scotland, of electing public school board members to supervise their children's education and local law enforcement officials such as county sheriffs, who played an important role in determining the outcome of strikes.[37]

Not only were the immigrant miners in Illinois able to vote in federal, state, and local elections; in addition, the political culture they entered was significantly different from the one they had left behind in Great Britain. U.S. political culture was marked as much by regional, ethnic, and racial differences as it was by class distinctions. To be sure, by 1865 there were already salient economic differences between the interests of most workers and farmers in Illinois and those of the merchants, railroad magnates, and factory owners who dominated the economic life of cities such as St. Louis and Chicago.[38] Generally speaking, however, politics in the immediate post–Civil War era were driven as much by a concern with land rights, public education and religion, and the legacy of slavery as they were by European notions of class.[39]

First-generation Scottish colliers such as John James and Daniel McLaughlin of Braidwood, or the German miners and artisans who settled in St. Clair County, had initially been attracted by the "free soil, free labor, free men" philosophy of the prewar Republican Party.[40] Recall that quite a few of the British colliers who entered the area before the Civil War fought for the Union army. Hence for some years they remained faithful to the Reconstruction policies of the postwar Republicans. Little Egypt and the southern Illinois counties, on the other hand, having been settled from the South, were largely Democratic. This region was inhabited partly by Jacksonian Democrats moving north from the hill country of Kentucky and Tennessee and partly by former adherents of slavery who sought to escape from the destruction caused by the war itself. For the most part, therefore, the first groups of miners who settled in Little Egypt went along with their rural coconstituents and voted Democratic.[41]

Whether they were Republicans or Democrats, however, these early immigrant miners held political attitudes that were shaped not by resentment toward a preexisting oligarchy of coal masters and landowners who had excluded them from the franchise but by a desire to make the best of the new democratic opportunities that had been presented to them. Some of the first Scottish immigrants to come to the Midwest had also purchased land.[42] Such men were likely to be as much concerned with the provisions of the Homestead Act (1862) and with the niceties of Illinois land law as they were with the political manipulations of the coal owners. Whatever their politics, however, the Illinois miners, unlike their Scottish counterparts, were now part of a mass, democratic two-party system. It was a system in which, in Amy Bridges's words, "partisan identity was 'larger' than ethnic or class identity, and not simply reflective of either of them." [43] In a general sense, these broader and more opportunistic attitudes toward politics undoubtedly helped to delay the growth of third-party sentiments among the British miners when they first settled in the Illinois coalfields.

It was on pragmatic issues such as mine safety that the colliers first began to enter politics in their immediate self-interest, whether they lived in the Old World or the New. Because none of the Scottish miners could vote before 1868, ameliorative mining legislation affecting all of the British coalfields was at first passed by aristocratic sympathizers in Parliament such as Lord Shaftesbury.[44] After the second Mines Act was passed in 1855, however, Lanarkshire's colliers, like those elsewhere in Great Britain, tried to make up for their exclusion from the franchise by exerting pressure on Parliament through indirect means. In this, as in so many other matters, Alexander McDonald took the lead. Delegate meetings of miners assembled in Glasgow to discuss the current state of mining laws and desirable amendments to them. After consulting with one another, these delegates drew up and circulated parliamentary petitions for the rank-and-file miners to sign. Then the colliers paid McDonald to travel down to London by train to present the petitions to Parliament and lobby M.P.s of all the major groupings for improvements in mining law.[45]

On his first visits to London during the late 1850s, McDonald linked up with other lobbyists for trade union legislation from elsewhere in Great Britain. He made particular friends with Lord Elcho, a Palmerstonian Whig, but he received help also from Arthur Kinnaird, a leading Scottish Liberal M.P. McDonald's 1859 visit, during which he managed to secure an interview with Prime Minister Henry Palmerston, helped to secure the passage of the 1860 Mines Act. This limited the use of boys down the pits, improved ventilation procedures, and permitted miners to choose their own checkweighmen.[46]

Reading of this victory in the American labor press a few weeks later, the pioneer miners of St. Clair County decided to follow the same tactic in Illinois. Unfair weighing of coal by agents of the operators was a perennial problem in many U.S. coalfields, just as it was in Britain, so in the fall of 1860 the St. Clair County miners decided to petition the Illinois General Assembly, then meeting in Springfield, for a checkweighman's law. A collier's representative was sent there, presented the petition, and spoke on its behalf to more than a dozen state representatives. A local paper subsequently noted: "About 1,400 of our best citizens in conjunction with the miners submitted a petition to the General Assembly for a mining law, where it was favorably acted upon."[47]

Such pressure group tactics were followed throughout the remainder of the 1860s on both sides of the ocean, with small groups of immigrant and native-born miners allying with other sympathetic workers in Illinois to follow the example of their British mentors. During the 1863 session of the Illinois General Assembly, for example, miners from St. Clair and La Salle Counties petitioned the General Assembly for a two-shaft bill, arguing that mines should have not one but two exit shafts. These miners cited a recent mining disaster that had occurred at the Hartley pit in Northumberland in support of their claim.[48] The political policies of the Lanarkshire and Illinois miners were even more closely aligned in October 1869, when Alexander McDonald himself came to Braidwood as part of a tour on which he visited his North American protégés.[49] Hearing that a constitutional convention was soon to be held in Springfield to revise the Illinois state charter, he met with John James, Daniel McLaughlin, and Andrew Cameron, the influential editor of the Chicago *Workingman's Advocate,* to plan strategy for the meeting. All four of these men were Scots.[50]

Ultimately the 1870 Illinois constitutional convention merely added a new section to the state constitution urging the General Assembly to enact mining legislation "when the same may be required."[51] This was an ambiguous result, since the assembly was left to decide when such laws should be passed, but the miners were pleased at being indirectly recognized in the state's constitution. They were still more gratified when John Hinchcliffe, elected to the General Assembly in 1871 as a Republican from Belleville, finally secured the passage of a two-shaft law. This Yorkshire-born tailor, who had for some years edited the *Weekly Miner,* became known as the "attorney for the miners." When he retired in 1873, Hinchcliffe was presented with a gold watch "by the working miners of Illinois . . . in recognition of his services in the enactment of legislation."[52] This was similar to the purses of money that were given to Alexander McDonald after he had completed his lobbying trips to Westminster.

On both sides of the Atlantic, then, miners began to exert their influence in politics by using similar pressure group tactics. In retrospect, however, Hinchcliffe's election to the Illinois General Assembly in 1871 looks as though it might have signaled the beginnings of a move toward greater political independence. As Reconstruction faded in the United States in the mid-1870s, the Republican Party in Illinois lost much of its pre–Civil War idealism. It

came increasingly under the control of railroad magnates and other powerful businesspeople in Chicago and elsewhere for whom free trade and the
defense of private property had become paramount.[53] In Lanarkshire, too,
workingmen disliked the control that coal and iron magnates were coming
to exert over the newly established Liberal Party.[54]

The Scottish miners were the first to move. In the fall of 1868 Alexander McDonald, taking advantage of the new Scottish Reform Act, put his
name forward as a parliamentary candidate for Kilmarnock Burghs, which
included a number of communities in the Lanarkshire coalfield. Although
nominally a Liberal, McDonald called himself a "people's candidate" in the
election.[55] Besides demanding a further extension of the franchise, he called
for a "ten-hours act," protection of trade union funds against civil suits, and
a workmen's compensation law, the last proposal being particularly popular
among the accident-prone miners. McDonald also distanced himself from
the official Liberal candidate, coal owner James Merry of Hamilton, who
had incurred the miners' wrath by continuing to use truck stores at his local
iron works.[56]

McDonald was forced to withdraw his candidacy at Kilmarnock Burghs
before the 1868 election took place. But six years later, in the general election of 1874, he was elected as a "Lib-Lab" M.P. for the coal and iron town of
Stafford, in the English Midlands (Lib-Labs were trade unionists who stood
for Parliament on the Liberal ticket but upheld a workingmen's platform).
Along with Thomas Burt, who was elected to Parliament by the Northumberland miners, these two became the first workingmen ever to be elected
to the British House of Commons.[57]

Just as the Scottish miners edged away from the upper-class Whigs and
self-made coal and iron magnates, such as James Merry, who dominated
the Liberal Party in the Lanarkshire coal towns, so too — as the 1870s wore
on — the miners of Illinois began to distance themselves from the business
leaders who now dominated the Republican Party in the northern part of the
state. This trend toward political independence became particularly noticeable during the severe depression of the mid-1870s, with its bitter mining and
railroad strikes. In the spring of 1874 the miners of Will County elected Scots-
born William Mooney to the General Assembly on a party variously designated as Independent, Farmer, or Illinois-Independent.[58] This paved the way
for the still more radical Greenback Labor Party movement of 1876-78.

The Greenback Labor Party briefly acquired national fame around a platform of cheap money, land reform, antimonopolism, and a desire to protect
workers engaged in "mining, manufacturing, and building pursuits."[59] Land
reform was still an attractive proposition for those midwestern colliers who

thought of becoming farmers. The party achieved one of its greatest successes in Illinois among the coal miners of Braidwood when a Greenback Labor ticket, headed by Daniel McLaughlin running for mayor, swept the township's offices in both 1877 and 1878. But the success did not last long. As already noted regarding the bitterly fought 1877 strike against the Chicago, Wilmington, and Vermilion Company, John Young, who had been elected town supervisor on the Greenback ticket, used his powers to impose a tax on the company's previously untaxed coal lands. Infuriated, the politically influential CW&V engineered a fusion ticket of Republicans and Democrats that removed the Greenbackers from office in the subsequent city elections.[60]

Despite these flurries of activity, the first decade of political activity among the Lanarkshire and Illinois miners does not tell us anything very definitive about the miners' ultimate political role on either side of the Atlantic. True, the Greenback Labor Party collapsed in Illinois after 1878, causing most miners to return to their previous political loyalties. By contrast, in 1874 and again in 1880, Alexander McDonald, running as a Lib-Lab, was elected to the House of Commons. He was a member for Stafford, however, not for any of the Lanarkshire mining towns. As a leader of the British Trades Union Congress, he was also now as much preoccupied with general labor reform as he was with mining legislation.[61] On neither side of the ocean did the miners yet show any real interest in breaking with the two-party system.

By the mid-1880s, however, the political situation in both places had begun to change. In 1886 the Knights of Labor, a labor federation that for a time was more hostile to the wage system than was the British Trades Union Congress, rose to dominance in the United States. In some respects the Knights of Labor were also more willing than the British Trades Union Congress to undertake independent political action.[62] The Knights of Labor expanded briefly into England, and in 1888 they even secured a temporary toehold among the miners in Scotland. The basis of their appeal on both sides of the ocean was land reform, cooperation, and the establishment of a broad-based form of labor organization that contained within it the seeds of modern industrial unionism.[63] Many of these reform ideas were initially generated in the United States and then traveled to Europe, instead of the other way around.[64]

The basis of this new transatlantic protest movement was fear of monopoly in the control of industry and land. The land and trust issues were both addressed by Henry George in his *Progress and Poverty* (1879), a book that was read in Britain, including southwest Scotland, almost as widely as it was in America. Indeed, at one point Keir Hardie stated that it was Henry George's idea of a single tax on land, and the popular lecture tours of Scotland and Ireland George undertook in 1882 and 1884, that set him on the road to socialism.[65]

In downstate Illinois, which aside from its mining industry was almost exclusively agricultural, the desire for land reform also intensified the movement to reserve public lands for settlers only rather than turn them over to railroads and private speculators. This call was taken up by the Knights of Labor and in the mid-1890s by the Populists, who coupled it with a demand for the nationalization of telegraphs, railroads, and mines.[66] In the Scottish coalfields the desire for land reform had a somewhat different thrust. It grew out of the anger of those colliers whose employers had sometimes refused to grant them wage increases because they owed mineral royalties to aristocratic lairds such as the duke of Hamilton. In 1884, for example, the issue of corporate wealth led the Irish land reformer Michael Davitt, who had a large following on both sides of the Atlantic, to found the Miners' National Labour League in Scotland. Its purpose was to campaign for the nationalization of mines and mineral royalties, as well as for state insurance for colliers injured in accidents.[67]

After these popular reform ideas had become known to the colliers in both countries, the issue arose of what impact they would have on the miners' attitudes toward independent labor politics. This question became particularly significant in Scotland after the passage of the Third Reform Act of 1884. This act added more than two hundred thousand voters to the franchise, including several thousand colliers. Although it still excluded large numbers of lodgers (a category that included many single miners),[68] it incorporated significant numbers of colliers into the body politic for the first time. Voting miners were now numerous enough in Lanarkshire to exercise an important influence in at least three newly established parliamentary constituencies: Mid-Lanark, Lanark North-East, and Lanark North-West. What would they do with their votes?

At first it seemed as though the Scottish colliers would make use of their newly won votes to press for independent political action more rapidly than their fellow miners in northern Illinois did. After acting as the Greenback mayor of Braidwood in 1877–78, for example, Daniel McLaughlin went on to serve a term in the Illinois General Assembly—but as a Republican. In fact, of the eleven miners who were elected to Springfield from the state's mining counties between 1874 and 1911, only one was an independent. The rest took their seats as either Democrats or Republicans.[69] This did not necessarily mean that they were conservative in their outlook. Besides proposing new mining laws, these miners' representatives favored other reform measures, such as factory legislation, eight-hour laws, and the exemption of unions from court-mandated injunctions.[70] As yet, however, the Illinois miners as a whole showed little inclination to step outside the existing two-party system.

In Lanarkshire, by contrast, the growth of collectivist ideas that resulted from the revival of British socialism in the 1880s, coupled with the surge of electoral activity that followed the passage of the 1884 Reform Act, spurred the founding of a small but significant social democratic movement. Besides Robert Smillie of Larkhall and Keir Hardie as secretary of the LCMU, its most important leader was William Small, a former Cambuslang draper turned socialist whose cottage at Blantyre became the venue for discussions of the mining question with such luminaries of the early socialist movement as William Morris, Henry Hyndman, and Edward Carpenter. In the 1885 general election Small urged the miners who could vote not to support any Liberal candidate who was an iron or coal master and to vote instead for other, more progressive Liberals. A year later William Small succeeded Keir Hardie as secretary of the LCMU. A branch of Henry Hyndman's Marxist Social Democratic Federation was also established in Glasgow about this time. Its main propagandists in the coalfield were J. Bruce Glasier and Andreas Scheu.[71]

The most important breakthrough, however, came in March 1888, when Keir Hardie stood as an independent labor candidate in a by-election (special election) at Mid-Lanark, a parliamentary constituency that contained all three Scottish mining towns discussed here. He ran on an overtly statist program that included compulsory arbitration, an eight-hour law, state-funded insurance and pensions for the miners, and a ministry of mines. Keir Hardie came at the bottom of the poll, receiving only 617 ballots to the victorious Liberal candidate's 3,647. But his independent stand, coming at a time when socialist ideas were gaining credence across the United Kingdom, alarmed the local Liberals and sent a shock wave through the British political establishment. Three months later, in August 1888, Keir Hardie, along with R. B. Cunninghame Graham and other key Scottish radicals, founded the Scottish Labour Party, with its headquarters in Glasgow. Tiny though it was, it secured the political support of at least some of the Lanarkshire miners.[72]

No such clear collectivist outcome resulted from the next phase of political endeavor in Illinois. The major U.S. third-party movement of the early 1890s was the People's Party, a farm-labor movement that appealed primarily to poor farmers in the South and West, not to the urban working class. Miners were not urban workers, however, and some elements of the Populist program held considerable appeal for them. Its Omaha platform of 1892, for example, included a demand for the nationalization of both the railroads and the mines.[73] Since absentee-owned railroad and mining corporations were the two largest employers in the small coal towns of downstate Illinois, any political effort that sought to exert public control over these two industrial giants was bound to create interest.

As a consequence, in 1894, at the height of the industrial depression, efforts were made to fashion a political alliance between the Socialist Labor Party, the Chicago trade union movement, and the disaffected miners and farmers of downstate Illinois. Although the Knights of Labor, which had earlier counted the miners among its most loyal supporters,[74] had by now declined drastically, its legacy of antimonopolistic ideas served as a bridge between each of the other groups that made up the Populist coalition. The Illinois State Federation of Labor called a strategy-planning conference for July 2, 1894, in Springfield. It was held in the midst of the Pullman strike, when Eugene Debs's American Railway Union — an industrial trade union like the UMWA — was being crushed by federal troops.[75] Even though conservative craft unionists from Chicago refused to accept the Marxist elements in the SLP program, Progressive social reformer Henry Demarest Lloyd's compromise proposal for a joint Labor-Populist ticket in the fall 1894 elections was adopted. Ever since the 1889 Spring Valley miners' strike, whose cause he had championed in *A Strike of Millionaires against Miners,* Lloyd had been a hero to the colliers.[76]

There was other evidence of a movement to the left among the miners of district 12 during 1894. In April, for example, just before the miners' national strike began, the UMWA national convention adopted in toto Chicago machinist Thomas J. Morgan's political program favoring independent political action, which was modeled in part on Keir Hardie's just-established Independent Labour Party in Britain. After the strike failed, the condition of the unemployed colliers in many of the Illinois mining counties became so bad that district 12 secretary-treasurer W. J. Guyman predicted in all seriousness that unless conditions improved, a revolutionary outbreak might occur.[77] Guyman himself became a Populist for a time, as did district 12 president J. A. Crawford. In November 1894, departing from his usual practice of endorsing sympathetic Democratic and Republican candidates, Crawford ran as a congressional candidate in Springfield on the joint Labor-Populist ticket.

During the fall 1894 campaign, Henry Demarest Lloyd — who admired the ILP's efforts to create a third party in Britain — also sought to update America's labor republican tradition by identifying it with the non-Marxist ideas of the British Fabians. Although these ideas came primarily from a group of English intellectuals, the gradualist social ideas of the English Fabians attracted the interest of at least some of the miners on both sides of the Atlantic. In addition, Lloyd urged his audiences to read the works of utopian writers Edward Bellamy and Laurence Gronlund, whose ideas were also popular in Great Britain.[78]

When the November 1894 election results were declared, however, the Illinois Labor-Populist ticket garnered few votes. In a few northern Illinois mining counties, the miners gave the ticket strong support. In Spring Valley, for example, 700 of the 973 votes cast for the Populists came from the colliers. Similar numbers were recorded in Streator, Braidwood, and Belleville. In the much larger city of Springfield, however, where few miners lived, district 12's president Crawford secured only 7 percent of the ballots, which was the same as the average Labor-Populist vote statewide. After the People's Party endorsed Democrat William Jennings Bryan for the presidency in 1896, save for the tiny Marxist SLP in Chicago, the independent political movement among Illinois workers ran out of steam.[79]

There were several reasons for this poor showing. In the South as well as in Colorado and the other Rocky Mountain states, where metal miners gave the Labor-Populist ticket strong support, approximately three hundred independent labor candidates initially entered the 1894 campaign.[80] This appeared to rebut Samuel Gompers' claim, which he made on behalf of the AFL, that official labor could not support the People's Party because it was composed "of employing farmers."[81] Nevertheless, as the election returns showed, despite their antimonopolist sympathies, the Populists were basically an agrarian debtor party that was hostile toward urban immigrants and suspicious of collectivism. Their strongest showing in downstate Illinois came in poor rural counties far from the main mining and industrial centers.[82] To make matters worse, even before the 1894 election, the Labor-Populist coalition was rent with ideological differences among the single-taxers, the Farmers Alliance, Chicago's conservative craft unionists (many of whom had strong ties to one or another of the two major parties), and the adherents of Thomas J. Morgan's socialist program. Plank 10 of this platform, which called for the collective ownership of industry, was unacceptable to the moderates.[83]

In this respect Thomas J. Morgan, despite his English background and his rejection of SLP national leader Daniel DeLeon's dogmatic sectarianism, proved to be a less skillful coalition builder than Keir Hardie was in Scotland. Despite his own collectivist views, Keir Hardie was always careful to draw the Lib-Labists along with him.[84] The organizational weakness of the Knights of Labor in downstate Illinois in the early 1890s was also a factor in the Labor-Populist debacle. The Knights of Labor, which had earlier included many district 12 members in its ranks, was the one body whose broad vision might possibly have provided the framework within which a viable labor-farmer political movement could have been born. As Leon Fink has shown, however, although the Knights supported third-party candidates when it suited them to do so, they were not ideologically committed to a separate working-class party.[85]

Nonetheless, the most obvious difference between the emerging social democratic movement in Scotland and the radical ferment in Illinois during this period was the Illinois miners' suspicious attitude toward the state's role in labor matters. Most industrial workers in Lanarkshire were by now fairly willing to invoke the government to redress the imbalance of power that had developed between themselves and the local iron magnates and coal owners, whereas the Illinois miners were much more hesitant. This difference showed up in the program the Knights of Labor put forward in Lanarkshire during their brief appearance among the miners there in the late 1880s, for it contained more statist proposals than did the one the organization issued in Illinois. The Sons of Labor in Scotland (the name the Knights of Labor adopted there) called for a graduated income tax, a national insurance fund, a "state rent" on land, and nationalization of the mines. The Illinois Knights, by contrast, endorsed only the nationalization of the mines.[86] The skepticism that most U.S. labor leaders entertained toward the idea of state control over industry at this time was expressed by William C. Pomeroy, leader of the Chicago craft unionists, during the course of a debate over the SLP's Marxist program that took place during the 1894 election campaign. Vigorously rejecting plank 10 of the Morgan platform, he stated that "the state was a worse taskmaster than the industrialists."[87] When they came to power later on, the radicals in district 12 of the UMWA did display a growing interest in the idea of mine nationalization, but this made them somewhat exceptional in the U.S. labor movement. Because they formed a part of the voluntarist majority in the AFL, the Chicago craft unionists were far more typical of the American trade union movement as a whole.[88]

Did the Illinois miners' failure to help establish a farmer-labor party in the mid-1890s mean that they had abandoned all efforts at independent labor politics? Did the founding of the Scottish Labour Party and the Keir Hardie by-election in Lanarkshire mean that the victory of socialism among the Scottish colliers was now assured? The answer to both of these questions is no. That kind of determinism is one of the most misleading aspects of the exceptionalist case.

For one thing, the boost given to the social democratic movement in Lanarkshire by the Mid-Lanark by-election and by the founding of the Scottish Labour Party in 1888 turned out to be somewhat fleeting. Like the Labor-Populists in the U.S. Midwest, instead of gaining momentum, the Scottish Labour Party failed to establish itself as a significant political force. This failure was partly due to the feebleness of the so-called new unionist movement in Glasgow at this time, partly due to the overall weakness of the trade union movement throughout Scotland, and partly due to an outbreak of sectarian quarreling in the socialists' own camp that was almost as damaging as the one that helped to destroy the Labor-Populist alliance in Illinois.[89]

New unionism was a movement toward general, rather than craft-based, unionism that in England proved later on to be an important building block for the establishment of the Labour Party. In Scotland, however, it never put down the same roots, despite major strikes on the Glasgow docks and by Lanarkshire's railwaymen in 1889 and 1891, respectively. As for sectarian quarreling, Keir Hardie became jealous because of an LCMU move to have William Small, rather than himself, appointed to a royal commission on mining royalties. He also quarreled with Chisholm Robertson, a Stirlingshire miners' leader who threatened to set up a rival miners' union in the east of Scotland and make it independent of Glasgow. As a result, when the 1892 general election came around, the Scottish Labour Party was hopelessly weak. It put forward very few candidates, and none of them won. Its remnants were absorbed into the ILP the following year.[90]

It is true that in Lanarkshire itself the forces of the Left were better prepared when, in April 1894, a second opportunity arose to run an independent labor candidate for Parliament in the mining constituency of Mid-Lanark. This time the candidate was ILP member Robert Smillie, the recently elected president of the Scottish Miners Federation. Because of his long-standing leadership of the Larkhall miners' union, Smillie was probably even better known in the Mid-Lanark constituency than Keir Hardie was. Besides enjoying the SMF's support, he received the endorsement of the powerful Glasgow Trades Council, as well as of John Cronin, the leader of the steelworkers union in Wishaw.[91]

Nevertheless, Smillie got only 1,221 votes, or 13 percent of the total, only a few percent more than Hardie had received in 1888. James Caldwell, the Liberal Party victor, received 3,965, or 45 percent of the ballots.[92] The basic problem was the strong support that most coal miners continued to give to the Liberal Party, which for many years had seen itself—and was seen by others—as the legitimate representative of the Scottish working class. Following the promulgation of the so-called Newcastle program by the Liberal

Party in 1892, such miners' proposals as the demand for state control over mineral royalties could still be contained within the framework of Gladstonian liberalism.[93]

If anything, indeed, support for the Liberal Party among the Lanarkshire colliers grew still stronger in the late 1880s and early 1890s as a result of Prime Minister William Gladstone's endorsement of Irish home rule in 1886. Although this move cost the Liberals the support of many skilled, Ulster-born Protestant miners and steelworkers in places such as Wishaw, who tended to favor either the Conservatives or the Liberal Unionists, the loss was more than offset by the acquisition of the Catholic Irish miners, who gave the Liberal Party their virtually unanimous support. For example, Michael Davitt, the head of the United Irish League, who had been sympathetic to Keir Hardie in 1888 even though he refused to endorse him, openly opposed Smillie's candidacy in 1894. He supported the Liberal Party over Irish home rule instead. In addition, because he was an Ulster Protestant (a category whose members generally favored Ireland's continued attachment to the British Crown), Smillie failed to secure the support of the Scottish Home Rule Association.[94]

All this enabled the Mid-Lanark Liberal Association, which had been thoroughly alarmed by Keir Hardie's break with the party in 1888, to breathe a collective sigh of relief. Like the Liberals throughout most of Britain, it regarded the Lib-Lab insurgency as a temporary difficulty that could be overcome by some fairly minor adjustments in the party's program. The Liberals "sympathised with the claims of the Labour Party," the association's leadership declared in June 1894. "But if the Labour Party were proud or conceited enough not to act through the Liberal Association they [the Liberals] could afford to ignore them and fight them to the last ditch."[95]

All in all, the first forty years of political activity by the miners in the Lanarkshire and the Illinois coalfields yielded somewhat ambiguous results. The leaders of both groups of colliers, sharing similar political aims, began with a similar political policy: pressuring their respective legislatures for mine safety laws and other labor legislation. In 1874 Alexander McDonald had been elected to Parliament as a Lib-Labist M.P., an office he retained until his death in 1881. But he was elected by an English constituency as a spokesperson for labor in general. His role in Parliament tells us little about the political opinions of the Lanarkshire miners as such. The Illinois miners, also, despite two brief ventures into third-party politics via the Greenbackers in 1878 and the Populists in 1894, showed no consistent desire to break with the two-party system. The parting of the transatlantic political ways had not yet seriously begun.

8

MOVING IN TANDEM TO THE LEFT?
SOCIALISM AND THE COLLIERS, 1900–1914

In January 1900 the Scottish Workers Parliamentary Committee, which was the functional equivalent of the Labour Party in England, was founded. Eighteen months later, in July 1901, the Socialist Party of America was established. The founding of these two organizations fundamentally altered the terms of the debate over independent labor politics in both Britain and America. Now the issue for activist colliers in Lanarkshire and Illinois was not limited to how and when to lobby for mining laws or whether to put up political candidates of their own at the local level. It was whether, and under what circumstances, to give their electoral support to a newly established political party of labor.[1]

The leaders of both the infant Labour Party and the SPA knew that if they were to have a real chance to break into the two-party system in their respective countries, they had to secure a mass trade union base. The AFL had rejected the socialist call for a separate labor party in 1894. Its leaders, from federation president Samuel Gompers on down, were for the most part hostile to the socialists on both ideological and pragmatic grounds. Instead, from the turn of the century onward, the AFL followed an official policy of nonpartisanship, although in practice it leaned increasingly towards the Democrats.[2] The fledgling Labour Party, by contrast, secured the affiliation of unions representing 325,000 English workers at its founding conference in 1900.[3] It thus seemed at first sight as though it would have a significant advantage over the SPA in the struggle to secure organized labor's vote.

In practice, however, this advantage was not as great as it appeared. The

English unions that initially affiliated with the Labour Party represented only one-eighth of the membership of the Trades Union Congress. Most of the other unions, including giants such as the MFGB and the textile unions concentrated in the north of England, either remained aloof from the new party or actively opposed it. Despite the Taff Vale court decision of 1901, which declared unions liable for civil damages resulting from strikes, not simply the miners but also the great majority of British workers who could vote at this time remained loyal to the Liberals.[4] In America, however, although the SPA did not receive the endorsement of any U.S. national unions at its founding convention, it did receive electoral support from a large minority of workers in organizations such as the International Association of Machinists, the ILGWU, the Brewery Workers Union, and the Western Federation of Miners.[5]

Under these circumstances securing the votes of the coal miners became a task of paramount importance for both the Labour Party in Britain and the Socialist Party of America in the United States. With almost a half-million members each, the MFGB and the UMWA were the two largest trade unions in the English-speaking world. It has been estimated that by 1910 miners provided over 10 percent of the total vote in no fewer than eighty-six parliamentary seats in South Wales, the English Midlands, and southwest Scotland.[6] In the three key Lanarkshire parliamentary constituencies, the percentage of voting colliers was even higher.[7] Similar numbers of politically active miners were concentrated in the mining counties of Pennsylvania, Alabama, Ohio, West Virginia, and Illinois.[8] Given their widespread concentration in specific geographical areas, it is no exaggeration to say that coal miners had a greater potential to influence the future of labor politics in Britain and America than did any other group of workers.

Given their potential political clout, then, how did the miners approach the subject of labor politics after 1900? How, too, did the newly emerging factor of syndicalism—or the demand for direct action at the pithead rather than parliamentary action at the ballot box—affect the ongoing process of class formation in the two countries? In the light of their common industrial grievances, did the miners of Lanarkshire and Illinois move together in tandem toward the political Left? Or did they show a tendency to move in opposite political directions in the years leading up to World War I?

As previously noted, it seemed likely, on the face of it, that in the race for miners' votes the Labour Party would have a decided advantage over the SPA not only at the national level but also in the coalfields of Lanarkshire and Illinois. Despite the opposition from anticollectivists, Lib-Labs, and even some Tories among Britain's miners, by 1914 most members of the MFGB's national executive board were radicals or socialists of one kind of another. In 1912 the LCMU's Robert Smillie — who had for some years been president of the Scottish Miners Federation — was elected head of the MFGB.[9] By this time, too, most members of the LCMU's executive board were Labour Party supporters, including David Gilmour, Joseph Sullivan (a Catholic miner of Irish descent), and county agents such as John Robertson and Duncan Graham. Most of these men later became Labour M.P.s.[10]

In the UMWA, however, the picture was much more mixed. President John Mitchell, who led the national union between 1899 and 1908, was an open advocate of free-enterprise capitalism. At one point friendly with Republican president Theodore Roosevelt, in 1908 he was briefly considered for the U.S. vice presidency on the Democratic ticket. In the following years Mitchell, who had many friends among the Illinois miners, became embroiled in a bitter quarrel with the socialists because of his role in the business-oriented National Civic Federation. Despite a potential for radicalization, many of the recently arrived new European immigrants who worked as machine miners in the company towns of eastern states such as Pennsylvania tended to vote as their employers and the local political machines directed them, if they voted at all. Black miners in places such as West Virginia, however, voted Republican.[11]

The socialists commanded more influence in Illinois district 12 than they did in any other state. Besides John H. Walker, socialists such as Duncan MacDonald, Adolph Germer, and Frank J. Hayes at one time or another were elected to statewide office. Nevertheless, they never secured a majority on the district executive board, and they were frequently opposed by conservatives such as Frank Farrington. In the northern part of the state many colliers continued to vote Republican, while in Little Egypt most remained faithful to the Democrats.[12]

In addition, the rural character of downstate Illinois and the isolated location of many coal camps seemed to make them less inviting targets for the socialists than the densely populated, mixed industry towns that covered much of the Clyde Valley. In places such as Wishaw, Motherwell, and Airdrie, miners from the local pits now worked as part of a mixed labor force that included workers toiling in nearby iron foundries, machine shops, and steel mills. Glasgow, too, with its small but burgeoning socialist movement, was much nearer — both culturally and geographically — to the Lanarkshire

mining towns than the cosmopolitan socialists of Chicago were to the isolated mining camps of central and southern Illinois.[13] As if all this were not
enough, in the spring of 1908 two further steps were taken — one in Lanarkshire, the other in Illinois district 12 — that appeared to increase the lead the
Scottish socialists had taken over their U.S. counterparts. These steps seemed
to rule out any likelihood that Illinois district 12 would give any significant
electoral support to the SPA.

The first step was taken in May 1908, when the MFGB as a whole voted to
affiliate with the British Labour Party. The vote in Scotland was 32,112 in favor
of affiliation and 25,823 against.[14] The second step — apparently contrary to
the first — was taken in June 1908, when district 12 of the UMWA voted to
join the nonpartisan Illinois State Federation of Labor.[15] These two moves
appeared to put district 12 and the LCMU on two quite different political
tracks. On the one hand, the Scottish miners, like the MFGB as a whole, were
now committed — officially, at least — to supporting the Labour Party's candidates for political office. The automatic checkoff of the Lanarkshire miners'
union dues in support of the Scottish Workers Parliamentary Committee
also gave the party a significant infusion of new funds. Hence the SWPC had
reason to hope that in future elections it would be able to draw disaffected
miners away from the Liberals and into the Labour camp. To put it another
way, once the MFGB had affiliated with the Labour Party, it seemed likely
that any new candidates the Labour Party put up in the Scottish mining constituencies would combine the previously separate Labour Party and Lib-Lab
votes into one solid bloc, thereby forming a united working-class front.[16]

On the other hand, district 12, by joining the Illinois State Federation of
Labor, appeared to commit itself to the AFL's nonpartisan policy of endorsing candidates of either major political party who agreed to support labor
legislation and of voting against those who opposed it. This was the celebrated "reward-your-friends, punish-your-enemies" political policy that the
AFL at first pursued seriously in the 1906 congressional elections.[17] For some
time Illinois district 12 had maintained its own legislative committee to lobby
for improvements to the Illinois state mining code.[18] Now, by linking itself
publicly to the ISFL, it appeared to have taken a deliberate step away from independent labor politics and to have reinforced its commitment to working
for reform within the existing two-party system.

Nor was this all. In 1909, shortly after affiliating with the ISFL, district 12
took another step away from class-based politics when it joined with the Illinois Coal Operators Association and Republican governor Charles Deneen
to create the Mining Investigation Commission. This was a bipartisan body

consisting of three miners, three coal operators, and three disinterested members of the public charged with preparing amendments to the Illinois state mining code and submitting them to the General Assembly for legislative action. Only legislation on which the commission unanimously agreed was submitted to the assembly, and it was usually passed without much discussion. For example, in its first year the Mining Investigation Commission proposed that fire-fighting equipment be stationed at all Illinois mines. Later on the commission successfully proposed a number of other amendments to the state's mining code.[19] Disagreements between the miners and the mine owners sometimes occurred in the commission's meetings. But by thrashing out these differences behind closed doors, the commission removed decisions about mining laws from the kind of public debate that took place in the House of Commons and thus prevented the socialists from exposing the true class interests of the coal operators.

The leaders of the socialist faction in district 12 feared that these new steps would disguise the nature of the growing class struggle between the union and the Illinois Coal Operators Association and deter union members from supporting the Socialist Party ticket. At the district's 1910 convention, one of the most active leaders of the socialist faction, Duncan MacDonald, criticized the union's new link with the Mining Investigation Commission on just these grounds. He poured scorn on the backroom deals that were negotiated between ISFL lobbyists and members of the state legislature and expressed his concern that district 12's own legislative committee would be corrupted by the "Chicago gang of craft leaders in blue suits who hang around the Springfield bars." District 12 should employ "another method than that of begging at the State House door," MacDonald stated. It should abandon old party wheeling and dealing and follow the independent path of the British Labour Party. MacDonald argued: "District 12's members should go into the political arena and secure for their own members and other workers these positions of trust by way of the ballot box, as our brothers across the sea have been doing for some time past." His proposal was defeated by 133 votes to 84.[20]

When put into comparative perspective, therefore, it seemed likely that the LCMU's 1908 decision to affiliate with the Labour Party would commit the Scottish miners to independent labor politics, whereas the miners of district 12 — because of their decision to join the nonpartisan ISFL — would doom the SPA to failure in the Illinois coalfields. Such, however, did not turn out to be the case. To the contrary, in the opening years of the twentieth century, the advocates of independent political action in Lanarkshire failed signally to attract more than a small minority of colliers to the Labour Party's cause. The Socialist Party of America, on the other hand, did much better among the colliers of Illinois district 12 than the preceding analysis suggests it would.

To prove this claim, it is necessary first to take a careful look at the fortunes of the Labour Party in Lanarkshire between 1900 and 1910 and then to compare them with the record of the SPA in the coalfields of Illinois. Soon after it was founded in January 1900, the Scottish Workers Parliamentary Committee adopted a platform that the colliers found quite attractive. It included old-age pensions, the nationalization of mining royalties, and increased taxation on "Land Values and . . . other forms of Unearned Income."[21] The last proposal was a popular idea, since it was aimed partly at the local Lanarkshire lairds such as the duke of Hamilton, on whose estates many miners still lived. The SWPC then nominated candidates to run in the next general election in all three of Lanarkshire's mining constituencies: Mid-Lanark, Lanark North-East, and Lanark North-West. The first one of these to become vacant was Lanark North-East, where Robert Smillie was again chosen to run as Labour's representative against both a Tory and a Liberal-Unionist candidate in a by-election set for September 1901.[22]

In 1901 Smillie seemed to have a much better chance of getting elected in Lanark North-East than he had at Mid-Lanark in 1894. Besides anticipating the support of the miners in the constituency, he secured the endorsement of the Steel Smelters Union, which was strong in places such as Motherwell, Airdrie, and Craigneuk. Still more advantageous was the fact that his Liberal-Unionist rival for the seat was the well-known imperialist Cecil Harmsworth, a man who supported continuing union between England and Ireland even though he favored progressive social policies. Harmsworth's hostility toward Irish home rule seemed likely to throw a large number of the constituency's Irish miners into the Labour camp. During the course of the campaign Smillie received the endorsement of the United Irish League, and several nationalist leaders from the Irish Parliamentary Party spoke on his behalf.[23]

As it turned out, however, Smillie was soundly defeated, coming in again at the bottom of the poll. The same thing happened in Lanark North-East in August 1904, when LCMU agent John Robertson ran for the same seat. Still more disconcerting was the outcome of the general election of 1906. In this contest, which in England saw Labour get twenty-seven of its candidates elected as M.P.s (as well as two in Scotland) and assert its independence as a separate political party, the LCMU contested no fewer than five parliamentary seats, more than any other county miners' union in the whole of Great

Britain.[24] The result was a disaster. In Lanarkshire all three of the union's candidates—John Robertson in Lanark North-East, Joseph Sullivan in Lanark North-West, and David Gilmour in Falkirk Burghs—again came in last behind both the Tories and the Liberals.[25]

The Labour candidates' failures to do better in southwest Scotland between 1901 and 1906 could no longer be blamed on the weakness of the miners' union, as it could after Smillie's defeat in Mid-Lanark in 1894. By 1906 the LCMU, which in 1894 had only about 8,000 members, included 26,482 paid-up miners in its ranks.[26] Part of the problem was organizational. In 1902, partly in response to Smillie's defeat the year before, the SWPC had been replaced by the Scottish Workers Representation Committee, a body that was supposed to provide improved logistical support for Labour candidates in Scotland. No sooner had the SWRC been formed, however, than a number of internal problems arose. One was that under the SWRC's rules (which differed from those of the Labour Party in England), financial contributions made to it by union members were designated as voluntary rather than compulsory (i.e., there was no pithead checkoff for the political payment of union dues). This resulted in more limited funds for election expenses than had been expected.[27]

After 1906 it seemed as though this setback would be canceled by gains that local Labour candidates, supported usually by a coalition consisting of radical trade unionists, ILP activists, and cooperative society leaders, made at the municipal level. In the municipal elections of 1907, for example, David Gilmour was elected to the town council in the LCMU headquarters city of Hamilton. Parish council gains were also made at Blantyre, Bellshill, Overton, Summerlee, and Stonehouse—places where the miners were heavily concentrated.[28] At the school board elections of March 1909, new seats were won in Blantyre, Cambuslang, Rutherglen, Bothwell, and Wishaw. In Wishaw a new recreation center was built with funds raised by the local ILP, and vigorous propaganda activity, including sales of John Wheatley's pro-socialist *Catholic Working Man* pamphlet, attempted to offset the antisocialist speeches of the so-called socialist smasher Father Puissant.[29] Father Puissant's vigorous antisocialist speeches during the course of the campaign show that the Catholic church was as fierce an opponent of socialism in Lanarkshire as it was in the United States.

Further progress was made when LCMU agent Duncan Graham discovered that through a tacit agreement between the local Liberal and Conservative Parties (who controlled the electoral registration process), the rental qualification for the lodger vote in the Mid-Lanark constituency had been set at £6 rather than the £2 rental value mandated by the Reform Act of 1884.

This rental qualification disqualified large numbers of miner-lodgers from voting. Graham exposed the agreement between the Tory and Liberal Parties, and he went on to challenge the whole basis of lodger representation under the current registration law, insisting that the rental value requirement be lowered. It is not possible to say exactly how many new colliers were added to the electoral rolls in Lanarkshire as a result of Duncan Graham's endeavors. Nevertheless, by 1913 their number was estimated to have increased thirteen-fold.[30] Each of these advances increased the self-confidence of the Labour Party in the Lanarkshire mining towns and provided its parliamentary candidates with an improved organizational base from which to work.

Hence when a new British general election was called in January 1910, the LCMU entertained high hopes not just of improving on its dismal showing in 1906 but of making a decisive breakthrough. Robert Smillie entered the lists once more in the miners' flagship constituency of Mid-Lanark. Joseph Sullivan also ran again, this time for Lanark North-East, and Lanark North-West was contested by Robert Small, a Harthill miners' agent who was a member of the left-wing Social Democratic Federation. Once again, however, the Labour Party's candidates were soundly defeated. In the mining constituency of East Fife, William Adamson was elected as the first Scottish miner's M.P., but this was poor compensation for the losses in the more densely populated Lanarkshire coalfield, where, as in 1906, all three Labour candidates came in at the bottom of the poll. Even Smillie could muster only about 25 percent of the vote. The setback was so serious that when a second British general election was called in December 1910, the LCMU lacked the heart to contest anything more than Mid-Lanark. The result was still another disaster. Not only did Smillie again come in last; he secured even fewer votes than he had in the January contest.[31]

These new defeats in Lanarkshire took place, it should be noted, against a background in which the Labour Party was continuing to make significant progress in England. Between 1906 and 1910 the party raised its representation in Parliament from twenty-nine to forty M.P.s and increased its trade union membership by more than one-third. Most of these successes took place in parliamentary constituencies where, under an agreement between the Labour and Liberal Parties, no Liberal ran in seats where a Labour candidate was standing, hence permitting a straight contest between the Labour and Tory candidates. This agreement was not always observed, however, and in 1907 the Labour Party scored a significant victory when it won the Colne and Jarrow by-elections against both Tory and Liberal opposition. Although the Labour Party continued to vote with the governing Liberal Party in the

House of Commons on most issues, it was slowly beginning to establish its own political identity.[32]

What had gone wrong? Why did the long-awaited Labour Party breakthrough fail to occur in 1910 even in Mid-Lanark, over twenty years after Keir Hardie's initial challenge to the Liberals, and in a constituency that—with the possible exception of West Yorkshire and South Wales—seemed to offer Labour candidates their best chance of winning anywhere in Great Britain? Besides organizational difficulties, a number of other reasons can be cited.

First of all, there were ongoing disagreements both inside and outside the coalition that made up the political Left in Scotland. These internal disagreements included quarrels between the ILP and the SDF, a strict Marxist body comparable to the American SLP that attacked the Labour Party for being excessively reformist. Local Labour Parties in several mining constituencies also failed to maintain an adequate level of organization between elections. In addition, there was the arrogant behavior of several LCMU leaders who tended to insist that only miners should be nominated as parliamentary candidates in the three main Lanarkshire constituencies, even though there were other elements of the Labour Party coalition to be considered.[33]

At this time the Labour Party experienced another set of internal difficulties that adversely affected its fortunes in the Lanarkshire coalfield. The most serious of these was a disagreement over the proper allocation of funds between the English and the Scottish branches of the party. Some Scottish trade unions with headquarters in England paid their political contributions to the Labour Party in London. Others, however, paid them to the SWRC in Edinburgh. To make more money available for elections north of the border, the SWRC asked Labour leaders not to levy dues on the Scottish members of their affiliated unions. The national secretary in London, however, wanted to follow the opposite policy—to require the Scottish unions to affiliate with, and pay their political dues to, the party office in London. The resulting quarrel, which dragged on for years, caused personal bitterness and cut back further on the funds available to the Scottish Labourites.[34] Another financial problem arose as a result of the Osborne Judgement of 1908. Handed down by the high court, that decision declared it illegal for unions automatically to deduct money from workers' pay for the Labour Party's political fund.[35]

More important than any of these internal difficulties, however, was the continuing grip that the Liberal Party and its ideas exerted on large sections of the Scottish (as well as the English) working class. There were several reasons for this. The basic point is that, despite the official connection that had been established between the LCMU and the Labour Party as a result of the affiliation vote in 1908, most Scottish miners still felt themselves under no obligation to vote Labour.[36] Many of them saw the agreement as being between Labour and the official MFGB national leaders, not one that necessarily committed the rank and file. But there were also ongoing ideological doubts. As in America, there was in the Scottish trade union movement a strong tradition of hostility toward government intervention in economic affairs. Hence socialist ideas, even those propounded by relatively moderate ILP leaders such as Robert Smillie and Keir Hardie, were still dubious in the eyes of the Lib-Lab element on the LCMU executive board.[37]

Consequently, Labour Party leaders in London ran into trouble in the years after 1908 when they tried to coerce the ten or so remaining Lib-Labist M.P.s in Parliament, several of whom were miners, into abandoning their Liberal Party connections and committing themselves fully to Labour. Several of these old-style Lib-Labs, indeed, including Charles Fenwick of Northumberland and John Wilson of Durham, refused point blank to sign the Labour Party's constitution because of its socialist content.[38] These men also had a following in Scotland. In addition, many Scottish colliers feared that voting Labour in a three-way electoral contest including a Liberal would split the working-class vote and let a hated Tory landowner or aristocrat into Parliament. This fear paradoxically grew stronger as the Labour Party itself gained strength.

Finally, there was the positive record of the Liberal government of 1906–10, as well as the ongoing appeal to the Lanarkshire miners of several important elements in the Liberal Party's traditional philosophy, including free trade and unemployment insurance. In some respects the record of the 1906–10 Liberal government was disappointing, given the large majority it enjoyed in the House of Commons. By the January 1910 election, however, it had passed the Trades Disputes Act (1906), which restored the trade unions' legal immunity from civil suits, and it had adopted a wide range of social reform measures ranging from old-age pensions to the eight-hour day in the mines.[39] Influenced by the "new Liberalism" of David Lloyd George, Liberal candidates in several of the Lanarkshire mining constituencies also advocated reforms that were popular among the colliers. In the January 1910 election in Lanark North-West, for example, Liberal candidate W. M. R. Pringle pulled votes away from the Labour candidate by favoring the nationalization of land values and railways.[40] At Mid-Lanark ten months later, Liberal candidate J. M. Whitehouse cut into Smillie's support when he came out in support of a new mines act and state arbitration in industrial disputes.[41]

More generally, the Liberal Party in Scotland showed a remarkable ability to retain the loyalty of workingmen in a wide variety of trades, despite the fact that it continued to be dominated by leaders drawn almost exclusively from the middle class. Social deference probably played a role here. In addition, Lloyd George's "People's Budget" of 1909, which imposed heavy new taxes on the rich, including landowners, was highly popular among those Lanarkshire miners who still saw men such as the duke of Hamilton as symbols of aristocratic oppression. When the budget's defeat in the House of Lords caused a constitutional crisis in the spring of 1910, most miners—like most other British workers—rallied behind the Liberal Party in its all-consuming struggle to limit the veto power of Parliament's upper house.[42]

In Lanarkshire this Liberal dominance was compounded by the ongoing issue of the Irish Catholic vote, which continued to tie this influential minority of colliers to the Liberal Party even more strongly than their Protestant fellows were bound to it. From Labour's point of view, at one level the Irish problem was simple. The Liberal Party, and the Liberal government that was in office from 1906 on, had the power to grant Ireland home rule. The Labour Party, which was a minority element in Parliament, did not. Hence Irish miners who set a high priority on home rule for Ireland were likely to vote Liberal even if they agreed with Labour on social and labor issues.[43] But the issue cut deeper than that. The divided Irish vote exposed the ongoing religious and cultural divide between the Orange and the Green, between Protestant and Catholic miners who—despite all their intermingling down the pit—still constituted two distinct political communities in most of the Lanarkshire coal towns. Many Protestant miners who tended to be anti-Catholic, or who opposed home rule for Ireland out of loyalty to the Crown, were likely to vote for Liberal Unionists such as Cecil Harmsworth, or even to vote Tory, rather than support Labour candidates such as Smillie. The Catholic element in the working class, however, was likely to vote for the Liberals on purely nationalist grounds, whomever the candidate was.[44]

Catholic miners who took seriously their parish priests' warnings about the atheistic implications of Marxism were also deterred from voting Labour on ideological grounds, just as Catholic miners who immigrated from southern and eastern Europe to the coalfields of downstate Illinois were deterred by their priests from voting for leftist parties. By 1906, however, fewer Irish colliers were ready to follow their church's conservative teachings on economic and political issues than had been so in earlier years. Most of them had now lived in the secular atmosphere of industrial Scotland and experienced the exhausting labor and dreadful housing conditions of its pit villages for more than two generations. Some of the Scots-Irish miners may also have been influenced toward radicalism by the rise of the militant, nationalistically oriented labor movement in Dublin and other Irish cities.[45] So by 1910 a growing minority of the Irish colliers, influenced by the views of Catholic socialist leader John Wheatley emanating from Glasgow, were willing to give the Labour Party's message a hearing instead of dismissing it out of hand.[46]

As World War I approached, however, and the debate over Irish home rule became even more heated,[47] both Protestant and Catholic colliers were subjected to still fiercer sectarian appeals. In the January 1910 election in Lanark North-East, for example, Tory candidate J. R. Wilson openly exploited the sectarian issue when he appealed for Protestant miners' votes at a meeting of the Orange Order in Bellshill. Before an audience containing many colliers, he declared himself "in favor of convent inspection, against carrying the Host in the streets, and . . . against any change in the King's oath."[48]

Sectarianism also prevented many Irish miners from voting Labour because United Irish League leaders expressed fears that, were they to endorse a Labour politician in a three-way contest between a Tory, a Liberal, and a Labour candidate in any of the Lanarkshire mining constituencies, the move would throw the election to an anti–home rule Tory. In the first 1910 election, for example, Keir Hardie, who was now a prominent Labour M.P.,[49] tried to gloss over nationalist divisions and unite the mining vote behind the Labour Party's local candidates. He expressed annoyance at the way in which the UIL had blindly endorsed the Liberals in all three Lanarkshire constituencies when, on economic and trade union matters, the interests of Protestant and Catholic miners were clearly the same. "The claims of the Irish people," Keir Hardie argued, "can only be won for them by the united action of the working class of Great Britain."[50] Nevertheless, this class argument was not yet convincing enough to make the Irish colliers abandon their support for the Liberals. The UIL responded to Keir Hardie's plea as follows: "To have sent it [the Irish vote] to Labour would have wasted it, and made a gift of all three seats to the Tories."[51]

Meanwhile, the Socialist Party of America did far better in the downstate Illinois mining counties in 1900–1914 than the earlier failure of third-party movements among miners would lead one to expect. One index of growing collier support was the socialist vote for state treasurer. In mining counties statewide, this rose more or less steadily from 5.91 percent in 1900 to 22.04 percent in 1912.[52] More telling was the vote for leading socialists running for office in Macoupin, Madison, and St. Clair Counties, where the largest numbers of radical miners were to be found. In the St. Clair County election of 1908, for example, Adolph Germer, who became national secretary of the

Socialist Party in 1916, received 11.68 percent of the vote when he ran against both a Republican and a Democratic opponent. In 1910 he raised this share to 31 percent. This was a higher figure than any miners' candidate had yet obtained in the three main Lanarkshire parliamentary constituencies. In that same year socialist Frank Hayes, who was to serve as president of the UMWA in 1917–19, got 24 percent of the vote when he ran for the General Assembly from Madison County.[53]

These totals were achieved despite the opposition of conservative district 12 leaders such as Secretary-Treasurer Frank Farrington, who attacked the socialists as "pie-in-the-sky aliens." Following the freewheeling, sometimes corrupt political practices of some others on the union's legislative committee, Farrington developed a habit of offering — without official authorization — district 12's endorsement to both Republican and Democratic candidates for local-level offices, sometimes in return for personal gain.[54] The rising socialist vote was also secured despite the disapproval of middle-class businesspeople and large-scale grain farmers, as well as of the Catholic priests in many of the downstate coal towns. Like the Catholic clergy among the Irish miners of Scotland, immigrant Catholic priests from southern and eastern Europe sought to insulate their recently arrived Slavic and Italian parishioners from any contact with the incubus of atheistic Marxism. Meeting in Staunton in June 1915, for example, the Macoupin County Catholic Federation passed a resolution urging "every Catholic [miner], . . . inasmuch as he is able, to oppose Socialism as generally taught by the Socialists."[55] Despite this warning, in Staunton's municipal elections that year socialist candidates averaged 25 percent of the local votes. In the spring of 1917 Louis Fickert, a tracklayer at Consolidated Mine No. 4, went on to win a seat on the city council as alderman for Staunton's second ward. Although Fickert was German, he secured quite a number of eastern European immigrant votes.[56]

In addition, the socialist vote in Illinois continued to grow despite the presence of another U.S. political movement that, though it took a form somewhat different from the "new Liberalism" then influencing British politics, nevertheless bore a strong resemblance to it. This was the Progressive movement, which exerted a major influence in both the Democratic and Republican Parties in the period before World War I. More urban than rural, the U.S. Progressive movement advocated many of the same democratic reforms and labor policies that Lloyd George's "new Liberalism" did in the United Kingdom. They included old-age pensions, workers' compensation, and removing legal disabilities from trade unions.[57] In downstate Illinois, by 1910 it seemed as though the Progressives might become strong enough to draw large numbers of radically inclined colliers away from the Socialist Party and cement their loyalty to the Progressive wing of one or the other of the two major parties.

Voting Progressive was particularly attractive to the older generation of Anglo-Saxon miners as well as to collier descendants of German Forty-Eighters in the St. Louis region. Both of these groups included miners who were repelled by the corrupt machine politics of men such as Farrington but could not quite bring themselves to vote for a putatively revolutionary party such as the SPA. These moderate radicals favored the direct election of senators, women's suffrage, and labor measures such as workmen's compensation laws. The SPA favored these proposals too, but Progressive candidates soon began to use what became known as the "wasted vote" argument to persuade labor voters to support them instead of the socialists.[58] In 1908 Hugo Kleckheimer, a stove-make and leader of the iron foundrymen's union in Belleville, urged the workingmen in his area, including the local miners, to vote for a Progressive Republican for the General Assembly instead of a socialist. To vote socialist, he said, would be to "ignore the realities of the day."[59]

This socialist-versus-Progressive dilemma also exercised the mind of UMWA district 12 president John H. Walker. Like Duncan MacDonald, Walker was a Scots-born ethical socialist of the Keir Hardie stripe.[60] He greatly admired the British Labour Party. Had it been left up to him, he, like Thomas J. Morgan and other moderates in the Chicago socialist movement, would have preferred to see a labor party of the British type established in the American Midwest rather than the ideologically more rigid SPA. By pursuing this vision Walker hoped to unify the labor and moderate reform vote. This preference can be seen in the various efforts he made to hold a referendum vote in the Illinois State Federation of Labor on the labor party question.[61]

Given his pragmatic bent, in 1908 Walker found himself torn between his desire to promote a separate labor party among the miners of district 12, on the one hand, and his practical wish to advance the miners' legislative agenda by supporting either the Progressives or favorably disposed politicians in one of the two major parties, on the other. In the November election of that year, Governor Charles Deneen, a Progressive Republican who had already been in the governor's mansion at Springfield for two years, came up for reelection. He had a prolabor record, having favored mine safety legislation, restrictions on the use of convict labor in factories, and other desirable measures. As a leading member of the Illinois Socialist Party, Walker should in theory have endorsed that party's nominee for state governor. Governor Deneen's opponent, however, Democratic nominee Adlai Stevenson, was a strong opponent of the United Mine Workers of America. So, to the irritation of more sectarian SPA leaders such as Adolph Germer, Walker endorsed Deneen for reelection.[62] As time went on, tensions between radicals who favored a labor party on the British model and socialists who preferred a social democratic party on German lines created increasing problems for the American Left.

On this matter, however, Walker and his labor party supporters appeared at this point to be a minority among the Illinois socialists. In the November 1912 elections, when Eugene Debs scored his highest vote for the U.S. presidency, the socialists did even better in the coal counties of downstate Illinois than they had in 1910. In that year a separate Progressive Party ticket, headed by former president Theodore Roosevelt, appeared on the Illinois ballot. Besides promoting antitrust legislation, the party advocated the vote for women, an eight-hour law, and a proposal to limit employers' use of antistrike injunctions against unions.[63] Nonetheless, Frank J. Hayes, running this time as a socialist in St. Clair County, received 38 percent of the vote, 12 percent more than his Progressive rival. Hayes lost only narrowly to the victorious Republican. Adolph Germer, who this time switched to Macoupin County, received 29 percent of the vote in his contest, again outscoring the Progressive.[64]

As in Lanarkshire, however, it was at the municipal level that the Socialist Party did best. Staunton was by no means the only coal-mining town in downstate Illinois to elect radicals to office in these years. Although details of their programs are scanty, thirteen coal towns are known to have elected socialist councilmen to office between 1908 and 1917. These places included Thayer and O'Fallon, in Macoupin and Madison Counties; Riverton, in Sangamon County; as well as Buckner and Herrin, in Williamson County.[65] The victories in the last two towns were significant, since the communities were located in culturally conservative Little Egypt, at the southern tip of Illinois. They show that the socialist surge was by no means confined to the coalfields in the central part of the state.[66]

In the 1916 elections, in the mining town of Mascoutah, two socialists joined a comrade already serving in city office. Similar results were obtained in Glen Carbon, as well as in the much larger coal town of Collinsville. Of the twelve socialist candidates who ran for office in Collinsville between 1915 and 1917, at least eight were coal miners. In Belleville, which possessed a more varied working class, four of eleven SPA candidates in the 1915 local elections were identified as miners.[67] Aside from intellectuals and other left-wing radicals, the main supporters of the Socialist Party in downstate Illinois appear to have been the so-called Old Immigrant workers, particularly German Americans and colliers from the British Isles. For instance, three Sauer brothers led the SPA ticket in Belleville in 1915, along with men with names such as Neuf, Wilson, McTavish, and Kniepkamp. Nevertheless, there are indications that more recent immigrants from southern and eastern Europe also gave some support. In Madison County native-born and German American socialists running for office were joined by men with Polish, Lithuanian, and Italian names.[68]

Little is known about relations between the advocates of socialism in district 12's coal towns and the small corn farmers in the surrounding countryside — no more than is known about parallel relations in southwest Scotland. The cultural and economic interests of the two groups were sometimes quite different, as the failure of the Populist-Labor alliance of 1894 showed. Nevertheless, it would be wrong to assume that miners and farmers in downstate Illinois could not be united behind a radical cause. One common enemy both groups still faced was the railroads, a factor not present in Scotland. Besides owning mining corporations, the railroad companies controlled local freight rates, which powerfully affected the local farmers' economic prospects. It should also be remembered that when Eugene Debs ran for president in 1908 and 1912, some of his highest totals were secured in the mixed lumber, rural, and coal-mining areas of Oklahoma and Texas.[69]

Hence, the Illinois Socialist Party platform included not only the nationalization of mines but also state ownership of grain elevators so as to mitigate the monopolistic control that the railroads tried to exert over the local prairie farmers' grain-marketing practices.[70] This reform was upheld earlier by the Populists as well. A list of those who purchased socialist newspapers in Macoupin County in 1909 shows that small-acre farmers, not miners, were the largest group of subscribers to the left-wing press. Colliers came second on the list, followed by railroad workers and skilled craftsman.[71]

Partly to counteract the growing influence of company-owned stores in the smaller Illinois mining towns, the consumers' cooperative movement also made rapid headway among the miners of district 12 in the pre–World War I years, just as it did in the mining towns of southwest Scotland. These stores were particularly valuable to the miners' wives. Because of their rural isolation, these women had even less choice of places to shop than the miners' wives did in the Lanarkshire coal towns. The largest number of retail cooperative stores were found in subdistricts 5, 7, and 9, which were also the main centers of socialist voting strength.[72] One of the earliest of these cooperative retail stores was established in Glen Carbon, in Madison County, in 1904. It was run by second-generation German and Scottish miners, the latter drawing on the traditions of retail cooperation they had brought from Scotland. Elements of a socialist counterculture could be found in the community activities provided by the Labor Temple in Staunton: stacks of groceries, miners' clothes, and dairy products filled the ground-floor co-op, and the second floor boasted a restaurant, a theater, a reading room, and a dance hall.[73]

By the time America entered World War I in April 1917, the Central States Cooperative Society, which was founded in East St. Louis in 1915, was operating over thirty such stores in the Illinois coalfields. Both John H. Walker and Duncan MacDonald admired this aspect of their native labor tradition. For a time Walker was president of the Central States Cooperative Society, and he used this position to persuade district 12 to invest its funds in the society, much as the LCMU did in the cooperative movement in Lanarkshire.[74]

By 1914 a significant socialist movement had grown up among the miners of Illinois district 12. At least in central Illinois, this movement bore a strong resemblance to the Labour Party movement that had emerged in the coal-mining towns of Lanarkshire. By this time the SPA had gained enough strength in the American Midwest to show that it was not a temporary, fly-by-night protest movement. It had put down genuine roots in the political life of the Illinois coal-mining communities, as can be seen in the retail cooperative stores it helped foster, in the support it gave local farmers in their efforts to acquire cooperatively owned grain elevators, and in the common cause it made with the railroad workers of the coal towns. For example, both miners and local socialists lent their support to the railroad shopcraft workers' strike that took place on the Illinois Central Railroad between 1911 and 1915.[75]

With the advantage of hindsight, it is easy to show that in 1914 the burgeoning U.S. socialist movement was about to enter a period of precipitous decline, whereas the British Labour Party was on the verge of making a dramatic leap upward. Between 1913 and 1916, for example, the SPA lost quite a lot of the nationwide electoral support it had garnered in previous years, in large part because of the Progressive reforms enacted by President Woodrow Wilson's first Democratic administration. These reforms included a 1913 law establishing the U.S. Department of Labor; the Clayton Act of 1914, which exempted unions from prosecution under the Sherman Antitrust Act; and the LaFollette Seaman's Act of 1915.[76]

Nonetheless, U.S. socialists were not unique in losing steam as a result of the Progressives' labor reforms; a similar slowdown could be detected in the Labour Party's electoral progress as a result of the "new Liberal" reforms that the Liberal Party's Lloyd George wing enacted in Great Britain. Because of World War I, no general election was held in the United Kingdom between

1910 and 1918, making it difficult to judge how well the Labour Party might have done among British miners had an election been held in these years. If by-elections (special elections) are any guide, however, they would not have done particularly well. In nearly all the by-elections that took place in Britain between 1910 and 1914, Labour continued to come in at the bottom of the poll. By 1914, in fact, after more than a dozen three-way contests among Tory, Liberal, and Labour candidates, several of which involved mining seats, Labour held fewer seats in Parliament than it had in 1910.[77]

Nonetheless, it would be going too far to conclude from this evidence that on the eve of World War I the SPA was in as strong an electoral position as the Labour Party was in Great Britain. By 1912 the SPA had elected approximately 1,200 municipal officials across the United States, among them seventy-nine mayors in twenty-four states. It had also voted thirty state legislators into office. But the party had elected only one candidate to the House of Representatives.[78] By this time the Labour Party had nearly forty M.P.s in the House of Commons. Also, despite its stand-pat position in Parliament, Labour had managed by this time to secure the financial and institutional support of its country's trade union movement on a scale that the SPA was never able to match.[79]

In addition to possessing an established bloc of M.P.s, moreover, the Labour Party now had a more extensive network of local party branches in the main Lanarkshire coal towns than the SPA did anywhere in Illinois, save possibly St. Clair County, east of St. Louis. Union support for Labour in Scotland was also enhanced by the passage of the Trade Union Act of 1913, which canceled out the Osborne Judgement by again permitting the automatic political checkoff of union dues.[80] This meant that the local Labour Party branches in Lanarkshire were better positioned to build on their earlier achievements in towns such as Hamilton, Larkhall, Wishaw, and Rutherglen than were the relatively sparse SPA branches with respect to similar efforts in downstate Illinois. The ILP's *Forward* newspaper, with sales approaching twenty thousand, had by now become a major propaganda asset in the coal towns of the Clyde Valley. Nothing approaching it was available in Illinois until Oscar Ameringer established the *Illinois Miner* in 1922.[81]

The improved vote that Labour received in the South Lanark by-election of February 1913 further boosted party morale. Although this constituency was partly rural and contained fewer colliers than the other mining seats, the Labour candidate came in with 38 percent of the vote.[82] This improved result prompted Robert Smillie to write a reflective article for *Forward* about the state of mining politics in southwest Scotland. Given the wealth of experience he had acquired by running for Parliament seven times in the previous twenty years, Smillie's opinion is worth quoting at some length:

> Ten years ago it would have been an impossibility. At that time the miners in the [South Lanark] division would not have listened to their officials speaking Labour politics. They believed the trade union had no right to interfere in politics and generally they supported the Liberal Party. Since then, the trade union [i.e., Osborne] decision, the minimum wage bill, the interference of the military [in mining strikes] and civilian oppression have opened up their eyes to the fact that the Liberal Party is as much the party of capitalism as the Tory Party. Therefore it is not surprising that hundreds of miners whom I have found to be Liberal a few years ago have thrown up Liberalism for good and have openly aligned themselves with the Labour Party.[83]

Finally, in the period immediately preceding World War I, neither class relations in general nor industrial relations in particular ever reached the same level of antagonism in Illinois that they did in the coal-mining regions of southwest Scotland. In part this deterioration in labor relations reflected what historian Standish Meacham has called the fear of an "impending clash" between classes that British society exhibited in these years.[84] This fear also resulted from the extensive civil disobedience that developed simultaneously in the women's suffrage movement, in the struggle for Irish home rule, and in national strikes on the docks, on the railroads, and in the mines. The fear was heightened still further by the constitutional crisis provoked when the House of Lords rejected Lloyd George's revolutionary 1909 budget, which imposed unprecedented taxes on the estates owned by the landed aristocracy. This crisis had no real analogue in the United States.

At the local level the strike wave that swept Britain in the pre–World War I years also helped to stimulate the emergence of a neosyndicalist movement among Lanarkshire's rank-and-file coal miners that showed considerably greater strength than did a similar one that appeared in Illinois district 12 during the same period. The syndicalists advocated industrial unionism, rank-and-file control of trade unions, and—in theory, at least—a general strike to do away with capitalism. In one sense, of course, because these syndicalist movements were ostensibly antipolitical, their emergence both in Britain and America (even though they were much smaller than those in Italy and France) implied a turning away from electoral politics and toward direct action at the workplace.[85] The greater strength of the syndicalist movement in the United Kingdom, however, and the deterioration of class relations from which it flowed, created a climate of opinion that made the Labour Party more likely to thrive than was the left-wing movement in the United States. In practice, most syndicalists in the Industrial Workers of the World, which was the leading syndicalist organization in the United States, voted socialist whatever their political predilections,[86] but so too did the much larger group of syndicalists in Britain.

In downstate Illinois the emergence of syndicalist ideas among the coal miners can be traced to the founding of the IWW — the Wobblies — in Chicago in 1905. This revolutionary body, which advocated a mixture of militant, all-inclusive industrial unionism and direct-action strikes, succeeded for a short time in establishing a few locals in the southern Illinois coalfields. It also gained a brief footing in the Singer sewing machine works in Glasgow a few years later.[87] These IWW branches did not last long on either side of the Atlantic, however, mainly because of the dual unionist policies that their parent body pursued in its relations with the AFL.[88] More important was the heightened level of dissatisfaction both toward the coal owners (because of tightening industrial discipline) and toward the elected leaders of Illinois district 12 (because of its bureaucratic practices and timid negotiating stance), emotions tapped by district 12's dissident radicals, such as Edward Wieck. Such sentiments exemplified growing disaffection among an increasingly militant body of colliers on both sides of the ocean.

As the syndicalist critics of the district 12 leadership saw it, the record of union president John H. Walker and the other political socialists — of whom much had been expected when they were first elected to office — was disappointing on three counts. First, instead of vigorously promoting the idea of industrial unionism in the AFL, they had acquiesced in the conservative craft union policies espoused by AFL president Samuel Gompers and his supporters on the labor federation's executive board. Second, they had compromised district 12's own democratic traditions by downplaying the role of the popularly elected pit committees in the life of the union. Third, they had engaged in class collaborationist tactics with the coal owners by the rigid and legalistic manner in which they implemented the Central Competitive Field Agreement. "Even with lauded progressive men at the head of the organization," wrote Wieck bitterly in 1912, district 12 was "becoming more and more . . . a vast machine which with the aid of complicated contracts can be in the interests of business." The answer, he wrote, was "to cease . . . bargaining and compromising and stand erect before all, recognizing no right of the mine owners, using every effective weapon including that of class conscious direct action."[89]

Out beyond the borders of Illinois, a number of mass strikes of the kind that Wieck had in mind did take place in America during 1912–14. Most notable among them were the IWW-led stoppage of textile workers in Lawrence, Mass., the railroad shop craft strike against the Harriman lines, and the UMWA's own major (and very bloody) coal strike in southern Colorado.[90] None of these U.S. strikes was national enough in its scope, however, or serious enough in its economic consequences, to pose the threat of class war on the same scale as did the great industrial conflicts that swept across Great Britain in the years leading up to World War I.

Between 1910 and 1912 a quick succession of three national strikes crippled three of Britain's basic industries—the docks, the railroads, and the mines. They were followed, in June 1914, by the establishment of the so-called Triple Alliance, a confederation of three of the country's largest and most powerful trade unions—the MFGB, the National Union of Railwaymen, and the Transport Workers Federation—that together encompassed more than three million workers. The purpose of the Triple Alliance, at least in theory, was to coordinate contract negotiations with the employers in each of its members' industries so that the agreements would all terminate at the same time. Had this policy actually been carried out, not only would it have given these unions the power to threaten the employers with a complete economic shutdown, but it also would have enabled the British trade union movement to dictate industrial policy to the government.[91] The U.S. labor movement never acquired a comparable ability to threaten the operations of the federal government, save possibly for a brief period during the course of the late 1930s and in World War II.

In turn, the establishment of the Triple Alliance in Britain strengthened the hand of the syndicalist minority in the Lanarkshire County Miners Union and gave it an authority that the syndicalists in Illinois district 12 lacked. Syndicalism's appeal to the colliers in the LCMU was enhanced by two other developments that had no analogue in the United States: the anger generated in the Scottish pits by the disappointing results of the British national coal strike of 1912 and the popularity of a direct-action pamphlet about mining trade unionism called *The Miners' Next Step*, which was published in the same year.[92]

The British national coal strike of 1912, which involved extensive violence, brought more than a million colliers—including over eighty thousand in Scotland—out of the pits behind the demand for a minimum wage law. Had it been enacted, this law would have guaranteed twenty-five pence a day for adult miners and ten pence for boys. Parliament did enact the principle of a minimum wage, but it left the actual wage levels for the mines to be determined by a series of regional arbitration boards. Despite this backpedaling, the MFGB as a whole called off the strike, even though the Scottish miners voted to continue it by a majority of 30,473 to 23,186.[93] Feeling betrayed, the Lanarkshire colliers displayed a degree of anger against their own trade union officers, as well as against the coal owners, that was a good deal stronger than that expressed by the dissidents in Illinois district 12. Soon after the 1912 strike was over, a large crowd gathered at a mine in Wishaw and attempted "in a most systematic manner to try and destroy the pithead."[94] In a Fife mining town a crowd of eight thousand colliers attacked several pits and in one instance smashed the windows in the pithead buildings. When a union official, dispatched to restore order, called the rioters hooligans, police had to rescue him from the crowd.[95]

Frustration at the outcome of the 1912 strike also caused a growing minority of militant young Lanarkshire miners to take seriously the message contained in *The Miners' Next Step.* This syndicalist pamphlet (which originated among dissidents in the South Wales Miners Federation) proposed not only that the MFGB, hitherto a loose confederation of county unions, be reorganized along industrial lines but also that the coal owners themselves be dispossessed not by nationalization of the mines but by a series of strikes that would bring the whole of British industry to a standstill.[96] In the years preceding World War I, not many Scottish colliers took this idea literally. Nonetheless, it stirred up opposition to the timid policies pursued by the paid agents of the LCMU, who had joined in calling off the 1912 strike and who were content to follow what seemed to many to be the pusillanimous political path of the Labour Party. Illinois district 12 experienced far less rancor toward its leadership. In August 1912 a large demonstration of rank-and-file miners was held in Hamilton, organized by a body called the "Miners' Indignation and Reform Committee." It was addressed by a number of speakers, including W. F. Hay, one of the authors of *The Miners' Next Step.* One speaker claimed that there was "not a more autocratic organization" than the Lanarkshire County Miners Union. At the conclusion of the demonstration, resolutions were passed calling for the LCMU's entire reconstruction along democratic, industrial-union lines.[97]

Taking these two different national trajectories into account, what should we conclude about the relative state of class relations in the coalfields of Lanarkshire and central and southern Illinois on the eve of World War I? The weaker state of the Socialist Party's local branches in Illinois, coupled with the limited attraction of syndicalist ideas in the American Midwest compared to the Clyde Valley, implies that class-conscious militancy, on both the industrial and the political fronts, advanced more rapidly in the LCMU than in UMWA district 12 at this time. Writ large, these diverging tendencies suggest that the radical Left would have a far less auspicious future in America than in Great Britain during the stormy World War I years to follow.

In August 1914, however, the consequences of this emerging gap in the development of class consciousness in the two labor movements were still hidden from view. Much political water had flowed beneath the bridges on both sides of the Atlantic since 1900, when the socialists had first begun appealing for support among the miners of Illinois district 12, and the Labour Party had followed the same course through its efforts to exert political influence within the LCMU. It may not be quite true to say that the advocates of class-conscious action, whether at the ballot box or down the pit, had moved in tandem in these two coal-mining districts during the preceding decade and a half, but they had come fairly close to doing so.

To put it another way, a distinct difference had now appeared in the process of class formation among the miners on each side of the Atlantic — a difference indicating that their politics had begun to part ways. But World War I itself, and much else besides, had to be gone through before that parting of the ways was to be complete.

9

DENOUEMENT: WORLD WAR I, LABOUR PARTY TRIUMPH, AND THE COLLAPSE OF THE LEFT IN ILLINOIS, 1914–24

In 1914 the more advanced position of the socialist element in the LCMU compared to that of the radical faction in Illinois district 12, coupled with the more embittered state of industrial relations in Britain generally, suggested that a gap in working-class militancy was emerging between the miners on the opposite sides of the Atlantic. Instead of narrowing, this political and economic gap widened during the industrial turmoil that took place during and after World War I. The Labour Party made a series of dramatic breakthroughs in the British general elections of 1918 and 1922. As a result, it became a major force in the social and political life of the Lanarkshire coal towns. On the other side of the ocean, the Socialist Party of America suffered a near-total collapse in the coalfields of downstate Illinois, as it did throughout the United States.

This political gap widened still further in the immediate postwar years. In the British general election of January 1924, the Labour Party not only retained all four mining seats it had acquired in southwest Scotland in 1922 but also won enough other seats in Parliament to be able to form a minority government. In the Illinois coalfields, by contrast, the radical faction in UMWA district 12 was unable to demonstrate a comparable degree of strength when Senator Robert LaFollette ran as an independent reform candidate in the presidential election of November 1924.[1] Although it was not seen this way at the time, these defeats in the postwar years signaled the end of the socialist effort to capture the support of the largest and electorally most important trade union in the American labor movement.

Never again, save for the 1930s, when a small minority of miners voted socialist or communist, did America's colliers reach the level of third-party activism they attained in the first two decades of the twentieth century. Given the political power of the colliers, this retreat from independent labor politics in America — and the corresponding rise in support that the British miners gave to the Labour Party — had a profound effect in differentiating America's labor movement from Great Britain's and, indeed, from the labor movement in Europe as a whole.

How and why did this dramatic political parting of the ways take place? Were the sudden emergence of the Labour Party as a major force in southwest Scotland and the collapse of the third-party movement in Illinois due to internal developments such as differences in trade union strategy and tactics? Did they result from socioeconomic factors such as the greater role the postwar crisis played in heightening class tensions in British society? Or were they, perhaps, due to structural changes in British politics that took place during and after World War I?

Great Britain declared war on the Central Powers in August 1914. The United States followed suit almost three years later, in April 1917. Despite this difference in timing, miners in both Lanarkshire and downstate Illinois responded similarly to the outbreak of war: most patriotically supported it, but others expressed growing anger and doubt as the sacrifices required for the war effort sank in. During the first phase of World War I, full employment, rising wages, and both governments' solicitude toward their trade unions so as to ensure high levels of production guaranteed the loyal support of the great bulk of the miners on both sides of the ocean. In both Lanarkshire and Illinois large numbers of colliers volunteered for the armed forces. By the end of 1915, for example, 10,166 men, amounting to 19 percent of the mine labor force, had joined up in Lanarkshire.[2] By the end of 1917, 8,400 miners from Illinois — about 13 percent of the colliers — had entered the military.[3]

Soon afterward, however, disillusionment began to set in, even though it was muted for a time by patriotic disclaimers on the part of union leaders on both sides of the ocean. A leading cause of discontent was inflation. Between 1914 and 1919 the purchasing power of the average Illinois collier's wage fell by more than 20 percent.[4] A similar development occurred in southwest Scotland.[5] Dissidents in both Lanarkshire and Illinois also complained that their union leaders sacrificed the interests of the rank and file on the altar of national duty and increased production. In September 1916, for example, Thomas Gray of Craighead and Manus Duddy of Blantyre, two leaders of the militant minority who had recently been elected to the LCMU's executive council, urged that an "idle day" be held in the Lanarkshire pits to protest government inaction over inflation and the coal owners' excessive profiteering.[6] This idea was turned aside in favor of a general trade union conference in Glasgow to consider the rising cost of food, milk, and coal, which affected all workers in the Clyde Basin. Demands were also made for higher pensions for the widows of disabled miners.[7]

After this, although patriotism remained the order of the day for most miners, protests against unfair treatment continued to escalate. Another request for an "idle day" was made by Gray and Duddy in the spring of 1917. When it was turned down, several hundred miners from pits in Wishaw, Blantyre, Motherwell, and Airdrie walked out in protest.[8] Complaints were also registered by rank-and-file Scottish colliers over the selection procedures used in military conscription and the acute shortage of affordable housing.[9]

Although day-to-day life was not as difficult in the Illinois coalfields as it was in southwest Scotland, a significant protest movement also took root there. Between August and October 1917, for example, over forty thousand person-hours were lost to production as a consequence of wildcat strikes.[10] As in Lanarkshire, these strikes resulted from increasing anger over the coal owners' excessive profits, the failure of wages to keep up with prices, and the increased safety problems that resulted from longer hours and the heightened pace of work. Although overall accident and death rates remained roughly constant throughout the war in both Illinois and southwest Scotland, the pressure on miners to produce more coal increased workplace tensions in both places.[11]

Another source of coal miners' anger on both sides of the Atlantic was the increased use of coal-cutting machines during the conflict. Both the British and American governments encouraged the use of these machines to improve the output of vital coal supplies for the war effort. The number of coal-cutting machines listed in the Illinois Bureau of Labor Statistics's *Coal Reports* rose from 272 in 38 mines in 1888 to 4,762 in 185 mines in 1925. Most of these new machines were installed during World War I.[12] Between 1913 and 1918 the number of cutting machines used in the Scottish pits rose as well, from 876 to 1,081.[13] The colliers worried that the machines would decrease both mine safety and skill requirements. Reflecting on the machines' negative impact on his work rhythms, one miner from Glen Carbon, in central Illinois, stated, "They were over there fightin', and we were over here beatin' our brains out [with the cutting machines] working every day."[14]

These growing tensions between miners and the government and between union leaders and the rank and file grew worse in 1917 after authorities in both Britain and America decided to put their nations' coal-mining industries under government control for the remainder of the war. Some miners welcomed this development in the hope that the state would prove to be a better taskmaster than had the private coal owners. But it did not turn out that way. In the United Kingdom a coal controller was appointed in March 1917 with powers to regulate personnel, production, and wage levels.[15] He quickly got into a dispute with the LCMU over wage rates, output targets, and exemptions from military service.[16] In Illinois state control over the coal industry began in May 1917 with the creation of the Illinois State Council of Defense.[17] The main cause of escalating tension in district 12, however, came in October 1917, when the U.S. Fuel Administration mandated the so-called Washington Agreement, with the UMWA and the coal operators as cosigners.

The Washington Agreement awarded U.S. miners a wage increase, but it also permitted another rise in coal prices, and it froze wages at the new level for the duration of the conflict. The colliers were particularly annoyed by a penalty clause against striking intended to ensure continuous production, with fines to be automatically deducted from the miners' paychecks.[18] Reaction was more hostile in Illinois than in any other mining state. In the fall of 1917 more than ten thousand miners in Macoupin, Madison, Montgomery, Bond, and St. Clair Counties walked out rather than obey the Washington Agreement. They demanded that the compact, which had been negotiated by the UMWA's national leaders over the heads of the rank and file, be submitted to a referendum vote of the membership. Frank Farrington, who had by now become president of district 12, refused to do this. Invoking the authority of the federal government, he forced the striking miners back to work.[19]

The anger of the miners toward their respective governments during the war was compounded by the sense of betrayal they felt at their treatment after it. Colliers in both Britain and America felt they had made disproportionate sacrifices to fulfill their countries' needs for adequate energy supplies. Like workers in other industries, they believed that after the armistice was signed in November 1918, they were entitled to some kind of special reward, either in the form of wage increases or relief from the various privations and shortages they had suffered during the war.[20]

The most important request the MFGB made of the British government after World War I was for nationalization of the mines. The union had favored this policy ever since the 1890s, and after the war it renewed the demand with greater intensity. It did so partly on ideological grounds and partly as a means of resolving the problem of falling demand now facing the industry.

Early in 1919 the MFGB urged the British government not to return the coal mines to private hands but rather to award the miners a 30 percent wage increase and to introduce parliamentary legislation to nationalize the mines. Instead Prime Minister Lloyd George's coalition government appointed the Sankey Coal Commission to consider the future of the industry. In its report the commission proposed a seven-hour day and a wage increase, but it was divided over the question of nationalization. Although a majority of the commission favored such a measure, the minority did not.[21]

When it came to consider the Sankey commission's report in the summer of 1919, Prime Minister Lloyd George's government accepted the minority's recommendations opposing nationalization rather than those of the majority favoring it. Its members angry and frustrated, the MFGB refused to back down on its demand. To make matters worse, soon thereafter the British government abruptly abandoned state control of the mines, returning the industry to private hands. It soon became clear that in the interests of profitability, the coal owners were determined to drive wages back down to their prewar level. A bitter lockout ensued in 1920. It lasted for three months and ended in a humiliating defeat for the colliers. In Lanarkshire, as elsewhere, this loss was rendered all the more galling by the extensive use of violence on the part of police and soldiers against the strikers, as well as by the failure of the Triple Alliance to come to the aid of the colliers with a sympathy strike.[22]

Developments were similar in the United States. Most miners in Illinois district 12 assumed that the Washington Agreement, with its frozen wage levels and prohibition on strikes, would end once the war was over. Because no formal peace treaty with Germany was signed until later, however, the agreement continued until March 1920, more than fifteen months after hostilities ceased. Faced with this prospect the September 1919 UMWA convention, under pressure from the radicals in district 12, urged newly appointed UMWA president John L. Lewis to extract some concessions from the government. He was instructed to press for the abrogation of the Washington Agreement, a 60 percent wage increase, a five-day week, and nationalization of the mines. If these demands were not met, Lewis was authorized to call a national coal strike on November 1, 1919.[23] Offered a 14 percent wage increase but nothing more, Lewis issued a strike order, only to withdraw it in the face of a court injunction secured by the federal government. UMWA members were infuriated that the court order issued by Attorney General A. Mitchell Palmer was based on the 1917 Lever Act, a law intended to deal with wartime industrial conditions, not with peacetime industry. After Palmer had secured the injunction, he raised tensions even further by putting federal troops on alert in West Virginia and dispatching FBI agents to the UMWA's national headquarters in Indianapolis to make sure that the union complied. Faced with this kind of pressure, John L. Lewis had little choice but to back down.[24]

Given these adverse developments at the national level in their respective countries, it was hardly surprising that rank-and-file colliers both in the LCMU and in Illinois district 12 became even more disaffected. In southwest Scotland the miners' determination to fight back against government double-dealing and their union leaders' unwillingness or inability to bring them any relief was reinforced by the example of the so-called Red Clyde. This wartime social movement consisted largely of insurgent shop stewards in the Clyde Workers Committee who rallied Glasgow's engineering and munitions workers against skill dilution, housing shortages, and government manipulation during the course of the conflict.[25]

The most important index of this new militant mood among rank-and-file miners was a further rise in the influence of syndicalist ideas on both sides of the ocean. As early as July 1917 the Miners Unofficial Reform Committee had met in Hamilton, Scotland, to formulate a set of policies as an alternative to those pursued by the union's official leaders. This committee issued a manifesto noting the harmful effects of the new coal-cutting machines, the growing competition among large-scale coal owners, and the "continual struggle to reduce the time taken to produce coal."[26] The manifesto went on to demand that more power be put in the hands of the LCMU's pit committees, that agents and other union officials be elected annually instead of being appointed by the top leadership, and that the entire MFGB be restructured so that "a genuine British Miners' Industrial Union" could be brought into being.[27] James MacDougall, a young radical who was a protégé of Scottish revolutionary John MacLean, played an important role in this 1917 meeting. MacDougall and MacLean together conducted Marxist education classes among the miners of Fife and Lanarkshire.[28] "It is worthy of remark," wrote MacDougall concerning the gathering, that "a prominent part was played in this conference by Lanarkshire men who had had experience as officials or as members of the United Mineworkers Union of America, either in Illinois or in British Columbia."[29]

The climax in this opening round of postwar protests, as far as the Lanarkshire colliers were concerned, came in late January 1919. The Miners Unofficial Reform Committee, seeking to increase pressure on the government over wage increases, called the miners out on their largest unofficial strike so far. On January 29, 1919, an angry crowd of miners invaded the LCMU headquarters in Hamilton, threw documents out the window, and raised the red flag of revolution over the balcony. Two days later miners from Earnock and Hamilton Palace collieries, near Blantyre (two of the largest and most heavily mechanized pits in southwest Scotland), smashed up the office at Hamilton Palace pit, assaulted a police officer, and marched on to Bellshill, where they were turned back by a large contingent of police. The militants were persuaded to return to work by county agent John Robertson. The fact that men from Blantyre played such an important role in these protests showed how easily mass action could be sparked at highly industrialized pits.[30]

This insurgency in southwest Scotland was fully matched by the dissident protests in southwestern Illinois's subdistricts 5, 7, and 9. In July 1919 the imprisonment of American war protester Tom Mooney sparked a widespread unofficial strike that lasted for several weeks.[31] A few days later, in early August, the colliers of St. Clair County held two mass meetings in Belleville's Priester Park. They demanded that, among other things, the UMWA leadership either renegotiate the Washington Agreement or declare it nonbinding. Because the union's international executive board and the federal government had cooperated extensively over coal policy during the war, the insurgents denounced the UMWA leadership as "the apologists for and the beneficiaries of" a capitalist system that was now in crisis.[32] In addition, the miners at the first Priester Park meeting adopted a resolution urging that the next annual convention of the UMWA call a nationwide congress, "there to demand of the capitalist class that all instruments of industries be turned over to the working class." [33] The second meeting rejected the pleas of various district 12 and international union officials for a return to work. Instead, it passed a resolution requesting a special convention to consider the wage scale. When this was rejected by district president Frank Farrington, the Belleville men, joined by insurgents from subdistricts 5 and 6, sent "Crusaders" marching into other areas of the central and southern Illinois coalfields to publicize their grievances. By the end of August 1919, as many as twenty thousand colliers, constituting more than a quarter of district 12's entire membership, had come out on wildcat strikes.[34]

During these protests the Illinois insurgents, much like their Scottish counterparts, began to set up alternative democratic structures within district 12 to protest the bureaucratic policies of the statewide leadership and to bring about trade union reform. At the August 3, 1919, mass meeting in Belleville, a fifty-person policy committee headed by Luke Coffey and Henry Schilling was appointed to spread the demand for a special district 12 convention to reconsider what those assembled deemed to be the union's undemocratic methods of government. Soon afterward it was replaced by a statewide rank-and-file policy committee, which included elected representatives from other coalfields in Illinois. This statewide committee made plans to call a special district convention of its own. Such a convention would undoubtedly have met had not UMWA president John L. Lewis met in the interim with government and industry officials to discuss the Washington Agreement at the national level.[35]

Late in 1920 matters were made still worse by the onset of a serious depression in the coal industry in both Britain and the United States. The causes differed in the two places, but on the U.S. side this recession was to last for more than a decade. In Illinois the root cause, besides a decline in the demand for coal due to the termination of wartime orders, was productive overcapacity. Because of the disproportionate loss of investment capital entailed in closing a mine, many coal operators there had developed the habit of sinking a larger number of pits than were necessary to meet demand. They opened them for production only when coal prices reached a profitable level, thereby leaving large numbers of pits—along with their employees—idle for long periods of time.[36] Between 1915 and 1919, for example, the average number of days worked each year in the Illinois pits fell from 187 to 169, while the number of miners available for work increased from 33,610 to 82,927.[37] After 1920 the situation in Illinois grew still worse when the demand for coal dropped and an open-shop drive by coal owners elsewhere in the country brought large quantities of cheap nonunion coal into the Chicago and St. Louis markets. Wages fell, and the number of unemployed miners rapidly increased.[38]

In southwest Scotland the crisis was even graver. There, the problem of overcapacity was compounded by the much larger number of army veterans who came back from World War I seeking jobs, by a long-term but persistent decline in the competitive position of the Lanarkshire mines compared to those in eastern Scotland, and by the loss of export markets—a problem that did not exist in Illinois.[39]

By 1921 the unemployment rate among Illinois's miners had reached 28 percent. In southwest Scotland it was only a few points lower. In fact, suffering was probably more acute in heavily industrialized Lanarkshire than it was in the more rural coal towns of downstate Illinois, where many colliers had access to farm produce and to the chicken coops and vegetable gardens they had set up behind their homes. By the end of that year, so many miners and metalworkers had lost their jobs in the Lanarkshire towns of Motherwell and Wishaw that, according to one historian, the two places had become "a social and economic disaster."[40]

Given the injustices that both the British and American colliers believed they had suffered at the hands of their respective governments during World War I and the extensive unemployment they experienced after it, one might suppose that miners on both sides of the Atlantic would have continued to channel their economic discontent into continued, or even enhanced, support for some form of independent political action. In Lanarkshire the postwar industrial unrest did indeed translate into a further—and this time decisive—shift toward the Labour Party. In Illinois district 12, however, the political Left came close to collapsing.

In Illinois the SPA vote for state treasurer among the miners, which had reached a high of 22 percent in 1912, fell to 17 percent in 1914. It went down even further in the next few years, falling to 9 percent in 1918 and 7 percent in 1920.[41] In the state elections of 1914 and 1916, Socialist Party candidates for the state legislature in St. Clair, Madison, Macoupin, and Saline Counties continued to do quite well. Nevertheless, in the fall 1918 elections in St. Clair County, the flagship radical community where Adolph Germer had come near to victory in 1910 and 1912, they polled a miserable 12.5 percent of the vote—the best they did anywhere in the state.[42]

Furthermore, no new socialists were elected to municipal office in the Illinois coal towns after the spring elections of 1917. To the contrary, virtually all those previously elected lost their positions. It is unclear just when each of the socialist municipal officers were turned out of office by the voters, but Canton appears to have been typical of these towns. Unlike the socialist mayors of most other mining communities, Mayor Homer Whalen of Canton supported America's entry into World War I. Nevertheless, the fact that he favored America's participation in the war did not save his political skin. Soon after his socialist administration advocated recognizing Soviet Russia in February 1918, the town voted him out of office in favor of a fusion ticket of local Republicans and Democrats.[43]

In Lanarkshire, by contrast, the Labour Party's postwar political fortunes improved dramatically. When Britain's first postwar general election took place in December 1918, the Labour Party did not do particularly well at the national level. It was hampered by the suddenness of the election, a defective electoral register, and the enormous popularity of Prime Minister Lloyd George's governing coalition. The result was a complete victory for the coalition government's ticket, a mixture of prowar Liberals and Conservatives. The Labour Party won only fifty-seven seats in the new Parliament.[44] Nonetheless, this modest national result concealed a marked change in the political loyalties of the Lanarkshire miners. As a result of the election, the Labour Party achieved its first major breakthrough when LCMU political agent Duncan Graham won in the newly created parliamentary constituency of Hamilton, the site of the union's headquarters. Graham secured 42 percent of the vote in a four-way contest.[45] Nor was this all. Instead of coming in at the bottom of the poll, as they had before the war, Labour candidates came in a strong second in no fewer than three of Lanarkshire's other parliamentary seats. Indeed, in the nearby mining town of Bothwell, LCMU agent John Robertson failed to be elected only by a hair's breadth.[46] Still more remarkable was the fact that, nationwide, twenty-five of the Labour Party's fifty-seven seats in the new Parliament were held by miners.[47]

Four years later, in the general election of 1922, Labour's modest 1918 breakthrough in Lanarkshire turned into a smashing victory. By this time the popularity of Prime Minister Lloyd George's coalition government, which had been returned to office triumphantly in 1918, had faded. Its harsh treatment of the postwar labor unrest on the railroads, in the mines, and elsewhere, along with other setbacks, cost it much of the support it had garnered during the war. As a result the coalition broke up, and a new general election was called in November 1922. This time the Tory, or Unionist Party, and the Liberal and the Labour Parties, together with some independent Liberals who had not been part of the coalition, faced off against one another as separate entities.[48]

Some miners, discouraged by the Triple Alliance's failure to come to their aid when a new mining strike was threatened on "Black Friday" in April 1921, succumbed to apathy and despair.[49] For the majority of Lanarkshire miners, however, the 1922 election campaign became a call to action. The Labour Party was aided in the Clyde Valley coal towns by the vigorous campaigning of local ILP members, as well as the fiery rhetoric of visiting speakers from Glasgow such as John MacLean, John Wheatley, and Nora Connolly. (Nora Connolly was the daughter of Irish revolutionary James Connolly, who had spent much time working on behalf of the IWW in America before the war and who was killed in the failed Irish Easter uprising of 1916.)[50] The result of all this in the 1922 election was a massive shift to the Left not only by the Lanarkshire miners but also by thousands of other workers in the region who voted Labour for the first time.

Not only was Duncan Graham, the LCMU's political agent, returned for a second time as Labour M.P. for Hamilton with an increased majority, but three other Lanarkshire miners' leaders were elected to Parliament, from Bothwell, Coatbridge, and North Lanark: LCMU president John Robertson; union vice president James C. Welsh; and Joseph Sullivan, the son of an Irish miner who represented the Scottish miners on the MFGB's executive committee. Motherwell even returned a Communist to Parliament, one of only three ever elected to the House of Commons. He was J. T. W. Newbold, a Lancashire-born lecturer at the Scottish Labour College who managed to retain the Labour Party's endorsement at Motherwell despite a general prohibition against permitting Communists to run for Parliament on its ticket.[51] W. Wright was also elected Labour M.P. for Rutherglen. In all, six Labour M.P.s were elected from the Lanarkshire coalfield. This was the largest group of Labour Party members elected from a single industrial area in the whole of Great Britain.[52]

After more than a dozen years of procrastination, the Lanarkshire colliers of the MFGB had turned against the Liberals and endorsed the Labour Party with a vengeance. The socialists in Illinois, however, had been thoroughly discredited. What caused the coal miners of Lanarkshire and Illinois district 12, as well as workers in Britain and America generally, to diverge so suddenly and dramatically in their attitudes toward the political Left?

No single argument can explain the remarkable shift that occurred in the Lanarkshire miners' political loyalties to the Labour Party, on the one hand, and the collapse of socialist support among the colliers of Illinois, on the other. Three different sets of reasons, involving three different levels of analysis, are needed. The first set of reasons is socioeconomic, by which I mean that the repercussions of World War I exacted a greater economic and psychological toll from the miners of Lanarkshire than they did from those in Illinois district 12. The second set of reasons is sociocultural. It derives from the more divisive impact that demands for patriotic conformity, and fears of disloyalty among "enemy alien" immigrants, had on the political outlook of the American mine labor force compared to the British.

The third reason for the dramatic upward shift in the fortunes of the Labour Party in southwest Scotland was political-structural. It derives from the split that occurred in Britain's governing Liberal Party in 1916, the extension of the political franchise that resulted from the passage of the Fourth Reform Act in 1918, and the ability of the Labour Party to take advantage of both of these developments to grow from a small third party into the main political representative of the British working class. Nothing comparable to these developments occurred in the United States.

Up to a point, the increased sacrifices that World War I demanded from working people were similar on both sides of the Atlantic. Because the United States was a combatant for only eighteen months, however, government regulations there were milder, and lasted for a much shorter period of time, than they did in Great Britain. For example, the system of compulsory food rationing in Britain was much more stringent than the voluntary system of controls over consumer goods instituted in the United States.[53] Miners in both countries complained equally about inflation and war profiteering, but the smaller size of the meat ration in Britain, in particular, was important to a group of men who expended an enormous amount of physical energy performing their daily tasks. Since the colliers of downstate Illinois had greater access to local farm produce, they weathered the shortages caused by World War I and the subsequent depression in the coal industry more easily than their Scottish counterparts could.

Another domestic matter more important to Lanarkshire colliers than to those in the American Midwest was the issue of housing and rent control. Like food rationing, this was a matter of particular concern to the colliers' wives. It is true that many of the miners in downstate Illinois lived in small, rural, wooden structures without modern plumbing or electricity, but these houses were still better than those in southwest Scotland, where both the shortage of miners' housing and its deplorable state had by now become a national scandal.[54] Several major rent strikes, with which the miners expressed strong sympathy, took place in Glasgow during the war. The minutes of the bimonthly meetings of the LCMU's executive council in 1917 and 1918 are full of resolutions demanding government action either to upgrade the existing stock of miners' rows or to subsidize a program of public housing.[55] It was Labour, more than any other British political party, that became the true champion of housing reform. "The housing issue," writes one historian, "did more than anything else to galvanise political consciousness in communities such as Craigneuk"—a slum area lying between Wishaw and Motherwell— "so that by the end of wartime, Craigneuk was to gain a deserved reputation for left-wing politics."[56]

In addition, there was the significantly larger number of Scottish miners who were killed or permanently injured in the long years of bloody and inconclusive trench warfare on the western front. Exact figures comparing war-related miners' deaths for the two areas are lacking. Nevertheless, it stands to reason that in four years of war the Lanarkshire colliers lost a larger proportion of their comrades to injury and death than Illinois district 12 did in a mere eighteen months of conflict. The LCMU council minutes refer far more frequently to the loss of life among conscripted miners, and to the need for pensions for war widows, than do the comparable sources for Illinois.[57] In turn, Scotland's more numerous wartime losses made the Lanarkshire miners' disagreements over the merits of participating in the war sharper than similar rifts in district 12. Since the rise and fall of antiwar sentiment had a powerful effect in shaping the fortunes of the Left on both sides of the ocean, it is necessary to understand clearly how both the Labour Party and the SPA viewed the conflict.

The Labour Party, like the worldwide socialist movement in general, was divided in its attitude toward Britain's participation in World War I. A majority officially supported the war from the beginning, but a growing minority, including quite a few members of the LCMU, either actively opposed Britain's role in the war or went along with it only reluctantly. Through 1915 this opposition element largely kept quiet, but in 1916 and 1917, when the casualty lists lengthened and victory seemed as far off as ever, their skepticism hardened into a series of bitter disputes with the coal controller over which miners, and how many, should be conscripted into the armed forces. (The coal controller was one of the government officials charged with running the mines.) Increasingly they openly supported the large minority on the left wing of the Labour Party who opposed Prime Minister Lloyd George's policy of victory at any cost and favored a negotiated settlement.[58]

The American Left was also ambivalent about World War I. Many Progressives, particularly in the isolationist Midwest, wanted the United States to stay out. In 1915 and 1916 this element included the official leadership of the AFL as well as the great majority of American trade unionists. Once President Wilson committed the United States to war in April 1917, however, most workers, including the majority of coal miners, closed ranks behind the war effort. The Socialist Party of America, on the other hand—unlike Britain's Labour Party—came out unequivocally against U.S. participation in the conflict on the grounds that it was a contest between capitalist powers in which the working class had no interest.[59] Hence the socialists in the Illinois coalfields were completely unprepared for the subsequent massive outpouring of patriotic loyalty in support of America's participation, especially after President Wilson clothed it in the mantle of a crusade for democracy. For a short time afterward a minority of the miners in district 12 continued to express public anger at the Selective Service Act of April 1918, and they also chafed at the various government restrictions that accompanied the demands for increased wartime productivity. In the face of an unprecedented display of jingoistic patriotism, however, these colliers soon learned to keep silent.[60] Under these circumstances the SPA's opposition to the war, even though it concealed a significant minority within the party who favored it, proved to be a serious liability for the radical element in Illinois district 12. The antiwar stand of most of the socialists who had been elected to municipal office in the coal towns of downstate Illinois before the war was the main reason they were dismissed from office.[61]

There were two additional reasons explaining why antiwar sentiment was less destructive for the Left in southwest Scotland than in the coalfields of Illinois. The first stemmed, paradoxically, from the fact that the majority in the Labour Party supported Britain's participation in the war from the time it was first declared in August 1914. This meant that, however bitter the disagreements between its pro- and antiwar factions, the party as a whole was not discredited by being antiwar, as the SPA was. The second and more important reason was that two prominent leaders of Labour's prowar faction—one of them being John Hodge of the steelworkers—were included in the first coalition government established by Liberal prime minister Herbert Asquith in May 1915.[62] The presence of these trade union leaders in the government not only provided British unions with a means of influencing state policy; it also lent the Labour Party a degree of respectability—and hence acceptance among the British voters—that the SPA was never able to achieve.

Nonetheless, the problem of antiwar sentiment among the socialist faction in Illinois district 12 cut even deeper than this. In downstate Illinois large numbers of miners were of Slavic and Italian, as well as German and British, descent. Under the pressure of hysterical patriotism, it mattered little to those who demanded loyalty to the U.S. cause that the Italian and Russian governments were both allies of the United States, at least until Russia withdrew from the conflict. Not just German or Austrian American miners but any immigrant collier who expressed doubt about America's role in the conflict was placed outside the pale of respectability. Save for some of the Irish, however, most British immigrant miners enthusiastically supported the Allied cause, thereby exacerbating the radical-conservative split within the union. A good example of just how destructive these disagreements could be for the socialists—and of how differences that in Britain were primarily political became suffused with elements of nativism and interethnic hatred in America—is provided by the break that occurred in November 1917 between German-born Adolph Germer and the Scots-born former Illinois district 12 president John H. Walker, who was now head of the prowar Illinois State Federation of Labor.[63]

Adolph Germer, who had left the pits the previous year to become national secretary of the Socialist Party of America, had earlier blamed Walker for having endorsed President Woodrow Wilson as well as Illinois Democratic governor Edward F. Dunne for reelection in the 1916 fall election instead of the Socialist Party's candidates for these offices. In fact, in December 1916 Walker had been expelled from the SPA for his deviations from the party line. Now Walker had become one of labor's chief representatives on the Illinois State Council of Defense, where he collaborated with some of Illinois's biggest capitalists in the prosecution of the war.[64]

When they quarreled again over Walker's support for the war and Germer's opposition to it, however, the fight concerned not simply Walker's endorsement of "profiteering capitalists" on the ISCD but also Germer's German background and his supposedly un-American conduct. In an exchange of letters, Germer accused Walker of "fawning at the feet" of the capitalist class,[65] to which Walker caustically replied: "I want you and your like, who want to bring about improvements for the working people by making the German Kaiser the Emperor of the WORLD, and put everybody under the heels of his Military Machine, to know, that there isn't anything I can think of or do, that I won't do, to prevent you from accomplishing your purpose." [66]

These letters were private. Not at all private were the hysterical accusations of treachery that prowar native-born or second-generation U.S. miners made against socialist colliers of German or Italian descent, who were accused of everything from spying for Germany to planting dynamite in the mines so as to sabotage the war effort. In the process all the radicals in Illinois district 12, whatever their ethnic background or political opinions, were tarred with the brush of disloyalty. In the summer of 1918 in Staunton, Mount Olive, and other former bastions of socialist strength, nativist hysteria got so bad that several immigrant radicals were beaten, tarred and feathered, and forced to kiss the American flag even though there was no evidence that they were disloyal.[67] At the March 1918 district 12 convention, Severine Oberdan, an Italian miner who had been indicted for sedition under the Espionage Act because of his antiwar views, was prevented from appealing to the membership for legal aid when he was found to be a member of the antiwar IWW.[68] The witch-hunt culminated in March 1918, when Robert Prager, a German American miner accused of spying and sabotage, was dragged from prison and hanged by an angry mob in Collinsville.[69]

As a result of all this, the SPA, in addition to suffering electoral setbacks because of its antiwar stance, now found itself self-destructing from within because of its ethnic and cultural divisions. The situation was made still worse by the Russian Revolution in October 1917, which was considerably more popular among the Lanarkshire miners than it was among the colliers of Illinois district 12. This time it was the Slavic immigrant miners in downstate Illinois—many of whom were wrongly thought to support the new Bolshevik government in Russia—who came under attack. As the Red Scare mounted in America, the socialists found themselves denounced at every turn. Another consequence of the more virulent character of the U.S. Red Scare compared to the one in Great Britain was the greater severity with which the federal government punished those who criticized America's entry into the war or who professed support for the Russian Revolution. In 1917 and 1918 the British government, making use of the Defense of the Realm Act, imprisoned a number of antiwar activists, including Scottish supporters of the Russian Revolution such as John MacLean.[70] Nevertheless, the British government's measures were far milder than the June 1917 Sedition Act and the Espionage Act of May 1918, which Congress passed in response to a wave of popular antiradical hysteria.[71]

Besides restricting antiwar statements, these two U.S. laws imposed much more severe limits on citizens' free speech than did the relevant clauses of the British Defense of the Realm Act. They were used ruthlessly to arrest and try both any antiwar radicals in district 12 who publicly voiced support for the IWW and the Socialist Party and virtually the entire national leadership of these two organizations. By the summer of 1918 IWW leader Bill Haywood, socialist presidential candidate Eugene Debs, Congressman Victor Berger of Milwaukee, and district 12's own Adolph Germer had all been tried and convicted of breaking the provisions of these acts or of conspiring to obstruct the draft.[72] The effect was to reduce the Socialist Party in Illinois, as well as elsewhere in the United States, to political impotence.

The third factor that explains the Labour Party's rapid rise to influence in the Lanarkshire coal towns during World War I and its electoral successes after it was the reorganization of British politics resulting from the 1916 split in the Liberal Party and the subsequent passage of the Fourth Parliamentary Reform Act in 1918. This law extended the franchise to all adult British males, as well as to some females. Taken together, these two events brought about a major realignment in British politics that led ultimately to the displacement of the Liberals by Labour as the majority party of the British working class.[73] There was no equivalent for these events in America. In southwest Scotland the consequence was that by the early 1920s even those Lanarkshire miners who still favored the Liberal Party found themselves under strong pressure to support Labour candidates. In the Illinois coalfields, by contrast, even those miners who still considered themselves socialists after the war found themselves reverting, *faute de mieux,* to one or another of the two major U.S. political parties.

The details of the Liberal Party split need not detain us here. Suffice it to say that in December 1916, Lloyd George helped to engineer a coup against Liberal prime minister Asquith that led to the second British wartime coalition government, in which Lloyd George himself became prime minister. This coalition included not only prowar Liberals and Tories but also several Labour ministers, who from this time on were given a more active role in the running of the war. Arthur Henderson secured a seat in the war cabinet, John Hodge of the steelworkers was made minister of labour, and G. N. Barnes of the Amalgamated Society of Engineers became minister of pensions.[74]

The addition of these new Labour ministers to the British cabinet further enhanced the party's viability and visibility nationwide. Even more important, Labour's new position in the government provided Britain's trade unions, including the Miners Federation of Great Britain, with a means of influencing government policy. In turn this gave the LCMU, like other county unions in the MFGB, a further incentive to strengthen its relations with the local Labour Party and to encourage its members to vote Labour.[75]

While the Reform Act of 1918 was being debated, a parliamentary commission was established to determine the boundaries of the new parliamentary constituencies. It was a measure of the Labour Party's newfound political strength and of the LCMU's commitment to the party's cause that Duncan Graham, the union's political agent, appeared before this commission several times and gave detailed reports to the LCMU executive council on its deliberations.[76] The county of Lanarkshire, which had previously contained only the constituencies of Mid-Lanark, Lanark North-West, and Lanark North-East, was given seven parliamentary seats. Six of them contained significant numbers of miners. Of course, not all miners who were admitted to the franchise voted Labour simply because they were given the vote as a result of the Reform Act of 1918. In fact, in 1918 many if not most of them voted for one or another of the Lloyd George coalition government's candidates, which included Tories, Labourites, and Liberals. Even in 1922 many miners still voted Liberal.[77]

By early 1919, however, there was a marked contrast between the position of strength that the Labour Party had attained in Lanarkshire and the position of weakness to which the Socialist Party had been relegated in the coalfields of downstate Illinois. In southwest Scotland the Labour Party had already made an important breakthrough in the 1918 general election, and it was poised on the edge of still greater success. In downstate Illinois, by contrast, most of the SPA's leaders had been either arrested or voluntarily silenced by the effect of the Espionage and Sedition Acts. Internal strife within the party at the national level was rampant, and relations with organized labor were more problematic than ever before.[78]

To say this is not to underestimate the force of the labor unrest that swept across the United States in the months after World War I ended or the social and economic turmoil that accompanied its return to the peacetime world. For example, extensive violence accompanied the AFL's failed attempt — via its Steel Workers Organizing Committee — to set up an industrial union in the steel industry in the fall of 1919. Other national strikes took place on the railroads as well as in the mines. Indeed, in attempting to capitalize on their wartime gains and to resist their employers' counterattacks, more American workers came out on strike in 1919 than in any year since 1886.[79] By this time, however, there was no longer a viable Socialist Party to take advantage of this industrial turmoil, even if the trade union movement had been disposed to vote for it. The infant Workers or Communist Party was as yet too small and weak to have a significant impact. Quite a lot of the social turmoil that took place in America during and immediately after World War I was also affected as much by the politics of race as it was by the politics of class. Britain's Labour Party escaped such troubles. It had grown from a small, weak trade union party into a mass political organization capable of appealing to a wide segment of the electorate. Ethnic and racial issues were relatively insignificant.

In comparison to the major political crisis that gripped the British Liberal Party during and after World War I, which was in part class driven, postwar industrial turmoil had a relatively minor impact on the American political system. When Wilsonian Progressivism collapsed or went underground at the end of 1919, most American workers went back to voting for one or the other of the two major political parties. One index of this political continuity is provided by the results of the midterm congressional elections that took place in Illinois in November 1918. Instead of turning away from the two main parties, as many of their British comrades did at this time, most of the colliers in the downstate coal counties reverted to voting for orthodox political candidates of the Democratic or Republican Parties. Even in St. Clair County, which in the prewar years had been a bastion of Socialist strength, the German American colliers followed a similar pattern. For the most part, they silently punished the Democrats for having taken America into war by voting Republican, not Socialist.[80]

Several other factors also explain the rapid growth of class-conscious sentiments in the Lanarkshire coal towns in the post–World War I period. One factor was the important boost to working-class unity in southwest Scotland provided by the internal reforms that the Labour Party as a whole instituted in 1918. These reforms included a provision for individual party membership, among other things. This meant that although the trade unions, the ILP, and the various other groups that made up the Labour Party all retained their separate identities, they worked together as a social movement to a greater extent than they had done before.[81]

A second unifying factor was the accession of large numbers of working-class women to the electoral rolls in southwest Scotland as a result of the 1918 Reform Act and their emergence as significant players in the internal life of the party. Like their counterparts in America, most leaders of the female suffrage movement in Great Britain were middle class, but former LCMU leader

Keir Hardie, among other Labour leaders, had long championed women's rights.[82] In addition, every day during the war several hundred Clyde Valley women workers, including some of the miners' daughters, traveled by train from the coal towns to Glasgow to work in the munitions factories. This brought at least some of them into contact with militant activists working for women's suffrage and other social reforms. The consciousness of the miners' wives was also raised by their role in the wartime rent strikes, their position in the new movement for miners' housing, and their position as consumers in the now powerful retail cooperative movement. Since the coal town co-ops were themselves affiliated with the Labour Party, this too provided an important avenue for promoting the position of women within the Lanarkshire branches of the party. By 1924 the Labour Party had twenty-four women's branches in Scotland, several of them located in the Lanarkshire coal towns.[83]

Less is known about the political activities of the miners' wives and daughters in downstate Illinois during this period. What little can be gleaned from the sources suggests that the movement for class-conscious political action was far smaller and weaker among the women there than it was in southwest Scotland. Some of the miners' daughters in the northern Illinois coalfield worked as domestics in Chicago or, if they lived near enough, in the metalworking shops of East St. Louis, in the west-central part of the state.[84] Nevertheless, few of these women appear to have had any contact with urban labor or the women's suffrage movement during or after World War I. One exception was Agnes Burns Wieck, wife of Edward Wieck, who became part of the circle of female Progressives acting under the leadership of Jane Addams during the conflict.[85] Another was Mother (Mary) Jones, who occasionally visited the Illinois coalfields. Although highly militant on a wide variety of issues, however, Mother Jones opposed female suffrage.[86]

As in southwest Scotland, the cooperative retail stores in the Illinois coal towns provided the colliers' wives with a collectivist focus for their activities, and some also possessed women's clubs. Still, these co-ops had no formal connection to the labor movement, as did similar bodies in Lanarkshire. Still less were they part of a mass political movement like the Labour Party. Miners' wives in downstate Illinois were just as courageous on the picket line as were their counterparts in southwest Scotland. Especially for the wives of Italian, Polish, and other Slavic colliers, however, the Catholic church and the local immigrant nationalist clubs were the main focal points of their social lives. It was not until the 1930s that more than a small number of them became active in local politics.[87]

After 1920 the retail co-ops in southern Illinois also went into a period of decline. This development contrasted sharply both with the Clyde Valley cooperative movement's rapid postwar growth and with the broadening political relationship that had now emerged between the co-ops and the Labour Party in the Lanarkshire coal towns. One reason for the decline of retail co-ops in the American Midwest was incompetence and malfeasance on the part of a number of cooperative store managers, which led the leaders of district 12 to cease investing money both in the Central States Cooperative Society and in individual cooperative societies in coal towns throughout the state. The number of retail shops in Illinois operated by the Central States Cooperative Society fell from a high of forty-six in 1917 to a low of eighteen in 1922. Equally interesting is the second reason for this decline: the growing popularity of privately run grocery chain stores such as Piggly Wiggly, which began to compete successfully with the co-ops and with other retail stores in the coal towns not long after World War I. These chain stores succeeded not just through superior marketing techniques but also because of the growing popularity of a style of consumer-driven, free-enterprise capitalism that flourished even in the rural areas of states such as Illinois in the 1920s.[88]

A third, highly important reason for the growing cohesion of the Lanarkshire working class in the postwar period was the partial resolution, at long last, of the Irish problem. Owing to the activities of John Wheatley's Catholic Socialist Society, even before 1914 some Irish miners had already begun to abandon their suspicious attitudes toward the collectivist policies of the Labour Party. This process of political accommodation between the two groups was further enhanced by new, cross-cultural bonds that were forged between Catholic and Protestant colliers during the postwar coal strikes, as well as by the Labour Party's opposition to Prime Minister Lloyd George's coercive policies in Ireland in 1919 and 1920.[89] The decisive shift in Irish coal-mining opinion, however, came after the negotiation of the Irish Treaty of December 1921. While it left the six Protestant-dominated counties of Ulster as part of Great Britain, this treaty established the Irish Free State, which covered the southern portion of the island. Another development that helped to draw Irish Catholic miners into the Labour Party was the more even-handed approach that the United Irish League—the main secular body of Irish opinion in Scotland—adopted toward Labour in the elections following World War I. Before 1914, when either a by-election or a general election was called in one of the Lanarkshire mining seats, the UIL nearly always endorsed the Liberal candidate. After 1918, however, as the Liberal Party began to lose its dominant position on the left wing of British politics, the UIL quite frequently endorsed Labour as the more promising option.[90]

Thus, the signing of the Irish Treaty removed one of the last obstacles preventing the Irish Catholic miners from accepting their full working-class identity and voting Labour alongside their Protestant fellows. As the *Glasgow Observer,* the main Catholic newspaper in Glasgow, put it in an editorial just before the general election of November 1922: "The Catholics of this country are chiefly workers. They belong to the toiling masses and therefore they are *prima facie* sympathetic towards the Labour movement and towards a sane and sound Labour policy." [91]

This growing rapprochement between Protestant and Catholic workers in the Labour Party's cause in southwest Scotland stood in sharp contrast to the ethnic and religious divisions that reappeared in the coal towns of southern Illinois's Little Egypt region during the same years. Social relations between the largely Baptist, native-born miners who had moved up from Kentucky and Tennessee into Williamson, Franklin, and Saline Counties in earlier decades and the Italian and Slavic Catholics who had been brought in to work the pits alongside them had always been somewhat problematic. For as long as prosperity reigned in Little Egypt, the two groups lived side by side with a fair degree of harmony. [92] But when the unemployment, wage cuts, and racial conflicts brought about by the postwar transition to a peacetime economy began to bite, the precarious social compact in Little Egypt broke down. It was further undercut by the renewed flow of immigrants from southern and eastern Europe into the southern Illinois coalfields that began in 1919 and by the flowering of the Prohibition movement, which came into its own with the passage of the 1919 constitutional amendment banning the manufacture and sale of beer, wine, and liquor. Tensions generated by the closing of liquor stores in towns such as Herrin, Benton, and West Frankfurt in Williamson, Franklin, and Saline Counties, coupled with the appearance of illegal stills, pitted the "dry" native-born fundamentalist Protestant colliers against the Slavic and Italian Catholic "wets."

Still more serious in provoking social tensions was the Ku Klux Klan's widening popularity in Little Egypt. Moving rapidly up from the South, by 1922 the KKK had become the dominant social institution in many of Little Egypt's poverty-stricken coal towns. The KKK in this period was as much anti-immigrant and anti-Catholic as it was antiblack. The so-called Herrin massacre of June 1922, in which union miners from subdistrict 10 shot and killed a number of strikebreakers who had been brought in to break an ongoing national mining strike, partly resulted from the KKK's influence. [93]

Consequently, instead of turning against the coal owners in the economic crisis that now gripped the coal industry, the ethnically fragmented colliers of Franklin and Williamson Counties began to turn against each other in local elections. Despite the official disapproval of the district 12 leadership, Protestant Klan members — some of whom were miners themselves — vandalized Italian Catholic churches, beat up immigrant miners who flouted the local Prohibition laws, and excoriated anyone with "communist connections." Under these circumstances, which contrasted starkly to those in southwest Scotland, the overriding issue in Little Egypt elections became not class differences with the coal owners but the candidates' stands on such matters as temperance, immigration restriction, and the activities of the Ku Klux Klan itself.[94]

In the light of the Labour Party's emergence as a powerful force among Lanarkshire's miners between 1914 and 1922, and the apparent collapse of support for the SPA in the Illinois coalfields, it seems reasonable to conclude that by the latter date the colliers in the two countries had embarked on two entirely separate paths, and that the political parting of the ways—with the LCMU fully behind the Labour Party and Illinois district 12 remaining nonpartisan—was already complete.

The benefit of hindsight shows this conclusion to be largely justified. In the British general election of January 1924, the Labour Party secured enough seats in the House of Commons to form a minority government, even though it was dependent on parliamentary support from the Liberals. No fewer than 44 of the 191 seats that Labour won in that election came from constituencies in which the miners played a decisive role. This showed once again how politically potent the mining vote was. Nine months later, in November 1924, Senator Robert M. LaFollette of Wisconsin ran as independent candidate for the U.S. presidency on behalf of the Conference for Progressive Political Action. He was endorsed by both the AFL and the remaining elements of the SPA, as well by numerous prewar reformers and Progressives. Although LaFollette secured more than three million votes nationwide, however, in the coal towns of downstate Illinois he secured a vote that was significantly lower than the one obtained by the Socialists in their heyday between 1908 and 1918.[95]

This disappointing result, and the subsequent failure of the CPPA to transform itself into a viable third American political party, helped to confirm the American coal miners' unwillingness to follow the British example and commit permanently to third-party action. These efforts at postwar revival are nevertheless worth examining briefly, if only because of the additional light they shed on the different political orientations of the British and American trade union movements.

In March 1919, with the SPA reeling from the effects of the Red Scare, John Fitzpatrick and Edwin Nockels of the Chicago Federation of Labor

helped the Illinois State Federation of Labor secure the passage of a referendum favoring the establishment of a new, broadly based national labor
party.[96] This was something that district 12 president John H. Walker had
tried in 1910, but it had failed. Much of the impetus for the new party came
from prewar socialists and advocates of reform in the American labor movement who admired the British Labour Party and who sought to build on
its example. For example, the call sent out to the various trade unions and
other groups that established the new party in March 1919 referred to British
Labour as the model to emulate. Noting the party's successes at the general
election of December 1918, it pointed out "the advisability of forming in Illinois an independent labor party along the lines of the British Labor Party
but adapted to American conditions." [97] At the party's founding convention
John H. Walker was chosen as national vice chair, and Frank Esper, secretary of the Illinois branch, became national secretary. Duncan MacDonald,
another former socialist officeholder in district 12 — and now president of
the ISFL as a whole — was made Illinois state chairman. Altogether 78 of the
400 Illinois delegates to the convention were miners. They came from former
strongholds of socialist influence all across the state, including coal towns
such as Streator in northern Illinois, Collinsville in Madison County, and
West Frankfurt in Little Egypt.[98]

At first it seemed as if the rank-and-file miners of Illinois district 12 would
also react favorably to these new third-party efforts. At its March 1920 convention district 12 endorsed most of the social and economic planks that
had been included in the platform for the new party, now called the Farmer-
Labor Party to appeal to farmers in Illinois and elsewhere in the Midwest.
Then it took up a motion proposed by Frank Hefferly of Collinsville to commit district 12 to the political checkoff of union dues. This proposal, which
was modeled explicitly on the political checkoff used by the trade unions in
Great Britain, would have automatically donated a portion of the miners'
union dues to the Farmer-Labor Party. Debate on the proposal was heated.
Its opponents pointed to the AFL's nonpartisan traditions and to the fact that
the colliers of Illinois were divided in their political loyalties, arguing that
for district 12 to adopt the checkoff would be to split the union wide open
and to spend the union's dues improperly.[99]

In the end the checkoff proposal was defeated by 314 votes to 286.[100] Given
the fact that district 12 was one of the Farmer-Labor Party's largest potential donors, the defeat of this proposal was a serious setback. Nevertheless,
the supporters of third-party action persisted. They tried to build popular
support around demands for mine nationalization and old age pensions, the
need for new legislative measures to improve the state's mining code, and the

demand that industrial employers in Illinois cease using court-issued labor injunctions to roll back the gains the AFL unions had made during World War I.[101]

The critical year, as far as relations between Illinois district 12 and the Farmer-Labor Party were concerned, was 1920. The Washington Agreement was still operative, the strike defeats of 1919 were still fresh in the miners' memories, and as in Scotland the economic problems of the coal industry were becoming more and more serious. Like many in Lanarkshire, a minority of the Illinois colliers also supported the "Hands off Russia" campaign. They demonstrated this support by calling on authorities to withdraw from Soviet Russia the American and British troops sent there to overthrow the new Soviet regime.[102] From Springfield in the middle of the state to Little Egypt in the south, a core group of militant miners attended political rallies calling for Irish independence, the defeat of police bills in the Illinois state legislature, and the release of jailed antiwar protesters such as Eugene Debs and Tom Mooney. As in Britain, hopes were still high for some new form of industrial democracy that would provide workers with a greater share of the profits from industry and protect them against the counterattack that employers in both countries were now making to restore the prewar status quo.[103]

From the Farmer-Labor party's perspective, however, the results of this political agitation were disappointing. In the spring of 1920 third-party slates were run in almost a dozen of the coal towns where the SPA had been strong before World War I. As before, most of these towns were in Macoupin, Madison, and St. Clair Counties in southwestern Illinois, but a few Farmer-Labor candidates were put up in Franklin, Saline, and Williamson Counties in Little Egypt, to which the coal industry's center of gravity was now shifting. As far as can be ascertained, however, municipal victories were secured in only three isolated instances: in the mixed coal and industrial towns of Belleville and East St. Louis, and in Harrisburg, in the south of Illinois.[104]

Still more disappointing were the results of John H. Walker's run for governor of Illinois on the Farmer-Labor Party ticket in the fall of 1920. As vice chair of the party, a political moderate, and a well-known labor leader, he might have been expected to do well even in some of the state's rural counties, where a farm depression was also beginning to bite. He did not. Walker got 17 percent of the vote in Macoupin County and did fairly well in a number of other coal-mining areas, but he got almost no votes anywhere else.[105] Unlike the workers in Glasgow, who were starting to vote for the Labour Party in large numbers, Chicago's huge working class cast fewer than five thousand votes of its almost one million for the Farmer-Labor Party. Instead, most of Illinois's labor voters protested the Democratic administration's 1919 antilabor crusade by voting Republican. "Workers disregarded the Farmer-Labor party appeal," explained the *New Majority*, "and vented their revenge on the Wilson administration for its effort to smash labor in the coal, steel, and railroad strikes by voting for [Republican presidential candidate] Harding."[106]

By 1921 the inability of district 12's radicals to secure any political results through third-party action left them even more vulnerable than before to the pleas of the more conservative elements in the Illinois State Federation of Labor, who had always preferred to secure labor legislation by exerting pressure on sympathetic Democrats and Republicans in the Illinois General Assembly in Springfield. In turn, this exposed the Achilles' heel that limited the growth of independent labor politics in the American Midwest ever since district 12 had affiliated with the ISFL in 1908: the greater effectiveness of the AFL's "reward-your-friends, punish-your-enemies" political policy over that of third-party action. The socialists' argument against this policy—that it condemned the unions to accepting political crumbs from the capitalist table—was no less cogent in the postwar period than it had been ten years before. With the collapse of both the SPA and the Farmer-Labor Party, however, and with the U.S. labor movement generally struggling to survive in a hostile business climate, the argument became increasingly difficult to uphold.[107]

As in the pre-1914 period, when he wavered between supporting the SPA and endorsing Progressive politicians such as Democratic governor Dunne, John H. Walker and his activities played a central role in the final triumph of nonpartisan politics in district 12. As president of the ISFL, Walker was once again the most powerful trade union leader in the state. His final apostasy, as far as the radical Left was concerned, began in 1921, when the Joint Labor Legislative Board, which was the ISFL's main lobbying arm in the state legislature, complained that by putting forward its own, independent political slate the previous fall, the Farmer-Labor Party had brought about the defeat of two of labor's "best friends" in the General Assembly, R. G. Soderstrom of Streator and K. C. Ronalds of Harrisburg, both of whom were pro-labor Republicans.[108]

As a result of these warnings, as well as of his earlier doubts, Walker began to deemphasize third-party politics in his speeches up and down the state.[109] At the same time the JLLB refined its lobbying tactics when the General Assembly met in Springfield. Late in 1921, for example, it began publishing a political newsletter that tabulated the votes of General Assembly members, both Republican and Democrat, on all bills of interest to labor. In 1921 these bills included an anticonstabulary measure, an anti-injunction law, and numerous amendments to the state's mining code. At election time the JLLB also issued leaflets urging union members to vote against any legislator, of either party, who had voted against the political reforms favored by the ISFL in the previous session and to vote for any candidate who had supported them. Beginning in 1921 the JLLB solicited funds from the ISFL's member unions to back up its AFL-endorsed nonpartisan policy.[110]

These two developments, coupled with pressure from AFL president Gompers, finally persuaded Walker to abandon his independent approach to political action, as well as his openly expressed support for the ethical form of socialism that, years before, had also fueled Keir Hardie's political beliefs in Walker's native Scotland. In a speech given to the January 1922 district 12 convention, Walker argued that if the Illinois miners persisted in cutting themselves off from the two major parties by founding an independent political movement, they would lose all the political clout they had built up over the years with friendly Republicans and Democrats in Springfield. "From experience men get new light, and they change their views," Walker said. The best policy was to "stick together" and abide by the nonpartisan political policies of the AFL.[111]

Walker's views were endorsed by a large majority of district 12's delegates.[112] As previously indicated, a small number of voters supported the independent presidential ticket of the Conference for Progressive Political Action in November 1924. Without the official support of district 12, however, they were never likely to get very far.[113] In effect, the January 1922 district 12 convention's decision to endorse the AFL's nonpartisan political policy ended the miners' experiment with independent labor politics. The parting of the ways between Scotland and Illinois was now complete.

CONCLUSION: COMPARATIVE CLASS FORMATION AND THE COLLIERS WHO CROSSED THE SEA

The preceding chapters traced the fortunes of a select group of coal miners, first in their native Scotland and then both there and in the American Midwest, over a period of one hundred years. Because of the extensive influence that the organized miners played in the development of British and American industrial relations, it is legitimate to ask what new light this comparative study sheds on the differential development of the U.S. and British labor movements, on the question of American exceptionalism, and on the process of class formation as a whole.

The coal industries of both Lanarkshire and northern and southern Illinois went through three similar stages of economic development, although these stages were staggered somewhat because Scottish industrialization began earlier. The first stage, which lasted from about 1830 to 1870, was a period of small-scale, shallow pits where the technology was primitive and the production process was controlled almost entirely by the miners themselves.[1] During the second stage the competitive pressures of an expanded market prompted the introduction of shaft mines and new steam-driven machinery, which led to an increase in the division of labor. In the third period, which began in the 1880s and continued until after 1924, the scale of mining was expanded still further, machine mining was introduced, and industrial discipline became still more strict.

The consequence of this shared history of economic development, at several different levels, was a growing separation of class interests in the coal industry on each side of the ocean, both in the workplace and in the community. In developmental terms this polarization reached its peak in the highly industrialized coal mines of Blantyre, Scotland, and Spring Valley, Illinois, in the decades leading up to World War I. Both towns possessed a half-dozen large-scale, deep-shaft coal mines employing hundreds of men working under the longwall method with coal-cutting machines and other modern equipment. Most of the colliers in these pits were semi-proletarians rather than artisan-colliers, as their predecessors in the coalfields had been one hundred years before. Newcomer-rebels were less common than they had been earlier, since by this time both the British and the American coal industries were nearing their peaks of production. Geographically speaking, by 1914 modern methods of production had also spread not only to older coal towns such as Larkhall and Wishaw in the Clyde Valley, and to the remaining coal towns in northern Illinois, but also to much of the rest of the coal industry throughout southern Scotland and the American Midwest.

It is true, as Roy Church and Quentin Outram have pointed out, that mining strikes are frequently idiosyncratic and that the development of solidarity among colliers does not follow a linear pattern.[2] Nevertheless, the third stage of economic development in the industry, between 1880 and 1924, provided the most likely context for full-scale class polarization to take place. Among the employers the result was tighter industrial discipline, separate employer federations, and an increasingly hostile attitude toward trade unions on both sides of the Atlantic.

Among the miners the emergence of modern class relations in the coal industry accelerated the breakdown of social deference, especially for the nineteenth-century cadre of artisan-colliers. In southwest Scotland the separation of the workers' and owners' class interests introduced a new level of hostility into the already polarized relations that had characterized the preexisting social and economic hierarchy. No such preexisting social and economic hierarchy was present on the midwestern prairie when the Scottish miners first settled there in 1865. At this time the mining industry in northern Illinois was also in a more primitive state than it was in Lanarkshire, enabling the immigrant colliers to recapture the high degree of workplace autonomy they had once enjoyed at home. Nevertheless, in America this utopian republican order of small-scale coalpits and easy social relations was quickly undermined by the same set of industrial changes that had fostered the rise of class antagonism between the miners and the mine owners of southwest Scotland.

At first, in a vain attempt to maintain good relations with the employers, artisan-colliers such as Alexander McDonald in southwest Scotland and John James and Daniel McLaughlin in the northern Illinois coalfield maintained a policy of arbitration and conciliation and selective strikes. In the industrial crises of the early 1870s, however, these policies were found wanting in the United States just as they were in Great Britain. A series of bitter, regionwide strikes broke out on both sides of the Atlantic, and they resulted in a similar sense of alienation and defeat. The class-harmony ideal, which had been cherished even more deeply in America than in Britain,[3] now came under attack in both Lanarkshire and northern Illinois. Its decline was symbolized in Lanarkshire by the repudiation of Alexander McDonald's leadership in 1873–74 and in northern Illinois by the quarrel between John James and Daniel McLaughlin during the 1877 Braidwood strike.

In southwest Scotland in the years that followed, the whole apparatus of mid-Victorian class collaborationist trade unionism was slowly abandoned, to be replaced, under the leadership of Keir Hardie and others, by a class-conscious trade union philosophy emphasizing national coal unions, state intervention in the coal industry, and aggressive use of the strike. This was followed, after 1900, by the consolidation and rapid growth of the Lanarkshire County Miners Union. Its increased numbers gave the union much greater ability both to determine the outcome of collective bargaining negotiations with the employers and to influence the political process.

Much the same development occurred in Illinois. As in Scotland, the colliers' unions had to undergo a lengthy period of employer opposition before they were able to organize more than a small fraction of the local labor force. The number of strike defeats and lockouts they sustained along the way, however, particularly during the depression years of the mid-1870s and mid-1890s, was almost identical to what it was in Lanarkshire. The Spring Valley lockout of 1889, for example, and the humiliating defeat of the American national coal strike in 1894 were especially disillusioning for immigrant miners who had come to believe that a democratic republic would never permit the capitalist class to engage in the kind of oppressive behavior that the colliers had confronted back home.

The growth of union bureaucracy and the emergence of a career-oriented cadre of union officers also led to the rise of similar syndicalist movements in both the LCMU and Illinois district 12 in the years leading up to World War I, particularly among the semi-proletarians and newcomer-rebels. Indeed, the movement toward militant industrial unionism was in some ways more advanced among the midwestern colliers than it was among the Scottish ones. During the war the insurgent syndicalist movement, sometimes called the Miners' Minority Movement in Scotland, was admittedly larger in Lanarkshire than in Illinois. Still, the anger and frustration that colliers felt at their governments' wartime manipulation of the coal industry, particularly at the inept way in which both Prime Minister Lloyd George and President Woodrow Wilson returned the industry to private hands in 1919–20, was expressed just as vehemently in the Illinois coalfield as it was in southwest Scotland.

Nevertheless, in class terms the Illinois miners' political and cultural response to the rise of corporate power in the coal industry was a good deal more ambiguous than that of the Lanarkshire miners. After the repudiation of McDonaldism in the 1870s, and still more after the bitter strike defeat of 1894, it seemed almost natural for Keir Hardie to invoke collectivist solutions to the problems facing Scottish miners. Despite an almost identical history of employer exploitation at the workplace, however, it took much longer for the Illinois miners to turn toward radical politics, and when they did, they did not embrace the socialist alternative to the existing capitalist system as extensively or as consistently as their Scottish counterparts. Was there anything in the circumstances of the colliers on the American side of the Atlantic, either in the workplace or in the community, that made them less inclined to embrace a collective political response to industrial exploitation than were miners in Scotland?

By 1914 the leaders of the LCMU and of Illinois district 12 of the UMWA had forged among their followers in Lanarkshire and northern Illinois, respectively, a nearly indistinguishable brand of solidarity both in the community and down the pit. Contrary to the standard opinion, ethnic differences did not create more problems for miner solidarity in Illinois than in southwest Scotland.[4] Established Scottish artisan-colliers initially viewed the unskilled Irish emigrants whom the coal masters brought into the Lanarkshire pits in the 1840s and 1850s with the same mixture of fear and suspicion that British immigrant miners displayed toward the peasant recruits whom U.S. coal owners brought into the midwestern mines from eastern and southern Europe in the 1880s and 1890s. Despite initial hostility, however, and the higher proportion of new European immigrants in America compared to Scotland, these cultural differences and the residential segregation they fostered were no more inimical to class formation in the Illinois coal-mining regions than they were in Lanarkshire.

Indeed, it can even be argued that the political and cultural divisions that emerged between Protestant miners and their Irish Catholic counterparts in Lanarkshire were more, rather than less, damaging to the development of long-term class loyalties in southwest Scotland than were the ethnic conflicts that developed between the British colliers and the Italians and Slavs in the Illinois coalfield. In the latter case community solidarity was inhibited by cultural and linguistic divisions that faded with the passage of time, and with the imposition of a self-conscious "Americanization movement" at the time of World War I for which there was no equivalent in Scottish society. In the former, despite the common use of the English language, ethnic and religious divisions were kept alive by the presence of an active Irish nationalist movement that sought consciously to keep the Protestant and Catholic communities apart.

Moreover, I do not believe, contra Sean Wilentz and other scholars who debated the subject of exceptionalism in the early 1980s, that it was the persistence of working-class republicanism among the laboring class in America that undercut the Illinois miners' willingness to embrace a collectivist solution to their problems. My evidence suggests that militant republicanism did not became a viable U.S. substitute for more orthodox forms of European class consciousness.[5] As is made clear by the despairing speech about the inadequacy of republican ideology that Daniel McLaughlin made following the 1877 strike defeat, the search for new answers to their predicament became just as pressing for the Illinois colliers during the depression years of 1873–96 as it was for the Scottish miners. The obsolete character of "General" Alexander Bradley's rhetoric concerning the virtues of joint stewardship over the coal industry during the 1897 strike illustrates the same point, as do Henry Demarest Lloyd's efforts to recast the U.S. radical tradition during the 1894 Labor-Populist episode by identifying it more closely with the collectivist ideas of Keir Hardie's ILP and with the non-Marxist ideas of the British Fabians.

Nevertheless, the Scottish colliers who settled in the American Midwest after 1865 enjoyed at least two social and economic advantages that rendered them less likely to embrace collectivist policies than were the British miners they had left behind. The first was their superior standard of living. The 1884 report of the Illinois Bureau of Labor Statistics clearly shows that in terms of home ownership, food purchases, and other domestic comforts, colliers' living standards were significantly higher in the northern Illinois coalfield than they were in southwest Scotland. During the 1880s money wages in the Streator pits were more than 50 percent higher than in Wishaw.

Second, anecdotal as well as statistical evidence shows that upward mobility rates among the first-generation colliers who settled in Braidwood and Streator were far higher than they were for the miners of Wishaw and Larkhall. The evidence suggests that within a few years a significant minority of the most talented leaders among the Illinois miners, taking advantage of a superior public education system, became engineers, professional men, or even mine owners themselves. Save for the few colliers who graduated from the Glasgow School of Mines, however, until the 1930s the only avenue of upward mobility for most Lanarkshire miners was to become a union officer, a shop assistant, or possibly a professional soccer player. Restrictions such as these reinforced the rigid character of the preindustrial Scottish social hierarchy and set severe limits to what even the most ambitious among the Lanarkshire miners could hope to achieve.

It is true that by the end of the century the Illinois miners had lost some of the social and economic advantages that they had earlier enjoyed over their Lanarkshire counterparts. Wage levels remained higher than in Scotland, but home ownership rates declined, industrial discipline intensified, and as the power of the mining companies increased, the former frontier coal communities of the American Midwest took on more of the characteristics of the eastern company towns. Nor should it be assumed, simply because many first-generation Lanarkshire colliers had left the pits by 1890, that no other groups of Illinois miners had any interest in advocating collectivist solutions to the miners' predicament. For example, in her study of the relationship between ethnicity and radicalism in the southern Illinois coal counties, Stephane Booth found that the Italian and Slavic miners were just as likely as the older generation of immigrant miners to vote for the Socialist Party in the pre–World War I era and for the Farmer-Labor parties that emerged just after it.[6]

However, the post–World War I vote for these parties was very small. These votes did not compensate for the fact that by 1890 a significant minority of the founding generation of British miners had either left the state of Illinois or moved up and out of the pits altogether. This development was bound to dilute the class-conscious sentiments of the Illinois mining community as a whole. It confirms the evidence adduced by Stephan Thernstrom and other scholars about the importance of greater U.S. social and geographical mobility in weakening class ties at the community level.[7] The presence of former colliers among the supervisors, pit bosses, and middle-class professionals with whom the post-1890 generation of immigrant miners came into contact undoubtedly blurred the class distinctions that existed in the coal towns. The fact that the radicals in district 12 were at pains to expel the

Mine Managers Association from the ranks of the Illinois State Federation of Labor in 1907 is clear evidence of this.

The most marked contrast between the LCMU and Illinois district 12 in their political reactions to the rise of corporate power in the coal industry, however, came in their differential responses to electoral politics and the role of the state. A distinction should be drawn here between the process of class formation at the workplace and in the community and support for an independent political party of labor. It is perfectly possible to conceive of a rising class consciousness and the growth of a militant trade union movement at the workplace, on the one hand, and a refusal to endorse a political party of labor, on the other.

Indeed, this is the basis of a general distinction that Ira Katznelson and others have drawn between the development of labor politics in America and that in a number of European countries.[8] In Germany, for example, where the unions were to some extent a creature of the Social Democratic Party, decisions about collective bargaining and electoral politics were often made by the same men in the same industrial and political context.[9] In America, however, decisions about politics and trade union matters were more likely to be kept separate. From this point of view, Britain occupied an intermediate position between the United States and Germany. In America, as in Britain, most workers at first adopted a hands-off, voluntarist attitude toward the state rather than a collectivist approach. Over the long run, however, even though the British miners were suspicious of state power, their doubts were not great enough to prevent them from joining the Labour Party, whereas U.S. miners' suspicions kept them from supporting a similar party in their own country. Having grown up in the volunteerist traditions of the AFL, the miners of Illinois district 12 had by 1919 become so skeptical about statist solutions that they were unwilling to follow the example of their Scottish fellows to more than a limited extent.

This point becomes clear when one compares the electoral tactics pursued by the miners' unions in Lanarkshire with those used by the Illinois colliers from the inception of miners' political activism in the mid-nineteenth century up to the triumph of the Labour Party in southwest Scotland in the 1922 general election. At first, while the political ideas of Alexander McDonald held sway, the two groups' political tactics were more or less the same. In the 1860s and 1870s miners on both sides of the Atlantic lobbied legislative bodies, whether Parliament, in Westminster, or the Illinois General Assembly, in Springfield, for mine safety legislation. They followed this up by electing McDonald to Parliament and William Mooney and John Hinchcliffe to the Illinois General Assembly.

Soon thereafter, however, the political behavior of the colliers in southwest Scotland began to diverge from that of miners in the Illinois coalfield. The Illinois colliers elected approximately ten more miners to the Illinois state legislature between 1880 and 1910, but all of them were either Democrats or Republicans. The Labor-Populist Party's failure to make any serious gains in the downstate mining counties of Illinois in the state elections of 1894 was due in part to ideological conflicts between the political groups that made up the coalition. It was due far more, however, to the fact that the leaders of the labor movement in Chicago, who carried more political clout than the downstate colliers did at this time, were already heavily implicated in the machine politics of both the Democratic and the Republican Parties. In the summer of 1894 William C. Pomeroy, the corrupt leader of the Chicago Trades and Labor Assembly, even used Democratic Party funds in an effort to break up the Labor-Populist alliance.[10] This tactic confirms Martin Shefter's remark that "the institutionalization of the trade union and the political machine established the characteristic manner in which class conflicts in the United States could be channeled and thereby contained."[11]

Because most Scottish miners could not vote until at least 1884, moreover, they were not so deeply socialized into a preexisting two-party system where they could readily influence one or the other of the two major parties in their own interests. As a consequence, once they did get the vote, the Lanarkshire miners had a somewhat greater incentive to support a political party of their own. From Keir Hardie's by-election effort in 1888 onward, the leaders of the LCMU consistently strove to elect members of their union to local municipal councils as well as to Parliament under the aegis of the Labour Party. For many years they failed in these endeavors, partly because of the divided Irish vote but mainly because of the rank and file's attachment to the Liberal Party. Nevertheless, even though the Labour Party was overshadowed by the "new liberalism" of Lloyd George, by 1914 it had made itself into a valuable ally of the MFGB by championing such matters as worker's compensation, the reversal of the Taff Vale and Osborne Judgements, and the eight-hour day in the mines.

Meanwhile, between 1908 and 1916, the mining communities of central and southern Illinois gave significant support to the Socialist Party of America. A genuine socialist movement took root there, whose aims included the development of retail cooperatives, the extension of union democracy, and the socialization of municipal services. Even as it did so, however, other political developments occurred that rendered the socialists' task increasingly difficult. One such development was Illinois district 12's affiliation with the nonpartisan Illinois State Federation of Labor in 1908. Another was the establishment of the Miners Legislative Committee, which sent district 12 representatives to Springfield to lobby for mining legislation. Both these moves drew the Illinois colliers deeper and deeper into the AFL's nonpartisan policy of political lobbying and cross-party voting as the best way to secure improvements in the state's mining code. The polarization of politics along class lines in Illinois was weakened still further by the establishment of the Mining Investigation Commission in 1909.[12]

Then came the intensification of industrial conflict on both sides of the Atlantic on the eve of World War I. The Lawrence textile strike of 1912, the Ludlow massacre of 1914, and the national strike that took place in the American mines four years earlier contributed to a sharp rise in class conflict in America. Nevertheless, the economic threat posed by the Triple Alliance, linked to the crisis over Irish home rule and the reform of the House of Lords, created the sense of "an impending clash" in Britain that had no real equivalent in the United States.

Despite these differences in the intensity of class conflict at the workplace, it was the workers' differential responses to the stresses imposed by World War I, not a prior event, that finally elevated the Labour Party to its dominant position in British labor politics and doomed the Socialist Party of America to insignificance.[13] The key development in Britain was the 1916 split in the Liberal Party, which revealed the limits of British liberalism and provided Labour with a chance to participate in government that was never open to American socialists. The greater social and economic price that World War I exacted from British workers also confirmed a growing number of colliers in their support for the Labour Party and helped temporarily to shift Britain's political agenda to the Left. Despite differences of opinion over whether America should enter the conflict, World War I produced no comparable crisis there within the ruling Democratic Party. Instead, as a result of racial turmoil, the revival of anti-immigrant hostility, and the greater virulence of the Red Scare in America compared to Great Britain, the U.S. political agenda shifted rapidly to the Right. In 1920, with the collapse of Progressivism, most of the disaffected miners in Illinois expressed their anger with President Wilson's treatment of them during the war by shifting their votes back to the Republican Party, not by voting for the Farmer-Labor Party. In that sense it was a concrete historical event, not some special characteristic of the American polity, that precipitated the final parting of the political ways between the Lanarkshire County Miners Union and Illinois district 12 of the UMWA.

Nevertheless, the inability of either the SPA, the Farmer-Labor Party, or the CPPA to attract the majority of district 12's miners also suggests that, in addition to adventitious historical events such as World War I, several structural and ideological differences between the political traditions of Britain and America also prevented U.S. colliers from adopting a collectivist response to the industrialization process. As was already suggested, one difference was the socialization of the American miners into the preexisting two-party system. By 1919 this process had enabled district 12's legislative committee, using the AFL's "reward-your-friends, punish-your-enemies" political policy, to secure from the Illinois state legislature a mining code every bit as good as the one provided by Parliament.[14]

The second structural difference arose from democratic reforms introduced into the American political system during the Progressive Era, particularly the system of primary elections. These reforms encouraged radical candidates from both the Left and the Right to enter the primaries of both major political parties while ensuring that a moderate who represented the widest range of Democratic or Republican opinions would be selected as the candidate in the general election.[15] This put the candidates of minority organizations such as the Socialist Party at an automatic disadvantage. John H. Walker referred to this problem in a letter he wrote to MFGB president Robert Smillie in September 1920, when Walker was about to run for Illinois governor on the Farmer-Labor ticket. Responding to Smillie's interest in the revival of independent labor politics in Chicago in the postwar era, Walker wrote: "I am not hopeful that I could get a large vote for governor of Illinois. Unlike you in your parliamentary system, we have a way here for the laborites in Chicago to put their men in the Democratic primaries. This means they will be listened to, without thinking of me and the farm-laborites at all."[16]

The third difference between the voting behavior of British and American miners — a difference prompted, this time, by ideological considerations — arose from the point already made about their contrasting attitudes toward the state. The American miners, like those in Britain, experienced state power in both a positive and a negative way and in roughly equal proportions. On the negative side, they were antagonized by the use of court injunctions to limit the activities of their trade unions and by the use of state militia to break their strikes. Nevertheless, colliers in both countries also benefited from general labor laws passed by their respective national governments and from the safety and collective bargaining legislation that was designed especially to satisfy their needs.[17] When it came to all-out socialist collectivist measures such as the nationalization of industry, however, the American colliers were far more hesitant than their British counterparts to endorse such an outcome. Hence they were less likely to embrace a left-wing political party that advocated collectivist goals.

This difference of outlook is most clearly illustrated by the contrasting stands that the LCMU and Illinois district 12 adopted toward the question of mine nationalization. At first glance there seems to have been little difference between the two unions' positions on the issue. The 1892 Omaha platform of the People's Party, for example, which district 12 endorsed in its support for the Labor-Populist alliance in 1894, came out for nationalizing mines in the United States only a few years after Keir Hardie had advocated the same idea for Britain. Nonetheless, these apparent similarities disguised significant differences. Union president John L. Lewis easily scuttled the 1919 UMWA convention's decision in favor of mine nationalization.[18] Most leaders of the MFGB, on the other hand, never wavered in their support for the idea. In fact, their disaffection with the British coalition government in 1919 (and hence with the Liberal Party) was partly predicated on Prime Minister Lloyd George's rejection of the majority Sankey Commission's report in favor of mine nationalization that same year.[19]

At the regional level, the most revealing evidence of the Illinois miners' greater unwillingness to embrace the idea of collective ownership (and hence of state control over industry) came in the post–World War I debate about mine nationalization that took place in both the LCMU and district 12. Even when they favored it, most Illinois miners who took part in the debate saw nationalization not as a means for bringing the coal industry under state control but as a mechanism whereby rank-and-file miners could replace *de facto* control over their individual workplaces by legally recognized control. This was a syndicalist approach to the issue, not a statist one, and it corroborates the opinions of previous scholars who have viewed the American radical tradition as neo-anarchist rather than neocollectivist.[20]

In a similar discussion about the nationalization of the British mines that took place in the LCMU's executive committee in the winter of 1923, the miners's attitudes were significantly different. In Lanarkshire mine nationalization was favored on the grounds that once the Labour Party got into power, it would "be able to make Parliament do our [the miners'] bidding, not follow the will of the capitalists."[21] This showed the British miners' greater willingness to use their electoral clout to secure power *in* the state, rather than, as in America, to use the state simply to *influence* government policy in the miners' direction.

The overall conclusion to be drawn from this study is not that the miners who crossed the sea from Scotland to Illinois followed an identical path in the development of modern working-class consciousness. Aside from anything else, the political and economic crisis generated by World War I cut deeper in Clydeside than it did in the American Midwest. For that, as well as for other reasons, independent labor politics took root in southwest Scotland in ways they never did in the mining regions of Illinois.

This difference in political outcome was important for the future of party politics in both Britain and America. Because they finally joined and then became a mainstay of an independent party of labor, the British miners cut themselves off from the cultural hegemony of the two main British political parties, and they played a major role in the Labour Party's accession to power. This ultimately enabled the Scottish miners' M.P.s, as part of the Labour Party, to help fashion a welfare state in Britain that was far more extensive than the one that UMWA president John L. Lewis, along with the CIO, helped to create by supporting the Democratic Party in the New Deal period of the 1930s. In this sense, the class experience cut deeper and had more profound consequences for the development of national politics in Britain than it did in America.[22]

Nevertheless, this comparative study suggests at least two additional reasons for abandoning the exceptionalist paradigm in future interpretations of U.S. labor politics. The first is that to judge the degree of class consciousness among workers solely by the presence or absence of an independent political party of labor, as many exceptionalist scholars do, is to wear the wrong set of glasses. It obscures common traditions of militancy at the workplace and in the community on both sides of the Atlantic that resulted from the same industrialization process and brought about many of the same movements of social protest. The correct way to approach the problem is to study the goals laid down by the workers themselves and then to see how far they were able to fulfill them within the means they had at their disposal, not to investigate how far they corresponded to some a priori definition of liberal or radical ideology.

Second, as the previous chapters make clear, the reform program espoused by the miners of Illinois, with the important exception of mine nationalization, was in most respects similar to the one upheld by the colliers in Lanarkshire. In the post–World War I era, for example, miners on both sides of the Atlantic advocated some form of industrial democracy that included old age pensions, the vote for women, improved workers' compensation laws, release of political prisoners incarcerated during the war, and a "hands-off" policy toward Soviet Russia. The difference between the political positions of the LCMU and Illinois district 12 consisted not so much in contrasting visions of social progress for their respective countries but in the different means by which those visions were to be achieved.

On the U.S. side of the ocean, the logic of the open franchise, the cross-class character of the existing two-party system, and a long history of mass participatory democracy pushed the miners into using the AFL's lobbying methods to bring about social change. On the British side of the ocean, in a more narrowly based electoral system dominated by class-based political parties from which they had earlier been excluded, the colliers used the Labour Party to press for roughly comparable aims. In the last analysis, therefore, it was the differing nature of the British and American two-party systems, coupled with divergent attitudes toward the role of the state in industry and the crisis created by World War I, that brought about the parting of the political ways. It had little to do with any fundamental difference in the respective levels of class consciousness among the miners themselves.

Notes

INTRODUCTION

1. *Glasgow Sentinel,* May 1, 1865, p. 6; ibid., October 14, 1867, p. 5; Herbert Gutman, "Five Letters of Immigrant Workers from Scotland to the United States, 1867–1869: William Latta, Daniel M'Lachlan, and Allan Pinkerton," *Labor History* 9:2 (Spring 1968): 384–408.

2. Katherine A. Harvey, *The Best-Dressed Miners: Life and Labor in the Maryland Coal Region, 1835–1910* (Ithaca, N.Y.: Cornell University Press, 1969), 81–83, 94–95; Rowland A. Berthoff, *British Immigrants in Industrial America, 1790–1950* (Cambridge, Mass.: Harvard University Press, 1953), chap. 6.

3. *Glasgow Sentinel,* May 7, 1865, p. 5.

4. For general histories of the MFGB and the UMWA, see R. Page Arnot, *The Miners, Years of Struggle: A History of the Miners Federation of Great Britain (from 1910 Onwards)* (London: George Allen and Unwin, 1953); Maier B. Fox, *United We Stand: The United Mine Workers of America, 1890–1990* (Washington, D.C.: United Mine Workers of America, 1990).

5. Louis Hartz, *The Liberal Tradition: An Interpretation of American Political Thought since the Revolution* (San Diego, Calif.: Harcourt Brace Jovanovich, 1991); Seymour M. Lipset, *American Exceptionalism: A Double-Edged Sword* (New York: Norton, 1996); Richard Ostreicher, "Urban Working-Class Political Behavior and Theories of American Electoral Politics, 1870–1940," *Journal of American History* 74:4 (Spring 1988): 1257–86; Mike Davis, "Why the U.S. Working Class Is Different," *New Left Review* 123 (May 1980): 5–44; Victoria C. Hattam, *Labor Visions and State Power: The Origins of Business Unionism in the United States* (Princeton, N.J.: Princeton University Press, 1993).

6. The most interesting debate among social historians over the merits of exceptionalism in analyzing U.S. labor history remains that among Sean Wilentz, Nick Salvatore, Michael Hanagan, and Steven Sapolsky in *International Labor and Working Class History* 26 (Fall 1984): 1–26 and 27 (Spring 1985): 35–38.

7. For other critiques of the exceptionalist paradigm, see Eric Foner, "Why Is There No Socialism in the United States?" *History Workshop* 17 (Spring 1984): 57–80; Rick Halpern and Jonathan Morris, eds., *American Exceptionalism? U.S. Working-Class Formation in an International Perspective* (London: Macmillan, 1996); and Ira Katznelson and Aristide Zolberg, eds., *Working-Class Formation: Nineteenth-Century Patterns in Western Europe and the United States* (Princeton, N.J.: Princeton University Press, 1986). For my own opinions, see John H. M. Laslett, "Pluralism, Liberalism and History: Seymour Martin Lipset and His Worldview," *Transaction/SOCIETY* 20:5 (July–August 1983): 64–68.

8. Gary Marks, *Unions in Politics: Britain, Germany, and the United States in the Nineteenth and Early Twentieth Centuries* (Princeton, N.J.: Princeton University Press, 1989); Leon Fink, *Workingmen's Democracy: The Knights of Labor and American Democracy* (Urbana: University of Illinois Press, 1983); Kim Voss, *The Knights of Labor and Class Formation in the Nineteenth Century* (Ithaca, N.Y.: Cornell University Press, 1993).

9. Katznelson and Zolberg, eds., *Working-Class Formation,* 399. See also Theda Skocpol and Margaret Somers, "The Uses of Comparative History in Macrosocial Inquiry," *Comparative Studies in Society and History* 22 (April 1980): 174–97.

10. Werner Sombart, *Why Is There No Socialism in the United States?* ed. and with an intro. by C. T. Husbands (White Plains, N.Y.: M. E. Sharpe, 1976); Selig Perlman, *A Theory of the Labor Movement* (repr., New York: Augustus M. Kelley, 1966); Philip S. Foner, *History of the Labor Movement in the United States,* 11 vols. (New York: International, 1947–85), vol. 1.

11. This point can be made about many, although not all, of Lipset's works on the topic. See, e.g., Seymour M. Lipset, *The First New Nation: The United States in Historical and Comparative Perspective* (New York: Norton, 1979). However, Lipset's *Agrarian Socialism: The Cooperative Commonwealth Federation in Saskatchewan—A Study in Political Sociology* (Berkeley: University of California Press, 1950), which compares radical agrarian movements in Saskatchewan and North Dakota, is a work of genuine comparative history.

12. Exceptions to this tendency include Peter Shergold, *Working-Class Life: The "American Standard" in Comparative Perspective, 1899–1914* (Pittsburgh: University of Pittsburgh Press, 1982); Gerald Friedman, *State-Making and Labor Movements: France and the United States, 1876–1914* (Ithaca, N.Y.: Cornell University Press, 1998).

13. Sean Wilentz, "Against Exceptionalism: Class Consciousness and the American Labor Movement," *International Labor and Working Class History* 26 (Fall 1984): 5.

14. Aristide Zolberg, "How Many Exceptionalisms?" in *Working-Class Formation,* ed. Katznelson and Zolberg, 398–404.

15. David Brion Davis, *The Problem of Slavery in Western Culture*, 2 vols. (Ithaca, N.Y.: Cornell University Press, 1967).

16. Richard J. Evans, *The Feminists: Women's Emancipation Movements in Europe, America, and Australasia, 1840–1920* (London: Croom Helm, 1977).

17. Ann Orloff, *The Politics of Pensions: A Comparative Analysis of Britain, Canada, and the United States* (Madison: University of Wisconsin Press, 1993).

18. Friedrich Lenger, "Beyond Exceptionalism: Notes on the Artisanal Phase of the Labour Movement in France, England, Germany, and the United States," *International Review of Social History* 36 (1991): 1–23.

19. For a work that demonstrates the traditions of international solidarity among coal miners in many different countries, see Klaus Tenfelde, ed., *Sozialgeschichte des Bergbaus im 19. und 20. Jahrhundert* (Munich: C. H. Beck, 1992).

20. Eric D. Weitz, "Class Formation and Labor Protest in the Mining Communities of Southern Illinois and the Ruhr, 1890–1925," *Labor History* 27:1 (Winter 1985–86): 85–105.

21. For a study of German coal miners' unions that does take these variables into account, see Marks, *Unions in Politics*, chap. 5.

22. Roger Fagge, *Power, Culture, and Conflict in the Coalfields: West Virginia and South Wales, 1900–1922* (Manchester, U.K.: Manchester University Press, 1996).

23. See my review of Fagge's book in *International Labor and Working Class History* 53 (Spring 1998): 252–55. For additional discussions of comparative coal-mining history, see Roy Church and Quentin Outram, *Strikes and Solidarity: Coalfield Conflict in Britain, 1889–1966* (Cambridge: Cambridge University Press, 1998), 252–59.

24. James Holt, "Trade Unionism in the British and U.S. Steel Industries, 1880–1914," *Labor History* 18:1 (Winter 1977): 6–35.

25. Jeffrey Haydu, *Between Craft and Class: Skilled Workers and Factory Politics in the United States and Britain, 1890–1922* (Berkeley: University of California Press, 1988).

26. For a recent study that examines the differences between exceptionalism, comparative history, and transnational history, see George Frederickson, "From Exceptionalism to Variety: Recent Developments in Cross-National Comparative History," *Journal of American History* 80:2 (September 1995): 587–604.

CHAPTER 1: SOCIAL STRUCTURE AND CLASS IN EARLY SCOTTISH MINING VILLAGES

1. Robert Duncan, *Wishaw: Life and Labour in a Lanarkshire Industrial Community, 1790–1914* (Motherwell: Department of Leisure Services, 1986), 6–7; Jack McLellan, *Larkhall: Its Historical Development* (Larkhall: H. Mathew, 1979), 24–36; Alan Campbell, *The Lanarkshire Miners: A Social History of Their Trade Unions, 1775–1874* (Edinburgh: John Donald, 1979), 157–61; Anthony Slaven, *The Development of the West of Scotland, 1750–1960* (London: Routledge and Kegan Paul, 1975), 92–103.

2. *Scottish Ordinance Survey Maps, Wishaw and Larkhall* (1864).

3. Campbell, *Lanarkshire Miners,* 157–61; Norman Murray, *The Scottish Hand-Loom Weavers, 1790–1850: A Social History* (Edinburgh: John Donald, 1978), chap. 2; *Third Statistical Account of Scotland* (Edinburgh: William Blackwood and Sons, 1845), 721–25.

4. Sydney Checkland, *Dictionary of Scottish Business Biography, 1860–1960,* 2 vols. (Aberdeen: Aberdeen University Press, 1986), 1:30–33, 51–52.

5. Checkland, *Dictionary,* 1:46–48; Duncan, *Wishaw,* 38–46; Slaven, *Development,* 116–17.

6. Duncan, *Wishaw,* 14–18; R. D. Corrins, "William Baird and Company, Coal and Iron Masters, 1830–1914" (Ph.D. diss., University of Strathclyde, 1974), 91–103.

7. Duncan, *Wishaw,* 15–16.

8. Campbell, *Lanarkshire Miners,* 151–52.

9. Alan Campbell, "Honourable Men and Degraded Slaves: A Comparative Study of Trade Unionism in Two Lanarkshire Mining Communities, c. 1830–1874," in *Independent Collier: The Coal Miner as Archetypal Proletarian Revisited,* ed. Royden Harrison (Hassocks, U.K.: Harvester, 1978), 102.

10. Scottish Population Census, Cambusnethan, Hamilton, Dalserf, and Stonehouse Parishes, 1851, 1861, 1871.

11. Clark Kerr and Abraham Siegel, "The Inter-Industry Propensity to Strike: An International Comparison," in *Industrial Conflict,* ed. Arthur Kornhauser, Robert Dubin, and Arthur M. Ross (New York: McGraw-Hill, 1954), 189–212.

12. See, e.g., the criticisms of the "isolated-mass" hypothesis advanced in Harrison, ed., *Independent Collier,* 1–16; and in Roy Church and Quentin Outram, *Strikes and Solidarity: Coalfield Conflict in Britain, 1889–1966* (Cambridge: Cambridge University Press, 1998), chap. 8.

13. For critiques of the isolated-mass thesis that refer to Spain, West Virginia, and South Wales, see Roger Fagge, "A Comparison of South Wales and West Virginia, 1900–1922," and Adrian Shubert, "A Divided Community: The Social Development of the Asturian Coalfields to 1934," both in *Sozialgeschichte des Bergbaus im 19. und 20 Jahrhundert,* ed. Klaus Tenfelde (Munich: C. H. Beck, 1992), 105–22, 204–93.

14. Scottish Population Census, Larkhall and Hamilton Parishes, 1861.

15. Scottish Population Census, Cambusnethan Parish, 1851.

16. Scottish Population Census, Larkhall Parish, 1851, 1861, 1871.

17. Scottish Population Census, Stonehouse Parish, 1871.

18. McLellan, *Larkhall,* 18–19.

19. *Glasgow Herald,* September 14, 1871, p. 4; D. F. MacDonald, *Scotland's Shifting Population, 1770–1850* (Glasgow: Jackson and Son, 1937), chap. 4.

20. Scottish Population Census, Cambusnethan, Hamilton, Dalserf and Stonehouse Parishes, 1851, 1861, 1871.

21. Scottish Population Census, Cambusnethan, Hamilton, Dalserf and Stonehouse Parishes, 1881.

22. Scottish Population Census, Cambusnethan, Hamilton, Dalserf and Stonehouse Parishes, 1871.

23. James E. Handley, *The Irish in Scotland, 1798–1848* (Cork: Cork University Press, 1945), chaps. 2–3.

24. Ibid., 64.

25. For a discussion of religious and cultural divisions between Scottish and Irish miners, see Campbell, *Lanarkshire Miners,* chap. 7; and H. Senior, *Orangeism in Ireland and Britain, 1795–1836* (London: Routledge and Kegan Paul, 1966), 53–81.

26. See, e.g., John Benson, *British Coal Miners in the Nineteenth Century: A Social History* (New York: Holmes and Maier, 1980), chap. 4; M. Jones, "Changes in Industry Population and Settlement in the Exposed Coalfield of South Yorkshire, 1840–1908" (M.A. thesis, University of Nottingham, 1966), 214–38.

27. See the discussion on this point by Seymour M. Lipset and Stephan Thernstrom in *Failure of a Dream? Essays in the History of American Socialism,* ed. John H. M. Laslett and S. M. Lipset (Berkeley: University of California Press, 1985), chap. 12.

28. On "flitting" see Benson, *British Coal Miners,* 17–18.

29. Scottish Population Census, Cambusnethan, Dalziel, Larkhall, Hamilton, Dalserf, and Stonehouse Parishes, 1851, 1861, 1871.

30. Harrison, ed., *Independent Collier,* 8–12. For a Marxist interpretation, see Anna Rochester, *Labor and Coal* (New York: International, 1931).

31. Campbell, *Lanarkshire Miners,* chap. 8.

32. Alan Campbell and Fred Reid, "The Independent Collier in Scotland," in *Independent Collier,* ed. Harrison, chap. 2.

33. Quoted in ibid., 38.

34. Quoted in ibid., 40. Henry Pelling is the main proponent of the view that the typical miner was unskilled; see Henry Pelling, *Popular Politics and Society in Late Victorian Britain* (London: Macmillan, 1968), 47.

35. Campbell and Reid, "Independent Collier," 52.

36. Ibid., 65–66; Campbell, *Lanarkshire Miners,* 227–36; Bro. Tom Honeyman, ed., *Good Templary in Scotland: Its Works and Workers, 1869–1894* (Glasgow: Aird and Coghill, 1917), 12–15; Elspeth King, *Scotland Sober and Free: The Temperance Movement, 1829–1979* (Glasgow: Glasgow Museums and Art Galleries, 1979), 8–12.

37. Kellog Durland, *Among the Fife Miners* (London: Swan and Sonnenschein, 1904), 105–16.

38. See records of the Larkhall and Millheugh Friendly Society, Larkhall St. Thomas Lodge, Quarter Colliers Friendly Society, Newarthill Friendly Society, etc. in Larkhall; and those of Wishaw Friendly Society, Wishaw Iron Works Annual Friendly Society, etc. in Wishaw.

39. John Gordon, "On the State of Education among the Mining Population of Lanarkshire," *Transactions of the the National Association for the Promotion of Social Science* 2 (1860): 370–79.

40. *Glasgow Herald,* March 25, 1867, p. 4.

41. *Colliery Manager and Journal of Mining Engineering* 1:9 (September 18, 1885): 164–65.

42. For discussions of class harmony on both sides of the Atlantic in this period, see Asa Briggs, "The Language of 'Class' in Early Nineteenth-Century England," in *Essays in Labour History,* ed. Asa Briggs and John Saville (London: Macmillan, 1960), 58–65; and Martin J. Burke, *The Conundrum of Class: Public Discourse on the Social Order in America* (Chicago: University of Chicago Press, 1995), chap. 5.

43. Campbell and Reid, "Independent Collier," 64–65.

44. R. W. Dron, *The Coalfields of Scotland* (Edinburgh: R. W. MacKay, 1902), 48–53.

45. Raymond Challinor, "Alexander McDonald and the Miners," in *Our History,* Pamphlet 46 (N.p.: Communist Party of Great Britain, 1967–68).

46. William Cloughan, *A Series of Letters on the Restriction of Labour and Its Effects in the Mines of Lanarkshire* (Coatbridge, U.K., 1846), 12.

47. "Rules and Practices of the Wishaw Miners Association" (1857).

48. Campbell, *Lanarkshire Miners,* 41.

49. See, e.g., the discussion of the growing division of labor in the mines in T. G. Nasmyth, "Changing Work Arrangements in the Scottish Pits since the 1860s," *Transactions of the Mining Institute of Scotland* 3 (1881): 63–88.

50. James T. Barrowman, "New Categories of Workers in the Lanarkshire Coalfield," *Proceedings of the Philosophical Society of Glasgow* 22 (1882–83): 8–18.

51. Some of these differences in interest between different categories of miners are recounted in Durland, *Among the Fife Miners,* 15–37, 60–80.

52. A good description of the longwall system of mining and its implications for the organization of the work force can be found in Keith Dix, *Work Relations in the Coal Industry: The Hand-Loading Era, 1880–1930* (Morgantown, W. Va.: Institute for Labor Studies, 1977), 7–9.

53. *Coal Mines Inspectors Reports (Eastern and Western Districts of Scotland)* (1873), 166–69.

54. *Glasgow Sentinel,* February 9, 1868, p. 4.

55. *Coal Mines Inspectors Reports* (1881), 208–9.

56. Gordon Wilson, "The Strike Policy of the Miners of the West of Scotland, 1842–74," in *Essays in Scottish Labour History: A Tribute to W. H. Marwick,* ed. Ian MacDougall (Edinburgh: John Donald, 1986), 29–64.

57. Robert Haddow, "The Miners of Scotland," *The Nineteenth Century* 24 (September 1888): 359–67.

58. Quoted in Campbell and Reid, "Independent Collier," 60.

59. Haddow, "Miners of Scotland," 360.

60. *Airdrie, Coatbridge, Bathgate and Wishaw Advertiser,* May 2, 1864, p. 3.

61. Haddow, "Miners of Scotland," 363–64.

62. By 1870 the number of oncost workers employed in the Lanarkshire coalfield had reached 9,408, which was 23 percent of the mine labor force as a whole; see *Coal Mines Inspectors Reports* (1871), 119.

63. A striking example of this solidarity can be seen in the reaction of miners all across Scotland to the Blantyre pit disaster of October 1877, when a firedamp explo-

sion killed 207 men and boys. Colliers from more than thirty surrounding communities contributed volunteers, food, and money to the rescue effort, and contributions to the relief fund came from mining towns as far away as Australia, Canada, and the United States. See H. Duckham and B. Duckham, *Great Pit Disasters* (Newton Abbott, U.K.: Hanham, 1973), 140–48.

64. For the idea of the mining town as an "occupational community," see Martin Bulmer, "Sociological Models of the Mining Community," *Sociological Review* 23:1 (February 1975): 61–92; N. Dennis, P. Henriques, and C. Slaughter, *Coal Is Our Life* (London: Tavistock, 1956).

65. This generalization is based on indirect evidence drawn from newspaper accounts and novels. The similarity between Scottish and Irish surnames recorded in the Scottish population census makes it impossible to determine with any accuracy the ethnic backgrounds of Scottish and Irish marriage partners.

66. Gordon Wilson, *Alexander McDonald, Leader of the Miners* (Aberdeen: Aberdeen University Press, 1982), 41–42.

69. "Report on the Founding and Development of the Glasgow School of Mines," *Transactions of the Mining Institute of Scotland* 3 (1881): 124–43.

68. Scottish Population Census, Cambusnethan, Dalziel, Larkhall, Hamilton, Dalserf, and Stonehouse Parishes, 1851, 1861, 1871.

69. For the link between shared predispositions, collective action, and human agency in in the process of class formation, see Ira Katznelson and Aristide Zolberg, eds., *Working-Class Formation: Nineteenth-Century Patterns in Western Europe and the United States* (Princeton, N.J.: Princeton University Press, 1986), 14–20.

CHAPTER 2: CONFLICT AND ACCOMMODATION IN LANARKSHIRE, 1830–64

1. *Report of the Commissioners Appointed to Inquire into the State of the Population in the Mining Districts* (1844), 218.

2. Lord Shaftesbury played a significant role in shaping modern mining legislation in Britain, beginning with the removal of women from the pits in the early 1840s, but he was also an evangelical aristocrat who believed firmly that employers should maintain social control over their employees. See Georgina Battiscombe, *Shaftesbury: A Biography of the Seventh Earl, 1801–1885* (London: Constable, 1974), chaps. 10, 13–15.

3. Alan B. Campbell, *The Lanarkshire Miners: A Social History of Their Trade Unions, 1775–1874* (Edinburgh: John Donald, 1979), chap. 7.

4. Quoted in ibid., 215.

5. John T. Wilson, *Report by the County Medical Officer of Lanark on the Housing Conditions of Miners* (Glasgow: Robert Anderson, 1910), 40–41.

6. Robert Duncan, *Wishaw: Life and Labour in a Lanarkshire Industrial Community, 1790–1914* (Motherwell: Department of Leisure Services, 1986), 117–18.

7. See, e.g., the series of retrospective reports on miners' housing in the *North British Daily Mail* for May–June 1883.

8. *Wishaw Press,* May 18, 1870, p. 3.

9. For a discussion of the role of miners' wives in nineteenth-century coal-mining communities, see John Benson, *British Coalminers in the Nineteenth Century: A Social History* (New York: Holmes and Meier, 1980), chap. 5.

10. Kellog Durland, *Among the Fife Miners* (London: Swan and Sonnenschein, 1904), 52.

11. Duncan, *Wishaw,* 72–78.

12. Campbell, *Lanarkshire Miners,* 215–16.

13. John Conaghan, "The Truck System in North Lanarkshire, 1831–1887" (B.A. thesis, University of Strathclyde, 1977), 43.

14. Brian Harrison, *Drink and the Victorians: The Temperance Question in England, 1815–1872* (Pittsburgh: University of Pittsburgh Press, 1971), chap. 1.

15. Donald J. Withrington, "The Churches in Scotland, c. 1870: Towards a New Social Conscience," *Scottish Church History Records* 19 (1977): part 3, 162–68.

16. John Gordon, "On the State of Education among the Mining Population of Lanarkshire," *Transactions of the National Association for the Promotion of Social Science* (1860): 370–79.

17. Duncan, *Wishaw,* 131–38; *Hamilton Advertiser,* September 14, 1864, p. 4.

18. *Wishaw Press,* December 20, 1873, p. 3.

19. For a discussion of the period of serfdom in the Scottish coal mines and the miners' reactions to it, see B. F. Duckham, *A History of the Scottish Coal Industry,* 2 vols. (Newton Abbott, U.K.: Harvester, 1970), vol. 1, esp. chaps. 9–10.

20. Duncan, *Wishaw,* 73–74.

21. J. I. Brash, ed., *Papers on Scottish Electoral Politics, 1832–1854* (Edinburgh: T. and A. Constable, 1974), ix–xxxviii.

22. Jack McLellan, *Larkhall: Its Historical Development* (Larkhall: H. Mathew and Co., 1979), 14.

23. Burgh of Wishaw, Council Minute Books (1855), 14–15.

24. For a discussion of mass protest against the inadequacy of workers' housing in modern industrial Scotland, see Joseph Melling, *People's Struggle for Housing in West Scotland, 1890–1916* (Edinburgh: Polygon, 1983).

25. Campbell, *Lanarkshire Miners,* 134–35.

26. Records of the Victualling Society of Larkhall (1873), 4–5.

27. Elspeth King, *Scotland Sober and Free: The Temperance Movement, 1820–1979* (Glasgow: Glasgow Museums and Art Galleries, 1979), 16–23.

28. Conaghan, "Truck System," 41–43.

29. Quoted in Gordon Wilson, *Alexander McDonald, Leader of the Miners* (Aberdeen: Aberdeen University Press, 1982), 115.

30. Robert Howie, *The Churches and the Churchless in Scotland, Facts and Figures* (Glasgow: David Bryce and Son, 1893), 79–80; *Catholic Directory for the Clergy and Laity of Scotland* (1877), Mitchell Library, Glasgow.

31. Aside from hostility toward employer manipulation, other reasons for the decline in working-class church attendance in southwest Scotland in this period included increasing disbelief in the literal truth of the Bible, the loss of the Church of Scotland's prerogatives regarding education and poor-law relief, and the lack of new churches in industrialized areas. See Withrington, "Churches in Scotland," 155–61; T. C. Smout, *A Century of the Scottish People, 1830–1950* (London: Collins, 1986), 81–84; Andrew Drummond and James Bullock, *The Church in Late Victorian Scotland, 1874–1900* (Edinburgh: St. Andrews, 1978), 180–214.

32. Scottish Population Census, Cambusnethan, Hamilton, and Dalserf Parishes, 1861.

33. *Glasgow Sentinel,* June 5, 1860, p. 4.

34. Campbell, *Lanarkshire Miners,* 218.

35. Duncan, *Wishaw,* 134.

36. The early history of producers' and consumers' cooperation in southwest Scotland can be traced in the pages of the *Glasgow Sentinel* and in the life of its most famous early advocate, Alexander Campbell, who at one time was an Owenite missionary. See W. H. Marwick, *The Life of Alexander Campbell* (Glasgow: Glasgow and District Cooperative Association, 1964).

37. Robert Bullock, *A Century of Economic Striving: A History of the Inception, Aspirations, Progress, and Personalities of the Larkhall Victualling Society* (Glasgow: Scottish Cooperative Wholesale Society, 1922), 15–36.

38. Bullock, *Century of Economic Striving,* 28.

39. *Hamilton Advertiser,* January 14, 1860, p. 3; ibid., July 9, 1863, p. 4.

40. Duncan, *Wishaw,* 166.

41. For further details on Alexander Campbell's life, see Joyce M. Bellamy and John Saville, eds., *Dictionary of Labour Biography,* 5 vols. (London: Macmillan, 1972), 1:65–68.

42. Campbell, *Lanarkshire Miners,* 220–21; Duncan, *Wishaw,* 27–28; Conaghan, "Truck System," 42–79.

43. Duncan, *Wishaw,* 27–28.

44. W. Hamish Fraser, "A Newspaper for Its Generation: *The Glasgow Sentinel,* 1850–1877," *Journal of the Scottish Labour History Society* 4 (July 1971): 20.

45. Fraser, "A Newspaper," 24; *Glasgow Sentinel,* August 4, 1860, p. 3; Wilson, *Alexander McDonald,* 88–89.

46. Fraser, "A Newspaper," 20.

47. Ibid.

48. *Glasgow Sentinel,* February 4, 1855, p. 4; ibid., December 9, 1859, p. 3.

49. Robert W. Dron, *The Coal-Fields of Scotland* (London: Blackie and Son, 1902), 111.

50. James Barrowman, *Some Chapters in the History of Scotch Mining and Miners* (Hamilton, U.K.: W. Naismith, 1889), 10–13; William Moore, "Observations on the Supply of Coal and Ironstone, from the Mineral Fields of the West of Scotland," *Proceedings of the Philosophical Society of Glasgow* 1 (1882–83): 292–306.

51. Alan Campbell and Fred Reid, "The Independent Collier in Scotland," in *Independent Collier: The Coal Miner as Archetypal Proletarian Miner Revisited,* ed. Royden Harrison (Hassocks, U.K.: Harvester, 1978), 69.

52. Dron, *Coal-Fields of Scotland,* 109–18; Barrowman, *Some Chapters,* 28–42.

53. Barrowman, *Some Chapters,* 31–34. For a more general study of the introduction of modern business methods into the British coal industry, see Arthur J. Taylor, "Labour Productivity and Technological Innovation in the British Coal Industry, 1850–1914," *Economic History Review,* 2d ser., 14:1 (1961): 53.

54. *Report of the Commissioners Appointed to Inquire into the State of the Population in the Mining Districts* (1847–48), 244–45.

55. Gordon Wilson, "The Strike Policy of the Miners of the West of Scotland, 1842–74," in *Essays in Scottish Labour History: A Tribute to W. H. Marwick,* ed. Ian MacDougall (Edinburgh: John Donald, 1986), 45–46.

56. Wilson, *Alexander McDonald,* 28.

57. *Report of the Commissioners* (1847–48), 244. See also Campbell, *Lanarkshire Miners,* 250.

58. The number of deaths per thousand tons of coal raised declined in both Wishaw and Larkhall between 1851 and 1875, although it fell more rapidly in Larkhall than it did in Wishaw, possibly because of the higher proportion of gassy pits there. The number of injuries per thousand tons of coal raised also declined, but by a small percentage. See Duncan, *Wishaw,* 66; *Report of the Commissioners* (1852–53), 484; *Coal Mines Inspectors Reports (Eastern and Western Districts of Scotland)* (1854–55), 668–69; ibid. (1864), 345.

59. *Coal Mines Inspectors Reports* (1854–55), 668.

60. *Coal Mines Inspectors Reports* (1864), 345.

61. See cumulative statistics on death and injuries resulting from roof falls in this period listed in *Coal Mines Inspectors Reports* (1864), 344–46. In Wishaw they ranged from fourteen to twenty-three per year, and in Larkhall, from eight to sixteen.

62. *Coal Mines Inspectors Reports* (1859, sess. 2), 421.

63. James Barrowman, "Scotch Mining Legislation," *Transactions of the Mining Institute of Scotland* 10 (1888–89): 70–71.

64. *Coal Mines Inspectors Reports* (1856), 302.

65. Ibid.

66. Ibid.

67. *Report from Select Committee on Mines* (1866), appendix B, 536. See also Wilson, "Strike Policy," 150–51.

68. See p. 71–74.

69. Campbell, *Lanarkshire Miners,* 348.

70. Ibid., 260; Wilson, *Alexander McDonald,* 67–83.

71. Duncan, *Wishaw,* 83.

72. *Glasgow Sentinel,* August 24, 1856, pp. 4.

73. Duncan, *Wishaw,* 31.

74. *Wishaw Press,* April 14, 1869, p. 4.

75. Campbell, *Lanarkshire Miners,* 157; *Hamilton Advertiser,* September 8, 1864, p. 7.

76. See, in addition, Alan Campbell's argument regarding the greater weakness of the miners' union in Coatbridge, which had a larger proportion of Irish in the iron-works than did Larkhall, which was socially more homogeneous. See Alan Campbell, "Honourable Men and Degraded Slaves: A Comparative Study of Trade Unionism in Two Lanarkshire Mining Communities, c. 1830–1874," in *Independent Collier,* ed. Harrison, chap. 2.

77. See, e.g., Selig Perlman, *A Theory of the Labor Movement* (repr., New York: Augustus M. Kelley, 1966), 162–69.

78. A more balanced view of the role of ethnic and religious differences in in-fluencing the development of class consciousness in the American labor movement is provided by Richard J. Oestreicher in his *Solidarity and Fragmentation: Working People and Class Consciousness in Detroit, 1875–1900* (Urbana: University of Illinois Press, 1986).

79. Campbell, *Lanarkshire Miners,* chap. 11.

80. Ibid., appendix 7.

81. Ibid., 281.

82. Quoted in ibid., 284.

83. *Glasgow Sentinel,* February 4, 1864, p. 3.

84. Campbell, *Lanarkshire Miners,* 280.

85. *Glasgow Sentinel,* January 28, 1865, p. 4.

86. Ibid.

87. Wilson, "Strike Policy," 47.

88. R. C. Clements, "Trade Unions and Emigration, 1840–80," *Population Studies* 9:2 (November 1955): 167–79.

89. Alexander McDonald, "Report to the Members of the National Union on the Conditions and Prospects of Labour in the United States," manuscript in Bishopsgate Institute, London.

CHAPTER 3: CROSSING THE OCEAN

1. W. A. Carruthers, *Emigration from the British Isles* (London: D. S. King, 1929), 119–32; R. V. Clements, "Trade Unions and Emigration, 1840–80," *Population Studies* 9:2 (November 1955): 169; Charlotte Erickson, "The Encouragement of Emigration by British Trade Unions, 1850–1900," *Population Studies* 3:3 (December 1949): 267–68.

2. Clements, "Trade Unions and Emigration," 169–70; Erickson, "Encouragement of Emigration," 269–71.

3. Alan B. Campbell, *The Lanarkshire Miners: A Social History of Their Trade Unions, 1775–1874* (Edinburgh: John Donald, 1979), 256–57.

4. *Glasgow Sentinel,* February 11, 1865, p. 5.

5. *Glasgow Sentinel,* April 15, 1865, p. 4. See also Gordon Wilson, *Alexander McDonald, Leader of the Miners* (Aberdeen: Aberdeen University Press, 1982), 112–13.

6. *Glasgow Sentinel,* April 22, 1865, p. 5.

7. Quoted in Campbell, *Lanarkshire Miners,* 269.

8. For an interesting account of the trip down the Clyde, the embarkation on an ocean-going steamer, and the experience of steerage passengers crossing the Atlantic in this period, see Robert Louis Stevenson's recounting of his journey from Glasgow to California in 1879, in Andrew Noble, ed., *From the Clyde to California: Robert Louis Stevenson's Emigrant Journey* (Aberdeen: Aberdeen University Press, 1985), 37–70. See also letters to the *Glasgow Sentinel* written by Daniel McLaughlin, who later became an important miners' leader in northern Illinois, describing his journey from Glasgow to New York in 1869. They are reproduced in Herbert Gutman, "Five Letters of Immigrants Workers from Scotland to the United States, 1867–1869: William Latta, Daniel M'Lachlan, and Allan Pinkerton," *Labor History* 9:2 (Spring 1968): 384–408.

9. *Glasgow Sentinel,* November 9, 1867, p. 4.

10. Maldwyn A. Jones, *Destination America* (New York: Holt, Rinehart and Winston, 1976), 30–39.

11. Quoted in ibid., 42.

12. Ibid., 44.

13. W. Hamish Fraser, "A Newspaper for Its Generation: *The Glasgow Sentinel,* 1850–1877," *Journal of the Scottish Labour History Society* 4 (July 1971): 19; Bernard Aspinwall, *Portable Utopias: Glasgow and the United States, 1820–1920* (Aberdeen: Aberdeen University Press, 1984), chap. 1.

14. Fraser, "A Newspaper," 18–31; Aspinwall, *Portable Utopias,* chap. 1; Ray Boston, *British Chartists in America, 1839–1900* (Manchester, U.K.: Manchester University Press, 1971), chaps. 3, 5–6; *Glasgow Sentinel,* October 21, 1865, p. 6; Royden Harrison, *Before the Socialists: Studies in Labour and Politics, 1861–1881* (London: Routledge and Kegan Paul, 1965), 64.

15. *Glasgow Sentinel,* October 21, 1865, p. 6.

16. *Glasgow Sentinel,* September 29, 1863, p. 4. See also David Montgomery, *Beyond Equality: Labor and the Radical Republicans, 1862–1872* (Urbana: University of Illinois Press, 1981), 86; Martin J. Burke, *The Conundrum of Class: Public Discourse on the Social Order in America* (Chicago: University of Chicago Press, 1995), chaps. 4–5.

17. Boston, *British Chartists,* 89.

18. Ibid., 91; Edward A. Wieck, *The American Miners Association: A Record of the Origins of Coal Miners' Unions in the United States* (New York: Russell Sage Foundation, 1940), 86.

19. Wieck, *American Miners Association,* 57.

20. *Glasgow Sentinel,* May 24, 1856, pp. 4–5.

21. Mark Wyman, *Immigrants in the Valley: Irish, Germans, and Americans in the*

Upper Mississippi Country, 1830–1860 (Chicago: Nelson-Hall, 1984), 79–101; David Byrnie, "Irish Immigration and Settlement in Illinois, 1845–1880" (M.A. thesis, Illinois State University, 1959), chaps. 3–4.

22. Paul W. Gates, *The Illinois Central Railroad and Its Colonization Work* (Cambridge, Mass.: Harvard University Press, 1934), 223–24.

23. Wieck, *American Miners Association,* 113–14; Clifton K. Yearley, *Britons in American Labor: A History of the Influence of the United Kingdom Immigrants on American Labor, 1820–1914* (Baltimore: Johns Hopkins University Press, 1957), 125–26.

24. Wilson, *Alexander McDonald,* 113–14.

25. Charlotte Erickson, *American Industry and the European Immigrant, 1860–1865* (Cambridge, Mass.: Harvard University Press, 1957), 23–28.

26. *Glasgow Sentinel,* August 20, 1864, p. 4.

27. *Glasgow Sentinel,* September 4, 1864, p. 4.

28. *Glasgow Sentinel,* September 10, 1984, p. 3.

29. Ibid.

30. Wilson, *Alexander McDonald,* 112.

31. *Glasgow Sentinel,* June 25, 1864, p. 5.

32. Amy Z. Gottlieb, "The Regulation of the Coal Mining Industry in Illinois, with Special Reference to the Influence of British Miners and British Precedents, 1870–1911" (Ph.D. diss., University of London, 1975), 41–42.

33. *Glasgow Sentinel,* October 22, 1864, p. 5; ibid., December 24, 1864, p. 6.

34. Gottlieb, "Regulation," 43–44; *Glasgow Sentinel,* April 29, 1865, p. 5; ibid., May 13, 1865, p. 5.

35. Yearley, *Britons in American Labor,* 136–37.

36. Ibid.; Erickson, *American Industry,* 50; *Glasgow Sentinel,* June 24, 1865, p. 4.

37. *Glasgow Sentinel,* June 24, 1865, p. 4.

38. Ibid.

39. Yearley, *Britons in American Labor,* 137; Herbert Gutman, *Power and Culture: Essays on the American Working Class,* ed. Ira Berlin (New York: New Press, 1987), 119.

40. *Glasgow Sentinel,* July 1, 1865, p. 4.

41. Quote in Gottlieb, "Regulation," 48.

42. *Glasgow Sentinel,* October 28, 1865, p. 6.

43. *Glasgow Sentinel,* September 23, 1865, p. 4.

44. For the migration of American and British immigrant miners to the Midwest from the coalfields of Maryland and Pennsylvania, see Katherine A. Harvey, *The Best-Dressed Miners: Life and Labor in the Maryland Coal Region, 1835–1910* (Ithaca, N.Y.: Cornell University Press, 1969), 341–48; Frank J. Warne, *The Immigrant Invasion* (New York: Dodd and Meade, 1913), chap. 1.

45. Quoted in Richard P. Joyce, " 'Old Man' McLaughlin: Miners' Leader from Illinois," unpublished paper, Wilmington, Ill., 1986, 2.

46. Ibid.

47. Yearley wrongly gives 1868 as the year when Daniel McLaughlin emigrated to Braidwood. For the correct date, which is 1869, see *Journal of United Labor,* September 4, 1869, p. 2.

48. Quoted in Herbert Gutman, *Work, Culture, and Society in Industrializing America* (New York: Knopf, 1976), 396.

CHAPTER 4: HEYDAY OF PICK MINING IN THE AMERICAN MIDWEST

1. George Woodruff, et al., *The History of Will County, Illinois* (Chicago: William Le Baron, 1878), 466.

2. John H. M. Laslett, "British Immigrant Colliers and the Origins and Early Development of the UMWA, 1870–1912," in *The United Mine Workers of America: A Model of Industrial Solidarity?* ed. Laslett (University Park: Pennsylvania State University Press, 1996), chap. 2; Frank J. Warne, *The Slav Invasion and the Mine Workers: A Study in Immigration* (Philadelphia: J. B. Lippincott, 1904), chap. 5.

3. Amy Z. Gottlieb, "Immigration of British Coal Miners in the Civil War Decade," *International Review of Social History* 23, part 3 (1989): 372.

4. Paula Angle, *Biography in Black: A History of Streator, Illinois* (Streator: Weber, 1962), 26–27.

5. *Braidwood Centennial, 100 Years, 1865–1965* (Braidwood: n.p., 1965), 24.

6. Richard P. Joyce, "Miners on the Prairie: Life and Labor in the Wilmington, Illinois, Coal Field, 1866–1897" (M.A. thesis, Illinois State University, 1980), 12–13; Herbert Gutman, "Labor in the Land of Lincoln: Coal Miners on the Prairie," in *Power and Culture: Essays on the History of the American Working Class,* ed. Ira Berlin (New York: New Press, 1987), 121–23. For Braidwood's satellite coal towns in Grundy County in this period, see Helen S. Ulrich, *This Is Grundy County: Its History from Beginning to 1968* (Dixon, Ill.: Rogers, 1968), esp. 141–42.

7. Angle, *Biography in Black,* 28–29. See also Ralph Plumb to George W. Morrell, June 22, 1867, George W. Morrell Papers, Box 2.

8. Ralph Plumb to George W. Morrell, January 29, 1869, Morrell Papers, box 2.

9. Article on the history of Streator in *Streator Daily Free Press,* August 9, 1923, p. 2.

10. *Compendium of Ninth U.S. Census* (1880) (Washington, D.C.: Government Printing Office, 1881), part 1, 105, 114.

11. *Glasgow Sentinel,* November 9, 1867, p. 2; ibid., November 23, 1867, p. 3; ibid., December 7, 1867, p. 4; ibid., October 9, 1867, p. 4; ibid., November 20, 1869, p. 3; ibid., October 1869, p. 3; ibid., October 2, 1876, p. 4; ibid., October 28, 1876, p. 4; *Workingman's Advocate,* November 3, 1867, p. 2; ibid., November 14, 1869, p. 4.

12. U.S. Population Census, Reed Township (Braidwood) and Bruce Township (Streator), 1880.

13. U.S. Population Census, Reed Township and Bruce Township, 1880.

14. *Workingman's Advocate,* October 21, 1868, p. 3.

15. Angle, *Biography in Black,* 37; Modesto J. Donna, *The Braidwood Story* (Braidwood: n.p., 1957), 25.

16. For the early migration into the Braidwood area by Italian and Slavic peasants, who in the 1870s amounted to no more than a few hundred, see Maurice Marchello, *Black Coal for White Bread: Up from the Prairie Mines* (New York: Vintage, 1972), 39–41.

17. *Wilmington Advocate,* November 16, 1877, p. 2, cited in Joyce, "Miners on the Prairie," 45.

18. By the early 1890s, as mining operations in Braidwood moved further west, many of the miners' homes were moved to Diamond, Coal City, Eileen, and Carbon Hill. See Donna, *Braidwood Story,* 53.

19. *Streator, Illinois Centennial* (Streator: n.p. 1968), 5.

20. Beginning in the 1870s the State of Illinois developed a code of mining laws that was as good as the one in Great Britain, but in the years just after the Civil War it was inadequate. For details, see Amy Z. Gottlieb, "The Regulation of the Coal Mining Industry in Illinois, 1870–1911, with Special Reference to the Influence of British Miners and British Precedents" (Ph.D. diss., University of London, 1975).

21. *Glasgow Sentinel,* February 4, 1867, p. 3.

22. Streator historian Paula Angle mentions fear of illnesses such as typhoid, smallpox, and diphtheria, but she cites no instances of these diseases. See Angle, *Biography in Black,* 38.

23. Ibid., 42; Joyce, "Miners on the Prairie"; *The City of Streator: Resources and Advantages* (Streator: Business Men's Association, 1887), 8.

24. Joyce, "Miners on the Prairie," 43–44.

25. Donna, *The Braidwood Story,* 74–76; *Streator: Resources and Advantages,* 9–10.

26. H. K. Barnard, *Anton the Martyr* (Chicago: Marion, 1923), 31–32.

27. Linden H. Mulford, "The Industrial History of Streator, Illinois" (M.A. thesis, University of Illinois, 1941), 23–38.

28. *Braidwood Centennial,* 41.

29. U.S. Population Census, Reed Township (Braidwood) and Bruce Township (Streator), 1880.

30. U.S. Population Census, Bruce Township, 1880.

31. Mulford, "Industrial History," 23–28.

32. U.S. Population Census, Bruce Township (Streator), 1880, 1900; Mulford, "Industrial History," 28.

33. Mulford, "Industrial History," 34–35; George E. Barnett, *Chapters on Machinery and Labor* (Cambridge, Mass.: Harvard University Press, 1926), 60–66.

34. *Streator Times-Press,* July 27, 1964, p. 5.

35. See Angle, *Biography in Black,* 43–44; Charlotte Erickson, *American Industry and the European Immigrant, 1860–1885* (Cambridge, Mass.: Harvard University Press, 1957), 140–45.

36. Mulford, "Industrial History," 62–63.

37. U.S. Population Census, Bruce Township, 1880.

38. *The Story of Streator* (Streator: n.p. 1958), 21; Steven B. Vardy, *The Hungarian-Americans* (Boston: Twayne, 1985), 32–33.

39. Emily Balch, *Our Slavic Fellow Citizens* (New York: Arno, 1969), 210–36.

40. *Historia Cikvi Sv. Trojice Streator, Illinois* (Streator: Svedoki, 1914), 14–18. For the Italians, see Elena Madonna, "Italian Settlers in Northern Illinois," *Black Diamond* 33:18 (October 1904): 950–55.

41. Alex Gottfried, *Boss Cermack of Chicago: A Study of Political Leadership* (Seattle: University of Washington Press, 1942), 14.

42. Edward A. Steiner, *From Alien to Citizen: The Story of My Life in America* (New York: Fleming H. Revell, 1923), 188–92.

43. Angle, *Biography in Black*, 89.

44. Marchello, *Black Coal for White Bread*, 50.

45. Berlin, *Power and Culture*, 123.

46. *Wilmington Advocate*, April 23, 1873, quoted in Joyce, "Miners on the Prairie," 37.

47. "Notes on Knights of Labor Assemblies," Edward A. Wieck Collection, Box 15, Folders A and B.

48. Illinois Bureau of Labor Statistics, *Third Annual Report* (Springfield: H. W. Rokker, 1884), 433.

49. *Chicago Times*, July 31, 1877, quoted in Berlin, *Power and Culture*, 135.

50. Significant hostility developed between white British immigrant miners and African American strikebreakers who were brought in to break the 1877 northern Illinois coal strike. See *Report of Special Committee on Labor to Illinois General Assembly* (Springfield: State of Illinois, 1879), 48–77.

51. Bureau of Labor Statistics, *Third Annual Report*, 434.

52. Ibid., 432.

53. Ibid., 433–34.

54. Ibid.

55. Amy Z. Gottlieb, "British Coal Miners: A Demographic Study of Braidwood and Streator, Illinois," *Journal of the Illinois State Historical Society* 72:3 (August 1979): 192.

56. Ibid.

57. Pick miners enjoyed maximum earning capacity in their twenties and thirties. After this their physical powers, and hence their output of coal, slowly declined. There were also marked differences in skill levels among miners. For example, in his 1882 report for eastern Scotland, the mine inspector divided the miners in his district into first-class miners and average miners. A first-class miner in the Wishaw area earned £75 4p ($362), whereas an average miner earned only £56 13p ($273). See *Coal Mines Inspectors Reports (Eastern and Western Districts of Scotland)* (1882), 236–37.

58. On both sides of the Atlantic, fall and winter were busy seasons and summer was slack owing to a fall in the demand for coal for domestic heating. For this comparison, I estimated the average number of days worked by miners in Wishaw to be 271 and in Streator to be 256. See *Coal Mines Inspectors Reports* (1882), 236; ibid.

(1884), 314; ibid. (1886), 186; ibid. (1888), 412; ibid. (1890–91), 381; Illinois Bureau of Labor Statistics, *Seventh Annual Report* (Springfield: H. W. Rokker, 1888), 419–30.

59. In Wishaw deductions from the miner's pay packet included not only 2p a week for pick sharpening but other deductions for attendance of the miners' children at the coal company school and payment for the company doctor should the miner be injured at work. As far as I have been able to ascertain, no such deductions were taken from the Streator miners' pay packet *(Hamilton Advertiser,* June 4, 1888, p. 4).

60. Because of the small percentage of miners' wives and daughters who worked outside the house in mining towns such as Wishaw and Streator, and because of the lack of reliable data on their earnings, female contributions to the miners' family income have been omitted from this calculation.

61. The wage data on which this comparison is based are drawn from the Illinois Bureau of Labor Statistics' first, third, and seventh annual reports (1882, 123; 1884, 191; and 1888, 84) and from *Coal Mines Inspectors Reports* (1881), 236–37; ibid. (1885), 92–93; ibid. (1891), 497–98.

62. Philip S. Bagwell and G. E. Mingay, *Britain and America, 1850–1939: A Study of Economic Change* (London: Routledge and Kegan Paul, 1970), 96–97.

63. *Chicago Tribune,* June 8, 1874, quoted in Berlin, *Power and Culture,* 136.

64. Berlin, *Power and Culture,* 137–38.

65. *Hamilton Advertiser,* June 28, 1888, p. 4; ibid., October 10, 1892, p. 2; *Wishaw Press,* January 8, 1881, p. 8.

66. Woodruff, *History of Will County,* 751–65.

67. Ibid., 765.

68. Ibid., 754–59.

69. *Story of Streator,* 55.

70. *Rotary Spokesman,* June 15, 1923, cited in Donald O. Clark, "John Elias Williams (1858–1919) — Labor Peacemaker: A Study in the Life of an Early Illinois Mediator and Arbitrator and His Impact upon the American Labor Movement" (M.A. thesis, University of Illinois, 1957), 15.

71. In 1889 Streator miners took advantage of the election of Daniel McLaughlin as chairman of the state legislature's Committee on Mines and Mining to lobby Governor Fifer for the appointment of their preferred candidates as mine inspectors. This continued a practice that had been going on for some years. See Gottlieb, "Regulation," 93–94.

72. *La Salle County General Directory for 1872-3: Bruce Township and City of Streator* (Joliet, Ill.: Republican Steam Printing House, 1872); *Beasley's Streator Directory for 1876-7* (Streator: W. W. Bean, 1876); *A Directory of the Residences and Business Houses of Streator, Ill.* (Streator: Free Press, 1888).

73. Gottlieb, "Regulation," 92.

74. *Story of Streator,* 28–33; Angle, *Biography in Black,* 41–43; 50–52.

75. Quoted in Berlin, *Power and Culture,* 130.

76. *Streator Times-Press,* July 27, 1964, p. 4.

77. Tom Tippett, *Horse Shoe Bottoms* (New York: Harper Bros. 1935), 4.

78. Ibid., 16.

79. Ibid., 38.

80. John Williams, quoted in *Story of Streator,* 12.

81. Edward A. Wieck, *The American Miners Association: A Record of the Origins of Coal Miners' Unions in the United States* (New York: Russell Sage Foundation, 1940), 68–69.

82. Ibid., 85.

83. Andrew Roy, *A History of the Coal Miners of the United States* (Westport, Conn.: Greenwood, 1970), 156–60.

84. For the fusing of Scottish Jacobinism, Chartism, and antimonarchist sentiment with American republicanism, see *Glasgow Sentinel,* February 14, 1858, p. 4; ibid., March 13, 1862, pp. 3–4; Henry Pelling, *America and the British Left, from Bright to Bevan* (London: Macmillan, 1958), chap. 3; and James D. Young, "Changing Images of American Democracy and the Scottish Labor Movement," *International Review of Social History* 18, part 1 (1973): 69–72.

85. *Workingman's Advocate,* January 4, 1867, p. 3.

86. Letter from "Union Miner" to *Belleville Democrat,* May 16, 1863, cited in Wieck, *American Miners Association,* 112.

87. Letter from "Union Miner" to *Belleville Democrat,* June 12, 1864 (quoting editorial in *Weekly Miner*), cited in Wieck, *American Miners Association,* 112–13.

CHAPTER 5: STRIKES, INTERNAL CONFLICT, AND THE DECLINE OF THE CLASS-HARMONY IDEAL, 1872–82

1. *Glasgow Sentinel,* January 14, 1871, p. 4.

2. *Hamilton Advertiser,* December 28, 1872, p. 1.

3. Andrew Roy, *A History of the Coal Miners of the United States* (Westport, Conn.: Greenwood, 1970), 164.

4. *Glasgow Sentinel,* January 28, 1876, p. 3.

5. In Fred Reid, *Keir Hardie: The Making of a Socialist* (London: Croom Helm, 1978), 97.

6. Robert Duncan, *Wishaw: Life and Labour in a Lanarkshire Industrial Community: 1790–1914* (Motherwell: Department of Leisure Services, 1986), 52–53; R. H. Campbell, *Scotland since 1707: The Rise of an Industrial Society* (Edinburgh: John Donald, 1985), 174–75.

7. "Notes on the Malleability of Pig Iron," *Collier Manager and Journal of Mining Engineering* 1:9 (September 1885): 2–3.

8. Louis Bloch, *Labor Agreements in Coal Mines: A Case Study of the Administration of Agreements between Miners and Operators' Organizations in the Bituminous Coal Mines of Illinois* (New York: Russell Sage Foundation, 1931), chaps. 1–2.

9. Harry M. Dixon, "The Illinois Coal Mining Industry" (Ph.D. diss., University of Illinois, 1951), 72–74; Richard P. Joyce, "Miners on the Prairie: Life and Labor in the

Wilmington, Illinois, Coal Field, 1866–1897" (M.A. thesis, Illinois State University, 1980), 15–17.

10. Herbert Gutman, "Labor in the Land of Lincoln: Coal Miners on the Prairie," in *Power and Culture: Essays on the American Working Class*, ed. Ira Berlin (New York: New Press, 1987), 122–23; "Report of the Directors of the Chicago, Wilmington and Vermilion Coal Company," 7, Chicago Historical Society.

11. Gutman, "Labor," 122–23.

12. Henry D. Lloyd, *A Strike of Millionaires against Miners; or, The Story of Spring Valley* (Chicago: Bedford-Clarke, 1890), 156–57.

13. Gutman, "Labor," 144.

14. Ibid.

15. T. J. Byers, "The Scottish Economy during the 'Great Depression,' 1873–1896, with Special Reference to the Heavy Industries of the Southwest" (M. Litt. thesis, University of Glasgow, 1963), 119–20; Maier Fox, *United We Stand: The United Mine Workers of America, 1890–1930* (Washington, D.C.: United Mine Workers of America, 1990), 81–84.

16. Reid, *Keir Hardie,* 26.

17. *Glasgow Herald,* November 8, 1879, p. 4.

18. *Wilmington Advocate,* April 4, 1874, p. 3.

19. In Joyce, "Miners on the Prairie," 71.

20. Detailed accounts of the 1872 and 1874 miners' strikes in Lanarkshire are given in Royden Harrison, ed., *Independent Collier: The Coal Miner as Archetypal Proletarian Revisited* (Hassocks, U.K.: Harvester, 1978), chap. 5.

21. The extensive analysis of the 1874 strike in northern Illinois was provided by Herbert Gutman in his article "The Braidwood Lockout of 1874," *Journal of the Illinois State Historical Society* 53 (1960): 5–28.

22. Gutman, "Labor," 166.

23. Ibid., 166–91.

24. Reid, *Keir Hardie,* 49–50.

25. Ibid., 50.

26. *Hamilton Advertiser,* December 12, 1872, p. 3.

27. Joyce, "Miners on the Prairie," 71.

28. *Hamilton Advertiser,* December 19, 1872, p. 4.

29. Fred Reid, "Alexander MacDonald and the Crisis of the Independent Collier," in *Independent Collier,* ed. Harrison, 160.

30. *Streator Times-Press,* July 9, 1874, p. 3.

31. *Wilmington Advocate,* July 11, 1874, p. 2.

32. Gutman, "Labor," 171–73.

33. In *The Story of Streator* (Streator: n.p., 1958), 31.

34. T. C. Smout, *A Century of the Scottish People, 1830–1950* (London: Collins, 1986), 102.

35. In February 1873, for example, the *Hamilton Advertiser* reported that shopkeepers had met in the local town hall to consider extending credit to the unemployed

and that a leading grocer condemned the local miners as "a feckless, ill-dressed band of men whose turbulent manners strike fear in our regular customers" (*Hamilton Advertiser,* February 14, 1873, p. 4).

36. Ian S. Wood, "Irish Nationalism and Radical Politics in Scotland, 1880–1906" *Journal of the Scottish Labour History Society* 2 (June 1975): 52.

37. For the Liberal Party as a socializing agent between artisans and middle-class reformers in southwest Scotland, see James G. Kellas, "The Liberal Party in Scotland, 1885–1895" (Ph.D. diss., University College, London, 1961), chap. 1.

38. *Chicago Tribune,* August 24, 1877, p. 3.

39. *Workingmen's Advocate,* July 2, 1877, p. 2.

40. "Knights of Labor Assemblies in Illinois," Edward A Wieck Collection, Box 28, File 6.

41. *Wilmington Advocate,* October 9, 1879, p. 3.

42. For a study detailing the greater power of the labor movement in the United States compared to Britain in the 1880s, see John H. M. Laslett, "Haymarket, Henry George, and the Labor Upsurge in Britain and America during the Late 1880s," *International Labor and Working Class History* 29 (Spring 1986): 68–82.

43. Gerald R. Grob, *Workers and Utopia: A Study of Ideological Conflict in the American Labor Movement* (Evanston, Ill.: Northwestern Universty Press, 1961), chap. 3.

44. *Hamilton Advertiser,* December 10, 1872, p. 3.

45. Ibid.

46. Reid, "Alexander MacDonald," 168.

47. Ibid.

48. *Hamilton Advertiser,* December 17, 1872, p. 3; ibid., January 9, 1873, p. 1.

49. The price of pig iron on the Glasgow market was used as the benchmark for setting miners' wages because the large amounts of coal used in the production of pig iron exerted a powerful influence over coal prices.

50. In the 1879–80 Lanarkshire strike, McDonald's proposal for a sliding scale, this time with the Dunlop Iron Company, caused even more of a furor because the price of pig iron had by then fallen even lower on the Glasgow market. Had his proposal been accepted, it would have brought the miner a wage of only 18½p a day, which was insufficient to support a single man, let alone a collier with family. See Reid, "Alexander MacDonald," 171–72; *Hamilton Advertiser,* December 11, 1879, p. 3.

51. Reid, "Alexander MacDonald," 166.

52. *Hamilton Advertiser,* March 30, 1874, p. 1.

53. For the Scottish miners' practice of gathering to decide on policy or hear reports from delegate meeings, see Gordon Wilson, "The Miners of the West of Scotland and Their Trade Unions, 1842–1874" (Ph.D. diss., University of Glasgow, 1977), 81–83.

54. Reid, "Alexander MacDonald," 173.

55. *Hamilton Advertiser,* April 11, 1874, p .1.

56. Reid, *Keir Hardie*, 51–52.

57. *National Labor Tribune*, January 12, 1879, p. 2.

58. Ibid.

59. *Workingman's Advocate*, January 18, 1878, p. 1.

60. Tom Tippett, *Horse Shoe Bottoms* (New York: Harper Bros., 1935), 84–88.

61. Ibid., 91–92.

62. Ibid., 101–2.

63. Reid, "Alexander MacDonald," 173.

64. Gordon Wilson, *Alexander McDonald, Leader of the Miners* (Aberdeen: Aberdeen University Press, 1982), 156–58.

65. Ibid., 205–7.

66. Ibid.

67. Ibid., 206.

68. Gutman, "Labor," 194.

69. Ibid., 196.

70. Ibid.

71. Ibid., 197.

72. Edward Pinkowski, *John Siney: The Miners Martyr* (Philadelphia: Sunshine, 1963), 209.

73. Ibid., 215–23.

74. Gutman, "Labor," 196–97.

75. Ibid., 204.

CHAPTER 6: NEW TECHNOLOGY, NEW IMMIGRANTS, AND GROWING CLASS CONFLICT

1. Anthony Slaven, *The Development of the West of Scotland, 1750–1960* (London: Routledge and Kegan Paul, 1975), 123, 167.

2. Harry M. Dixon, "The Illinois Coal Mining Industry" (Ph.D. diss., University of Illinois, 1951), 40–52.

3. Dixon, "Illinois Coal Mining," 50–51; Slaven, *Development*, 166–67.

4. For general histories of Blantyre, see Rev. Stewart Wright, *Annals of Blantyre* (Glasgow: Wilson and McCormick, 1885); C. Pridgeon, "Notes on the History of Blantyre" (1977) (typescript in Hamilton Reference Library). The most complete history of Spring Valley in this period is Karl Fivek, "From Company Town to Miners' Town: Spring Valley, Illinois, 1885–1905" (Certificate of Advanced Study, Northern Illinois University, 1976). See also *Spring Valley, Illinois, 1886–1986: An Ethnic Heritage Built from Coal* (Spring Valley: Spring Valley Centennial Committee, 1986).

5. John R. Commons, "Slavs in the Bituminous Mines of Illinois," *Charities* 13:10 (December 1904): 224–25; Frank J. Warne, *The Slav Invasion and the Mine Workers: A Study in Immigration* (Philadelphia: J. B. Lippincott, 1904), 19–29.

6. Kenneth Lunn, "Reactions to Lithuanians and Polish Immigrants in the Lanark-

shire Coalfield, 1880–1914," in *Hosts, Immigrants, and Minorities: Historical Responses to Newcomers in British Society, 1870–1914*, ed. Kenneth Lunn (Folkestone, U.K.: Dawson, 1980), 108–14.

7. *Third Statistical Account,* 267–68.

8. T. Robert Moore, "Recent Developments in the Hamilton Coalfield," *Proceedings of the Philosophical Society of Glasgow* 32 (1893): 56–57; Michael Colligan, "Blantyre: A Geographical Study in Economic and Social Development" (B.S. honours thesis, University of Strathclyde, 1983), 17–18; Anthony Slaven, "Coal Mining Enterprises in the West of Scotland in the Nineteenth Century: The Dixon Enterprises" (B.Litt., University of Glasgow, 1966), 111–14.

9. Keith Dix, "Work Relations in the Coal Industry: The Hand-Loading Era, 1880–1930," *West Virginia University Bulletin,* ser. 78 (January 1978): 111–14.

10. Moore, "Recent Developments," 56.

11. Ibid., 56–57.

12. "History of Spring Valley," typescript in Bernice Sweeney Collection, 1–4.

13. Ibid., 3; *Spring Valley, Illinois,* 41–48.

14. *Spring Valley Gazette,* June 4, 1888, p. 4.

15. *Chicago Tribune,* October 14, 1889, p .8.

16. Fivek, "From Company Town," 15–18.

17. Keith Dix, *What's a Coal Miner to Do? The Mechanization of Coal Mining* (Pittsburgh: Pittsburgh University Press, 1988), 61–69.

18. Illinois Bureau of Labor Statistics, *Sixth Annual Report* (Springfield: H. W. Rokker, 1888), 49; idem, *Tenth Annual Report* (Springfield: H. W. Rokker, 1891), 26–27.

19. Arthur J. Taylor, "Labour Productivity and Technological Innovation in the British Coal Industry, 1850–1914," *Economic History Review,* 2d ser., 19:1 (1961): 57.

20. Dix, *What's a Miner to Do?* 4–5.

21. Carter Goodrich, *The Miners' Freedom* (Boston: Marshall Jones, 1925), 41–43.

22. Dix, *What's a Miner to Do?* 121. See also William Graebner, *Coal-Mine Safety in the Progressive Period: The Political Economy of Reform* (Lexington: University Press of Kentucky, 1976), chap. 3.

23. Illinois Bureau of Labor Statistics, *Tenth Annual Report* (Springfield: H. W. Rokker, 1891), 231.

24. *United Mine Workers Journal,* January 28, 1904, p. 3; ibid., February 5, 1904, p. 3.

25. W. D. Stewart, *Mines, Machines, and Men* (Edinburgh: A. W. Ramsey, 1935), 34–35.

26. Illinois Bureau of Labor Statistics, *Seventh Annual Report* (Springfield: H. W. Rokker, 1888), 14.

27. Illinois Bureau of Labor Statistics, *First Biennial Report* (Springfield: H. W. Rokker, 1892), 14.

28. Fivek, "From Company Town," 4.

29. Bureau of Labor Statistics, *First Biennial Report,* 14.

30. *The Story of Streator* (Streator: n.p. 1958), 31.

31. *Spring Valley, Illinois,* 62–63.

32. "The Growth of Ladd," typescript in Bernice Sweeney Collection, 4–5.

33. *Spring Valley Gazette,* December 18, 1897, 4.

34. For a retrospective report on Lanarkshire coal company housing that exposed the appalling conditions of the miners' rows in Wishaw and Blantyre, see J. Wilson, *Report by the County Medical Officer of Lanark on the Housing Conditions of Miners* (Glasgow, 1910), 127.

35. Colligan, "Blantyre," 28–29.

36. Lunn, "Reactions to Lithuanians," 309–10; A. Kaupas, "The Lithuanians in America," *Charities* 13:10 (December 3, 1914): 231–32.

37. Joseph Rouceck, "Lithuanian Immigrants in the American Midwest," *American Journal of Sociology* 41:4 (January 1936): 447–51; David R. Wyn, "Trade Unions and the 'New' Immigration: A Study of the United Mine Workers of America, 1890–1920" (Ph.D. diss., University of London, 1976), 94–99.

38. Sarah J. Allen, "Immigrant Population of Spring Valley," unpublished paper, Bernice Sweeney Collection, 9–11.

39. Quoted in Wyn, "Trade Unions," 106.

40. Illinois Bureau of Labor Statistics, *Supplemental Report* (Springfield: Bureau of labor Statistics, 1894), 133.

41. Allen, "Immigrant Population," 4–7.

42. Lunn, "Reactions to Lithuanians," 310–13.

43. Ibid., 315.

44. Ibid., 325.

45. Wyn, "Trade Unions," chaps. 1–2.

46. Earl R. Beckner, *A History of Illinois Labor Legislation* (Chicago: University of Chicago Press, 1929), 332–36.

47. Louis Bloch, *Labor Agreements in the Coal Mines: A Case Study of the Administration of Agreements between Miners and Operators' Organizations in the Bituminous Mines of Illinois* (New York: Russell Sage Foundation, 1931), 114–15.

48. Commons, "Slavs in Bituminous Mines," 224. For further elaboration on this point, see my essay "A Model of Industrial Solidarity? Interpreting the UMWA's First Hundred Years, 1890–1990," in *The United Mine Workers of America: A Model of Industrial Solidarity?* ed. Laslett (University Park: Pennsylvania State University Press, 1996), 14–18.

49. "The Coal Miner in the Strike of 1897," in Illinois Bureau of Labor Statistics, *Sixteenth Annual Report* (Springfield: Philips Bros., 1898), 162.

50. Ibid., 166.

51. Record Book of UMWA Local 8215, 116.

52. Commons, "Slavs in Bituminous Mines," 228–29.

53. Craig Phelan, "John Mitchell and the Politics of the Trade Agreement, 1898–1917," in *United Mine Workers of America,* ed. Laslett, 74–90.

54. *Chicago Chronicle,* December 15, 1902, p. 4.

55. For a general analysis of the rise of ethnic and racial prejudice in the American labor movement, see Gwendolyn Mink, *Old Labor and New Immigrants in American Politcal Development: Union, Party, and State, 1875–1920* (Ithaca, N.Y.: Cornell University Press, 1986), chap. 2.

56. Herbert Hill, " 'Myth-Making as Labor History': Herbert Gutman and the United Mine Workers of America," *International Journal of Politics, Culture, and Society* 2 (Winter 1988): 132–41.

57. For another analysis that confirms this hypothesis, see Mildred A. Beik, *The Miners of Windber: The Struggles of New Immigrants for Unionization, 1890s–1930s* (University Park: Pennsylvania State University Press, 1996), 84–91.

58. Philip S. Bagwell and G. E. Mingay, *Britain and America: A Study of Economic Change, 1850–1939* (London: Routledge and Kegan Paul, 1970), 63–68.

59. *Glasgow Weekly Mail*, February 12, 1887, p. 5.

60. Fred Reid, *Keir Hardie* (London: Croom Helm, 1979), 88–89; *Glasgow Weekly Mail*, February 26, 1887, p. 1.

61. *Glasgow Weekly Mail*, February 18, 1887, p. 5.

62. Ibid.

63. Reid, *Keir Hardie*, 93.

64. Henry D. Lloyd, *A Strike of Millionaires against Miners; or, The Story of the Spring Valley* (Chicago: Bedford-Clarke, 1890), 55.

65. Ibid., 55–56.

66. Ibid., 61, 63; Chester M. Destler, *Henry Demarest Lloyd and the Empire of Reform* (Philadelphia: University of Pennsylvania Press, 1973), 227.

67. Destler, *Henry Demarest Lloyd*, 228.

68. Lloyd, *A Strike of Millionaires*, 88–89.

69. Ibid.

70. Ibid., 104.

71. Destler, *Henry Demarest Lloyd*, 231.

72. In John H. M. Laslett, *Labor and the Left: A Study of Socialist and Radical Influences in the American Labor Movement, 1881–1924* (New York: Basic Books, 1970), 197–98.

73. Carlos A. Schwantes, *Coxey's Army: An American Odyssey* (Lincoln: University of Nebraska Press, 1985), 172–79.

74. Quoted in Laslett, *Labor and the Left*, 198.

75. R. Page Arnot, *A History of the Scottish Miners, from the Earliest Times* (London: George Allen and Unwin, 1955), 74–75.

76. Ibid., 75; *Glasgow Herald*, September 12, 1894, p. 5.

77. *Spring Valley Gazette*, August 4, 1894, p. 4.

78. Richard P. Joyce, "Miners of the Prairie: Life and Labor in the Wilmington, Illinois, Coal Field, 1866–1897" (M.A. thesis, Illinois State University, 1980), 165.

79. *Glasgow Herald*, September 18, 1894, p. 3.

80. Quoted in Arnot, *A History*, 75.

81. Quoted in the appendix to Lloyd, *A Strike of Millionaires*, 290–91.

82. Reid, *Keir Hardie,* 84.

83. See pp. 168–69.

CHAPTER 7: MASS UNIONISM AND EARLY VENTURES INTO POLITICS

1. *Glasgow Herald,* October 14, 1894, p. 8; R. Page Arnot, *A History of the Scottish Miners, from the Earliest Times* (London: George Allen and Unwin, 1955), 86–88; David J. McDonald and Edward A. Lynch, *Coal and Unionism: A History of the American Coal Miners Unions* (Silver Springs, Colo.: Cornelius, 1939), 41.

2. *Proceedings of the Twentieth Annual Convention of the United Mine Workers of America, District 12* (Springfield: United Mine Workers, 1910), 184–85.

3. Roy Church, with the assistance of Alan Hall and John Kanefsky, *The History of the British Coal Industry,* vol. 3: *1830–1913, Victorian Pre-eminence* (Oxford: Clarendon, 1986), 198.

4. Anthony Slaven, *The Development of the West of Scotland, 1750–1960* (London: Routledge and Kegan Paul, 1975), 166–69; Alan Campbell, "Colliery Mechanization and the Lanarkshire Miners," *Bulletin of the Society for the Study of Labour History* 49 (1984): 37.

5. "A Compilation of the Reports of the Mining Industry of Illinois from the Earliest Records to 1954," *Report of the Illinois Department of Mines and Minerals, 1955* (Springfield: State of Illinois, 1955), 13–16, 28–34, 83, 91.

6. "Report on the Disaster at Cherry, Illinois," *Laws of the State of Illinois Enacted by the Forty-Seventh General Assembly* (Springfield: State of Illinois, 1911), 385–427.

7. Grace Abbott, "The Immigrant and Coal Mining Communities of Illinois," in *Bulletin of the Immigrants Commission,* no. 2 (Springfield: Department of Registration and Education, State of Illinois, 1920), chap. 3.

8. Stephane E. Booth, "The Relationship between Radicalism and Ethnicity in Southern Illinois Coalfields, 1870–1940" (Ph.D. diss., Illinois State University, 1983), appendix A.

9. John R. Commons, "Immigrants as Trade Union Officers in the United Mine Workers of America, 1897–1912," *Charities* 16:4 (July 1918): 362–68; *Proceedings of the Twenty-Second Annual Convention of District 12, UMWA* (Springfield: United Mine Workers, 1912), 184–86. Using an unknown method, Commons listed UMWA district officers by ethnic denomination in Illinois, Pennsylvania, and Colorado. They are supplemented here by a retrospective listing of district 12 officers included in the 1912 district proceedings.

10. Commons, "Immigrants as Union Officers," 362–68. It is not clear how Commons distinguished between the Scots and the Irish-named officeholders.

11. "Introductory Pamphlet," Duncan McDonald Collection; Anthony B. Barrette, "John Walker, Labor Leader of Illinois, 1905–1933" (M.A. thesis, Eastern Illinois University, 1967), 4–15, 18–23, 32–48.

12. Carl Weinberg, "The Tug of War: Labor, Loyalty, and Rebellion in the Southwestern Illinois Coalfields, 1914–1920" (Ph.D. diss., Yale University, 1995), 53.

13. Ibid., 53–57; Booth, "Radicalism and Ethnicity," 81.

14. Donald F. Tingley, *The Structuring of a State: The History of Illinois, 1899–1928* (Urbana: University of Illinois Press, 1970), 57–58; Booth, "Radicalism and Ethnicity," 84–91.

15. Edward Wieck, *The American Miners Association: A Record of the Origins of Coal Miners' Unions in the United States* (New York: Russell Sage Foundation, 1940), chap. 3; E. Sharpe, *The Story of Granite City* (Granite City, Ill.: G. Hickson, 1921), 13–18; John M. Coggeshall, "Ethnic Persistence with Modification: The German-Americans of Southwest Illinois" (Ph.D. diss., Southern Illinois University, 1984), chap. 6.

16. T. E. Savage, "The Geology and Resources of Herrin, Illinois, Triangle," *Illinois State Geological Survey Bulletin* 16 (1918): 267–85.

17. Daniel J. Prosser, "Coal Towns in Egypt: Portrait of an Illinois Mining Region, 1890–1930" (Ph.D. diss., Northwestern University, 1973), 3–22, 68–79, 115–17.

18. Quoted in John H. M. Laslett, *Labor and the Left: A Study of Socialist and Radical Influences in the American Labor Movement, 1881–1924* (New York: Basic Books, 1970), 198.

19. Laslett, *Labor and the Left,* 198–99; McDonald and Lynch, *Coal and Unionism,* 46.

20. For the workings of the Central Competitive Field Agreement and of district 12's role in it, see Louis Bloch, *Labor Agreements in Coal Mines: A Case Study of the Administration of Agreements between Miners and Operators' Organizations in the Bituminous Coal Mines of Illinois* (New York: Russell Sage Foundation, 1931), chaps. 1–2. For the operation of the Joint Conciliation Board in Scotland, see Arnot, *A History,* 98–101.

21. In 1898, in the aftermath of the 1897 strike, F. W. Lukins of the Chicago-Virden Coal Company and other antiunion coal operators in central Illinois imported black strikebreakers from Alabama to prevent district 12 from unionizing the miners at Pana and Virden. The resulting violence between African American strikebreakers and armed white miners exacerbated racial hostility between the two groups. Nevertheless, both district 12's leaders and the black community realized the dangers of letting the situation get out of hand. Jack Hunter, president of district 12, protected the black miners at Virden from the violence that threatened them, and the Alabama branch of the Afro-American Labor Protective Association passed a resolution in support of their fellow miners who had moved north to Pana. After the Pana and Virden incidents, relations between black and white miners improved. For a fuller account, see Weinberg, "Tug of War," 83–91; John H. Keiser, "Black Strikebreakers and Racism in Illinois, 1865–1900," *Journal of the Illinois State Historical Society* 65:2 (Autumn 1972): 313–26; and Ronald Lewis, *Black Coal Miners in America: Race, Class, and Community Conflict, 1780–1980* (Lexington: University Press of Kentucky, 1987), 79–81.

22. Weinberg, "Tug of War," 75; Abbott, "Immigrant and Coal Mining Communities," chap. 3.

23. John H. Keiser, "The Union Miners Cemetery at Mt. Olive, Illinois: A Spirit-Thread of Labor History," *Journal of the Illinois State Historical Society* 62:3 (Summer 1969): 229–66; Edward A. Wieck, "General Alexander Bradley," *American Mercury* 8 (May 1926): 69–70.

24. *Proceedings of the Fourteenth Biennial Convention of the Illinois State Federation of Labor*, Springfield, 1907, 114–16.

25. For details of the 1910 strike in Illinois and the 1912 strike in Scotland, see "Special Report on 1910 Coal Strike in Illinois," *United Mine Workers Journal*, February 14, 1911, pp. 3–9; Arnot, *A History*, chap. 6; and Roy Church and Quentin Outram, *Strikes and Solidarity: Coalfield Conflict in Britain, 1889–1966* (Cambridge: Cambridge University Press, 1998), chap. 7.

26. Bloch, *Labor Agreements*, chap. 9; Arnot, *A History*, 100–106, 115–20.

27. Lorin L. Cary, "Adolph Germer: From Labor Agitator to Labor Professional" (Ph.D. diss., University of Wisconsin, 1968), chap. 1; David Thoreau Wieck, *Woman from Spillertown: A Memoir of Agnes Burns Wieck* (Carbondale: Southern Illinois University Press, 1992), 57–58; Lanarkshire County Miners Union, Minutes of Council Meetings, April 24, 1902; ibid., July 31, 1902; Lanarkshire County Miners Union, *Report and Balance Sheet for the Period Ending 30th June, 1906*, 5–6, National Library of Scotland, deposit 227.

28. *Hamilton Advertiser*, August 3, 1912, p. 4.

29. Edward Wieck, "Pit Committees in District 12," Edward Wieck Collection, Box 87, File 2; See also Keith Dix, *What's a Coal Miner to Do? The Mechanization of Coal Mining* (Pittsburgh: University of Pittsburgh Press, 1988), 123–25.

30. See, e.g., the discussions that took place about enforcing union agreements in the LCMU meetings in the summer and fall of 1905, Minutes of Council Meetings, June 5 and Sept. 13, 1905, National Library of Scotland, deposit 227.

31. Barrette, "John Walker," 21–24; Joyce M. Bellamy and John Saville, eds., *Dictionary of Labour Biography*, 5 vols. (London: Macmillan, 1976), 3:167–68.

32. Michael Dyer, *Respectable Citizens: The Scottish Electoral System*, 2 vols. (Aberdeen: Aberdeen University Press, 1996), 1: chaps 2–3; H. J. Hanham, *Elections and Party Management: Politics in the Time of Disraeli and Gladstone* (London: Longmans, Green 1959), ix–x, 160–62.

33. For a general history of Chartism, see David J. V. Jones, *Chartism and the Chartists* (London: Allen Lane, 1975).

34. Alan B. Campbell, *The Lanarkshire Miners: A Social History of Their Trade Unions, 1775–1874* (Edinburgh: John Donald, 1979), 84–85; F. C. Mather, *Public Order in the Age of the Chartists* (New York: Augustus M. Kelley, 1967), 80–81.

35. James Johnston, *The History of the Working Classes in Scotland* (Trowbridge, U.K.: Rowman and Littlefield, 1974), 251–52.

36. W. Hamish Fraser, "A Newspaper for Its Generation: The Glasgow Sentinel, 1850–1877," *Journal of the Scottish Labour History Society* 4 (July 1971): 24–25.

37. Maurice R. Marchello, *Black Coal for White Bread: Up from the Prairie Coal Mines* (New York: Vintage, 1972), 46–47. For a general introduction to working-class politics in Illinois in the post–Civil War period, see John H. Keiser, *Building for the Centuries, 1865 to 1898* (Urbana: University of Illinois Press, 1977), chap. 3.

38. For the early economic history of St. Louis and Chicago, see Wyatt W. Winton, *The Economic Rivalry between St. Louis and Chicago* (New York: Columbia University Press, 1947).

39. Mark Wyman, *Immigrants in the Valley: Irish, Germans, and Americans in the Upper Mississippi Country, 1830–1860* (Chicago: Nelson-Howell, 1984), 166–72.

40. For a discussion of these early Republican ideals, see Eric Foner, *Free Soil, Free Labor, Free Men: The Ideology of the Republican Party before the Civil War* (New York: Oxford University Press, 1970), 160–71.

41. James T. Przybylski, "Twentieth-Century Elections in Illinois: Patterns of Partisan Change" (Ph.D. diss., University of Illinois, 1974), 26–27.

42. See pp. 65–66.

43. Amy Bridges, "Becoming American: The Working Class in the United States before the Civil War," in *Working-Class Formation: Nineteenth-Century Patterns in Western Europe and the United States,* ed. Ira Katznelson and Aristide R. Zolberg (Princeton, N.J.: Princeton University Press, 1986), 191.

44. Joan Clifford, *Shaftesbury, Fighter for the Poor* (London: Marshall Pickering, 1993), 88–92, 114–19.

45. Gordon Wilson, *Alexander McDonald, Leader of the Miners* (Aberdeen: Aberdeen University Press, 1982), 98–100.

46. Ibid., 100–101.

47. In Wieck, *American Miners Association,* 241.

48. Amy Z. Gottlieb, "The Regulation of the Coal Mining Industry in Illinois, with Special Reference to the Influence of British Miners and British Precedents, 1870–1911" (Ph.D. diss., University of London, 1975), 102.

49. Wilson, *Alexander McDonald,* 99.

50. *Workingman's Advocate,* October 14, 1869, p. 4.

51. Earl R. Beckner, *A History of Labor Legislation in Illinois* (Chicago: University of Chicago Press, 1929), 291.

52. Cited in Wieck, *American Miners Association,* 196–97.

53. Keiser, *Building for the Centuries,* 76; Samuel Morton, "Railroad Magnates, Workers, and Liberal Republicans in the Illinois State Elections of 1872," *Journal of the Illinois State Historical Society* 60:4 (November 1954): 202–23.

54. W. Hamish Fraser, "Trade Unions, Reform, and the General Election of 1868 in Scotland," *Scottish Historical Review* 50:2 (October 1971): 228–41.

55. Wilson, *Alexander McDonald,* 135–36.

56. Ibid., 136.

57. Ibid., 159–60. For a description of the Lib-Labs, see Roy Gregory, *The Miners and British Politics, 1906–1914* (London: Oxford University Press, 1968), chap. 3.

58. Herbert Gutman, "Labor in the Land of Lincoln: Coal Miners on the Prairie," in *Power and Culture: Essays in the American Working Class,* ed. Ira Berlin (New York: New Press, 1987), 138.

59. Max C. Kelley, "The Greenback Labor Party in Illinois, 1876–1884" (M.A. thesis, University of Illinois, 1926), 26.

60. Gutman, "Labor," 139.

61. Wilson, *Alexander McDonald,* chap. 12.

62. For the political policies of the Knights of Labor, see Leon Fink, *Workingmen's Democracy: The Knights of Labor and American Politics* (Urbana: University of Illinois Press, 1983).

63. For the Knights of Labor in England, see Henry Pelling, "The Knights of Labor in Britain, 1880–1904," *Economic History Review* 9:2 (1959): 313–31. For the influence of the Knights of Labor among the Scottish miners, see Fred Reid, *Keir Hardie: The Making of a Socialist* (London: Croom Helm, 1978), appendix 2.

64. John H. M. Laslett, "Haymarket, Henry George, and the Labor Upsurge in Britain and America in the Late 1880s," *International Labor and Working Class History* 29 (Spring 1986): 68–82; Henry Pelling, *America and the British Left, from Bright to Bevan* (London: Macmillan, 1958), chap. 4.

65. Reid, *Keir Hardie,* 84; Pow Key Sohn, "Henry George on Two Continents: A Comparative Study of the Diffusion of Ideas," *Comparative Studies in Society and History* 2 (1959–60): 85–109.

66. Nathan Fine, *Labor and Farmer Parties in the United States, 1828–1928* (New York: Rand School of Social Science, 1928), 74–75.

67. Reid, *Keir Hardie,* 80.

68. In theory the 1884 Reform Act gave the vote to all male householders in Britain, whether owners or tenants, including the large proportion of the mine labor force who were lodgers. Significant numbers of miner lodgers were disqualified, however, either because they moved too frequently to fulfill the residency requirements or because they had to occupy lodgings valued at £10 or more per annum. Nevertheless, after 1885 it is likely that between one-third and one-half of all adult miners living in the three main Lanarkshire parliamentary constituences were able to vote. See Henry Pelling, *Social Geography of British Elections, 1895–1910* (New York: St. Martin's, 1967), 7–8; Neal Blewitt, "The Franchise in the United Kingdom, 1885–1918," *Past and Present* 32 (December 1965): 27–56.

69. Amy Z. Gottlieb, "A Demographic Study of Braidwood and Streator, Illinois," *Journal of the Illinois State Historical Society* 42 (August 1979): 185.

70. Beckner, *Labor Legislation in Illinois,* 290–91.

71. Reid, *Keir Hardie,* 80.

72. Ibid., chap. 5; J. G. Kellas, "The Mid-Lanark By-Election (1888) and the Scottish Labour Party (1888–95)," *Parliamentary Affairs* 18 (1965): 318–29.

73. John D. Hicks, *The Populist Revolt* (Lincoln: University of Nebraska Press, 1932), 440.

74. For the exceptional support that coal miners all over the country gave to the Knights of Labor in the late 1880s and early 1890s, see Jonathan Garlock, "A Structural Analysis of the Knights of Labor: A Prolegomenon to the History of the Producing Classes" (Ph.D. diss., University of Rochester, 1974), 124–36.

75. For the defeat of the 1894 Pullman strike and the affinity that many miners felt toward the railroad workers, see Almont Lindsey, *The Pullman Strike: The Story of a Unique Experiment and of a Great Labor Upheaval* (Chicago: University of Chicago Press, 1942), 135–38.

76. Chester M. Destler, *American Radicalism, 1866–1901* (Chicago: Quadrangle Books, 1966), 168–73; Destler, *Henry Demarest Lloyd and the Empire of Reform* (Philadelphia: University of Pennsylvania Press, 1963), 485–87.

77. Laslett, *Labor and the Left,* 197.

78. Destler, *American Radicalism,* 176–77; Laslett, *Labor and the Left,* 200–201.

79. Destler, *American Radicalism,* 208–11.

80. Philip S. Foner, *History of the Labor Movement in the United States,* 11 vols. (New York: International, 1947–85), 2:336–38.

81. Samuel Gompers, "Organized Labor in the Campaign," *North American Review* 155 (July 1892): 94.

82. The highest countywide votes received by the People's Party in the Illinois state elections of 1894 were secured in a tier of impoverished rural counties to the north of Little Egypt, where few miners or urban workers lived. See Joanne E. Wheeler, "The Origins of Populism in the Political Structure of a Midwestern State: Partisan Preferences in Illinois, 1876–1892" (Ph.D. diss., SUNY-Buffalo, 1976), 170–79; *List of State Officers of the State of Illinois* (Springfield: Philips Bros., 1900), 403–6.

83. Destler, *American Labor Radicalism,* chap. 4.

84. Reid, *Keir Hardie,* 80–85.

85. Fink, *Workingmen's Democracy.*

86. Reid, *Keir Hardie,* appendix 2; Amy Z. Gottlieb, "Coal Miners and Knights of Labor in Illinois," unpublished paper, University of Illinois, 1979, 3–4.

87. Quoted in Eugene Staley, *History of the Illinois State Federation of Labor* (Chicago: University of Chicago Press, 1930), 194.

88. For a general discussion of the role of voluntarism, or hostility toward state intervention in industry, in the AFL's political outlook, see Michael Rogin, "Voluntarism: The Political Functions of an Anti-Political Doctrine," in *The American Labor Movement,* ed. David Brody (New York: Harper and Row, 1971), 100–118.

89. Jean Forest, "Scottish Labour Party, 1888–1894" (B.A. honours thesis, University of Strathclyde, 1979), chap. 4.

90. Reid, *Keir Hardie,* 120–21; *Hamilton Advertiser,* September 27, 1890, p. 4; ibid., January 10, 1891, p. 4.

91. Robert Smillie, *My Life with Labour* (London: Hilton and Jones, 1924), 43–44; *Labour Leader,* March 31, 1891, p. 6.

92. F. W. S. Craig, ed., *British Parliamentary Election Results, 1885–1910* (London: Macmillan, 1974), 547.

93. Jack Reynolds, *Liberalism and the Rise of Labour, 1890–1918* (New York: St. Martin's, 1984), 214–21.

94. *Labour Leader*, April 7, 1894, p. 3; J. G. Kellas, "The Liberal Party in Scotland, 1885–1895" (Ph.D. diss., University College, London, 1961), 181–93.

95. *Labour Leader*, June 16, 1894, p. 5.

CHAPTER 8: MOVING IN TANDEM TO THE LEFT?

1. The standard history of the SPA is David Shannon, *The Socialist Party of America: A History* (New York: Macmillan, 1955). For the Labour Party, see Henry Pelling, *A Short History of the Labour Party* (London: Macmillan, 1972).

2. Marc Karson, *American Labor Unions and Politics, 1900–1918* (Carbondale: Southern Illinois University Press, 1958), chaps. 1–3; Philip S. Foner, *History of the Labor Movement in the United States*, 11 vols. (New York: International, 1947–85), 2: chaps. 10–11, 3: chaps. 12–14.

3. Henry Pelling, *The Origins of the Labour Party, 1880–1900* (London: Macmillan, 1954), appendix B.

4. Pelling, *A Short History*, 10–12.

5. John H. M. Laslett, *Labor and the Left: A Study of Socialist and Radical Influences in the American Labor Movement, 1881–1924* (New York: Basic Books, 1970).

6. Roy Gregory, *The Miners and British Politics, 1900–1914* (London: Oxford University Press, 1968), 11.

7. Ibid., 96.

8. See Michael Nash, *Conflict and Accommodation: Coal Miners, Steel Workers, and Socialism, 1890–1920* (Westport, Conn.: Greenwood, 1982); Maier Fox, *United We Stand: The United Mine Workers of America* (Washington, D.C.: United Mine Workers of America, 1990), 99, 104–5.

9. Gregory, *Miners and British Politics*, 84–87.

10. For biographical vignettes of Sullivan and Gilmour, see William Knox, ed., *Scottish Labour Leaders 1918–39: A Biographical Dictionary* (Edinburgh: Mainstream, 1984), 127, 257. For Robertson and Graham, see Gordon Brown, "Some Problems Connected with the Rise of the Labour Party in the West of Scotland, 1872–1914" (M.A. thesis, University of Strathclyde, 1972), 12–15.

11. Marguerite Green, *The National Civic Federation and the American Labor Movement, 1900–1925* (Westport, Conn.: Greenwood, 1973), 85–87; Craig Phelan, *Divided Loyalties: The Public and Private Life of a Labor Leader* (Albany: State University of New York Press, 1994), chaps. 2–3.

12. Anthony B. Barrette, "John H. Walker, Labor Leader of Illinois, 1905–1933" (M.A. thesis, Eastern Illinois University, 1967), 28–34.

13. Eric Weitz, "Class Formation and Labor Protest in the Mining Communities of Southern Illinois and the Ruhr," *Labor History* 27:1 (Winter 1985–86): 85–105; Donald F. Tingley, *The Structuring of a State: The History of Illinois, 1899 to 1928* (Urbana: University of Illinois Press, 1980), chaps. 1–2.

14. Gregory, *Miners and British Politics,* 20–32.

15. Eugene Staley, *History of the Illinois State Federation of Labor* (Chicago: University of Chicago Press, 1928), 180.

16. Gregory, *Miners and British Politics,* 35–36.

17. Karson, *American Labor Unions,* chap. 3.

18. Earl R. Beckner, *A History of Illinois Labor Legislation* (Chicago: University of Chicago Press, 1929), 296–97.

19. Staley, *Illinois State Federation,* 269; Beckner, *A History,* 298–302.

20. *Proceedings of the Twentieth Annual Convention of the United Mine Workers of America, District 12* (Springfield: United Mine Workers, 1910), 47–51.

21. W. Hamish Fraser, "The Labour Party Party in Scotland," in *The First Labour Party, 1906–1914,* ed. K. D. Brown (London: Croom Helm, 1985), 38.

22. Ibid., 28.

23. *Hamilton Advertiser,* September 4, 1901, p. 4; *Glasgow Observer,* September 5, 1901, p. 8.

24. Fraser, "Labour Party in Scotland," 28.

25. F. W. S. Craig, *British Parliamentary Election Results, 1885–1910* (London: Macmillan, 1974), 502, 548, 549.

26. Eric Johnson, "Report on Trade Unions," *Board of Trade,* ser. 14, no. 12 (London: H.M. Stationery Office, 1907), 38.

27. Frank Bealey and Henry Pelling, *Labour and Politics, 1900–1906* (London: Macmillan, 1958), appendix B.

28. Brown, "Some Problems," 61–64.

29. *Forward,* April 10, 1909, p. 4. John Wheatley, a former Baillieston miner of Irish background who was later to hold office in two Labour governments, was the most important Catholic socialist in the Glasgow ILP. His Catholic Socialist Society (1906) was instrumental in persuading a growing minority of Catholic miners to overcome their opposition to socialism and in some case to embrace it. See Ian S. Wood, *John Wheatley* (Manchester, U.K.: Manchester University Press, 1980), 121–27.

30. Fraser, "Labour Party in Scotland," 57–58.

31. *Forward,* December 28, 1910, p. 3; Fraser, "Labour Party in Scotland," 52–53; Craig, *Parliamentary Election Results,* 547–49.

32. Ross McKibbin, *The Evolution of the British Labour Party, 1910–1924* (New York: Oxford University Press, 1974), chaps. 1–2.

33. Fraser, "Labour Party in Scotland," 53; Brown, "Some Problems," 65–68; I. G. C. Hutchison, *A Political History of Scotland, 1832–1924: Parties, Elections, and Issues* (Edinburgh: John Donald, 1986), 253–63.

34. Pelling, *Labour and Politics,* appendix B; Hutchison, *Political History,* 252–54.

35. The Osborne Judgement hurt the finances of the Scottish Labour Party only indirectly, for the SWRC's rules disallowed the political checkoff of union dues. Because the judgment cut back on the trade union income of the Labour Party in England, however, the party there became less willing to pass on any money

to the SWRC in Scotland. See Henry Pelling, *A History of British Trade Unionism* (Harmondsworth: Penguin, 1963), 130–32.

36. Gregory, *Miners and British Politics,* 63–68.

37. For a discussion of British trade union attitudes toward the state, see Ben Roberts, *The Trades Union Congress 1868–1921* (London: George Allen and Unwin, 1958), chap. 3.

38. Gregory, *Miners and British Politics,* 117–23.

39. Chris Cook, *A Short History of the Liberal Party, 1900–1984* (London: Macmillan, 1984), 48.

40. *Forward,* January 18, 1910, p. 7.

41. *Glasgow Herald,* December 6, 1910, p. 7.

42. Brown, "Some Problems," 68; Fraser, "Labour Party in Scotland," 59–60. For further discussions of the Liberal philosophy's continuing appeal to working-class voters in Edwardian Britain, see George L. Bernstein, *Liberalism and Liberal Politics in Edwardian England* (London: Allen and Unwin, 1986); and Peter Clarke, *Liberals and Social Democrats* (New York: Cambridge University Press, 1978).

43. Henry Pelling, *Social Geography of British Elections, 1885–1910* (New York: St. Martin's, 1967), 408–13.

44. David Howell, *British Workers and the Independent Labour Party, 1898–1906* (New York: St. Martin's, 1983), 166.

45. C. Desmond Greaves, *The Life and Times of James Connolly* (London: Lawrence and Wishart, 1961), chap. 11.

46. Wood, *John Wheatley,* 21–35.

47. In 1912 the Liberal government introduced a new home rule bill so bitterly opposed by Conservatives and Liberal Unionists in England and Protestant Loyalists in Ulster that it threatened to bring civil war to Northern Ireland. For brief accounts, see Cook, *A Short History,* 56–57; Tony Gray, *The Orange Order* (London: Bodley Head, 1972), 165–69.

48. *Glasgow Observer,* January 15, 1910, p. 5. "Carrying the Host in the streets" referred to some priests' practice of carrying the holy sacrament when they participated in public demonstrations.

49. Fred Reid, *Keir Hardie* (London: Croom Helm, 1978), 104–5.

50. *Glasgow Observer,* February 5, 1910, p. 5.

51. *Glasgow Observer,* February 12, 1910, p. 8.

52. Lee M. Wolfle, "Radical Third-Party Voting among Coal Miners, 1896–1940" (Ph.D. diss., University of Michigan, 1976), 74.

53. *Illinois Blue Book 1909* (Springfield: State of Illinois, 1910), 418–44; *Illinois Blue Book 1910* (Springfield: State of Illinois, 1912), 372–96.

54. *Proceedings of the Twenty-Sixth Annual and First Biennial Convention of the UMWA, District 12* (Springfield: United Mine Workers, 1916), 44–68, 205–6; Frank Farrington to Harriet Reid, October 5, 1914, Duncan MacDonald Collection, Illinois State Library, Box 1, Folder 1.

55. The Macoupin County Catholic Federation was influenced, as many other

American trade unions were in the early years of the century, by the propaganda of David Goldstein, an antisocialist crusader who toured the United States several times urging workers to reject the doctrines of atheistic Marxism. For the quotation, see Carl Weinberg, "The Tug of War: Labor, Loyalty, and Rebellion in the Southwestern Illinois Coalfields, 1914–1920" (Ph.D. diss., Yale University, 1995), 301. For a more extended discussion of Catholic antisocialist propaganda, see Henry Bedford, *Socialism and the Workers of Massachusetts, 1886–1912* (Amherst: University of Massachusetts Press, 1968), chap. 4.

56. Weinberg, "Tug of War," 297–98.

57. For a discussion of the influence of the Progressive movement within the Illinois Democratic and Republican parties, see Tingley, *Structuring of a State*, chap. 6.

58. For a discussion of the "wasted vote" argument, see James Weinstein, *The Decline of Socialism in America, 1912–1924* (New York: Monthly Review Press, 1967), 86–87.

59. *Belleville Democrat*, September 14, 1908, cited in Edward A. Wieck, *The American Miners' Association: A Record of the Origin of Coal Miners' Unions in the United States* (New York: Russell Sage Foundation, 1940), 240.

60. John H. Walker and Keir Hardie met at least once, at the 1912 International Miners Federation in London. Walker retained a sentimental attachment to all things Scottish, as can be seen in his love of Robert Burns's poetry and his visit back home to his native town of Binnie Hill, near Glasgow, in 1920. See John H. Walker Collection, Illinois Historical Survey, Box 76, Folder 1–3; Barrette, "John H. Walker," 80.

61. In 1910 Walker prevailed on the ISFL to hold a referendum vote on whether it should take the initiative in establishing a labor party in Illinois. Only seventy out of more than two hundred unions affiliated to the ISFL voted on this resolution, however, and it was defeated by 3,154 votes to 1,795. See Staley, *Illinois State Federation*, 233.

62. Tingley, *Structuring of a State*, 172–73.

63. James T. Przybylski, "Twentieth-Century Elections in Illinois: Patterns of Partisan Change" (Ph.D. diss., University of Illinois, 1974), 33–35.

64. *Illinois Blue Book 1912* (Springfield: State of Illinois, 1912), 114–15.

65. Robert F. Hoxie, "The Rising Tide of Socialism — A Study," *Journal of Political Economy* 19:3 (October 1911): 609–31.

66. For further evidence of socialist influence in the Little Egypt area of southern Illinois, see Stephane E. Booth, "The Relationship between Radicalism and Ethnicity in Southern Illinois Coalfield, 1870–1940" (Ph.D. diss., Illinois State University, 1983), parts 3–4.

67. Weinberg, "Tug of War," 298–300.

68. Ibid., 300–301. For the role of southern and eastern Europeans among the socialists of district 12, see also Booth, "Radicalism and Ethnicity," 129–47.

69. For relations between socialists and farmers in the farming communities of Oklahoma and Texas, and also in the mining towns of the southwest, see James R.

Green, *Grass-Roots Socialism: Radical Movements in the Southwest, 1895–1943* (Baton Rouge: Louisiana State University Press, 1978), 53–86, 193–204.

70. "Socialist State Plaform, 1906," Wieck Collection, Box 9, Folder 1.

71. "Names of Subscribers to Socialist Papers," Wieck Collection, Box 9, Folder 1. See also Victor Hicken, "Mine Union Radicalism in Macoupin and Montgomery Counties," *Western Illinois Regional Studies* 3:2 (Fall 1980): 173–89.

72. Colston E. Warne, *The Consumers Cooperative Movement in Illinois* (Chicago: University of Chicago Press, 1926), appendix D.

73. Ibid., 24.

74. Ibid., 34–35.

75. David L. Lightner, "Labor on the Illinois Central Railroad" (Ph.D. diss., Cornell University, 1969), 105–16.

76. Karson, *American Labor Unions,* chap. 6.

77. Cook, *A Short History,* 58–62.

78. Weinstein, *Decline of Socialism,* 93–103.

79. McKibbin, *Evolution,* 122–23.

80. Pelling, *British Trade Unionism,* 132.

81. Oscar Ameringer, *If You Don't Weaken: The Autobiography of Oscar Ameringer* (Norman: University of Oklahoma Press, 1983), chap. 12.

82. Craig, *British Parliamentary Elections,* 549.

83. *Forward,* March 29, 1913, p. 4.

84. Standish Meacham, *A Life Apart: The English Working Class, 1890–1914* (London: Thames and Hudson, 1977), 219.

85. For a brief comparative history of anarchosyndicalism, with some discussion of the United States, see George Woodcock, *Anarchism: A Brief History of Libertarian Movements* (Cleveland: Meridian Books, 1962).

86. For relations between socialists and IWW members in the United States, see Joseph Conlin, *Bread and Roses Too: Studies of the Wobblies* (Westport, Conn.: Greenwood, 1969), chap. 5.

87. Patrick Renshaw, *The Wobblies: The Story of Syndicalism in the United States* (Garden City, N.Y.: Doubleday, 1967), 88–89.

88. Laslett, *Labor and the Left,* 209–11.

89. Wieck, "Industrial Unionism," in Wieck Collection, Box 1, Folder 5. See also Keith Dix, *What's a Miner to Do? The Mechanization of Coal Mining* (Pittsburgh: University of Pittsburgh Press, 1988), 119–25.

90. James R. Green, *The World of the Worker: Labor in Twentieth-Century America* (New York: Hill and Wang, 1980), 87–90. See also David Montgomery, *Workers Control in America: Studies in the History of Work, Technology, and Labor Struggles* (New York: Cambridge University Press, 1979), chap. 4; Priscilla Long, *Where the Sun Never Shines: A History of America's Bloody Coal Industry* (New York: Paragon House, 1989), chap. 12; Jeremy Brecher, *Strike!* (San Francisco: Straight Arrow Books, 1972).

91. Roberts, *Trades Union Congress,* 267–68. For a contemporary account that

refers extensively to the miners, see George R. Carter, *The Triple Alliance of Industrial Unionism* (Huddersfield, U.K.: Advertiser, 1917).

92. For an analysis of *The Miners' Next Step* and its significance, see Hywel Francis and David Smith, *The Fed: A History of the South Wales Miners Federation in the Twentieth Century* (London: Lawrence and Wishart, 1980), 13–16.

93. R. Page Arnot, *A History of the Scottish Miners, from the Earliest Times* (London: George Allen and Unwin, 1955), 112–29.

94. Alan Campbell, "The Social History of Political Conflict in the Scots Coalfields, 1910–1939," in *Miners, Unions, and Politics, 1910–1947,* ed. Alan Campbell, Nina Fishman, and David Howell (Aldershot, U.K.: Scolar, 1996), 161.

95. Ibid.

96. For a detailed account of the unofficial reform committees that the publication of *The Miners Next Step* spawned in various British coalfields, including Lanarkshire, in the years after 1912, see David Egan, " 'A Cult of Their Own': Syndicalism and *The Miners Next Step,*" in *Miners, Union, and Politics,* ed. Campbell, Fishman, and Howell, 13–33.

97. Campbell, "Social History," 162.

CHAPTER 9: DENOUEMENT

1. For a general description of these political developments, see I. G. C. Hutchison, *A Political History of Scotland, 1832–1924: Parties, Elections, and Issues* (Edinburgh: John Donald, 1986), chap. 9; G. D. Cole, *A History of the Labour Party from 1914* (London: Routledge and Kegan Paul, 1948), chaps. 3–5.

2. W. R. Scott and J. Cunnison, *The Industries of the Clyde during the War* (Oxford: Clarendon, 1924), 29.

3. *Proceedings of the Twenty-Eighth Annual and Second Biennial Convention of the United Mine Workers of America, District 12, UMWA* (Springfield: District 12, 1918), 219–19.

4. Isador Lubin, *Miners' Wages and the Cost of Coal* (New York: McGraw-Hill, 1924), 230.

5. Scott and Cunnison, *Industries of the Clyde,* 169–70.

6. Lanarkshire County Miners Union, Minutes of Council Meetings, September 28, 1916, p. 7, National Library of Scotland, deposit 227.

7. LCMU Council Minutes, October 8, 1916, p. 4.

8. LCMU Council Minutes, May 30, 1917, p. 3.

9. Scott and Cunnison, *Industries of the Clyde,* 165–67, 171–72; LCMU Council Minutes, August 4, 1917, p. 2; ibid., September 20, 1917, p. 3; Chris Wrigley, *David Lloyd George and the British Labour Movement, Peace, and War* (New York: Barnes and Noble, 1976), chaps. 9–10, 14.

10. Figures cited in Carl Weinberg, "The Tug of War: Labor, Loyalty, and Rebellion in the Southwestern Illinois Coalfields, 1914–1920" (Ph.D. diss., Yale University, 1995), 348.

11. William Graebner, *Coal-Mining Safety in the Progressive Era* (Lexington: University Press of Kentucky, 1976), 57–58, 130; Barry Supple, *The History of the British Coal Industry, 1913–1946*, 3 vols. (Oxford: Clarendon, 1987), 4:426–42.

12. Harold W. Perrigo, "Factional Strife in Illinois District No. 12, United Mine Workers of America, 1919 to 1933" (Ph.D. diss., University of Wisconsin, 1933), 8–11, 14.

13. Alan Campbell, "Colliery Mechanization and the Lanarkshire Miners," *Bulletin of the Society for the Study of Labor History* 49 (1984): 37–45.

14. Quoted in Weinberg, "Tug of War," 355.

15. Supple, *British Coal Industry*, 78–93.

16. Scott and Cunnison, *Industries of the Clyde*, 31–32; LCMU Council Minutes, May 26, 1917, p. 4; ibid., August 16, 1917, p. 5.

17. Marguerite E. Jenison, *The War-Time Organization of Illinois* (Springfield: Illinois State Historical Society, 1923), 256–57; Donald F. Tingley, *The Structuring of a State: The History of Illinois, 1899–1928* (Urbana: University of Illinois Press, 1980), 199.

18. Gordon S. Watkins, *Labor Problems and Labor Adminstration in the United States during the World War* (Urbana: University of Illinois, 1920), 148–49.

19. Weinberg, "Tug of War," 389–97.

20. Philip S. Bagwell and G. E. Mingay, *Britain and America, 1850–1939: A Study of Economic Change* (London: Routledge and Kegan Paul, 1970), 244–46.

21. R. Page Arnot, *A History of the Scottish Miners Miners, from Earliest Times* (London: George Allen and Unwin, 1955), 144–60; G. D. Cole, *Labour in the Coal Mining Industry (1914–1921)* (Oxford: Oxford University Press, 1923), chaps. 3–4.

22. Supple, *British Coal Industry*, 194–201; Cole, *Labour in Coal Mining*, 77–87.

23. Marion Savage, *Industrial Unionism in America* (New York: Ronald, 1923), 96–97; Melvyn Dubofsky and Warren Van Tine, *John L. Lewis: A Biography* (New York: New York Times Book Co., 1977), 48–55.

24. Dubofsky and Van Tine, *John L. Lewis*, 55–57.

25. Cole, *Labour in Coal Mining*, 84–91; Sylvia Kopald, *Rebellion in Labour Unions* (New York: Boni and Liveright, 1924), 84–101; Iain McLean, *The Legend of Red Clydeside* (Edinburgh: John Donald, 1983), 186–97; James Hinton, *The First Shops Stewards Movement* (London: George Allen and Unwin, 1973).

26. Alan Campbell, "The Social History of Political Conflict in the Scots Coalfields, 1910–1939," in *Miners, Unions, and Politics, 1910–47*, ed. Alan Campbell, Nina Fishman, and David Howell (Aldershot, U.K.: Scolar, 1996), 162.

27. J. D. MacDougall, "The Scottish Coalminers," *The Nineteenth Century* 102 (July–December, 1927): 767.

28. Campbell, "Social History," 162; Nan Milton, *John MacLean* (Bristol: Pluto, 1973), 154–57.

29. MacDougall, "Scottish Coalminers," 767.

30. *Hamilton Advertiser*, February 1, 1919, p. 4; ibid., February 8, 1919, p. 3; MacDougall, "Scottish Coalminers," 772–73.

31. Labor activist Tom Mooney had been arrested in San Fransisco in 1916 after an antipreparedness parade. In a display of international workers' solidarity, Mooney's name was bracketed at demonstrations in Glasgow with that of imprisoned Scottish antiwar protester John MacLean. See Richard Frost, *The Mooney Case* (Stanford, Calif.: Stanford University Press, 1968), 321–24; Harry McShane, *Glasgow, 1919: The Story of the 40 Hours Strike* (Kirkintilloch, U.K.: n.p., n.d.) 27.

32. Kopald, *Rebellion*, 53, 74–75.

33. Ibid., 75.

34. Ibid.; Harold W. Perrigo, "Factional Strife," 8–11.

35. Kopald, *Rebellion*, 75–77; Perrigo, "Factional Strife," 10–14.

36. Malcom Brown and John Webb, "Seven Stranded Coal Towns: A Study of an American Depressed Area," in *U.S. Works Project Administration Research Monograph* 23 (Washington, D.C.: Government Printing Office, 1941), 53–54.

37. Louis Bloch, *Coal Miners Insecurity* (New York: Russell Sage Foundation, 1922), 20.

38. Brown and Webb, "Seven Stranded Coal Towns," 56–61.

39. Cole, *Labour in Coal Mining*, 41–53; Supple, *British Coal Industry*, 185–94; Campbell, "Social History," 150–54; Alan Campbell, "From Independent Collier to Militant Miner: Tradition and Change in the Trade Union Consciousness of the Scottish Miners, 1874–1919," unpublished paper, Liverpool University, 1988, 3–9.

40. Robert Duncan, *Steelopolis: The Making of Motherwell, c. 1750–1939* (Motherwell: Department of Leisure Services, 1991), 93.

41. Lee M. Wolfle, "Radical Third-Party Voting among Coal Miners, 1896–1940" (Ph.D. diss., University of Michigan, 1976), 74.

42. *Illinois Blue Book, 1919–1920* (Springfield: State of Illinois, 1921), 662–65.

43. Errol W. Stevens, "The Socialist Party of America in Municipal Politics: Canton, Illinois, 1911–1920," *Journal of the Illinois State Historical Society* 72:4 (November 1979): 257–58.

44. Henry Pelling, *A Short History of the Labour Party* (London: Macmillan, 1972), 46–47.

45. F. W. S. Craig, ed., *British Parliamentary Election Results, 1918–1949* (London: Macmillan, 1977), 632.

46. McLean, *Red Clydeside*, 160.

47. Pelling, *A Short History*, 46.

48. Kenneth O. Morgan, *The Age of Lloyd George: The Liberal Party and British Politics, 1890–1919* (London: George Allen and Unwin, 1975), 81–96.

49. Cole, *Labour in Coal Mining*, 193–220.

50. Austen Morgan, *James Connolly: A Political Biography* (Manchester, U.K.: Manchester University Press, 1988), 133–34, 146–48.

51. Duncan, *Steelopolis*, 164–68; Robert Duncan, " 'Motherwell for Moscow': Walton Newbold, Revolutionary Politics, and the Labour Movement in a Lanarkshire Constituency, 1918–1922," *Scottish Labour History Society Journal* 28 (1993): 60–64.

52. Duncan, " 'Motherwell for Moscow,' " 56–64; William Knox, ed., *Scottish Labour Leaders, 1918–39* (Edinburgh: Mainstream, 1984), 127, 257, 271–72; Craig, ed., *British Parliamentary Elections*, 630–36.

53. On rationing and the supply of food in Britain and America during World War I, compare the evidence provided by William C. Mullendorf in his *History of the United States Food Administration, 1917–1919* (Stanford, Calif.: Stanford University Press, 1941) with that given by Noel Whiteside in "The British Population at War," in *Britain and the First World War,* ed. John Turner (London: Unwin Hyman, 1988), 85–98.

54. Brown and Webb, "Seven Stranded Coal Towns," 61–64; Joseph Melling, *People's Struggle for Housing in West Scotland, 1890–1916* (Edinburgh: Polygon, 1983).

55. See, e.g., LCMU Council Minutes, May 1, 1916, p. 4; ibid., February 4, 1917, p. 3; ibid., November 29, 1917, p. 9.

56. Robert Duncan, *Wishaw: Life and Labour in a Lanarkshire Industrial Community, 1790–1914* (Motherwell: Department of Leisure Services, 1986), 126–27.

57. See, e.g., LCMU Council Minutes, May 14, 1916, p. 3; ibid., April 12, 1917, p. 5.

58. In 1917 Duddy, McAnulty, and other radicals on the LCMU council protested the appointment of union secretary David Gilmour to the National Service Advisory Board, a government body that supervised the work of these recruiting courts, and they secured a referendum vote by the miners that forced Gilmour to withdraw from the position. See LCMU Council Minutes, May 26, 1917, pp. 5–6; ibid., July 28, 1917, p. 3; ibid., August 16, 1917, p. 8; ibid., November 24, 1917, p. 5. See also Cole, *History of the Labour Party,* 33–41.

59. James Weinstein, *The Decline of Socialism in America, 1912–1925* (New York: Monthly Review Press, 1967), 145–46.

60. Weinberg, "Tug of War," 237–68.

61. Stevens, "Socialist Party," 254–56.

62. Cole, *History of the Labour Party 1914,* 88–91; Carl F. Brand, *British Labour's Rise to Power* (Stanford, Calif.: Stanford University Press, 1941), 116–28.

63. John H. M. Laslett, "End of an Alliance: Selected Correspondence between Socialist Party Secretary Adolph Germer and U.M.W. of A. Leaders in World War One," *Labor History* 12:4 (Fall 1971): 570–95.

64. Ibib., 587. For Walker's role on the Illinois State Council of Defense, see Tingley, *Structuring of a State,* 199–202.

65. Quoted in Laslett, "End of an Alliance," 579.

66. Quoted in ibid.

67. Weinberg, "Tug of War," 434–49.

68. John H. M. Laslett, "Swan Song or New Social Movement? Socialism and Illinois District 12, United Mine Workers of America, 1919–1926," in *Socialism in the Heartland: The Midwestern Experience, 1900–1915,* ed. Donald T. Critchlow (Notre Dame, Ind.: Notre Dame University Press, 1985), 199.

69. Weinberg, "Tug of War," chap. 9.

70. Nan Milton, *John MacLean* (Bristol: Pluto, 1973), 112–18.

71. David Shannon, *The Socialist Party of America: A History* (New York: Macmillan, 1955), 109–10.

72. Robert K. Murray, *Red Scare: A Study in National Hysteria, 1919–1920* (New York: McGraw-Hill, 1955), chap. 2.

73. For general accounts of the Liberal Party split and its consequences for the rise of the Labour Party, see Keith Laybourn and Jack Reynolds, *Liberalism and the Rise of Labour, 1890–1918* (New York: St. Martin's, 1984); Chris Cook, "Labour and the Downfall of the Liberal Party," in *Crisis and Controversy: Essays in Honour of A. J. P. Taylor,* ed. Alan Sked and Chris Cook (London: Macmillan, 1976), 38–65.

74. Brand, *British Labour's Rise,* 40–42; Trevor Wilson, *The Downfall of the Liberal Party, 1914–35* (London: Collins, 1966), chap. 2.

75. Wrigley, *David Lloyd George,* 113–21; LCMU Council Minutes, January 10, 1916, p. 7; ibid., March 31, 1917, p. 3; ibid., May 26, 1917, p. 10; H. C. G. Mathew, R. I. McKibbin, and J. A. Jay, "The Franchise Factor in the Rise of the Labour Party," *English Historical Review* 91:361 (October 1976): 723–52.

76. LCMU Council Minutes, November 24, 1917, p. 3; ibid., December 13, 1917, pp. 14–18.

77. There is much debate among British historians over the reason that Labour displaced the Liberals as the major party of the Left between 1914 and 1924. Some argue that this displacement was a "natural" consequence of the Reform Act of 1918; others, that numerous additional factors were involved. See Mathew, McKibbin, and Jay, "The Franchise Factor," 731–50; Laybourn and Reynolds, *Liberalism and the Rise of Labour,* 160–234; P. F. Clarke, "Liberals, Labour, and the Franchise," *English Historical Review* 92:3 (June 1977): 582–90; Duncan Tanner, "The Parliamentary Electoral System, the 'Fourth' Reform Act, and the Rise of Labour in England and Wales," *Bulletin of the Institute of of Historical Research* 56:134 (November 1983): 205–19; and B. A. Waites, "The Effect of the First World War on Class and Status in England, 1910–1920," *Journal of Contemporary History* 11 (1976): 27–48.

78. Shannon, *Socialist Party,* 118–22; Tingley, *Structuring of a State,* 217–20.

79. Joseph A. McCartin, *Labor's Great War: The Struggle for Industrial Democracy and the Origins of Modern American Labor Relations, 1912–1921* (Chapel Hill: University of North Carolina Press, 1997), chaps. 7–8.

80. Tingley, *Structuring of a State,* 227–28; James Przybylski, "Twentieth-Century Elections in Illinois: Patterns of Partisan Change" (Ph.D. diss., University of Illinois, 1974); *Illinois Blue Book, 1919–1920,* 314–15.

81. Cole, *History of the Labour Party,* 160–62.

82. For Keir Hardie's views on women's rights, see Kenneth O. Morgan, *Keir Hardie* (London: Oxford University Press, 1967), 141–44.

83. Hutchison, *Political History of Scotland,* 288–90; Melling, *People's Struggle,* 248–58; Esther Breitenbach and Eleanor Gordon, eds., *Out of Bounds: Women in Scottish Society, 1800–1945* (Edinburgh: University of Edinburgh Press, 1992), chaps. 4–5.

84. "Miners' Wives in St. Clair County, 1900–1930," in *Concerning Coal: Tidbits about Illinois Coal for Public Consumption* 1:2 (Winter 1992): 2.

85. David Thoreau Wieck, *Woman from Spillertown: A Memoir of Agnes Burns Wieck* (Carbondale: Southern Illinois University Press, 1992), chap. 3.

86. Dale Featherling, *Mother Jones: The Miners Angel* (Carbondale: Southern Illinois University Press, 1974), 36–42, 86–88.

87. Carl D. Oblinger, *Divided Kingdom: Work, Community, and the Mining Wars in the Central Illinois Coal Fields during the Great Depression* (Springfield: Illinois State Historical Society, 1991), 68–83.

88. Brown and Webb, "Seven Stranded Coal Towns," 72–74; Colston E. Warne, *The Consumers Cooperative Movement in Illinois* (Chicago: University of Chicago Press, 1936), 14–18, 341–42.

89. Cole, *History of the Labour Party*, 122; John Hannon, *The Life of John Wheatley* (Trowbridge, U.K.: Redwood Burn, 1988), chaps. 7–8.

90. Gordon Brown, "The Labour Party and Political Change in Scotland, 1918–1929: Politics of Five Elections" (Ph.D. diss., University of Edinburgh, 1981), 116–17.

91. Quoted in Hutchison, *Political History of Scotland*, 287–88.

92. Daniel J. Prosser, "Coal Towns in Egypt: Portrait of an Illinois Mining Region, 1890–1930" (Ph.D. diss., Northwestern University, 1973), chaps. 2–3.

93. Paul M. Angle, *Bloody Williamson: A Chapter of American Lawlessness* (New York: Knopf, 1980), chap. 5.

94. Prosser, "Coal Towns in Egypt," 123–41; Kenneth T. Jackson, *The Ku Klux Klan in the Cities, 1915–1930* (New York: Oxford University Press, 1967), chap. 1.

95. Nathan Fine, *Labor and Farmer Parties in the United States, 1828–1928* (New York: Rand School of Social Science, 1928), chap. 12. See also Kenneth C. McKay, *The Progressive Movement of 1924* (New York: Columbia University Press, 1947).

96. Staley, *Illinois State Federation*, 361–64; Alan C. Green, "The Labor Party Movement in Illinois, 1919–1924" (M.A. thesis, Southern Illinois University, 1928), chaps. 2–3.

97. Staley, *Illinois State Federation*, 362.

98. Green, "Labor Party Movement," 41–44; Fine, *Labor and Farmer Parties*, chap. 12.

99. *Proceedings of the Thirtieth Consecutive and Third Biennial Convention of the United Mine Workers of America, District 12* (Springfield: United Mine Workers, 1920), 204–6.

100. Ibid., 207.

101. Staley, *Illinois State Federation*, 361; Green, "Labor Party Movement," 53–54; Warne, *Consumers Cooperative Movement*, chap. 5; Laslett, "Swan Song?" 188–90.

102. Although sympathetic support for the Russian Revolution had a more immediate and widespread impact in southwest Scotland than it did in Illinois, many U.S. workers opposed any Allied intervention in Russia in 1919 aimed at unseating the Bolsheviks. See McShane, *Glasgow, 1919*, 24–29; Milton, *John MacLean*, 145–71; Ko-

pald, *Rebellion*, 81–82; Theodore Draper, *American Communism and Soviet Russia: The Formative Period* (New York: Viking, 1960), 23–25.

103. Kopald, *Rebellion*, 84–87; Laslett, "Swan Song?" 189–91; Richard Frost, *The Mooney Case* (Stanford, Calif.: Stanford University Press, 1968), 321–24; Milton Derber, *The American Idea of Industrial Democracy* (Urbana: University of Illinois Press, 1970).

104. John J. Hough, "The Progressive Campaign of 1924 in Illinois: A Vote Analysis" (M.A. thesis, Southern Illinois University, 1965), 12–13; "Minutes of Belleville Trades and Labor Assembly," April 15, 1920, Belleville Trade and Labor Assembly Collection, Illinois State Historical Society, Springfield, Box 2.

105. Green, "Labor Party Movement," 92; Hough, "Progressive Campaign of 1924," 14.

106. Quoted in Staley, *Illinois State Federation*, 378.

107. Ibid., 383–84; Green, "Labor Party Movement," 61–68.

108. Staley, *Illinois State Federation*, 380.

109. For example, in a speech he made to an audience of Farmer-Labor supporters in East St. Louis on February 21, 1921, Walker stated: "We would all like to go the better route and have representatives of our own in the government to bring about a better world, but we cannot do this and at the same time work with others" (Walker to Walter Nesbitt, February 28, 1921, John H. Walker Collection, Box 76, Folder 41).

110. Staley, *Illinois State Federation*, chap. 24; *ISFL Weekly Newsletter* 9:23 (May 3, 1921): 4–5.

111. *Proceedings of the Thirty-Second Consecutive and Fourth Biennial Convention of the United Mine Workers of America, District 12* (Springfield: United Mine Workers, 1922), 184.

112. *Proceedings of the Thirtieth Convention*, 189.

113. McKay, *Progressive Movement*, 71–124; Staley, *Illinois State Federation*, 389–90; Hough, "Progressive Campaign of 1924," 8–12.

CONCLUSION

1. These dates denote the first period of industrial growth for both the Scottish and the Illinois coalfields. The actual span of years was 1830–60 in Scotland and 1850–70 in the United States.

2. Roy Church and Quentin Outram, *Strikes and Solidarity: Coalfield Conflict in Britain, 1889–1966* (Cambridge: Cambridge University Press, 1998), chap. 1.

3. Although many in late Victorian England voiced considerable anxiety about the deterioration of class relations that resulted from increasing strikes and the displacement of "new model" unionism by the more assertive "new unionism" of the 1890s, the threat that emerging class conflict posed to this ideal caused even greater concern in America. This concern stemmed from the deep-seated American belief, which had no real equivalent in Britain, that a democratic republic guarantees certain rights to the "republican workingman" that were threatened by the rise of post–Civil

War capitalism. For an interesting discussion, see Martin J. Burke, *The Conundrum of Class: Public Discourse on the Social Order in America* (Chicago: University of Chicago Press, 1995).

4. One of the clichés about the weakness of class-conscious movements in the United States is that the greater ethnic diversity of the American labor force inhibited labor solidarity. See Werner Sombart, *Why Is There No Socialism in the United States?* (White Plains, N.Y.: International Arts and Sciences, 1976); Charles Leinenweber, "Socialism and Ethnicity," in *Failure of a Dream? Essays in the History of American Socialism,* ed. John H. M. Laslett and Seymour M. Lipset (Berkeley: University of California Press, 1985), chap. 7; Richard J. Oestreicher, *Solidarity and Fragmentation: Working People and Class Consciousness in Detroit, 1875–1900* (Urbana: University of Illinois Press, 1986).

5. For Wilentz's views, see Sean Wilentz, "Against Exceptionalism: Class Consciousness and the American Labor Movement," *International Labor and Working Class History* 26 (Fall 1984): 1–24.

6. Stephane E. Booth, "The Relationship between Radicalism and Ethnicity in Southern Illinois Coalfields, 1870–1940" (Ph.D. diss., Illinois State University, 1983), 297.

7. For Thernstrom's views, see Stephan Thernstrom, "Working-Class Social Mobility in Industrial America," in *Essays in Theory and History: An Approach to the Social Sciences,* ed. Melvin Richter (Cambridge, Mass.: Harvard University Press, 1970), 221–38.

8. Ira Katznelson, "Working-Class Formation: Constructing Cases and Comparisons," in *Working-Class Formation: Nineteenth-Century Patterns in Western Europe and the United States,* ed. Ira Katznelson and Aristide Zolberg (Princeton, N.J.: Princeton University Press, 1986), 27–28.

9. Adolph Sturmthal, *Unity and Diversity in European Labor Movements: An Introduction to Contemporary Labor Movements* (Glencoe, Ill.: Free Press, 1953), 45–53.

10. Chester M. Destler, *American Radicalism, 1865–1901* (Chicago: Quadrangle Books, 1946), 187–88; Eugene Staley, *History of the Illinois State Federation of Labor* (Chicago: University of Chicago Press, 1930), 87–93.

11. Martin Shefter, "Trade Unions and Political Machines: The Organization and Disorganization of the American Working Class in the Late Nineteenth Century," in *Working-Class Formation,* ed. Katznelson and Zolberg, 199.

12. In 1929 Earl R. Beckner, an industrial relations expert at the University of Chicago, wrote approvingly that "a spirit of agreement and mutual concession" prevailed at meetings of the Mining Investigation Commission. This spirit was clearly desirable from Beckner's point of view, but the drafting of mining legislation behind closed doors, and by a body whose mandate was to satisfy the public's interest rather than that of either the miners or the operators, obscured the basic class differences between them. See Earl R. Beckner, *A History of Labor Legislation in Illinois* (Chicago: University of Chicago Press, 1929), 299.

13. My position on this point differs fundamentally from that of Roy Gregory,

who argued that the British miners' basic decision to transfer their political loyalties from the Liberal Party to Labour had already been made by 1914. See Roy Gregory, *The Miners and British Politics, 1906–1914* (Oxford: Oxford University Press, 1968).

14. In 1919, according to Beckner, the Illinois state mining code, which by that time included a wide variety of laws on matters ranging from mine inspection to wash-houses and from the qualifications of shot-firers to the use of explosives, was "the equal of any in the world, including the mining laws of Great Britain." See Beckner, *Labor Legislation in Illinois,* 374.

15. For a discussion of primary elections' moderating effect on the candidates who ran for office on one or another of the two major party tickets, see E. E. Schatt-schneider, *Party Government* (New York: Rinehart, 1942), 85–86.

16. John H. Walker to Robert Smillie, September 21, 1920, John H. Walker Collection, Box 61, Folder 3.

17. For an assessment of the miners' relationship to the state, both negative and positive, see Melvyn Dubofsky, *The State and Labor in Modern America* (Chapel Hill: University of North Carolina Press, 1994), chap. 2; and Frank Tillyard, *The Worker and the State* (London: George Routledge, 1948), chaps. 2–3.

18. In 1921 Lewis appointed a UMWA committee to consider the feasibility of nationalizing America's mining industry, but he consistently undermined its efforts, criticized its attempts to cultivate support among socialists, and in 1922 effectively forced its members to resign. See Melvyn Dubofsky and Warren Van Tine, *John L. Lewis: A Biography* (New York: New York Times Book Co., 1977); John Brophy, *A Miner's Life* (Madison: University of Wisconsin Press, 1964), chap. 13.

19. Chris Wrigley, *Lloyd George and the Challenge of Labour: The Post-War Coalition, 1918–1922* (New York: Harvester-Wheatsheaf, 1990), chaps. 8–9.

20. *Proceedings of the Twenty-Eighth Consecutive and Second Biennial Convention of the United Mine Workers of America, District 12* (Springfield: United Mine Workers, 1918), 224–29. See also William M. Dick, *Labor and Socialism in America: The Gompers Era* (Port Washington, N.Y.: Kennikat, 1972).

21. Minutes of the Executive Committee of the LCMU, December 4, 1921, National Library of Scotland, deposit 227.

22. The degree to which class sentiments cut deeper in Britain than in the United States in the World War I period is discussed in Neville Kirk, *Labour and Society in Britain and the U.S.A.,* 2 vols. (Aldershot, U.K.: Scolar, 1994), 2:167–72, 229–64.

Bibliography of Primary Sources

SOUTHWEST SCOTLAND

Census Records

Census	Parish	Reel Number
1851	Cambusnethan	628
	Larkhall	638
	Dalserf	638
	Hamilton	647
	Stonehouse	660
1861	Cambusnethan	628
	Larkhall	638
	Dalserf	638
	Hamilton	647
	Stonehouse	656
1871	Cambusnethan	628
	Blantyre	624
	Larkhall	638
	Dalserf	638
	Hamilton	647
	Stonehouse	656
1881	Cambusnethan	628
	Blantyre	624
	Larkhall	638
	Dalserf	638
	Hamilton	647
	Stonehouse	656

Government Documents

Catalogue of Plans of Abandoned Mines. Vol. 5. Mines Dept., Board of Trade, 1931.
Miners' Eight Hour Day Committee: First Report of Departmental Committee. 1907.
Report from Select Committee into Operation of Act for the Regulation and Inspection of Mines, and into Complaints Contained in Petitions from the Miners of Great Britain. 1865, 1866.
Reports from Select Committee on Coal Mines:
> *Coal Mines Inspectors Reports (Eastern and Western Districts of Scotland).* 1854–55, vol. 15; 1856, vol. 18; 1859, sess. 2, vol. 12; 1864, pt. 1; 1866, appendix B; 1867, vol. 16; 1871, vol. 14; 1873, vol. 19; 1875, vol. 16; 1881, vol. 25; 1882, 21; 1884–85, vol. 15; 1886, vol. 16; 1888, vol. 30.
> *District Reports of Inspectors of Mines (Eastern and Western Districts of Scotland).* 1890–91, vol. 22.
> *Reports of the Commissioners Appointed to Inquire into the State of the Population in the Mining Districts.* 1844, vol. 15; 1847–48, vol. 26; 1854–55, vol. 15; 1864, vol. 24, pt. 1.
Report of the Royal Commission on the Housing of the Industrial Population of Scotland, Rural and Urban. 1917.
Report on the Blantyre Colliery Explosion. 1878.
Report on Trade Unions. Board of Trade, 1907.
Reports of the Mining Commissioner. 1846–52.
Royal Commission on Labour, Minutes of Evidence. 1892.
Royal Commission on Mines. 1909.
Wilson, J. *Report by the County Medical Officer of Lanark on the Housing Conditions of Miners.* Glasgow, 1910.

Archival Material

General

"Autobiography of Alexander Howison." John Burnett Collection, Brunel University Library, London. Access No. 354.
Blantyre Miners Association. Minutes. 1871–78. Scottish Record Office, Edinburgh. FS7/79.
"Conference of Members of Conciliation Board of Coalowners of Scotland, and Scottish Miners Federation." National Library of Scotland, Edinburgh. Accession 227.
"In the Mining Village of Yesterday." Strathclyde Regional Archives, Mitchell Library, Glasgow. TD 729/73.
Keir Hardie Letterbooks. National Library of Scotland, Edinburgh. Deposit 183.
Lanarkshire County Miners Union. *Minutes of Council Meetings.* 1904–19. National Library of Scotland, Edinburgh. Deposit 227.
———. *Reports and Balance Sheets.* 1904–6. National Library of Scotland, Edinburgh. Deposit 227/27.

McNeill and Thompson Papers. Archives Department, St. Andrews University.

"Meetings of the Lanarkshire Coal Masters Association." 1887. Scottish Record Office, Edinburgh. F32/32.

Miners Federation of Great Britain, National Conference Proceedings. 1893–94, 1901, 1905, 1907–8, 1912, 1919, 1922, 1924. British Library of Political and Economic Science, London School of Economics.

"Records of the Amalgamated Sons of Labour." Scottish Record Office, Edinburgh. FS7/75.

"Report of the First Annual Conference of the Scottish Workers Parliamentary Elections Committee." Manuscripts and Rare Books, London School of Economics.

"Report of the Scottish Executive of the Labour Party to the Scottish Advisory Council Meeting." 1916. National Library of Scotland, Edinburgh. Mf. Mss/137.

"Report on North-East Lanarkshire By-Election." 1911. Infancy of Labour Party Collection, Part 2, Folios 194–97, Manuscripts and Rare Books, London School of Economics.

"Representatives of the Coalowners of Scotland." 1889. Scottish Record Office, Edinburgh. FS8/88.

Scottish Liberal Association Collection. Candidates Election Manifestos, Manuscripts and Rare Books, University of Edinburgh.

Scottish Miners Federation Minutes. National Library of Scotland, Edinburgh. Deposit 111.

Scottish Women's Liberal Federation. *Annual Reports.* 1891–1900. Mitchell Library, Glasgow.

Smart, William. "Miners' Wages and the Sliding Scale." 1894. David Murray Collection, Department of Special Collections, University of Glasgow.

William Small Papers. National Library of Scotland, Edinburgh. Deposit 89.

Larkhall

"Balance Sheet of the Larkhall-Upperward of the Lanarkshire Miners Association." 1893. Hamilton Public Library.

Hamilton Estate Papers. Hamilton Public Library.

Larkhall Miners Association Minute Books. 1890–94. Hamilton Public Library.

Records of the Larkhall and Millheugh Friendly Society, Larkhall St. Thomas' Lodge, Quarter Colliers Friendly Society, and Newarthill Friendly Society. Scottish Record Office, Edinburgh. F24/1212, F24/887, FS1/16/185, FS24/926, FS1/16/186, FS24/102.

Records of the Victualling Society of Larkhall. Hamilton Public Library.

"Rules and Regulations of the Larkhall-Upperward of the Lanarkshire Miners Association." 1893. Hamilton Public Library.

Wishaw

"Applications for Parochial Relief." Cambusnethan Parish. 1891–93. Strathclyde Regional Archives, Mitchell Library, Glasgow. TD 26/34.

Council Minute Books. Motherwell Public Library.

"Rules and Practices of the Wishaw Miners Association." 1857. National Library of Scotland, Edinburgh. Deposit 30/41.

Newspapers

Airdrie, Coatbridge, Bathgate, and Wishaw Advertiser. 1857–64.

Colliery Guardian. 1889–94.

Colliery Manager and Journal of Mining Engineering. 1886–1905.

Forward. 1908–19.

Glasgow Free Press. 1851–52.

Glasgow Herald. 1864–1910.

Glasgow Observer. 1872–1910.

Glasgow Sentinel. 1852–76.

Glasgow Weekly Mail. 1885–88.

Hamilton Advertiser. 1860–1920.

Labour Leader. 1894–1914.

The Miner. 1887–88.

Miners' Watchman and Labour Sentinel. 1878.

Mining Engineering: An Illustrated Journal of Coalmining and Engineering. 1896–99.

Motherwell Times. 1883–95.

North British Daily Mail. 1879–84.

Wishaw Press. 1868–1917.

Wishaw Press and Advertiser. 1879–94.

Books and Pamphlets

An Address to the Working Miners of Scotland on Some of the Evils of the Present System, with Suggestions for Their Remedy. Edinburgh, 1847.

Alison, A. *Some Account of My Life and Writings.* Edinburgh, 1883.

Anderson, J. *Coal! A History of the Coal-Mining Industry in Scotland, with Special Reference to the Cambuslang District of Lanarkshire.* Glasgow, 1943.

Autobiography, Poems and Songs of Ellen Johnston, the "Factory Girl." Glasgow, 1867.

Barrowman, J. *A Glossary of Scotch Mining Terms.* Hamilton, 1886.

———. *Some Chapters on the History of Scotch Mining and Miners.* Hamilton, 1889.

Battison, G. *Wishaw Cooperative Society, Ltd.: A Record of Its Struggle, Progress, and Success from Its Inception in 1889.* Glasgow, 1939.

Bremner, D. *The Industries of Scotland: Their Rise, Progress, and Present Condition.* Edinburgh, 1869.

Brown, Rev. P. *Historical Sketches of the Parish of Cambusnethan.* Wishaw, 1893.

Bullock, R. *A Century of Economic Striving: A History of the Inception, Aspirations, Progress, and Personalities of the Larkhall Victualling Society.* Glasgow, 1922.

Carvel, J. *The Coltness Iron Company: A Study in Private Enterprise.* Edinburgh, 1948.

Catholic Directory for Clergy and Laity. Glasgow, 1879.

Cloughan, W. *A Series of Letters on the Restriction of Labour and Its Effects in the Mines of Lanarkshire*. Coatbridge, 1846.

Cochran-Patrick, R. W. *Early Records Relating to Mining in Scotland*. Edinburgh, 1878.

Cormack, I. L. *Old Bellshill, with Mossend, Holytown, and New Stevenston*. Wishaw, 1981.

Cunningham, A. S. *Reminiscences of Alexander McDonald, the Miners' Friend*. Dunfermline, 1902.

Directory for Blantyre and District, Including Cadzow, Eddlewood, Fernigair, Larkhall, Blantyre, High Blantyre, and Bothwell. Hamilton, 1909.

Directory for Hamilton and District, Including Larkhall. Hamilton, 1909.

Dron, R. W. *The Lanarkshire Coal-Field*. London, 1902.

Duncan, R. *Steelopolis: The Making of Motherwell, c. 1750–1939*. Motherwell, 1991.

———. *Wishaw: Life and Labour in a Lanarkshire Industrial Community, 1790–1914*. Motherwell, 1986.

Durland, K. *Among the Fife Miners*. London, 1904.

Edmonds, E. L., and O. P. Edmonds, eds. *I Was There: The Memoirs of H. S. Tremenheere*. Windsor, 1965.

Fisher, A. R. *Poems and Songs*. Larkhall, 1883.

Glasgow Green and Roundabout: A Tourist's Guide. Glasgow, 1982.

Groome, F., ed. *Ordinance Gazetteer of Scotland: A Survey of Scottish Topography, Statistical, Biographical, and Historical*. London, 1895.

Haddow, R. *Socialism in Scotland: Its Rise and Progress*. Edinburgh, 1920.

History of the Blantyre Cooperative Society, 1883–1933. Glasgow, 1934.

Hodge, J. *Workmen's Cottage to Windsor Castle*. London, 1931.

Howie, R. *The Churches and the Churchless in Scotland: Facts and Figures*. Glasgow, 1893.

Hunt, R. *Mineral Statistics of the United Kingdom, 1861–1881*. London, 1882.

Lanarkshire Business Directory, 1895. Hamilton, 1895.

Laslett, J. *Nature's Noblemen: The Fortunes of the Independent Collier in Scotland and the American Midwest, 1855–1889*. Los Angeles, 1983.

Lochhead, J. *Reminiscences of Larkhall*. Larkhall, 1980.

Lord Elcho and the Miners: Employers and Employed. London, 1867.

Lowe, D. *From Pit to Parliament: The Story of the Early Life of James Keir Hardie*. London, 1923.

———. *Souvenirs of Scottish Labour*. Glasgow, 1919.

MacGeorge, A. *The Bairds of Gartsherrie*. Glasgow, 1875.

MacLean, R., and Joseph Dickinson. *Report on the Blantyre Explosion*. London, 1878.

MacPherson, A. *Bothwell, Blantyre, and Uddingston*. Bothwell, 1862.

———. *Handbook of Hamilton and Blantyre*. Hamilton, 1862.

McGeown, P. *Heat the Furnace Seven Times More*. London, 1967.

McLellan, J. *Larkhall: Its Historical Development*. Larkhall, 1979.

McShane, H. *Glasgow, 1919: The Story of the 40 Hours Strike*. Kirkintilloch, 1974.

McWhirter, M. T. *Old Larkie Landmarks.* Larkhall, 1953.

Naismith, W. *Hamilton Directory for 1878–79.* Hamilton, 1879.

Neilson, J. *Chronicles of Cambusnethan.* Wishaw, 1911.

The New Statistical Account of Scotland. Edinburgh, 1845.

Official Catalog of Exhibits, Mining Exhibition in Glasgow in 1885. Hamilton, 1885.

Orr, T. *Historic and Descriptive Sketches of the Joint Burghs of Motherwell and Wishaw and Surrounding District.* Motherwell, 1925.

Peat and Forest's Directory of Hamilton, Blantyre, and Larkhall for 1894–1895. Hamilton, 1895.

Pomphrey's Directory of Wishaw, and Handbook of the Parish of Cambusnethan. Wishaw, 1893.

Pridgeon, C. *Notes on the History of Blantyre.* Blantyre, 1977.

Scottish Ordinance Survey Maps. 1859, 1864, 1899.

Stewart, T. *Among the Miners, Being Sketches in Prose and Verse, with Rhymes and Songs on Various Subjects.* Larkhall, 1893.

———. *Sketches in Prose and Verse.* Larkhall, 1893.

Third Statistical Account of Scotland. Edinburgh, 1845.

"A Traveller Underground." *Our Coal and Our Coal Pits.* Glasgow, 1853.

Welsh, J. C. *The Underworld: The Story of Robert Sinclair, Miner.* London, 1930.

Wright, Rev. S. *Annals of Blantyre.* Blantyre, 1885.

Articles

Barrowman, J. "The Health Conditions of Mining." *Transactions of the Mining Institute of Scotland* 10 (1888–89).

———. "New Categories of Workers in the Lanarkshire Coalfield." *Proceedings of the Philosophical Society of Glasgow* 22 (1882–83).

———. "Scotch Mining Legislation" and appendix. *Transactions of the Mining Institute of Scotland* 10 (1888–89).

Burnby, H. "The Iron and Steel Industries of the West of Scotland." *Proceedings of the Iron and Steel Institute* 2 (1901).

Burton, J. H. "Notes on the Practice of Truck in Scotland." *Transactions of the National Association for the Promotion of Social Science* 2 (1860).

"Discussion of Findings of Royal Commission on Mining Royalties." *Transactions of the Mining Institute of Scotland* 14 (1893–94).

Dixon, J. S. "Notes on Hamilton Palace Colliery." *Transactions of the Mining Institute of Scotland* 21 (1899–1900).

Gordon, J. "On the State of Education among the Mining Population of Lanarkshire." *Transactions of the National Association for the Promotion of Social Science* 2 (1860).

Haddow, R. "The Miners of Scotland." *The Nineteenth Century* 24 (September 1888).

Haldane, J. S. "The Causes of Death in Colliery Explosions." *Transactions of the Mining Institute of Scotland* 5 (1883–84).

"Inquiry into the Mining Villages in Scotland." *Glasgow Herald* (1875).

Irwin, M. H. "Women's Industries of Scotland." *Proceedings of the Philosophical Society of Glasgow* 36 (1896).

MacDougall, J. D. "The Scottish Coalminer." *The Nineteenth Century* 102 (1927).

Moore, T. "Recent Developments in the Hamilton Coalfield." *Proceedings of the Philosophical Society of Glasgow* 32 (1893).

Moore, W. "Observations on the Supply of Coal and Ironstone, from the Mineral Fields of the West of Scotland." *Proceedings of the Philosophical Society of Glasgow* 1 (1882–83).

Nasmyth, T. "Changing Work Arrangements in the Scottish Pits since the 1860s." *Transactions of the Mining Institute of Scotland* 22 (1881–82).

"Our Mining Population." *North British Review* 8 (1847).

Robson, J. T. "Explosions of Fire Damp." *Transactions of the Mining Institute of Scotland* 4 (1882–83).

"Social and Moral Condition of the Manufacturing Districts of Scotland." *Blackwood's Edinburgh Magazine* 50 (1841).

Dissertations and Theses

Black, G. M. "Scottish Liberal M.P.s, 1914–1924." B.A. hons. thesis, University of Strathclyde, 1980.

Brown, A. J. Y. "The Scots Coal Industry, 1854–1886." D.Litt. diss., University of Aberdeen, 1952.

Brown, G. "The Labour Party and Political Change in Scotland, 1918–1929: Politics of Five Elections." Ph.D. diss., University of Edinburgh, 1981.

———. "Some Problems Connected with the Rise of the Labour Party in the West of Scotland, 1872–1914." M.A. thesis, University of Strathclyde, 1972.

Byers, T. J. "The Scottish Economy during the 'Great Depression,' 1873–1896, with Special Reference to the Heavy Industries of the Southwest." M.Litt. thesis, University of Glasgow, 1963.

Campbell, R. H. "The Growth and Fluctuations of the Scottish Pig Iron Trade, 1828–1873." Ph.D. diss., University of Aberdeen, 1952.

Clements, R. V. "English Trade Unions and the Problem of Emigration." B.Litt. thesis, Oxford University, 1953.

Colligan, M. "Blantyre: A Geographical Study in Economic and Social Development." B.S. hons. thesis, University of Strathclyde, 1983.

Conaghan, J. "The Truck System in North Lanarkshire, 1831–1887." B.A. hons. thesis, University of Strathclyde, 1977.

Corrins, R. D. "William Baird and Co., Coal and Iron Masters, 1830–1914." Ph.D. diss., University of Strathclyde, 1974.

Forrest, J. "The Scottish Labour Party, 1888–1894." B.A. hons. thesis, University of Strathclyde, 1978.

Frame, A. B. "Problems of the Expanding Coal-Field in Mid-19th Century Lanarkshire." B.A. hons. thesis, University of Strathclyde, 1972.

Gibson, I. F. "The Economic History of the Scottish Iron and Steel Industry." Ph.D. diss., University of London, 1955.

Higgins, T. "The I.L.P. in Glasgow, with Particular Reference to the 1918 to 1924 General Elections." B.A. hons. thesis, University of Strathclyde, 1970.

Jones, D. L. "The Background and Motives of Scottish Emigration to the United States of America in the Period 1825–1861, with Special Reference to Emigrant Correspondence." Ph.D. diss., University of Edinburgh, 1970.

Jones, M. "Changes in Industry Population and Settlement in the Exposed Coalfield of South Yorkshire, 1840–1908." M.A. thesis, University of Nottingham, 1966.

Kellas, J. G. "The Liberal Party in Scotland, 1885–1895." Ph.D. diss., University College, London, 1961.

McDonagh, A. M. "Irish Immigrants and Labour Movements in Coatbridge and Airdrie, 1891–1931." B.A. hons. thesis, University of Strathclyde, 1977.

Noble, B. "Aspects of Lanarkshire Coal-Mining, 1873–96." B.A. hons. thesis, University of Strathclyde, 1974.

O'Malley, J. "The Drift towards Socialism by the Irish Catholic Community in Glasgow, 1880–1910, with Special Reference to the Role of John Wheatley and the Catholic Socialist Society." B.A. hons. thesis, University of Strathclyde, 1981.

O'Neill, J. "William Lloyd Garrison and the Anti-Slavery Movement in America and Scotland." B.A. hons. thesis, University of Strathclyde, 1979.

Radke, E. "The I.L.P. in Glasgow, 1893–1911." B.A. hons. thesis, University of Strathclyde, 1986.

Slaven, A. "Coal Mining in the West of Scotland in the Nineteenth Century: The Dixon Enterprises." B.Litt. thesis, University of Glasgow, 1966.

Stevenson, C. A. "The Attitudes of Left-Wing Parties, in Glasgow, to the Russian Revolution." B.A. hons. thesis, University of Strathclyde, 1977.

Wilson, A. "The Chartist Movement in Scotland." D.Phil. diss., Oxford University, 1955.

Wilson, G. "The Miners of the West of Scotland and Their Trade Unions, 1842–1874." Ph.D. diss., University of Glasgow, 1977.

Youngson-Brown, A. J. "The Scots Coal Industry." Ph.D. diss., University of Aberdeen, 1952.

ILLINOIS

Census Records

Census	County	Reel Number
1860	Bureau	653/158
	Will	653/180
	Will	653/238
	Grundy	653/181
	La Salle	653/196
	La Salle	653/197
	Livingston	653/199
1870	Bureau	593/190
	Will	593/291
	Will	593/292
	Grundy	593/225
	La Salle	593/243
	La Salle	593/244
	Livingston	593/247
1880	Bureau	T9/177
	Will	T9/260
	Will	T9/261
	Grundy	T9/209
	Grundy	T9/210
	La Salle	T9/222
	La Salle	T9/223
	La Salle	T9/224
	Livingston	T9/225
1900	Bureau	T623/238
	Bureau	T623/239
	Will	T623/353
	Will	T623/354
	Grundy	T623/303
	Grundy	T623/304
	La Salle	T623/315
	La Salle	T623/316
	La Salle	T623/317
	Livingston	T623/318

Government Documents

"Diamond Mine Disaster." *Journal of the Senate, Twenty-Third General Assembly.*
Springfield, 1883.
Illinois Bureau of Labor Statistics. *Annual Report.* Springfield, 1882–91.
Illinois Bureau of Labor Statistics. *Biennial Report.* Springfield, 1892–1926.
Illinois Bureau of Labor Statistics. *Coal in Illinois, 1894.* Springfield, 1895.
Illinois Bureau of Labor Statistics. *Coal Reports.* Springfield, 1894–1910.
Illinois Department of Mines and Minerals. *A Compilation of the Mining Industry of
Illinois, 1882–1930.* Springfield, 1931.
Illinois Governor's Commission. *Report on the Coal Miners' Strike and Lockout.*
Springfield, 1889.
Orendorff, A. *Biennial Report of the Adjutant-General of Illinois to the Commander-
in-Chief* (1893–1894). Springfield, 1895.
Report of Special Committee on Labor to Illinois General Assembly. Springfield, 1879.

Archival Material

General

Adolph Germer Collection. Illinois Historical Survey, University of Illinois, Urbana.
Belleville Trade and Labor Assembly Collection. Illinois State Library, Springfield.
Duncan MacDonald Collection. Manuscript Division, Illinois State Library, Spring-
field.
Edward Wieck Collection. Archives of Labor History and Urban Affairs, Walter P.
Reuther Library, Wayne State University, Detroit.
John H. Walker Collection. Illinois Historical Survey, University of Illinois, Urbana.
Maurice R. Marchello Papers. Immigration History Research Center, University of
Minnesota, St. Paul.
Illinois State Federation of Labor. *Newsletter.* 1917–24. Chicago Historical Society.
*Proceedings of Joint Convention, and Constitution and Laws of the National Progres-
sive Union of Miners and Mine Laborers.* 1888. Martin P. Catherwood Library,
Cornell University, Ithaca, N.Y.
*Proceedings of the Annual, Biennial, and Consecutive Conventions of District 12, United
Mine Workers of America.* 1899–1926. Martin P. Catherwood Library, Cornell
University, Ithaca, N.Y.
Proceedings of the Illinois State Federation of Labor. 1896–1900, 1904–1909, 1912–1918,
1920–1924. University Library, University of Illinois, Urbana.
Record Book of UMWA Local 8215. Archives, Southern Illinois University, Carbon-
dale.
*Report by A. MacDonald to the Members of the Miners' National Union on the Condi-
tion and Prospects of Labour in the United States.* Bishopsgate Institute, London.
43/38.
"Report of Directors of the Chicago, Wilmington, and Vermilion Co." 1881, 1888,
1896. Manuscripts Division, Chicago Historical Society.

Report on the Coal-Miners Strike and Lock-Out in Northern Illinois, by J. M. Gould and F. H. Wines, Commissioners Appointed by the Governor. 1889. University Library, University of Illinois, Urbana.

The Riots of 1877 in Illinois: An Official History of the Braidwood Campaign. Speeches and Papers by Illinoisans. Vol. B, 1878. Illinois Historical Survey, University of Illinois, Urbana.

Ruffin Drew Fletcher and Family Collection. Manuscript Division, Illinois State Library, Springfield.

William Mitch Papers. Historical Collections and Labor Archives, Pennsylvania State University, University Park.

Braidwood

Report and Proceedings of the Diamond Mine Widows and Orphans Relief Committee. 1883. Wilmington Public Library.

"Works Project Administration Interviews with Residents." 1934–35. Illinois Vertical File, Illinois State Library, Springfield.

Streator

Baptismal Records. St. Stephen's Parish Church, Streator.

George W. Morrell Papers. Manuscript Division, Illinois State Library, Springfield.

Miscellaneous Papers. La Salle County Historical Society.

Oral interviews conducted by the author, in his possession, with Thomas Gavasky (07/09/92); Thomas Centko (07/09/92); Anne Elko (07/10/92); Anthony Goura (07/10/92); Anthony Leskanich (07/10/92).

"Works Project Administration Interviews with Residents." 1934–35. Illinois Vertical File, Illinois State Library, Springfield.

Spring Valley

Bernice Sweeney Collection. Spring Valley Public Library.

Court Materials Concerning Spring Valley Riot and Miners' Strike, 1894–95. Supplied by A. Tonnozi, in author's possession.

"Minutes of Local Assembly 8617, Knights of Labor." 1888–94. Illinois Regional Depository, Illinois State University, Normal.

"Minutes of Miners and Mine Laborers Protective Association, Lodge No. 26." 1888–89. Illinois Regional Depository, Illinois State University, Normal.

Oral interviews conducted by the author, in his possession, with Leonard Baker (07/13/92); Bernard Bernaba (07/09/92); William Wimbiscus (07/13/92).

Newspapers

American Socialist. 1914–17.
L'Aurora. 1900–1901.
Black Diamond. 1889–98.
Bureau County Republican. 1886–97.
Chicago Chronicle. 1902.

Chicago Herald. 1894.

Chicago Inter-Ocean. 1901.

Chicago Socialist. 1908–19.

Chicago Tribune. 1877–1905.

Colliery Engineer. 1887–92.

Concerning Coal: Tidbits about Illinois Coal for Public Consumption. 1991–93.

Galesburg Labor News. 1896–98.

The Graphic. 1894.

Jednota. 1910–12, 1992.

Joliet Daily News. 1884–87.

Journal of United Labor. 1868–70.

Miners National Record. 1874–76.

Mining and Engineering Journal. 1886–98.

National Labor Tribune. 1868–86.

Spring Valley Gazette. 1888–1914, 1952–53, 1961–63.

Streator Daily Free Press. 1892–94, 1923.

Streator Times-Press. 1960–64.

Twin City Daily. 1887–94.

United Mine Workers Journal. 1894–1924.

Wilmington Advocate. 1882–1906.

Wilmington Independent. 1861–82.

Workingman's Advocate. 1868–79.

Books and Pamphlets

Agreement between Illinois Coal Operators Association and Illinois District 12, U.M.W. of A., 1912–1914. Springfield, 1914.

Angle, P. *Biography in Black: A History of Streator.* Streator, 1962.

Baldwin, E. *History of La Salle County, Illinois: A Sketch of the Pioneer Settlers of Each Town.* Chicago, 1877.

Barnard, H. K. *Anton the Martyr.* Chicago, 1933.

Barnett, G. E. *Chapters on Machinery and Labor.* Cambridge, Mass., 1926.

Barton, G. *Village of Braceville.* Braidwood, 1902.

Bateman, N., and P. Selby, eds. *Historical Encyclopedia of Illinois and History of Grundy County.* Chicago, 1914.

Bloch, L. *Labor Agreements in Coal Mines: A Case Study of the Administration of Agreements between Miners and Operators' Organizations in the Bituminous Coal Mines of Illinois.* New York, 1931.

Braidwood Centennial, 100 Years, 1865–1965. Braidwood, 1965.

Bukowczyk, J. *And My Children Did Not Know Me: A History of Polish-Americans.* Bloomington, Ill., 1987.

City Directory of Streator. Streator, 1872.

City of Streator: Its Resources and Advantages. Streator, 1887.

Coggeshall, J. M. " 'God Bless the Dutch'! The Emergence of a German-American Ethnic Group in St. Clair County, Illinois, 1838–1858." *Selected Papers in Illinois History.* Springfield, 1984.

Donna, M. J. *The Braidwood Story.* Braidwood, 1952.

Flaherty, E. A., ed. *Village of Ladd, 1880–1980: 100 Years Young and Still Growing.* Shawnee, Ill., 1991.

Fox, M. B. *United We Stand: The United Mine Workers of America, 1890–1990.* Washington, D.C., 1990.

Goodrich, C. *The Miner's Freedom: A Study of the Working Life in a Changing Industry.* Boston, 1925.

History of the Illinois Coal Operators Association. Springfield, 1921.

Husband, J. *A Year in a Coal-Mine.* Boston, 1911.

Illinois Bureau of Commerce and Manufacturing. Springfield, 1870.

Illinois Coal Operators Association. *A Brief Outline of 25 Years History.* Chicago, 1921.

Justi, H. *The Coal Mine Operator versus the Public.* Chicago, 1904.

Keiser, J. H. *Illinois Vignettes.* Springfield, 1977.

Lloyd, H. D. *A Strike of Millionaires against Miners.* Chicago, 1890.

Marcello, M. R. *Black Coal for White Bread: Up from the Prairie Coal Mine.* New York, 1972.

Maue, A. *History of Will County.* Joliet, 1928.

McNeill, G. E., ed. *The Labor Movement, the Problem of To-day.* New York, 1887.

Mitchell, J. *Organized Labor, Its Problems, Purposes and Ideals and the Present and Future of American Wage Earners.* Philadelphia, 1903.

Oblinger, C. D. *Divided Kingdom: Work, Community, and the Mining Wars in the Central Illinois Coal Fields during the Depression.* Springfield, 1991.

O'Byrne, M. C. *History of La Salle County.* Chicago, 1924.

Spring Valley, Illinois, 1886–1986: An Ethnic Heritage Made from Coal. Spring Valley, 1986.

Steiner, E. R. *From Alien to Citizen: The Story of My Life in America.* Chicago, 1944.

Stevens, W. W. *Past and Present of Will County.* Joliet, 1907.

Stone, R. "The Illinois Miners and the Birth of the Cooperative League." *Selected Papers in Illinois History.* Springfield, 1982.

Streator City and Business Directories. Streator, 1872, 1876, 1882, 1896, 1901–2.

Streator, Historical Centennial Program, 1868–1968. Streator, 1968.

St. Stephen's Parish Register. Streator, 1984.

Tippett, T. *Horse Shoe Bottoms.* New York, 1935.

Ullrich, H. S. *This Is Grundy County: Its History from Beginning to 1968.* Dixon, Ill., 1968.

Williams, J. E., ed. *The Story of Streator.* Streator, 1912.

Woodruff, G. *History of Will County.* Chicago, 1878.

Articles

Abbott, G. "The Immigrant and Coal Mining Communities of Illinois." *Bulletin of the Immigrants Commission,* no. 2 (1920).

Bauman, G. "Coal Miners, from Craftsmen to Industrial Workers." Unpublished paper. Los Angeles, 1977.

Clark, Q. "Modern Method of Opening Long-Wall." *Journal of the Illinois Mining Institute* 3 (1894–95).

"Coal Resources of District 1." *Bulletin of the Illinois State Geological Survey* 10 (1915).

Commons, J. R. "Slavs in the Bituminous Mines of Illinois." *Charities* 13 (December 1904).

Dix, K. "Work Relations in the Coal Industry: The Hand-Loading Era, 1880–1930." *West Virginia University Bulletin,* ser. 78 (January 1978).

Elliott, S. B. "An Epoch-Making Settlement between Labor and Capital: A Compilation of Letters, Reports, and Official Statements Regarding the Cherry Mining Disaster." *Forensic Quarterly* 8 (June 1910).

Fletcher, W. "The Introduction of Mining Machines." *Journal of the Illinois Mining Institute* 2 (1892–93).

Gottlieb, A. Z. "Coal Miners and Knights of Labor in Illinois." Unpublished paper. Urbana, Ill., 1977.

Hudson, T. "Mine Inspectors in Illinois." *Journal of the Illinois Mining Institute* 1 (1891–92).

Joyce, R. P. "Early Struggles in the Mines of Illinois, 1868–1900." Unpublished paper. Wilmington, Ill., 1981.

———. " 'Old Dan' McLaughlin: Miners' Leader from Illinois." Unpublished paper. Wilmington, Ill., 1984.

———. "The Spring Valley Race Riots of 1895: A Look at Ethnic Relations in the Coal Towns." Unpublished paper. Wilmington, Ill., 1987.

Kaupas, A. "The Lithuanians in America." *Charities* 13 (1904).

Kinneman, M. "John Mitchell in Illinois." *Illinois State Journal* 32 (September 1969).

Lovejoy, O. R. "The Anthracite Coal Industry — The Anthracite Coal Communities." *Charities* 13 (1904).

Macmillan, T. C. "The Scots and Their Descendants in Illinois." *Transactions of the Illinois State Historical Society* 26 (1919).

Manfreddini, D. M. "Italians Come to Herrin." *Journal of the Illinois State Historical Society* 37 (December 1944).

McPherson, P. S. "When Spring Valley Was Young." *Spring Valley Gazette,* November 24, 1952.

Panofsky, G. S. "A View of Two Major Centers of Italian Anarchism in the U.S.: Spring Valley and Chicago, Illinois." Unpublished paper. Northwestern University, 1987.

Rouceck, J. "Lithuanian Immigrants in the American Midwest." *American Journal of Sociology* 41 (1936).

Rovnianek, P. V. "The Slovaks in America." *Charities* 13 (1904).

Sheridan, F. "Italian, Slavic, and Hungarian Unskilled Immigrant Laborers." *U.S. Bureau of Labor Bulletin* 15 (September 1907).

"Short Course in Coal Mining for Coal Mine Employees." *University of Illinois Bulletin* 12 (1915).

Vecoli, R. "Italian Immigrants in Rural and Small-Town America." Unpublished paper. American Historical Association, 1981.

"Visit to No. 3 Shaft, C.W. & V. Coal Co." *Journal of the Illinois Mining Institute* 1 (1891–92).

Wheeler, H. D. "Machine Mining in the St. Louis Coal Regions." *School of Mines Quarterly* 9 (1888).

Dissertations and Theses

Barrette, A. B. "John H. Walker, Labor Leader of Illinois, 1905–1933." M.A. thesis, Eastern Illinois University, 1967.

Bassett, M. E. R. "The Socialist Party of America, 1912–1919: Years of Decline." Ph.D. diss., Duke University, 1970.

Bennett, D. L. "The Labor Movement of Streator, Illinois, 1868 to 1933." M.A. thesis, University of Illinois, 1966.

Booth, S. "The Relationship between Radicalism and Ethnicity in Southern Illinois Coalfields, 1870–1940." Ph.D. diss., Illinois State University, 1983.

Byrnie, D. "Irish Immigration and Settlement in Illinois, 1845–1880." M.A. thesis, Illinois State University, 1959.

Cary, L. L. "Adolph Germer: From Labor Agitator to Labor Professional." Ph.D. diss., University of Wisconsin, 1968.

Clark, D. O. "John Elias Williams (1858–1919) — Labor Peacemaker: A Study in the Life of an Early Illinois Mediator and Arbitrator and His Impact upon the American Labor Movement." M.A. thesis, University of Illinois, 1957.

Coggeshall, J. M. "Ethnic Persistence with Modification: The German-Americans of Southwest Illinois." Ph.D. diss., Southern Illinois University, 1984.

Costigan, D. D. "Irish Immigration and Settlement in Illinois, 1845–1880." M.S. thesis, Illinois State University, 1959.

Decherine, D. L. "Labor and Immigration in a Southern Illinois Coal Town, 1890–1937." M.A. thesis, Illinois State University, 1989.

Dixon, H. M. "The Illinois Coal Mining Industry." Ph.D. diss., University of Illinois, 1951.

Fenton, E. "Immigrants and Unions — A Case Study: Italians and American Labor, 1870–1912." Ph.D. diss., Harvard University, 1957.

Fivek, K. "From Company Town to Miners' Town: Spring Valley, 1885–1905." C.A.S. thesis, Northern Illinois University, 1976.

Garlock, J. "A Structural Analysis of the Knights of Labor: A Prolegomenon of the History of the Producing Classes." Ph.D. diss., University of Rochester, 1974.

Gottlieb, A. Z. "The Regulation of the Coal Mining Industry in Illinois, with Special Reference to the Influence of British Miners and British Precedents, 1870–1911." Ph.D. diss., University of London, 1975.

Gowaskie, J. A. "John Mitchell: A Study in Leadership." Ph.D. diss., Catholic University of America, 1968.

Green, A. C. "The Labor Party Movement in Illinois, 1919–1924." M.A. thesis, Southern Illinois University, 1928.

Green, C. R. "The Progressive Campaign of 1924 in Illinois, 1919–1924." M.A. thesis, University of Illinois, 1957.

Holford, D. M. "The Illinois Populists: Radical Politics at the Township Level, 1892." M.A. thesis, Eastern Illinois University, 1974.

Hough, J. J. "The Progressive Campaign of 1924 in Illinois: A Vote Analysis." M.A. thesis, Southern Illinois University, 1965.

Joyce, R. P. "Miners on the Prairie: Life and Labor in the Wilmington, Illinois, Coal Field, 1866–1897." M.A. thesis, Illinois State University, 1980.

Kelley, M. C. "Greenback Labor Party in Illinois, 1876–1884." M.A. thesis, University of Illinois, 1926.

Lightner, D. L. "Labor on the Illinois Central Railroad." Ph.D. diss., Cornell University, 1969.

Manahan, C. B. "An Urban Study of Spring Valley, Illinois." M.S. thesis, Illinois State University, 1963.

McCormick, M. R. "A Comparative Study of Coal Mining Communities in Northern Illinois and Southeastern Ohio in the Late Nineteenth Century." Ph.D. diss., Ohio State University, 1978.

Mulford, L. H. "The Industrial History of Streator, Illinois." M.A. thesis, University of Illinois, 1941.

Perrigo, H. W. "Factional Strife in Illinois District no. 12, United Mine Workers of America, 1919 to 1933." Ph.D. diss., University of Wisconsin, 1933.

Prosser, D. "Coal Towns in Egypt: Portrait of an Illinois Mining Region, 1890–1930." Ph.D. diss., Northwestern University, 1973.

Przybylski, J. T. "Twentieth-Century Elections in Illinois: Patterns of Partisan Change." Ph.D. diss., University of Illinois, 1974.

Scharnau, R. W. "Thomas J. Morgan and the Chicago Socialist Movement, 1876–1901." Ph.D. diss., Northern Illinois University, 1969.

Singer, A. J. " 'Which Side Are You On?' Ideological Conflict in the United Mine Workers of America, 1919–1928." Ph.D. diss., Rutgers University, 1982.

Weinberg, C. "The Tug of War: Labor, Loyalty, and Rebellion in the Southwestern Illinois Coalfields, 1914–1920." Ph.D. diss., Yale University, 1995.

Wheeler, J. E. "The Origins of Populism in the Political Structure of a Midwestern State: Partisan Preference in Illinois, 1876–1892." Ph.D. diss., SUNY-Buffalo, 1976.

Wolfle, C. "Radical Third-Party Voting among Coal Miners, 1896–1940." Ph.D. diss., University of Michigan, 1976.

Wyn, D. R. "Trade Unions and the 'New' Immigration: A Study of the United Mine Workers of America, 1890–1920." Ph.D. diss., London School of Economics, 1976.

Index

Note: Italicized page numbers refer to figures, tables, and maps.

absentee ownership, 104, 128–30, 168
accidents, 52, 164. *See also* disasters; safety
accommodationism: in management
    issues, 53–58; in social control issues,
    37–38, 43; in temperance, 37, 44–45
Adamson, William, 180
Addams, Jane, 214
AFL. *See* American Federation of Labor
    (AFL)
African Americans: politics of, 175; preju-
    dice against, 140, 156–57; as strike-
    breakers, 107, 216, 250n50, 260n21
Afro-American Labor Protective Associa-
    tion, 260n21
agriculture. *See* farmers
Airdrie (Scotland): emigration from, 80;
    mixed workforce of, 175, 178; temperance
    society in, 44; walkouts in, 198
air shafts, construction of, 97
alcohol. *See* drinking
alienation: ethnicity and, 82; growth of, 34,
    49, 83, 224. *See also* class consciousness
Alston, Robert, 120
Altgeld, John Peter, 146
AMA (American Miners Association), 64,
    66, 98, 119
American Federation of Labor (AFL):
    miners' unions' influence on, 10; politics

of, 173, 176, 217, 218, 220–21, 230, 231;
    steel organizing and, 212–13; Wobblies
    and, 192; WWI and, 208
American Miners Association (AMA), 64,
    66, 98, 119
American Railway Union, 168
Ameringer, Oscar, 190
Angle, Paula, 249n22
antimonarchist movement, 98, 99
apprenticeships, 33, 98
archetypal proletarian hypothesis, 24–25,
    34
artisan-colliers: autonomy of, 50–51, 53, 54,
    56–57, 96–97, 123, 131–32, 223; description
    of, 33, 120; firearms and, 82; hostility of,
    42–43, 223; origins of, 87; size of pits and,
    49; skills of, 131–32; status of, 34, 38
Asquith, Herbert, 209, 211
Associated Society of Scottish Mine
    Owners, 109
Auchinraith (Scotland), 126, 141
Australia, wages in, 117
Austro-Hungarian immigrants, 86–87, 154
Ayrshire (Scotland), 69, 114, 136–37

Bacon, Francis, 99
Baird, William, 18, 29, 51–52
Baird and Company: competition for, 103;

expansion of, 126; Irish workers for, 22; management techniques of, 50, 94, 106; strikebreakers for, 141

Balaclava mine (Elderslie), 69

Bargini, Enrico, 139

Barnard, H. K., 84

Barnes, G. N., 211

Barrowman, James, 30

Bartlett, Frances, 104

Bates, John, 64

Beckner, Earl R., 277n12, 278n14

Belgium, immigration from, 85

Belhaven, Lord (Wishaw House), 16–17, 42

Bellamy, Edward, 169

Belleville (Ill.): elections in, 187–88, 219; miners' meetings in, 202; union headquarters in, 155; union march and, 156–57

Belleville Democrat, on republicanism, 99

Bellshill (Scotland), 179, 184, 202

Bell's Rows (Scotland), 54

Benton (Ill.), 216

Berger, Victor, 211

Beveridge, John, 116, 120

Binnie Hill (Scotland), 268n60

"Black Friday," 205

blacklists: immigration to avoid, 59, 60, 69, 72; support for, 109; as weapon against unions, 118

Blantyre (Scotland): elections in, 179; housing in, 130; immigrants in, 126, 136; map of, 127; miner-owner confrontations in, 141–42, 198, 223; pit disaster in, 240–41n63; strikes in, 141–42, 158, 201–2; transformed to mining community, 10, 126–27

Bogle's Hole (Scotland), 67–68

Bohemian immigrants: ethnic tensions and, 86–87; settlement of, 135

Bo'Ness, West Lothian, lodge (Free Colliers), 56–57

Booth, Stephane, 227

Boston, immigrants' arrival at, 62, 72

Boston, Ray, 64

Bothwell (Scotland): elections in, 179, 205; mining in, 126–27

boys: education for, 26–27; legislation on use of, 162; occupations for, 30, 35

Braceville (Ill.), 91, 104

Bradley, "General" Alexander, 156–57, 226

Braidwood, James, 72, 77

Braidwood (Ill.): founding of, 10, 71–72; growth of, 77–78; housing in, 91; immigration to, 70, 72–73, 249n16; infrastructure of, 83–84; map of, 79; mayor of, 72, 121, 165; organizations in, 89–90; persistence rates in, 23; politics in, 165; population of, 79–82, 81; recession in, 105–6; as single-industry town, 84; social geography of, 82, 86; stores in, 92, 110, 118; strike support in, 110, 111, 121–22; union leadership in, 139; upward mobility in, 93, 227; value of coal companies in, 95–96

Brand, Robert, 114

Brewery Workers Union (U.S.), 174

brick workers, women as, 84–85

Bridges, Amy, 162

Bright, John, 49

British Trades Union Congress, 10, 35, 165, 174

brothering ceremony, 25

Brown, Michael, 116–17

brushers (redsmen), 30–31

Bryan, William Jennings, 169

Buchanan, Robert, 48

Buckner (Ill.), 187

building and loan associations, 91

Burns, Robert, 268n60

Burt, Thomas, 164

cage operators, 30–32, 49–50, 95–96

Caldwell, James, 171

Calvinism, influence of, 41

Cambuslang (Scotland), 179

Cambusnethan (Scotland), 47

Cameron, Andrew, 163

Campbell, Alan: on independent colliers, 24–27, 33; on miners' union, 245n76; romanticization by, 29–30

Campbell, Alexander, 47, 68, 243n36

canals, construction of, 22, 66

Canton (Ill.), 204

capitalism: critique of, 102, 147–48; development of corporate, 111–12; development of industrial, 97; differential development of, 5–6; disillusionment with, 118; miners vs. corporate, 155; strike against, 191; support for, 175; use of term, 120. See also absentee ownership; owners

Carbon Hill (Ill.), 249n18

Carey, Henry, 63

Carpenter, Edward, 167

Catholicism: concerns of, 111; cultural differences and, 85; education issues and, 46; influence on women, 214; liberalism's appeal and, 183–84; practices in, 267n48; secret societies opposed by, 56; socialism and, 179, 183–85, 266n29, 267–68n55; working-class identity and, 215–16

Catholic Socialist Society (Scotland), 215, 266n29

Catholic Working Man, as prosocialist, 179

Central Competitive Field Agreement (U.S.), 156–59, 192

Central States Cooperative Society (U.S.), 189, 215

Cermak, Anton, 84, 86–87

Challinor, Raymond, 28

Chartist movement, 51, 63–64, 98, 160

checkweighmen, 87, 162–63

Cherry mine fire, 152–53

Chicago (Ill.), 10, 78, 125

Chicago, Burlington, and Quincy Railroad, 133

Chicago, Milwaukee, and St. Paul Railroad, 104

Chicago, Wilmington, and Vermilion Company (CW&V): company stores and towns of, 118, 133; modernization of, 104–5; politics of, 165; railroad strikes and, 111; shutdowns of, 105, 108–9; strikes against, 106–7; technology used by, 131

Chicago and Alton Railroad, 78

Chicago and Northwestern Railroad, 155

Chicago and Wilmington Company, 78–79, 104

Chicago Federation of Labor, 154, 217–18

Chicago Trades and Labor Assembly, 229

Chicago Tribune, on lockout, 143

Chicago-Virden Coal Company, 260n21

Church, Roy, 223

churches: attendance at, 45, 243n31; establishment of, 87; strike support and, 110–11

Church of Scotland, 110–11

CIO (Congress of Industrial Organizations), 233

citizenship: educational goals and, 88; equality and, 99–100. *See also* voting

City of Glasgow (steamship), 62

Civil War (U.S.): coal shortage in, 67; coal strikes after, 70; miner shortage and, 66; organizations after, 89; recruitment for Union army in, 67–68, 73

class: church support for upper, 110–11; collaboration between, 28–29, 158; emergence of division in, 106–12, 119, 124, 223; fear of clash between, 191, 276–77n3;

miners' relations with middle, 92–94; polarization in, 140–48, 157, 223. *See also* class formation; class-harmony ideal (McDonaldism); owners; social control; working class

class consciousness: comparative approach to, 233–34; context for, 194–95; deterrents to, 226–28, 231; economic development and, 222–25; growth of, 106–12, 157–58, 213–16, 224; political parties and, 228–30; religion/ethnicity and, 7–8, 225–26; suffrage movement and, 160–61; weakness in U.S., 277n4; women's, 213–14; WWI and, 230–33

class formation: community solidarity and, 34–35, 225–26; comparative approach to, 5–12, 90; face-to-face relationships in, 23–24; historical context of, 36; religion and ethnicity in, 55–56, 225–26; shaft mining's impact on, 130–34; U.S. exceptionalism in, 4–5

class-harmony ideal (McDonaldism): demise of, 106–7, 144; repudiation of, 32, 112–24, 224, 225; strikes discouraged in, 98, 101–2, 107–8, 113–14, 224; support for, 54, 56, 98, 122, 157; tenets of, 27–29, 50, 63, 92–93, 97–98, 113

Clayton Act (U.S., 1914), 189

closed shop agreement, 156, 157

Cloughan, William, 29

Clyde Valley, emigration from, 3–5. *See also* Lanarkshire; River Clyde

Clyde Workers Committee, 201

coal: consumption of, 18–19, 125; markets for, 103, 114–15, 125, 152, 203, 222; prices of, 28, 51, 105; strikes and availability of, 114, 145; types and depths of, 49; unfair weighing of, 162–63

coal and iron masters: background of, 20, 35; housing owned by, 39–40; management techniques of, 37, 49–53, 105; social control by, 40–42; temperance concerns of, 44; wage cuts by, 60–61. *See also* owners

Coal and Iron Masters Association of the West of Scotland, 53

Coal City (Ill.), 104, 249n18

coal companies: absentee ownership of, 104, 128–30, 168; call for nationalization of, 166, 168, 170, 188, 199–200, 232–33, 278n18; closures of, 144; competition among, 201; developmental stategies of, 9–11; immigration negotiations and,

68–69; lockouts by, 142–45, 200, 223, 224; overcapacity of, 203; power of, 112; shutdowns by, 105, 108–9
coal-cutting machines: effects of, 131–32, 198, 201; function of, 130–32; introduction of, 123, 125, 133, 222
Coalfield Coal Company (Ill.), 104
coal industry: boom and bust in, 101–2; corporate power in, 225–30; depression in, 203, 207; deteriorating conditions in, 140–41; development of, 16–19, 30, 222–25; differential scale in, 19–20; economic problems in, 103–9; expansion of, 130–34, 222–23; extraction methods in, 31–32, 49; government control of (WWI), 199–201, 208, 225; limitations on production in, 127–28; modernization of, 103–4, 124, 223; occupations in, 29–32; output in, 28–29, 32, 50–51, 98; overcapacity in, 203; restructuring of, 152–53; seasonality of, 250–51n58. See also coal companies; shaft mines; wages
Coal Miners' Chartist Association (Scotland), 160
Coalville (Ill.), 86
Coatbridge (Scotland): elections in, 205; immigrants in, 136; location of, 18; miners' union in, 245n76
Coffey, Luke, 202
colliers (Scotland): autonomy of, 24–25, 31–32, 38, 50–51, 53, 54, 56–57, 222–23; class interests of, 123–24; customary rights of, 38–39; discipline resisted by, 53–58; grievances of, 37–38; heterogeneity of, 30–32; internal stratification of, 32–36; locally born vs. migrant, 21–22; number of, 125, 127, 129; owners as joint custodians with, 27–29, 56, 63, 97–98, 101–2, 226; patriotism of, 197; persistence rate of individual, 23–24; political independence of, 163–66; on responsibility for accidents, 52; rules for, 53; social control resisted by, 43–49; solidarity among, 34–35, 145, 223, 225–26; stereotypes of, 20–21, 24–27, 38; training and skills of, 25, 29, 30–31, 51, 250n57; types of, 29–32; unemployment in 1920s, 203; upward mobility of, 93; women as, 26; WWI and, 197–203, 207. See also artisan-colliers; colliers (U.S.); darg; families; immigrants/immigration; newcomer-rebels; semi-proletarians

colliers (U.S.): age and skills of, 250n57; autonomy of, 94–100, 222–23; departure from northern Illinois, 152–53; mandated training for, 138; number of, 104, 125, 129; origins of, 80–81, *81, 88;* output restricted by, 98; patriotism of, 197; political independence of, 163–66; proletarianization of, 126, 155; qualifications of, 98; social and economic advantages for, 90–94, 226–27; solidarity of, 82, 86, 87–90, 223, 225–26; tactics available to, 112–17; tensions among, 86–87; unemployment in 1920s, 203; upward mobility of, 92–94, 120, 122, 226–27; WWI and, 197–203, 207. See also artisan-colliers; colliers (Scotland); families; newcomer-rebels; semi-proletarians
Collinsville (Ill.), 187, 210
Colorado: migration to, 154; strike in, 193; union leadership in, 259n9
Coltness Iron Works (Newmains): education issues and, 46; establishment of, 17; hunting banned by, 39; Irish workers for, 18; management techniques of, 55; shift from iron to steel of, 103
Committee on Mines and Mining (Ill.), 251n71
Commons, John R., 139, 154, 259n9
communications: considered in immigrant destination choice, 66; electric signals in, 127
Communist Party (U.S.), 213
company stores: alternatives to, 46–47, 118, 188–89, 243n36; campaigns against, 46–48, 118, 164; establishment of, 118, 129, 133; indebtedness to, 40–41; liquor sales and, 41, 45; owners' advantages with, 41, 133–34, 143
company towns: establishment of, 155; growth of, 133–34
comparative studies: apples and oranges problem in, 7–9; approaches to, 5–12; on immigration, 3
Conference for Progressive Political Action (CPPA, U.S.), 201–2, 221, 231
Congress of Industrial Organizations (CIO), 233
Connecticut, metalworkers' movements in, 8
Connolly, James, 205
Connolly, Nora, 205
Conservative Party (U.K.), 179–80

consumerism, large-scale, 6, 215
consumer's cooperative movement, 188–89, 214–15
cooperative stores, 46–47, 118, 214–15, 243n36
Cowie Square (Scotland), 54
Coxey, "General" Jacob S., 145
CPPA (Conference for Progressive Political Action, U.S.), 201–2, 221, 231
Craigneuk (Scotland): housing in, 39, 207; immigrants in, 136; mining in, 126; social control in, 55; steel workers in, 178
Crawford, J. A., 168–69
Cregier, Dewitt, 143
Cronin, John, 171
Cullom, Shelby, 111
Cumming, Thomas Stewart, 91
CW&V. *See* Chicago, Wilmington, and Vermilion Company (CW&V)

Dalziel (Ill.), 133
darg: opposition to restricted, 50–51, 53; profits from exceeding, 57; renewed call for, 141, 142; size of, 33; support for restricted, 28–29, 32, 38, 50–51, 54, 98, 123
David, David Brion, 7
Davis, Rev. E. R., 110
Davitt, Michael, 166, 172
deaths and injuries: from new equipment, 52; number of, per ton of coal, 244n58; from roof falls, 244n61. *See also* accidents; disasters; safety
Debs, Eugene, 168, 187, 188, 211, 219
Defense of the Realm Act (U.K.), 210–11
DeLeon, Daniel, 144–45, 169
Democratic Party (U.S.): AFL and, 173; antilabor crusade of, 219–20; appeal of, 161; miners in, 166, 229
Deneen, Charles, 176–77, 186–87
Denny mines (Ayrshire), 69
Deskilling, 8
Devlin, Charles, 110, 128–30, 142
Diamond (Ill.), 249n18
Diamond Coal Company (Ill.), 104, 106
diet. *See* food
disasters: Blantyre, 240–41n63; Cherry mine, 152–53; Hartley pit, 163. *See also* accidents; deaths and injuries; fires
diseases: epidemic during lockout, 143; fear of, 249n22; sanitation and, 83
division of labor: changes in, 10, 30, 50, 222; in longwall system, 31–32, 50, 131–32

Dixon Coal Company (Scotland): evictions by, 120; expansion of, 126–27; management techniques of, 50, 106; strikebreakers for, 141
docks, strikes on, 171, 193
downstate Illinois coalfields: company towns in, 155; cooperative stores in, 188–89, 214–15; culture of, 155, 175–76, 203, 207; map of, 153; politics in, 161, 184–89; post-WWI protests in, 202–3; production in, 152–53, 198; socialism's decline in, 204, 208; strikes in, 202–3; syndicalism in, 192; union organizing of, 154–55; women's class consciousness in, 214. *See also* Little Egypt coalfield; St. Clair County coalfield (Ill.)
Drew, Samuel, 94
drift mines, 95–97, 96
drinking: cultural role of, 25–26; masculinity and, 45, 84; safety and, 37, 41, 44–45. *See also* Prohibition movement; temperance
Duddy, Manus, 158, 159, 197–98, 273n58
Dunlop, Colin. *See* Dunlop Iron Works (Scotland)
Dunlop Iron Works (Scotland), 19, 94, 254n50
Dunne, Edward F., 209, 220
Durland, Kellog, 26, 40

Earnock colliery (Scotland), 201–2
East Fife (Scotland), 180
East Lothian (Scotland), 114
East St. Louis (Ill.): businesses in, 155, 189; elections in, 219; growth of, 125
economy: coal industry development and, 222–25; cost of living and, 92; depression in (1880s–90s), 140–41, 144; recession in (1870s), 103–9, 123; recession in (1920s), 203; worker-employer relations in, 27–29; WWI inflation in, 197–98, 206–7. *See also* wages
education: attendance rates and, 45–46; boys in mines vs., 26–27; as common goal, 87–88; funds for, 88, 251n59; levels of, 35, 227; social control via, 41–42, 46; voting and, 161, 179
Edwardsville (Ill.), 155
Eileen (Ill.), 249n18
Elcho, Lord, 162
electoral politics: direct action vs., 191–92; growth of SPA and, 184–89; miners'

importance in, 173–75, 217; municipal, 179, 187–88, 204; problems for socialism in, 178–84; Scottish vs. U.S., 11, 228–30, 233–34. *See also specific parties and unions*

emigration. *See* immigrants/immigration; migration

engineers, 30, 31

enginemen, 50

England: emigration from, 9, 55, 93; lockout of miners in, 145; metalworkers' movements in, 8; strike support from, 145–46

equality, republicanism and, 99–100

Esper, Frank, 218

Espionage Act (U.S., 1918), 210, 211, 212

ethnicity: alienation and, 82; alliances across, 87–90, 137–40, 156–57, 225–26; division based in, 55–56, 86–87, 135–37, 156, 216–17; housing patterns and, 86, 135–36; job levels and, 87, *88;* marriage and, 34, 241n65; organizations based in, 87; prohibition and, 216–17; socialist support and, 187–88; technology's introduction and, 132; violence linked to, 26; WWI and, 209–11

Eureka Coal Company (Ill.), 93, 106, 110

Evans, Richard J., 7

Excelsior Iron Works (Scotland), 55

exceptionalist paradigm: concept of, xi; critique of, 4–5; rejection of, 12, 147–48, 226, 233–34

explosives, skills with, 135

Fabian movement, 168–69, 226

Fagge, Roger, 8

Fallbrook Coal Company (Pa.), 68–69

families: immigration and, 61–62; lockout's impact on, 142–44; solidarity among, 34–35, 240–41n63; statistics on, 81–82

Farcetti, Tomaso, 139

Farmer-Labor Party (U.S.): criticism of, 220; platform of, 218–19; rejection of, 230–31; speeches for, 276n109; worker support for, 227

farmers: alliances of, 91, 168, 169; common interests with, 188; third-party efforts and, 218. *See also* Farmer-Labor Party (U.S.)

Farmers Alliance, 169

Farrington, Frank, 175, 185, 186, 199, 202

FBI (Federal Bureau of Investigation), 200–201

feminism, comparative approach to, 7

Fenwick, Charles, 182

Fickert, Louis, 185

Fifer, Joseph W., 251n71

Fife (Scotland), 114, 194

Fink, Leon, 4, 5, 170

firedamp, explosion from, 240–41n63

firemen, 30, 50, 52

fires: equipment to fight, 177; migration after, 152–53; vulnerability to, 82–83

Fitzpatrick, John, 217–18

flitting, as tactic, 41, 69, 82

food: rationing of, 206–7; during strikes, 108; U.S. vs. Scottish, 91

Foreign Emigrant Aid Society of Boston, 66–69

Forward, as propaganda, 190

France: Germany compared with, 7; trade union members in, 6

Franklin, Benjamin, 99

Free Colliers (Order of Free Colliers), 56–57, 70

Free School Agitation Committee (Scotland), 46

Gardner (Ill.), 67, 106

Gartsherrie (Scotland), 18

Gemmell, Thomas, Sr., 69, 70, 71

George, Henry, 165–66

German Forty-Eighters, 186

German immigrants: destinations of, 154; ethnic tensions and, 86–87, 209–10; politics of, 161, 185, 186; as union leaders, 154

Germany: unions in, 7–8, 228; working-class votes in, 6

Germer, Adolph: conviction of, 211; ethnicity of, 154; militancy of, 158; politics of, 175, 187; votes for, 184–85, 187; WWI and, 209–10

Gillespie (Ill.), 154, 155

Gilmour, David, 146, 175, 179, 273n58

girls. *See* women; women workers

Gladstone, William, 172

Glasgow (Scotland): Braidwood's link to, 72, 77; colliers' meetings in, 57, 60, 101, 116, 162; emigration from, 61–62, 80, 246n8; industrialization of, 15, 21–22, 125; as market, 10, 18–19, 114–15; mixed workforce of, 175–76; rent strikes in, 207, 214; suffrage movement in, 160; temperance society in, 44; Wobblies in, 192; WWI agitation in, 201

Glasgow Iron and Steel Company, 103
Glasgow Observer, on working class, 216
Glasgow School of Mines, 35, 93, 227
Glasgow Sentinel: colliers' support for/by, 48–49, 54; on co-ops, 243n36; on employee/employer relations, 56–57; on Free Colliers, 57; immigrants' letters in, 60–61, 63, 66–67, 71, 83, 246n8; McDonald criticized in, 70–71
Glasgow Trades Council, 67, 171
Glasgow University, 35
Glasgow Weekly Mail, on miners' wages, 141
Glasier, J. Bruce, 167
glass making, 85–86, 152, 155
Glen Carbon (Ill.): coal-cutting machines in, 198; as company town, 155; cooperative store in, 188; elections in, 187
Goldstein, David, 267–68n55
Gompers, Samuel, 169, 173, 192, 221
Gordon, John, 27
government: attitudes toward intervention via, 117, 118, 170, 182, 228; class consciousness and, 7–8, 231–33; coal industry controlled by (WWI), 199–201, 208, 225; grain elevator control and, 188; inspectors from, 38, 52, 93, 251n71; responsibility of, 123; social control via, 42
Graham, Duncan: elections of, 204–5; politics of, 175; redrawing parliamentary seats and, 212; voting requirements investigated by, 179–80
Graham, R. B. Cunninghame, 167
Granite City (Ill.), 155
Gray, Thomas, 197–98
Great Britain. *See* United Kingdom
Greenback Labor Party (U.S.): goals of, 164–65; legacy of, 124; miners' support for, 121, 122
Gregory, Roy, 277–78n13
Grey, Sir George, 53
grocery store chains, 215
Gronlund, Laurence, 169
group consciousness, 27–29
Guyman, W. J., 168

Haddow, Robert, 32–33
Hamilton, duke of, 16–17, 19, 38–39
Hamilton Advertiser: complaints in, 83; on strike support, 253–54n35
Hamilton Palace colliery, 201–2
Hamilton (Scotland): Chartist clubs in, 160; elections in, 179, 204–5; emigration

from, 80, 134; Ladd (Ill.) compared to, 134; miners' demonstrations at, 158, 194, 201–2; strikes in, 106, 108
Hampshire and Baltimore Company (Md.), 68–71
Hanna, Mark, 102
Harding, Warren G., 220
Harmsworth, Cecil, 178, 183
Harrisburg (Ill.), 219
Hartley pit disaster, 163
Hartz, Louis, 4, 6
haulage workers, 30
Hay, W. F., 194
Haydu, Jeffrey, 8
Hayes, Frank J., 175, 185, 187
Haywood, Bill, 211
heaters, 21
Heenan, H. H., 110
Hefferly, Frank, 218
Henderson, Arthur, 211
Herrin (Ill.), 187, 216
hewers, 30–31
Hewitt, W. H., 110
Hinchcliffe, John, 66, 100, 163, 229
Hodge, John, 209, 211
Holt, James, 8
Holytown (Scotland), 51–52, 114
Homestead Act (1862), 161
Horse Shoe Bottoms (Tippett), 96, 119
Houldsworth, Henry, 17–18
hours: owner-controlled, 53, 105, 110; proposals on, 142, 200, 229; worker-controlled, 24, 56
housing: deteriorating conditions in, 132–35; ethnicity and patterns of, 86, 135–36; evictions from, 39, 51, 54, 57, 105, 120; as fire hazard, 82–83; gardens and, 25, 44, 91; for glassworkers, 85; home ownership and, 43–44, 78–79, 90–91, 132–33, 226; moveability of, 82, 249n18; occupations mixed in, 21, 82; resistance to company, 43–44; segregation in, 21; social control via, 39–40; U.S. vs. Scottish, 78–79, 90–91; WWI shortage in, 198, 207. *See also* miners' rows (housing)
Hunter, Jack, 260n21
Huntingdon, Father, 143
Hyndman, Henry, 167

idle day, calls for, 198
ILGWU (International Ladies Garment Workers Union), 174
illegitimacy rates, 26

Illinois: British-born miners in, 64, *64;* constitutional convention of, 163; education funds in, 88; ethnicity of union leadership in, 259n9; migration to, 72; mining laws in, 83, 249n20, 278n14; Scotland compared with, 66, 134, 155. *See also* downstate Illinois coalfields; Little Egypt coalfield; northern Illinois coalfield

Illinois and Michigan Canal, 66

Illinois Bureau of Labor Statistics: on ethnicity, 136; on housing, 90–91, 133; on technology use, 131, 198

Illinois Central Railroad: land of, 66, 155; links to, 78; opening of, 66; strikes and violence against, 146, 189

Illinois Coal Operators Association, 156–58, 176–77

Illinois district 12 (UMWA): alliances of, 148; alternative structures in, 202–3; discontent in, 158–59; divisions in, 209–10; ethnicity and, 9, 90, 137–39, 156–57; failures of, 192; government control and, 199–201; growth of, 156–57, 224; influence by, 3–4; leadership of, 154, 158, 159, 194; membership of, 151; militancy in, 157–59; national coal strike and, 144–45; organizing by, 154–55; politics of, 176–77, 184–89, 204, 220–21, 228–30; post-WWI protests in, 202–3; socialists in, 167–70, 177, 204, 206, 208, 209; solidarity in, 225–26; syndicalists in, 192–93; third-party efforts and, 218–21; WWI and, 209–11

Illinois General Assembly: advisory committee for, 176–77; checkweighmen's law passed by, 162–63; lobbying of, 220–21; miners in, 166–67, 229

Illinois Miner, founding of, 190

Illinois State Council of Defense, 199, 209

Illinois State Federation of Labor (ISFL): criticism of, 177; on labor party question, 186, 218, 268n61; leadership of, 154; lobbying of, 220–21; managers expelled from, 157, 228; politics of, 176, 220–21, 230; strategies of, 168; WWI and, 209

ILP. *See* Independent Labour Party (ILP, Scotland)

immigrants/immigration: blacklists avoided via, 59, 60, 69, 72; comparative study and, 3, 9; destinations of, 63–67, 135, 154; encouragement of, 58, 59–61, 67–68, 78–79; families and, 61–62; hostility toward, 55–56, 86–87, 135–37, 156, 216–17, 225–26; housing and, 78–79, 135–36; motivation for, 23, 58, 59–61; nationalist clubs of, 214; negotiations on, 69–71; politics of, 175; process of, 61–63, 246n8; proletarianization and, 126; summary of British, *64,* 64–65; union integration of, 9, 137–40, 154; WWI and, 209–10. *See also* ethnicity; migration

Independent Labour Party (ILP, Scotland): alliances of, 179, 226; election campaigning by, 205; newspaper of, 190; Scottish Labour Party absorbed by, 171; SDF dispute with, 181

Independent Order of Good Templars, 44, 84

individualism, condemnation of, 49

industrial discipline: colliers' autonomy vs., 24–25, 31–32, 38, 94–100, 222–23; imposed by owners, 130, 223; lockout to enforce, 143–44; resistance to, 53–58

industrialization: innovations' influence of, 18; market growth and, 15, 21–22, 125; mass strikes and, 202; social and political contexts of, 8

industrial unions. *See* mass unions

Industrial Workers of the World (IWW): as antiwar, 210, 211; founding of, 192; leadership of, 205; strikes of, 193

Inkerman mines (Glasgow), 69

insurance, call for miners', 142, 170, 182

International Association of Machinists, 174

International Ladies Garment Workers Union (ILGWU), 174

International Miners Federation, 268n60

Iowa (steamship), 62

Ireland: Easter uprising in, 205; emigration from (to America), 9; emigration from (to Scotland), 22, 29; home rule for, 111, 172, 178, 183–84, 191, 226, 230, 267n47; labor movement in, 183; treaty for, 215–16. *See also* Irish workers

Irish Free State, 215–16

Irish Parliamentary Party, 178

Irish Treaty (1921), 215–16

Irish workers: children of, 81; education issues and, 46; fear of, 38; housing and, 43, 135; hunting by, 39; immigration and, 9, 22, 29, 61, 72; jobs for, 18; Labour Party and, 215–16; McDonald criticized by, 70–71; motives of, 22, 32; opposition to, 56; skills of, 29, 30, 66; as strikebreakers,

22, 51; as union leaders, 154; voting by, 183–84

iron industry: coal prices for, 28; cultural divisions and, 55; economic problems in, 103–9; list and value of companies, *19;* occupations in, 21, 85

iron masters. *See* coal and iron masters

Iron Masters Association (Scotland), 109

iron ore: discovery of, 18; import of, 103; processing, 17–19; wages linked to price of, 114–15

ironworkers, strike support and, 114

isolated-mass hypothesis, 20–21, 23, 34

Italian immigrants: complaints against, 136; ethnic tensions and, 209–10; settlement of, 135, 136; socialism and, 185, 227; in strikes, 138; union recruitment of, 138–40

IWW. *See* Industrial Workers of the World (IWW)

Jacobinism, 98

James, John: background of, 69; fictional representation of, 119; on heroes, 99; immigration of, 69–70; leadership of, 71–73, 98, 101–2, 112; on out-of-work miners, 105–6; politics of, 161, 162; strike and, 121–22, 224

Joint Conciliation Board (Scotland), 156

Joint Labor Legislative Board (U.S.), 220–21

Jones, Mary "Mother," 214

judicial system, 42, 46, 89

Kangley, Edward, 133

Kansas, strikes in, 145

Katznelson, Ira, 5–6, 228

Keir Hardie, James: background of, 34–35, 122; on darg, 141; influences on, 165–66; McDonald criticized by, 102, 112; militancy of, 142, 147, 224, 225; on nationalization, 232; political action of, 167, 169, 170–71, 229; on sectarianism, 184; strikes and, 108, 120, 146–47; on wages, 117, 118, 136–37; Walker and, 268n60; on women's rights, 214

Kerr, Clark, 20, 23

King, James, 57, 70–71

Kinnaird, Arthur, 162

KKK (Ku Klux Klan), 216–17

Kleckheimer, Hugo, 186

Knights of Labor: class consciousness and, 111–12, 138; criticism of, 122; cross-cultural influence of, 89; decline of, 168,

169–70; on land reform, 166; power of, 165; in Scotland vs. United States, 170; on strikes, 113, 117–18

Ku Klux Klan (KKK), 216–17

labor force: controlling number in, 59–61, 98; limitations on, 29; restructuring of, 21–23; as single-industry vs. diversity in, 84–85; unskilled, 132

labor movements: alliances of, 148; ethnicity and, 140; growth of, 151; labor political parties and, 173–74; national context of, 7–9; occupations joined in, 89; post-WWI in U.S., 212–13; Scottish and U.S. linked, 63–64; third-party activism and, 197, 217–21. *See also* mass unions; trade unions; *specific organizations and parties*

labor philosophy, group conscious type of, 27–29. *See also* class-harmony ideal (McDonaldism)

Labor-Populist alliance, 124, 168–71, 188, 226, 229

Labor Temple (Staunton), 189

Labour Leader, on national coal strike, 146–47

Labour Party (U.K.): co-ops and, 214–15; funds for, 181, 266–67n35; government of, 196, 211–12, 217; growth of, 189, 190–91; Irish support for, 215–16; Liberals as competition for, 182–83; MFGB's choice of, 176; as model, 177, 186, 218; political reorganization and, 211–17; power of, 196–97; reforms of, 207, 213; success of, 178–79, 180–81, 204–6, 213, 217, 229, 230–31, 277–78n13; syndicalism and, 191–92; women in, 213–14; WWI and, 207–9. *See also* Scottish Labour Party (SLP); Scottish Workers Parliamentary Committee (SWPC)

Ladd (Ill.), 133–34, *134*

LaFollette, Robert M., 196, 217

LaFollette Seaman's Act (U.S., 1915), 189

lairds: in social hierarchy, 35; types of, 16–18

Lanark North-East, 178, 180, 184

Lanark North-West, 180, 182

Lanarkshire: Labour Party's success in, 204–6; parliamentary seats for, 212; post-WWI protests in, 201–2; sanitation in, 83; voting in, 166–70; women's class consciousness in, 213–14

Lanarkshire coalfield: breakdown of class-harmony ideal in, 112–17, 120–21; expansion of, 21–22, 125–26; extraction methods in, 31–32; geography of, 9; list and value of companies in, *19;* lockouts in, 200; map of, *2;* miner-owner confrontations in, 141–42; neosyndicalist movement in, 191; optimism in, 101; production of, 18, 125, 127–28, 198; restructuring of, 152; social democratic movement in, 167–68, 170–72; strikes in, 106–9, 113–15, 137, 147, 193–94; syndicalism in, 193–94; technology in, 131–32; types of mines in, 126. *See also* Blantyre (Scotland); colliers (Scotland); Larkhall (Scotland); social hierarchy; Wishaw (Scotland)

Lanarkshire Coal Owners Association, 107–8, 146

Lanarkshire County Miners Union (LCMU): alternative structures in, 201–2; candidates of, 178–79; criticism of, 193–94; divisions in, 141–42; governance of, 115–16, 120–21, 158, 159; government control and, 199–201; growth and expansion of, 116–17, 151–52, 224; on housing, 207; immigrants and, 137; influences on, 9; leadership of, 158, 159, 175, 181, 194, 198; negotiations of, 157; politics of, 177–81, 212, 217, 228–29; revolt against, 201–2; role of, 3–4; solidarity in, 225–26; strikes and, 107–8, 113, 194, 201–2; syndicalists in, 193–94; on WWI, 208

Lanarkshire Examiner, on immigrants, 137

land: attachments to, 24–25; availability of, 65, 91; coal company ownership of, 155; hunting on laird's, 38–39; politics of, 161–62, 164–66; railroad ownership and, 104, 155; values of, 182. *See also* farmers

language, as barrier, 90

Larkhall (Scotland): church attendance in, 45; coal mine development in, 10, 15, 19–20; deaths and injuries in, 244n58, 244n61; emigration from, 80; geography of, 15; housing in, 21, 25, 43–44, 90; map of, *17;* organizations in, 26; persistence rate in, 23–24; population of, 20, 22; schools in, 41–42; sliding wage scale and, 115; stores in, 40–41, 47; strikes in, 105, 106, 114; strike support in, 110–11; temperance societies in, 44; voters in, 43

Larkhall St. Thomas' Lodge, 26

Larkhall Victualling Society, 47

La Salle (Ill.), 65

Lawler, Frank, 143

LCMU. *See* Lanarkshire County Miners Union (LCMU)

Left: divergent shift in attitudes toward, 206–11, 217; Labour as party of, 274n77; Liberal influence and, 181–82; post-WWI fortunes of, 204–6. *See also specific parties and unions*

Legbrannock (Scotland), 46

legislation: on checkweighmen, 162–63; miners-operators committee on, 176–77; on mines inspection, 53, 55; mining code and, 278n14; proposals for, 164, 167, 170, 220–21, 233–34; reform efforts reflected in, 241n2; on shaft mines, 163; on women in mines, 26

Lever Act (U.S., 1917), 200–201

Lewis, John L.: on nationalization, 232, 278n18; Washington Agreement and, 200–201, 203; welfare state and, 233

liberalism: appeal of, 183–84; components of English, 111; construction of U.S., 4. *See also* Liberal Party (U.K.); Progressive movement (U.S.)

Liberal Party (U.K.): control of, 164; divisions in, 206, 211; individualism of, 49; reforms of, 182, 189–90; voter qualification and, 179–80; worker support for, 171–72, 174, 181–84, 191, 212, 215, 277–78n13

Lib-Labs: alliances of, 176, 180–81; attitudes toward, 172; Labour's courting of, 182; use of term, 164, 165

Lincoln, Abraham, 99, 100

Lipset, Seymour Martin, 4, 6, 236n11

Lithuanian immigrants, 135–37

Little Egypt coalfield: elections in, 187, 219; ethnicity and religion in, 140, 155–56, 216–17; extraction methods in, 155; map of, *153;* politics in, 161, 175

Lloyd, Henry Demarest: on absentee ownership, 104; politics of, 168–69; Populism and, 148, 226; radical writing of, 144, 147; SVCC's lockout and, 143–44

Lloyd, Thomas, 64, 66

Lloyd George, David: budget of, 183, 191; coal commission of, 200, 225, 232; coup of, 211; "new Liberalism" of, 182, 185, 189; opposition to, 205, 208, 215; popularity of, 204, 229

Lofty, Frank, 111
Loganlea (Scotland), 137
long pays system, 40–41, 48
longwall system, 31–32, 50, 131–32
Ludlow massacre, 230
Lukins, F. W., 260n21

MacDonald, Duncan, 154, 175, 177, 189, 218
MacDougall, James, 201
MacLean, John, 201, 205, 210–11, 272n31
Macoupin County Catholic Federation, 185, 267–68n55
Madison Coal Company (Ill.), 155
Malcolm, Henry, 113–14
Maltby, William, 93
Malthus, Thomas, 59
markets: expansion of, 103, 222; export, 103, 125, 152, 203; free trade in, 182; wages linked to, 114–15
Marks, Gary, 4
marriage: ethnicity and, 34, 241n65; housing patterns and, 86; social hierarchy maintained in, 35
Marxist Social Democratic Federation (Scotland), 167
Maryhill (Scotland), 72, 80, 115
Maryland: British colliers in, 3, 64, 64; coal companies in, 68–69; migration from, 72
Mascoutah (Ill.), 155, 187
masculinity, drinking and, 45, 84
mass unions: concept of, 171; need for, 138, 144, 147–48, 173–74; support for, 191–92; transition to, 159. See also syndicalist movement
McAnulty (collier), 273n58
McBride, John, 144, 145
McDonald, Alexander: background of, 33, 34–35, 51, 92, 94; as coal owner, 120; on colliers' origins, 80; criticism of, 102, 112, 115–16, 120–21, 224; on darg, 53, 101, 142; death of, 121; on education, 46; as hero, 99; immigration and, 58, 60–62, 68–71; on judicial system, 46; leadership of, 98, 162, 228–29; legacy of, 123, 157; newspaper and, 48; in Parliament, 35, 121, 164, 165, 172; strikes and, 107–8, 113–14; supporters of, 71, 72, 102; U.S. visit by, 163; wages and, 45, 114–15, 117, 254n50. See also class-harmony ideal (McDonaldism)
McDonald, Charlie, 67, 69
McDonald, James, 67, 121

McLaughlin, Daniel: elections of, 165, 166; immigration of, 72–73, 246n8, 248n47; leadership of, 112; politics of, 161, 162; radicalization of, 112–23; on state mining committee, 251n71; strike and, 111, 121–23, 224, 226
McTavish, John, 71
Meacham, Standish, 191
Merry, James, 164
Merry and Cunningham (Scotland): competition for, 103; establishment of, 18; expansion of, 126–27; immigrants hired by, 136–37; management techniques of, 94, 106
metalworkers, 8, 169
MFGB. See Miners Federation of Great Britain (MFGB)
Mid-Lanark (Scotland): elections in, 178, 180–82; liberalism in, 172; voter qualification in, 179–80
Mid-Lanark Liberal Association, 172
Midlothian (Scotland), 114
migration: coal industry restructuring and, 152–53; motivation in, 23; short vs. long distance in, 21–22; to western states, 72, 126, 154. See also immigrants/immigration
militancy: in archetypal proletarian concept, 24–25; gap in U.S. vs. Scottish, 196–97; growth of, 108, 115–16, 123–24, 147, 159, 192–94; in isolated-mass concept, 20–22; of leadership, 142, 147, 157–59, 192, 224, 225; in unions, 10, 138, 147, 157–59; WWI and, 197–203. See also trade unions
military, WWI and, 197–98, 207–8
militia: strike intervention by, 111, 146, 168; violence of, 200. See also police
Mill, John Stuart, 59
Miller, Henry J., 128, 130, 132
Miller, James, 43
Millheugh Friendly Society (Scotland), 26
Mine Managers' Association (U.S.), 157, 228
Miners Federation of Great Britain (MFGB): alliances of, 193; ethnicity and, 138; militancy of, 10; on nationalization, 199–200, 232; political parties and, 11, 174–75, 176, 229; power of, 3–4, 10, 159, 174, 212; restructuring of, 201; strikes and, 145–46, 193–94
Miners Legislative Committee (U.S.), 230
Miners' Minority Movement (Scotland), 225

Miners National Association (MNA), 89, 98, 101–2, 122
Miners National Association of Great Britain, 98
Miners' National Labour League (Scotland), 166
Miners National Union (Britain): on immigration, 60; leadership of, 120–21
Miner's Next Step, The (pamphlet), 193, 194
miners' rows (housing): conditions in, 39–40, 43–44, 133; discipline and, 130; evictions from, 39, 51, 54, 57, 105, 120; occupants of, 21; segregation of, 86
Miners Unofficial Reform Committee (Scotland), 201–2
Mines Acts (U.K.): 1842, 26; 1855, 162; 1860, 46, 162
Mines Inspection Act (1855), 53, 55
Mining Investigation Commission (U.S.), 176–77, 230, 277n12
Minonk (Ill.), 146
Mitchell, John, 139–40, 175
MNA. *See* Miners National Association (MNA)
monopolization: miners and farmers against, 188; political action against, 165–66
Mooney, Tom, 202, 219, 272n31
Mooney, William C., 88, 94, 164, 229
Moore, Ralph, 52
Moore, Robert, 128
Morgan, Thomas J., 168–70, 186
Morris, William, 167
Motherwell (Scotland): elections in, 205–6; mixed workforce of, 175, 178; strikes in, 106, 114; unemployment in, 203; walkouts in, 198
Mount Olive (Ill.): ethnicity in, 154; nativism in, 210; union march and, 156–57

Naismith, W., 25
National Civic Federation (U.S.), 102, 175
National Federation of Mine Owners and Mine Laborers (U.S.), 144
nationalization: of mines, call for, 166, 168, 170, 188, 199–200, 232–33, 278n18; of railroads, call for, 168, 182
National Labor Tribune, disillusionment voiced in, 118
National Reform League (Scotland), 160
National Service Advisory Board (Scotland), 273n58

National Union of Railwaymen (Britain), 193
negotiation/arbitration: failure of, 103, 106; militancy in, 157–59; rationale for, 27, 28–29, 117–18, 123, 224; rejection of, 107–9; of sliding wage scale, 114–15; unions' cooperation in, 193
Neilson, James, 18
neosyndicalist movement, 191
Newbold, J. T. W., 205–6
Newcastle program, 171–72
newcomer-rebels: description of, 33, 82; origins of, 87; technology and, 37–38
Newmains (Scotland), 17, 55, 80
New Monkland (Scotland), 121
Newsam, Frank, 91
newspapers, socialist-owned, 188. *See also specific newspapers*
New York, immigrants' arrival at, 62, 70
New York World, on lockout, 143
Nineteenth Century, writers for, 33
Nockels, Edwin, 217–18
northern Illinois coalfield: appeal of, 65–66; bitterness after national strike, 147; breakdown of class-harmony ideal in, 117–24; conditions in, 83; disasters in, 152–53; expansion of, 125–26; extraction methods in, 95; geography of, 9; immigration to, 3, 65–67; list and value of companies in, 94–96, *95,* 109–10; map of, *2;* market for, 10, 78; mine locations in, *79, 80,* 82; miner-owner confrontations in, 142–44; modernization in, 103–9; optimism in, 101; politics in, 169, 175; production of, 78, 104, 125, 127–28, 152; restructuring of, 152–53; sanitation in, 83; strikes in, 106–9, 122, 250n50; technology used in, 128, 131–32; types of mines in, 95–97, *96,* 126, 129–30. *See also* Braidwood (Ill.); Spring Valley (Ill.); Streator (Ill.)
North Lanark (Scotland), 205
Nova Scotia, immigrants' arrival in, 62

Oberdan, Severine, 210
occupational community: concept of, 34–35; ethnicity and, 87, *88;* hierarchy in, 85, 87; joined in labor movement, 89; upward mobility in, 92–94
Oestreicher, Richard J., 245n78
O'Fallon (Ill.), 187
Oglesby (Ill.), 146

Ohio: British-born miners in, *64;* migration from, 72; strikes in, 122, 145; wages in, 67

"Old Slope Mine," 78

oncost workers: number of employed, 240n62; status of, 34; strikes and, 114; tasks of, 30; wages of, 31

Orange Order, 184

Order of Free Colliers, 56–57, 70

organizations: building and loan, 91; cross-cultural type of, 89–90; cultural tensions among ethnic, 87; importance of, 26; secret type of, 56–57

Orloff, Ann, 7

Osborne Judgement (1908), 181, 190, 229, 266–67n35

Outram, Quentin, 223

oversman (supervisor), 31

Overton (Scotland), 179

Owen, Robert, 126

owners: absentee, 104, 128–30, 168; attitudes of, 38–39; church support for, 110–11; colliers as joint custodians with, 27–29, 56, 63, 97–98, 101–2, 226; dissatisfaction with, 192, 194; extraction methods preferred by, 31–32; fraudulent claims of, 46; negotiation rejected by, 107–9; overcapacity used by, 203; political interests of, 163–64; on responsibility for accidents, 52; social control imposed by, 37–43; solidarity of, 109; tactics against strikes, 22, 39, 51, 54, 57, 105, 118, 120; temperance concerns of, 44. *See also* coal and iron masters; company stores; social control

owners-colliers relations: absentee owners' impact on, 104, 128–30; agreement in U.S., 156, 199; changes in, 36, 104; class division's growth and, 106–10, 157–59, 223–24; confrontations in, 140–47; equitable cooperation in, 27–29, 56, 63, 97–98, 101–2; increased tension in, 49–53, 54–58, 105–6; republican approach to, 98–100, 101–2; in WWI, 199. *See also* class-harmony ideal (McDonaldism); negotiation/arbitration; strikes

Painters Addition (Ill.), 86

Palmer, A. Mitchell, 200–201

Palmerston, Henry, 162

Pana (Ill.), 260n21

Parliament: colliers in, 35, 121, 164, 165, 172, 175, 205; Communists in, 205–6;

constitutional crisis in, 183, 191; on education, 46; mine accidents and, 52; on mine regulations, 52–53, 162; on minimum wage, 193; redrawing boundaries of seats, 212; truck stores and, 47–48; workingmen in, 35, 121, 164

paternalism, in reform efforts, 38

patriotism, 197, 206, 208, 209

Pelling, Henry, 239n34

Pennsylvania: immigrant colliers in, 3, 60–61, 64, *64,* 70, 71; migration from, 72, 126; politics in, 175; strikes in, 122, 139; union leadership in, 259n9; wages in, 68

People, The, on national strike, 144–45

People's Party (U.S.), 167–68, 169, 232, 264n82

Perlman, Selig, 4

Philadelphia, immigrants' arrival at, 62

pick miners: age issues and, 250n57; as artisan-colliers, 33; autonomy of, 49–50, 96–97; migration westward of, 154; origins of, 87; tasks of, 31; technology's impact on, 130–32; wages of, 107

pig iron, price of, 115, 254nn. 49–50

pit bottomers, 30, 49–50

pit boys, 30

pit committees, 158–59, 201

Plumb, Col. Ralph, 77, 78

police: crackdown on hunting by, 38–39; social control via, 42; strike intervention by, 107–8, 111, 141–42, 146; violence of, 200; voting and, 161. *See also* militia

Polish immigrants: ethnic tensions and, 86–87, 136–37; housing and, 135; trade unions and, 138

political action: attitudes toward, 159–63, 165; call for, 147–48; choices in, 173–74; against company stores, 46–48; newspaper's role in, 48–49; opportunities for, 151–52; social democratic, 167–70; tactics in, 163–66. *See also* voting

politics: class consciousness and, 228–30; cross-ethnic alliances in, 89; gap in U.S. vs. Scottish socialist, 196–97; labor's party choices and, 173–78; reorganization of British, 211–17; third-party, 148, 167–68, 185, 197, 217–21; U.S. vs. British evolution of, 11, 63–64, 161. *See also* political action; voting; *specific parties*

Pomeroy, William C., 170, 229

Populism: alliances of, 148, 167–69; goals of, 166, 188; influences on, 144

Powderly, Terrence V., 113
Prager, Robert, 210
Pringle, W. M. R., 182
Progress and Poverty (George), 165–66
Progressive movement (U.S.): collapse of, 213, 230–31; reforms won by, 189, 231; socialism vs., 185–87; women in, 214
Prohibition movement, 216–17
Protestantism, politics of, 183–84
puddlers, 21
Puissant, Father, 179
Pullman strike, 168

Quarter (Scotland): housing in, 21, 25; iron works at, 19; location of, 15
quota. *See* darg

race, U.S. politics of, 213. *See also* African Americans
railroads: call for nationalization of, 168, 182; coal lands and, 104, 155; coal markets and, 78; company towns and, 133; construction of, 22, 66; establishment of, 18; farmers and miners vs., 188; immigrant settlement choices and, 66; strikes against, 111–12, 168, 171, 189, 193; violence against, 146
railroad workers, miners' link to, 155
Rankin, Robert, 68
Ratchford, Michael, 156
Red Clyde (group), 201
Redding Coal Company (Scotland), 56–57
Red Scare, 210–11, 217–18, 230
redsmen (brushers), 30–31
Reform Acts (U.K.): 1867, 42–43; 1868, 159–60; 1884, 111, 160, 166, 167, 179–80, 263n68; 1918, 206, 211, 212
Reid, Fred: on independent colliers, 24–27, 33; romanticization by, 29–30
religion: alliances across, 87–88, 89–90, 172, 215–16, 226; class consciousness and, 7–8, 225–26; division based in, 22, 34, 55–57, 85, 156, 183, 216–17; education issues and, 46; Prohibition and, 216–17; social control via, 41; temperance and, 44, 83–84; violence linked to, 26, 141. *See also* Catholicism; churches; organizations; Protestantism
republicanism: appeal of, 63–64; awareness of, 48–49; class consciousness and, 226; concept of, 276–77n3; miners and merchants linked in, 110; as old-fashioned,

157; owners-colliers relations and, 98–100, 101–2; Scottish heroes added to, 99
Republican Party (U.S.): appeal of, 161; control of, 163–64; miners in, 166, 175, 229; worker support for, 213, 220
River Clyde, in emigration journey, 61, 71, 246n8
Riverton (Ill.), 187
roads, funds for, 78
roadsmen, 50, 53
Robertson, Chisholm, 145–46, 171
Robertson, John, 175, 178–79, 202, 205
Ronalds, K. C., 220
roof falls, 52, 244n61
Roosevelt, Theodore, 139, 175, 187
Ross, David, 94
Rossi, Peter, 84
Russell, James, 56–57
Russian immigrants, 86–87
Russian Revolution (1917): impact on socialist parties, 6, 210; support for, 219, 234, 275–76n102
Rutherglen (Scotland): elections in, 179, 206; immigration from, 80; suffrage movement in, 160
Ryan, W. D., 139

safety: alcohol and, 37, 41, 44–45; ethnicity and, 136; mandated training and, 138; politics and, 162; regulations on, 83, 249n20; technology's impact on, 131–32. *See also* accidents; disasters
sale coal companies: markets for, 103; wages in, 106, 113, 114
Sankey Coal Commission (U.K.), 200, 232
Saunders, E. N., 128
Scheu, Andreas, 167
Schilling, Henry, 202
Scotland: Illinois compared with, 66, 134, 155; migration within, 22; national strikes in, 144, 145–46, 157; traditions of, 56, 99. *See also* immigrants/immigration
Scott, W. L., 128
Scott, William M., 143
Scottish Coal and Iron Miners Association, 29, 54
Scottish Education Act (1872), 35, 41–42, 110–11
Scottish Home Rule Association, 172
Scottish Labour Party (SLP): as coalition, 9; founding of, 167, 171; leadership of, 102; miners courted by, 11; as model, 168–69;

support for, 47. *See also* Scottish Workers Parliamentary Committee (SWPC)

Scottish Miners Federation: leadership of, 171; militancy of, 147; national strike and, 145–46

Scottish Workers Parliamentary Committee (SWPC): funds for, 176; problems of, 178–79; unions as base for, 173–75, 177–78

Scottish Workers Representation Committee (SWRC): funds for, 181, 266–67n35; problems of, 179–84

Seatonville (Ill.), 133, 134

secret societies, 56–57

Sedition Act (U.S., 1917), 211, 212

Selective Service Act (U.S., 1918), 208

semi-proletarians: description of, 33–34, 82, 223; origins of, 87; technology and, 37–38

sexuality, living conditions and, 26

Shaftesbury, Lord, 38, 162

shaft mines: class formation impacted by, 130–34; equipment for, 128; exit shafts for, 163; introduction of, *96*, 97, 129–30, 222

Shefter, Mark, 229

Sherman Antitrust Act (U.S.), 189

Shieldmuir (Scotland), 55

ships, steerage conditions on, 62–63

Shotts (Scotland), 47, 160

Shotts Iron Company, 52

Siegel, Abraham, 20, 23

Simpson, A. G., 41, 42, 44, 48, 114

Simpson's Square (Scotland), 54

Sinclair, Peter, 67–68, 69

Siney, John, 101–2, 119, 122

Sir William Wallace lodge (Free Colliers), 56

skills, as private property, 27–29

slavery, 7, 49

Slavic immigrants: ethnic tensions and, 86–87, 136, 210; settlement of, 135; socialism and, 185, 227; union recruitment of, 138–40

slope mines, 95–97, *96*

SLP. *See* Scottish Labour Party (SLP)

Small, Robert, 180

Small, William, 34–35, 148, 167, 171

Smillie, Robert: as collaborationist, 158; defeats of, 178–79, 180, 182, 183; elections of, 159, 171–72, 175; on labor party, 147–48; militancy of, 157; politics of, 167, 190–91, 231; union funds and, 145–46

Smith, Adam, 59–60, 61

Smith, Harry W., 112

social control: colliers' response to, 43–49; impact on strikes, 55; owners' imposition of, 37–43, 133–34. *See also* housing

Social Democratic Federation (Scotland), 180

social democratic movement: in Illinois, 167–70; precursor to, 117; in Scotland, 167–68, 170–72

social hierarchy: Scottish vs. U.S., 35, 110, 223; upward mobility in, 92–94, 226–27; work autonomy and, 97–98

socialism: Catholicism and, 179, 183–85, 266n29, 267–68n55; consumer's cooperative movement and, 188–89, 214–15; divergent shift in attitudes toward, 206–11, 217; Illinois miners' support for, 184–89; post-WWI fortunes of, 204–6, 227–28; problems for movement in Scotland, 178–84; Scottish vs. U.S., 173–78, 189–91, 194–95, 196–97, 225

Socialist Labor Party (SLP, U.S.), 168–70

Socialist Party of America (SPA): attempted revival of, 217–21; collapse of, 6, 196–97, 210–11, 212–13, 217–18, 220, 230–31; decline of, 189, 204; founding of, 173; growth of, 178, 184–85; leadership of, 154; miners courted by, 11; national coal strike and, 144; nature of, 9; platform of, 185–89; success of, 187–88, 189, 190; worker support for, 174, 175, 177, 227, 229–30; WWI and, 208–11

Society of Equitable Pioneers of Wishaw, 47

Soderstrom, R. G., 220

Sons of Labor in Scotland, 170

South Lanark (Scotland), 190–91

South Wales Miners Federation, 194

Soviet Union (USSR): "Hands off" campaign and, 219, 234, 275–76n102; recognition of, 204

Springfield (Ill.), 125, 169

Spring Valley (Ill.): founding of, 10, 126; housing in, 133–34, 136; immigrants in, 126; map of, *129;* miner-owner confrontations in, 142–44, 223; politics in, 169; social hierarchy in, 130; strikes in, 146; union leadership in, 139–40

Spring Valley Coal Company (SVCC): company towns of, 133–34; lockout by, 142–44, 223, 224; power of, 128–29; technology used by, 131; types of mines of, 129–30

Spring Valley Gazette, on shaft mines, 129–30
Spring Valley Townsite Company, 128, 132
Stafford (England), 164, 165
state. *See* government
Staunton (Ill.): elections in, 185, 187; ethnicity in, 154, 210; Labor Temple in, 189
St. Clair County coalfield (Ill.): British-born colliers in, 64, 65, 67; Civil War and, 66; elections in, 184, 204, 213; expansion of, 154–55; extraction methods in, 154–55; legislation and, 162–63; politics in, 161; railway links with, 66; strikebreakers in, 67; union in, 64, 65; Washington Agreement and, 202
steel industry, 103, 212–13
Steel Smelters Union, 178
Steel Workers Organizing Committee, 212–13
steelworkers' unions, 8, 171
Stephenson, George, 99
Stevenson, Adlai, 186–87
Stevenson, Robert Louis, 246n8
Steward, Sir Henry, 17
Stewart, W. D., 132
St. Louis, Alton, and Chicago Railroad, 66
Stonecraigs Row (Scotland), 21
Stonehouse (Scotland), 15, 160, 179
stoop-and-room method, 31
Streator, Ralph, 77
Streator (Ill.): businesses in, 85–86, 110, 118, 152; characteristics of, 10; cultural and religious differences in, 85–86; growth of, 77, 78; housing in, 86, 90–91, 133; infrastructure of, 83–84; list and value of companies in, 94–96, *95;* map of, *80;* organizations in, 89–90; persistence rates in, 23; population of, 79–82, *81;* recession in, 106; social geography of, 82, 86; strike in, 85–86; strike support in, 110; union leadership in, 139; upward mobility in, 93–94, 227; wages in, 92; wealth and diversity of, 84–85
streetcar lines (Ill.), 82
strikebreakers: African Americans as, 107, 216, 250n50, 260n21; British miners as, 67; Irish workers as, 22, 51; protection for, 141–42; refusal to be, 70, 71; whites as, 107
Strike of Millionaires against Miners, A (Lloyd), 144, 147, 168
strikes: choice of darg vs., 28–29; cross-ethnic alliance in, 138–39; demise of class-harmony doctrine and, 106–9; discouraged by labor leaders, 98, 101–2, 107–8, 113–14, 121–22, 158, 224; on docks, 171, 193; fear of class clash due to, 191; judicial system's role in, 89; for minimum wage, 151; on national level, 144–46, 156–57, 212–13, 224, 230; newcomer-rebels in, 33; non-miners' support for, 48, 85–86, 110, 111, 253–54n35; number of, 32, 51; owners' weapons against, 39, 51, 54, 57, 105, 120; penalty clause against in WWI, 199; post-WWI, 212–13; against railroads, 111–12, 168, 171, 189, 193; rent, 207, 214; responsibility for damages in, 174, 182; selective use of, 113–16, 224; violence in, 141–42, 146–47, 193–94, 200–202; wildcat, 158–59, 198, 202–3; willingness to hold, 35–36. *See also* negotiation/arbitration
Sullivan, John, 205
Sullivan, Joseph, 175, 179, 180
Summerlee (Scotland), 179
Sunnyside (Scotland), 41, 54–55
SVCC. *See* Spring Valley Coal Company (SVCC)
Sweet, Alanson L., 104, 107, 111
syndicalist movement: approach to trade unions, 159; growth of, 191–94, 224–25; nationalization and, 232; post-WWI, 201–2; precursor to, 48

Taff Vale decision, 174, 229
Tattie strike, 108, 120
taxes: on coal lands, 121–22; graduated income, 170; increased on rich, 183, 191; single, 169
Taylor, John, 128
technology: accidents due to, 52; autonomy impacted by, 131–32; dynamite vs. gunpowder, 49, 50; introduction of new (1850s–60s), 37–38, 49–53; introduction of new (1870s), 103, 222; introduction of new (1900s), 123, 125, 127–28, 129–30; weaving, 21. *See also* coal-cutting machines; shaft mines
temperance: accommodationist stance toward, 37, 44–45; liquor profits vs., 41; owners' interest in, 44; popularity of societies for, 26, 83–84; propaganda for, 47. *See also* drinking
textile workers, 126, 174, 193, 230. *See also* weavers/weaving

Thayer (Ill.), 187
Thernstrom, Stephan, 227
Thomson, Samuel, 120
timbermen, 30
Tippett, Tom, 96, 119
To Certain Rich Men (Lloyd), 143–44
Tories. *See* Conservative Party (U.K.); Unionist Party (U.K.)
Trades Dispute Act (U.K., 1906), 182
Trade Union Act (1913), 190
trade unions: alliances of, 168; civil suits and, 174, 182; class conflict channeled through, 229; entry money for, 29; generational differences in, 119–21; ideological differences in, 121–24; immigration assistance from, 58, 59–61, 68; impetus for, 111–12; leadership for, 33, 34–35, 194, 209, 224–25; newspaper and, 48–49; owners' opposition to, 105, 107, 223; percentage of workers in, 6; recognition of, 102, 156; rejection of, 107–9; reliance on, 54; rules and regulations of, 29; strength of, 44, 55; syndicalist interpretation of, 159; tactics available to, 112–17. *See also* militancy; negotiation/arbitration; strikes; *specific unions*
Transport Workers Federation (U.K.), 193
Tremenheere, H. S., 38, 50–51
Triple Alliance, 193, 200, 205, 230
Truck Act (U.K., 1831), 41, 45, 47–48, 160
truck stores. *See* company stores

UMWA. *See* United Mine Workers of America (UMWA)
underground face workers, 30
union dues, 156, 190, 218
Unionist Party (U.K.), 205
United Irish League, 172, 178, 184, 215
United Kingdom: national strikes in, 144, 145–46, 157, 193–94; trade union members in, 6. *See also* England; Ireland; Scotland; Wales
United Mine Workers of America (UMWA): criticism of, 202; ethnicity and, 136–40; growth of, 151–52; influence by, 3–4, 10, 11; militancy of, 10, 138, 147; national coal strike and, 144–45, 146; opposition to, 186–87; politics of, 168, 175, 176; power of, 159, 174; strike of, 193; Washington Agreement and, 200–201. *See also* Illinois district 12 (UMWA)
United States: appeal of, 63–67, 99–100, 135; class conflict feared in, 276–77n3;

national strikes in, 144–45, 156–57, 212–13, 224, 230; political continuity in, 211, 213, 217, 221, 228–31
U.S. Department of Labor, 189
U.S. Fuel Administration, 199
University of Illinois, 94

Vermilion Coal Company (Ill.), 77–79, 104
violence: alcohol and, 26; against strikebreakers, 260n21; in strikes, 141–42, 146–47, 193–94, 200–202
Virden (Ill.), 155, 260n21
Voss, Kim, 4, 5
voting: in Britain, 42–43, 159–61, 166–70, 206, 211, 263n68; by Irish workers, 183–84; miners' importance in, 173–75, 217; in United States, 63, 88, 160–63; violation of acts on, 179–80; "wasted vote" argument on, 186; by women, 191, 213–14

wages: average, 54; in coal boom, 101–2; deductions from, 40, 42, 46, 141; differences in, 66, 113, 114; factors in, 45, 91, 250n57, 251n59; fair, 123; for glassworkers, 85; immigration and, 61, 67–69, 136–37; job-based, 138; lockout to lower, 143–44; minimum, 117, 151, 157, 193; output restriction and, 28–29, 32, 50–51; payment of, 40–41, 48; political party funds from, 181, 190, 218; recession's impact on, 105; sliding scale of, 114–15, 117, 118, 254n50; strikes against cuts in, 106–8; strike support and, 145–46; threats to cut, 60–61; U.S. vs. Scottish, 91–92, 147, 226–27; wage-fund theory on, 59–60, 61; WWI and, 197, 199–200, 201
Wales: immigrants from, 93, 154; mining communities studied in, 8
Walker, James Monroe, 104
Walker, John H.: background of, 268n60; as collaborationist, 158; on cooperatives, 189; criticism of, 192, 209–10; election of, 159, 231; gubernatorial campaign of, 219–20; Keir Hardie and, 268n60; leadership of, 154; militancy of, 157; politics of, 175, 186–87, 218, 220–21, 268n61, 276n109; WWI and, 209–10
Ward, George, 136
Washington, George, 99
Washington Agreement (1917), 199, 200, 202, 203, 219
Watt, James, 99
Weaver, Daniel, 64

weavers/weaving: cooperative stores of, 47; decline in, 21, 39–40; housing for, 21, 44; immigration of, 59; role of, 15–16

Weekly Miner (Belleville, periodical), editor of, 66, 100, 163

Weitz, Eric, 7

welfare state, comparative approach to, 7

Wellhall estate (Hamilton), 120

Welsh, James C., 205

Welsh miners, 93, 154

Western Federation of Miners (U.S.), 174

West Frankfurt (Ill.), 216

West Virginia: mining communities studied in, 8; strike in, 70, 71

Whalen, Homer, 204

Wheatley, John, 179, 184, 205, 215, 266n29

Whistleberry (Scotland), 126

Whitebreast Coal Company (Ill.), 133–34

Whitehouse, J. M., 182

Wieck, Agnes Burns, 214

Wieck, Edward, 158, 159, 192, 214

Wilentz, Sean, 5, 226

Williams, John, 93, 97–98, 104, 130

Williams, Robert, 52

Wilmington Advocate: on Knights of Labor, 112; on out-of-work miners, 105–6

Wilmington Coal Mining and Manufacturing Company (Ill.), 104

Wilmington Star Coal Company (Ill.), 104, 106

Wilson, Gordon, 32

Wilson, J. R., 184

Wilson, John, 182

Wilson, Woodrow, 189, 208, 209, 220, 225, 230

Wilson and Company, 18

Wishaw (Scotland): characteristics of, 10, 41–42, 45–46, 55, 175; coal mine development in, 15–20; deaths and injuries in, 244n58, 244n61; elections in, 179; emigration from, 80; geography of, 15; heterogeneity of, 55; housing in, 21, 43–44, 133; map of, *16;* mixed workforce of, 175; organizations in, 26; persistence rate in, 23–24; police of, 38–39; population of,

18, 20, 22; shift from iron to steel in, 103; stores in, 40–41, 47; strikes in, 54–55, 105, 106, 114, 198; strike support in, 110–11; temperance societies in, 44; unemployment in, 203; voters in, 43; wages in, 92, 251n59

Wishaw and Coltness Railway, 18

Wishaw Iron Works Society, 26

Wishaw Miners Association, 29

Wishaw Press, complaints in, 83

Wobblies. *See* Industrial Workers of the World (IWW)

women: class consciousness of, 213–14; cooperative stores and, 188–89, 214–15; financial role of, 40–41; housing issues and, 26, 39, 207, 214; role of, 34; in Scotland vs. United States, 84; temperance and, 44; voting by, 191, 213–14

women workers: in brickmaking, 84–85; in mines, 26; occupations of, 35, 39–40, 84–85, 251n60

Woods, George, 95

working class: comparative approach to, 5–7; identity and, 215–16; Labour Party as choice of, 211; upper boundary for, 35; upward mobility and, 92–94, 226–27. *See also* class consciousness

Workingman's Advocate: editor of, 163; on national heroes, 99

World War I: class consciousness and, 230–33; differential socioeconomic impact of, 6, 197, 206–7, 233; miners' discontent in and after, 197–203; opposition to, 207–11; peace agreement in, 200; strikes prior to, 191–94; women workers in, 214. *See also* syndicalist movement

Wright, W., 206

Wyoming, migration to, 154

Yearley, Clifton, 248n47

yellow-dog contracts, 107

Young, John, 121–22, 165

Zolberg, Aristide, 5–6

JOHN H. M. LASLETT is a professor of history at the University of California at Los Angeles, where he teaches immigration and labor history. Born in England and educated at Oxford University, he is the author of several books, including *Labor and the Left: A Study of Socialist and Radical Influences in the American Labor Movement, 1881–1924* (Basic Books, 1970); the coauthor (with S. M. Lipset) of *Failure of a Dream? Essays in the History of American Socialism* (University of California Press, 1985); and the editor of *The United Mine Workers of America: A Model of Industrial Solidarity?* (Pennsylvania State University Press, 1996). He is completing a new interpretive work on American labor history set in a comparative framework entitled " 'Overlapping Diasporas': A Short Comparative History of the American Working Class" to be published by Princeton University Press.

The Working Class in American History

Worker City, Company Town: Iron and Cotton-Worker Protest in Troy and
   Cohoes, New York, 1855–84   *Daniel J. Walkowitz*
Life, Work, and Rebellion in the Coal Fields: The Southern West Virginia Miners,
   1880–1922   *David Alan Corbin*
Women and American Socialism, 1870–1920   *Mari Jo Buhle*
Lives of Their Own: Blacks, Italians, and Poles in Pittsburgh, 1900–1960
   John Bodnar, Roger Simon, and Michael P. Weber
Working-Class America: Essays on Labor, Community, and American Society
   Edited by Michael H. Frisch and Daniel J. Walkowitz
Eugene V. Debs: Citizen and Socialist   *Nick Salvatore*
American Labor and Immigration History, 1877–1920s: Recent European Research
   Edited by Dirk Hoerder
Workingmen's Democracy: The Knights of Labor and American Politics
   Leon Fink
The Electrical Workers: A History of Labor at General Electric and Westinghouse,
   1923–60   *Ronald W. Schatz*
The Mechanics of Baltimore: Workers and Politics in the Age of Revolution,
   1763–1812   *Charles G. Steffen*
The Practice of Solidarity: American Hat Finishers in the Nineteenth Century
   David Bensman
The Labor History Reader   *Edited by Daniel J. Leab*
Solidarity and Fragmentation: Working People and Class Consciousness in
   Detroit, 1875–1900   *Richard Oestreicher*
Counter Cultures: Saleswomen, Managers, and Customers in American
   Department Stores, 1890–1940   *Susan Porter Benson*
The New England Working Class and the New Labor History   *Edited by
   Herbert G. Gutman and Donald H. Bell*
Labor Leaders in America   *Edited by Melvyn Dubofsky and Warren Van Tine*
Barons of Labor: The San Francisco Building Trades and Union Power in the
   Progressive Era   *Michael Kazin*
Gender at Work: The Dynamics of Job Segregation by Sex during World War II
   Ruth Milkman
Once a Cigar Maker: Men, Women, and Work Culture in American Cigar
   Factories, 1900–1919   *Patricia A. Cooper*
A Generation of Boomers: The Pattern of Railroad Labor Conflict in
   Nineteenth-Century America   *Shelton Stromquist*

Work and Community in the Jungle: Chicago's Packinghouse Workers, 1894–1922
   James R. Barrett
Workers, Managers, and Welfare Capitalism: The Shoeworkers and Tanners of
   Endicott Johnson, 1890–1950   *Gerald Zahavi*
Men, Women, and Work: Class, Gender, and Protest in the New England Shoe
   Industry, 1780–1910   *Mary Blewett*
Workers on the Waterfront: Seamen, Longshoremen, and Unionism in the 1930s
   Bruce Nelson
German Workers in Chicago: A Documentary History of Working-Class Culture
   from 1850 to World War I   *Edited by Hartmut Keil and John B. Jentz*
On the Line: Essays in the History of Auto Work   *Edited by Nelson Lichtenstein
   and Stephen Meyer III*
Upheaval in the Quiet Zone: A History of Hospital Workers' Union, Local 1199
   Leon Fink and Brian Greenberg
Labor's Flaming Youth: Telephone Operators and Worker Militancy, 1878–1923
   Stephen H. Norwood
Another Civil War: Labor, Capital, and the State in the Anthracite Regions of
   Pennsylvania, 1840–68   *Grace Palladino*
Coal, Class, and Color: Blacks in Southern West Virginia, 1915–32
   Joe William Trotter, Jr.
For Democracy, Workers, and God: Labor Song-Poems and Labor Protest,
   1865–95   *Clark D. Halker*
Dishing It Out: Waitresses and Their Unions in the Twentieth Century
   Dorothy Sue Cobble
The Spirit of 1848: German Immigrants, Labor Conflict, and the Coming of the
   Civil War   *Bruce Levine*
Working Women of Collar City: Gender, Class, and Community in Troy, New
   York, 1864–86   *Carole Turbin*
Southern Labor and Black Civil Rights: Organizing Memphis Workers
   Michael K. Honey
Radicals of the Worst Sort: Laboring Women in Lawrence, Massachusetts,
   1860–1912   *Ardis Cameron*
Producers, Proletarians, and Politicians: Workers and Party Politics in Evansville
   and New Albany, Indiana, 1850–87   *Lawrence M. Lipin*
The New Left and Labor in the 1960s   *Peter B. Levy*
The Making of Western Labor Radicalism: Denver's Organized Workers,
   1878–1905   *David Brundage*
In Search of the Working Class: Essays in American Labor History and Political
   Culture   *Leon Fink*
Lawyers against Labor: From Individual Rights to Corporate Liberalism
   Daniel R. Ernst
"We Are All Leaders": The Alternative Unionism of the Early 1930s   *Edited by
   Staughton Lynd*

The Female Economy: The Millinery and Dressmaking Trades, 1860–1930
    Wendy Gamber
"Negro and White, Unite and Fight!": A Social History of Industrial Unionism in
    Meatpacking, 1930–90   *Roger Horowitz*
Power at Odds: The 1922 National Railroad Shopmen's Strike   *Colin J. Davis*
The Common Ground of Womanhood: Class, Gender, and Working Girls' Clubs,
    1884–1928   *Priscilla Murolo*
Marching Together: Women of the Brotherhood of Sleeping Car Porters
    Melinda Chateauvert
Down on the Killing Floor: Black and White Workers in Chicago's Packinghouses,
    1904–54   *Rick Halpern*
Labor and Urban Politics: Class Conflict and the Origins of Modern Liberalism in
    Chicago, 1864–97   *Richard Schneirov*
All That Glitters: Class, Conflict, and Community in Cripple Creek
    Elizabeth Jameson
Waterfront Workers: New Perspectives on Race and Class   *Edited by*
    Calvin Winslow
Labor Histories: Class, Politics, and the Working-Class Experience   *Edited by*
    Eric Arnesen, Julie Greene, and Bruce Laurie
The Pullman Strike and the Crisis of the 1890s: Essays on Labor and Politics
    Edited by Richard Schneirov, Shelton Stromquist, and Nick Salvatore
AlabamaNorth: African-American Migrants, Community, and Working-Class
    Activism in Cleveland, 1914–45   *Kimberley L. Phillips*
Imagining Internationalism in American and British Labor, 1939–49
    Victor Silverman
William Z. Foster and the Tragedy of American Radicalism   *James R. Barrett*
Colliers across the Sea: A Comparative Study of Class Formation in Scotland and
    the American Midwest, 1830–1924   *John H. M. Laslett*

Typeset in 10.5/13 Minion
with Minion/Polonais display
Designed by Paula Newcomb
Composed by Tseng Information Systems, Inc.
Manufactured by Cushing-Malloy, Inc.

University of Illinois Press
1325 South Oak Street
Champaign, IL 61820-6903
www.press.uillinois.edu